DATE DUE

ROBERT BROWNING

A Life After Death

ROBERT BROWNING

A Life After Death

•

Pamela Neville-Sington

Weidenfeld & Nicolson

LONDON

First published in Great Britain in 2004
by Weidenfeld & Nicolson

© 2004 Pamela Neville-Sington

A CIP catalogue record for this book
is available from the British Library.

ISBN 0 297 64396 7

Typeset by Selwood Systems, Midsomer Norton

Printed in Great Britain by Butler & Tanner Ltd,
Frome and London

Weidenfeld & Nicolson

The Orion Publishing Group Ltd
Orion House
5 Upper Saint Martin's Lane
London, WC2H 9EA

For David

VIS MEA

Contents

List of Illustrations

Acknowledgements

There are many libraries, archives, and individuals to whom I owe much gratitude for assisting me in my research and allowing me to quote from the letters and papers in their collections. First and foremost, I would like to thank the Armstrong Browning Library at Baylor University in Waco, Texas, for granting me a fellowship which enabled me to spend time exploring its extraordinary collection of manuscripts, books, and artefacts; its staff, the then Director Dr Mairi Rennie, the Librarian, Cynthia Burgess, and the Curator of Manuscripts, Rita Patteson, could not have been more helpful and welcoming. Philip Kelley, principal editor of *The Brownings' Correspondence* and of so many other indispensable works on the Brownings, was one of the most valuable resources at the Armstrong Browning Library, and I benefited greatly from our conversations. I would also like to thank John Murray for allowing me to look at Browning's letters to his publisher, George Smith, in the firm's wonderful front room and for permission to quote from those parts of the Brownings' correspondence over which he still holds copyright. My gratitude is due also to the Master and Fellows of Balliol College Library, Houghton Library at Harvard University, the British Library, Boston Public Library, New York Public Library, including the Henry W. and Albert A. Berg Collection of English and American Literature, the Royal Academy of Arts Library, The Alexander Turnbull Library, Wellington, New Zealand, Westminster Abbey Library, Eton College Library, London Library, the Institute of Historical Research and Senate House Library, University of London.

I have gained much knowledge and understanding of the Brownings through the lectures, meetings, and publications of the Browning Society and in my discussions with the scholars whom I have met through the Society in London, including Michael Meredith, Dr Scott Lewis and Dr

Berry Chevasco. Others whom I would like to thank are Norman and Susan Collings for a delightful day researching Pen and Fannie Browning's marriage in Kent; C. W. L. Wilson, who was so knowledgeable about Pembury Church; Kent College for Girls, Pembury, formerly Hawkwell Place, where Pen proposed to Fannie; Dr Marjorie Stone for being such good company in Waco and enlightening me on Elizabeth Barret Browning's poetry; Dr William Askins for allowing me to see his unpublished paper on the Brownings and the Eckleys; Julia Bolton Holloway for taking me around Casa Guidi and Bellosguardo in Florence; Celia and Enzo Cammaroto for their hospitality in Bagni di Lucca; Professor David Rosenthal for his knowledge of Hiram Powers, George Perkins Marsh, and other expatriates in Italy; Mary James, formerly of Bernard Quaritch, for drawing my attention to a few affordable first editions of Browning's poetry; Meg Ford of Christie's, London, for alerting me to an interesting Browning letter; Bailey and Elizabeth Bishop for their hospitality in Boston; Paul Scherer, David Alexander, and Roger Stoddard who kindly provided books relating to Browning; also Martin Chown and Harv Neville for various interesting titbits.

Last, but certainly not least, I would like to thank for all their help, support and guidance my agent, Peter Robinson at Curtis Brown, my original editor at Weidenfeld & Nicolson, Rebecca Wilson, my present editors, Francine Brody and Richard Milner and my copy-editor, Celia Levett.

Note

I tell Browning's story exclusively through contemporary sources: letters and reviews, diaries and newspaper accounts, as well as the writings of his friends turned biographers: Alexandra Orr, Lilian Whiting, and William Sharp. But, although I quote (with the original punctuation and spelling) only from the words of those who knew at first hand Browning and his world, I am enormously indebted to subsequent scholarship, especially William DeVane's *A Browning Handbook* (1936), Betty Miller's *Robert Browning: A Portrait* (1952), Maisie Ward's *Robert Browning and His World*, 2 vols. (1967–9), William Irvine and Park Honan's *The Book, the Ring, and the Poet* (1975), John Maynard's *Browning's Youth* (1977), Daniel Karlin's *The Courtship of Robert Browning and Elizabeth Barrett* (1985), and Clyde de L. Ryals' critical biography (1993).

　　　　　　. . . days decrease,
And autumn grows, autumn in everything.
Eh? The whole seems to fall into a shape
As if I saw alike my work and self
And all that I was born to be and do,
A twilight-piece.
　　　　　　　　　Browning, 'Andrea del Sarto'

Prologue

On a hot July day in 1861 in Florence, twelve-year-old Pen Browning sat in the barber's chair as the soft ringlets, so often stroked and petted by his mother, fell from under the scissors on to the stone floor. Elizabeth Barrett Browning had, despite her husband's protests, sought to prolong their son's infancy by keeping him in long hair and short breeches. But now, just days after her death, Robert Browning was doing what he had long wanted to do: 'Pen, the golden curls and fantastic dress, is gone just as Ba* is gone; he has short hair, worn boy-wise, long trousers, is a common boy all at once.'

Browning's entire world changed with Elizabeth's death. The forty-nine-year-old poet left Italy, his home for the last fifteen years – the whole of his married life – and returned to London with young Pen. 'There would be perhaps no more interesting chapter in his biography,' Henry James remarked of Browning, 'than that of his return from his long Italian absence, stricken and lonely (save for the place henceforth taken in his thoughts by his young son), to address himself to a future indefinite and obscure.'[1] In the course of researching Browning's life, I came to understand what James meant. The future was, indeed, a daunting prospect for the middle-aged widower. When they married, Elizabeth was the more famous poet. Robert looked to her as his Muse, yet in Italy his career languished while hers continued to flourish. By the time of her death, Robert had all but ceased to write poetry. His struggle over the next thirty years to come to terms with his loss and rebuild his life was a story waiting to be told. However, it was not one that fitted easily into the straitjacket of 'cradle to grave' biography.

I decided to take my cue from Henry James and begin my Life of

---

* The nickname Elizabeth was given as a child.

3

Robert Browning where his wife's ends. Robert did all he could to keep Elizabeth's spirit alive. He brought out new editions of her poetry while doing his best to ignore the gossip matching him with every eligible spinster in London. Yet, as Pen's sudden transformation from androgynous creature into common boy makes clear, Robert knew that he had to break free from Elizabeth's influence in order to find a way to survive – to live, possibly to love, and to write – without her. This conflict between the need to put his marriage behind him and the overwhelming desire to cling to his wife's memory is the central drama of Browning's life after Elizabeth's death. As the story unfolds, we witness his struggle to raise young Pen alone and to emerge as a poet in his own right. We also see a lonely man drawn dangerously close to three very different women – the sensitive and intelligent Julia Wedgwood, the handsome and impetuous Louisa, Lady Ashburton, and the adoring rich American, Katharine Bronson.

Although it does not follow a conventional format, this book is nevertheless a complete Life of Robert Browning, looking back as well as forward to gradually reveal the poet's character. This approach has allowed me to make the best use of the sources available, for little evidence survives from his childhood, and the story of the Brownings' marriage is known almost exclusively through his wife's letters – thus through her eyes, not his. Browning was many things to many people over the years. To the companions of his youth, he was a rising star, certain of success; to his fellow expatriates in Italy, he was simply the husband of the famous Mrs Browning; to his later friends and acquaintances, like Henry James, he was an unlikely literary lion who looked and spoke more like a bank manager than a poet. As I moved back and forth through Browning's life, these apparent contradictions dissolved, and a complete, very human, story emerged.

It is, after all, a journey in time which the lonely widower himself once made – facing up to the past before looking to the future.

CHAPTER ONE

'A Strange, Heavy Crown',
1861–5

On a June day in 1862 Robert Browning stood before 19 Warwick Crescent, a typical London house situated on a picturesque stretch of the Grand Junction Canal, as men unpacked the massive crates which had been sitting all those months in Florence gathering dust. Old pictures of saints looking out sadly from their black carved frames, Robert's own dark heavy furniture which had sat so awkwardly next to his wife Elizabeth's delicate pieces – these as well as a hundred charming nothings all passed through the threshold of the tall, narrow dwelling. Browning's manner was nervous and rapid. Standing approximately five feet six inches in his well-fitted black coat and trousers, his neatly brushed hair just touched with grey, he looked more like a prosperous man of business than a poet. Browning directed the men to set down Elizabeth's small decorative work table and her low deck armchair in the study, along with his own desk and ornately carved bookcase. Into the drawing room packers carried the tapestries and the wood and gilt mirror framed by two candle-bearing cupids.[1]

These objects had last seen the light of day in the Brownings' rooms on the *piano nobile* of the medieval Palazzo Guidi in Florence: their home for nearly the whole of their life together. On Elizabeth Barrett Browning's death, in June 1861, they had been shut away in crates and boxes, but not before Browning had commissioned a painting, by George Mignaty, of the room in Casa Guidi where Elizabeth had received friends, written letters, and composed verse. Then 'it was a sad house enough', wrote William Wetmore Story, the American sculptor, who had travelled from Rome for the funeral. 'There stood the table with her letters and her books as usual, and her little chair beside it, and in her portfolio, a half finished letter.' Browning had tenderly stowed his wife's writing case just as she left it, with her small beadwork purse, a miniature of Napoleon

III, and three numbers of the Italian newspaper *La Nazione*.[2] He had been equally careful with her books. Before packing one particular volume of her poetry which she had inscribed to him before their marriage, 'From EBB – September 2. 1845',* Robert mournfully scrawled on the same page ' – and this is July 26, 1861', followed by several lines of her poetry: 'Copied, alone in Casa Guidi, RB.'

Eventually the unpacking at Warwick Crescent was finished, down to the pictures and the old books which lined the stairs. 'I have got my poor old things from Florence & write this with the Bookcase beside me,' Robert wrote on 26 July 1862 to Isa Blagden, the Brownings' dearest friend and fellow expatriate; 'it is a sad business and I hardly know – or care to think – whether I like the things best here, or there, or at the bottom of the sea.' Several days later, perhaps while arranging the books in his study, he paused and wrote in his dead wife's New Testament a translation of the verse Dante had devoted to his beloved Beatrice: 'Thus I affirm, thus I am certain it is, that from this life I shall pass to another better, there, where that lady lives of whom my soul was enamoured' – signed and dated 31 July 1862. It was mere chance, he told the novelist William Thackeray when he met him walking with his daughter Annie in Kensington Gardens, whether he should live in London and join in social life, or go away to some quiet retreat and be seen no more.[3]

Browning's mind was full of such contradictions following Elizabeth's sudden and unexpected death. Throughout their fifteen years together, she had been all things to him, or so it had seemed: devoted wife and famed poet, cherished invalid and 'Guardian-Angel', the title of a poem Browning wrote shortly after their marriage. 'I am named and known by that moment's feat,' so Robert had written in another poem ('By the Fire-Side') of his and his wife's mutual declaration of love: 'There took my station and degree; / So grew my own small life complete, / As nature obtained her best of me – / One born to love you, sweet!'

Elizabeth had likened her husband's frequent mood swings to a chess-board, its squares either black or white, and never was this more in evidence than in the days, weeks, and months following her death. Before the funeral in Florence, when he was busy with those mercifully mind-numbing matters which attend death, Robert had managed to hold

---

* *A Drama of Exile* (*Reconstruction*, A325). The initials 'EBB' stand for her maiden name, Elizabeth Barrett Moulton-Barrett, as well as her married name.

himself together. 'She is with God, who takes from me the life of my life in one sense, – not so, in the truest,' he wrote to his sister Sarianna while his wife's body lay in the next room. 'My life is fixed and sure now. I shall live out the remainder in her direct influence, endeavoring to complete mine, miserably imperfect now, but so as to take the good she was meant to give me.' 'The future,' he continued, 'is nothing to me now, except inasmuch as it confirms and realizes the past.' He ended his letter to Sarianna: 'I shall now go in and sit with herself – my Ba, forever.' Yet, the very next day, 1 July, the forty-nine-year-old widower walked away from the cemetery convinced that he must make a clean break from the past or he would go mad: 'Life must now be begun anew – all the old cast off and the new one put on,' he told William Story.[4]

On the day of the funeral, shops in Florence were shut as a mark of respect. In the cool of evening, as the sun was setting, a crowd of Italians, English, and Americans followed the coffin, decked with crowns of white flowers and laurel, from Casa Guidi to the tiny Protestant cemetery in the Piazzale Donatello. The service was to be Church of England 'that I may hear those .. words at the beginning', Browning told Sarianna: 'I am the resurrection and the life, saith the Lord: he that believeth in me, though he were dead, yet shall he live: and whosoever liveth and believeth in me shall never die.' For the rest, Robert took nothing in but a flash of faces. William Story's impression was that the fat English parson blundered through it all.

The widower spent one last night alone at Casa Guidi. He laid his head on the table and remained senseless for what seemed an eternity. Husband and wife had hardly ever spent a night apart. Once, when Robert's early-evening train was cancelled on what was meant to be a day trip to Siena, he travelled home in a broken-down old vehicle with two priests. He did not arrive at Casa Guidi until three in the morning and, finding the gates locked, yelled up to Elizabeth, who ran down the corridor bare-footed to wake her maid Wilson and the wetnurse, who woke the porter, who opened the gates – and, as she later told her sister Henrietta, 'we were all right again.' Robert was always afraid lest she should be uneasy. Before their marriage he had counted the days – 'there are three days to wait,' he would tell Elizabeth – before his next visit to the Barretts' home in Wimpole Street.[5] He imagined himself in a strange state of suspended animation when he was not with her: 'So, I shall see her in three days / And just one night, but nights are short, / Then two long hours, and that is morn. / See how I come, unchanged, unworn! /

Feel, where my life broke off from thine, / How fresh the splinters keep and fine, – / Only a touch and we combine!'*

Robert had fallen in love with Elizabeth through her poetry before he had even laid eyes on her. Their extraordinary courtship began with the words, written in a letter dated 10 January 1845, 'I love your verses with all my heart, dear Miss Barrett.' Before he had reached the end, he exclaimed: 'I do, as I say, love these Books with all my heart – and I love you too.' Elizabeth had already declared her admiration for Browning's series of poems, *Bells and Pomegranates*,† which, she wrote in 'Lady Geraldine's Courtship' (1844), 'if cut deep down the middle, / Shows a heart within blood-tinctured, of a veined humanity!' Browning, as he admitted in that first letter, had nearly met her years before. John Kenyon, Elizabeth's cousin and an old friend of Robert's father, had asked the young poet one morning if he would like to be introduced to Miss Barrett. His cousin was a great invalid and saw no one – but, he confided, 'great souls jump at sympathy.'[6] However, she was too unwell that day, and the years had gone by.

Elizabeth was by far the better known – and more popular – poet. Critics and readers alike thought Robert's verse too obscure and difficult. Yet Elizabeth considered him a genius – 'a master in clenched passion .. concentrated passion .. burning through the metallic fissures of language', or so she tried to explain to Mary Russell Mitford, who remained sceptical. 'You half-frighten me from sending you Mr Browning's poetry,' Elizabeth told her: 'Promise me not to say again that it was a pity he missed being .. an attorney .. an engineer .. a merchant's clerk .. what trade was it?' In her own way, Elizabeth also was seeking to extend the bounds of verse, to write a new poem of a new class. Walter Savage Landor, Shelley's long-lived contemporary, thought both Miss Barrett and Mr Browning too fond of striking by strangeness: 'What is composition but consistency and compactness?' Elizabeth had heard such remarks, even the claim that *she* had written things harder to interpret than Browning himself. This led her to imagine – if they were ever to collaborate – the comments which would be directed to the 'critical Board of Trade, about visible darkness, multiplied by two, mounting into palpable obscurity'.[7] The comparison did not worry her.

---

* 'In Three Days'.
† Published in eight pamphlets between 1841 and 1846 and including *Pippa Passes*, *Dramatic Lyrics*, *Dramatic Romances and Lyrics*, and seven plays.

Hanging on her bedroom wall in Wimpole Street, beside the engravings of Wordsworth and Tennyson, was one of Browning, all taken from R. H. Horne's *A New Spirit of the Age* (1844) – a survey of contemporary literary figures to which Elizabeth had contributed.

Neither poet had been expecting love. Elizabeth was thirty-eight when she received Mr Browning's epistolary outburst. She had been an invalid for so long; she did not expect to live much longer, let alone entertain a lover. Robert, at thirty-two, was fixed in his bachelor ways and had made up his mind to the impossibility of loving any woman, or so he thought: 'How,' he would plead with Elizabeth, when she refused to countenance any talk of love, 'could I expect you?' Confined by ill health to her bedroom (or 'crypt', as she called it), Elizabeth shrank from visitors, especially Robert. She was afraid that her appearance and manner would not meet his expectations – whatever they were. 'There is nothing to see in me, – nothing to hear in me,' she insisted: 'the rest of me is nothing but a root, fit for the ground & the dark.' Yet, she was curious about Mr Browning and asked John Kenyon, who often spoke of one poet to the other, if the picture on her wall was a good likeness.[8]

Robert persisted, and after four months and several hundred letters – letters full of warmth and wit, learning, and poetry – she finally acceded to his wishes. One May afternoon in 1845 Browning was shown into Miss Barrett's room (but not before she had pulled down his portrait from the wall 'in a fit of shyness', then Tennyson's 'in a fit of justice'). Neither was disappointed, although both were a little surprised. Robert realised that the woman reclining on the sofa, with her luxurious dark ringlets and large, sparkling brown eyes, was not composed of pure ether, after all. Elizabeth had perhaps the greater shock, for the man announced as Mr Robert Browning did not have the bearing of a poet at all; he was too well groomed, rather bumptious, and certainly loud (a characteristic he had picked up from being around his father's half-brother Reuben who had lost his hearing through a blow to the head in a cricket match). Nevertheless, they each liked what they saw and heard. Robert's speech was as breathless and honest as his letters. Elizabeth, once she had conquered her nerves, was as clever and sincere in her conversation as in her writing.

Almost immediately after that first meeting, Robert, with all the grace of the proverbial bull in a china shop, dashed off a proposal of marriage – or words that could be taken as such. Elizabeth had worked hard to convince herself that she could never be happy or bring happiness to another. She had first fallen ill in her early teens. When she was twenty-two, her mother died unexpectedly. Elizabeth sought peace and tranquillity in reading, poetry, and morphine, her 'elixir'. The doctor had originally prescribed the opium-based drug during her childhood illness; she had continued to take it to steady her pulse and to sleep 'in a red hood of poppies'. She preferred to stay in her room where she felt secure. Her father, who indulged the whims of his talented, eldest daughter, cosseted her and grew to need – indeed, demand – Elizabeth's absolute dependence on him. It was an unhealthy relationship. Then came the worst blow of all. Her favourite brother Edward ('Bro') drowned in a tragic sailing accident, for which she irrationally blamed herself. She could neither speak nor shed a tear, but lay for weeks and months half unconscious, her mind wandering.[9]

Thus it was that when Robert proposed marriage to her, after only their first meeting, Elizabeth was shocked – almost angry – that anyone should try to tell her that she might love and be loved freely, with no accompanying sorrow, no conditions attached. Elizabeth begged him to forget at once and for ever his intemperate words; let them 'die out between *you & me alone*, like a misprint between you & the printer'. Elizabeth could not contemplate the future; she could have no future. But she, who had had so many sadnesses and so few pleasures in her life, desperately wanted their friendship to go on as it had before. 'We will,' she resolved for them both, 'shuffle the cards, & take patience, & begin the game again, if you please.'

Robert acquiesced – for a few months. But, by the end of the summer, he could keep still no longer: 'Let me say now – *this only once*,' he told Elizabeth at the end of August, ' – that I loved you from my soul, and gave you my life, so much of it as you would take, – and all that is *done*, not to be altered now.' Elizabeth again insisted that her life was a closed book, and a tragic one at that. What could she bring to him but anxiety and 'more sadness than you were born to'? 'We must leave this subject,' she insisted, '& I must trust you to leave it without one word more.' But Robert would not let it go this time, and within a matter of weeks Elizabeth had surrendered: 'Henceforward I am yours,' she declared on 26 September, 'whether friend or more than friend.' 'Only in meanwhile,' she added, 'you are most absolutely free .. "unentangled" (as they call it) by the breadth of a thread.'

'*My own, now!*' a triumphant Robert exclaimed; 'for there it is! .. oh, do not fear I am "*entangled*" – my crown is loose on my head, not nailed there.'

The engagement lasted a year during which time the visits, the letters, the lovemaking continued. For Elizabeth, it was like her own special fairy tale, and the postman's knock was the fairy's wand. She never wanted it to end. Her health dramatically improved. At Robert's urging, she cut down on her use of morphine. She would always insist that she did not take it for her 'spirits' – 'you must not think such a thing.'[10] Nevertheless, Elizabeth was psychologically, if not physically, dependent on the drug. But happiness is the most powerful drug of all. She found herself able to stroll about Regent's Park, and to step out of the house unaided and alone to post letters.

As for Browning, the waiting was sheer hell. He suffered more and more from terrible headaches and even nightmares. Not knowing what to do with himself, he began to indulge in superstitious nonsense. Once he picked up at random a book from the shelf and let it fall open, certain the words would guide him. It turned out to be an Italian grammar, of all things. 'What could it prove,' he told Elizabeth, 'but some assurance that you were in the Dative Case, or I, not in the ablative absolute?' He would have been thankful to find such a word as 'conjunction' or 'possessive pronoun'. But the phrase which stood out, tucked away under 'promiscuous' exercises for translation, was: '*If we love in the other world as we do in this, I shall love thee to eternity.*' Repeating the words, a bedazzled Elizabeth declared to her lover: 'I *shall.*'[11]

His parents and sister knew, but Robert longed to tell certain friends about their engagement. Elizabeth insisted that it remain a closely guarded secret; she had told her sisters Henrietta and Arabel, but no one else. Above all, her father must not find out, for she knew that he would never entrust the care of his precious hothouse flower to another man. He absolutely forbade his children – even his sons – to marry. It was an eccentricity ' – or something beyond', Elizabeth tried to explain to Robert.[12]

As the summer of 1846 drew to a close, Browning felt it was now or never. Surely, he argued, Elizabeth must realise that her delicate health would not allow them to travel in the winter months. She reluctantly agreed. They had already decided to marry first, then wait a few days before crossing the English Channel together. They would stop over in Paris en route to their final destination, Italy. The doctors had long recommended Italy, with its (usually) warm, sunny clime, for the invalid, but Mr Barrett had, perversely, forbidden her to go. The weeks and days leading up to the marriage bordered on the farcical. An observant aunt had guessed the truth about 'Elizabeth's poet' (as Mr Browning was called within the family circle) and teased her about it in front of her father. Robert then came down with a fever. Just when he had recovered and begun to look at train and boat timetables, Elizabeth's beloved cocker spaniel, Flush, was kidnapped. She was advised on all sides – even, to her horror, by Robert – not to give in to the blackguards. But she would not forsake Flush and, after much drama, the ransom was paid and the dog returned.

Then, on 10 September, Mr Barrett announced that the family would be leaving London while the house on Wimpole Street was being refurbished. There was no more time left. Robert and Elizabeth were married two days later at St Marylebone Parish Church, in the presence of only his cousin and her maid Wilson. They departed in separate cabs, to the verger's astonishment. The newlyweds did not see each other for a week; Robert refused to act out the charade of asking for 'Miss Barrett' on his wife's doorstep. It was one of the most painful and anxious weeks of his life, he later told Mrs Sutherland (Alexandra) Orr, his friend and biographer. At last, on 19 September 1846, they left as man and wife for the Continent.

Although they were beyond the reach of Mr Barrett, Robert was all too aware that he now faced an even greater danger. Would Elizabeth's frail body survive the Channel crossing, the overland journey to Paris and cheap lodgings there? They were now as poor as church mice. Each had borrowed some money from family and friends; Elizabeth had some investment income. As for the sale of their poetry, she earned relatively little from it, Robert even less. He could not yet provide for her financially – would he be able to care for her, keep her safe? He had not even managed to get the train timetables to Southampton straight; it was Elizabeth, his fragile charge, who had caught the mistake. If something were to happen to her – if she were to die, God forbid, before they had even reached Italy – how could Robert forgive himself? So anxious was he en route to Paris that he insisted on carrying his wife from the diligence, through a sea of strange faces, to the travellers' waiting room, and back again. Once in Paris, however, Elizabeth was able to reassure her husband that she might venture – on her own two feet – beyond the hotel lobby; they might even visit the Louvre together and dine out at a restaurant.

While in the French capital, the Brownings sought out a mutual friend, Mrs Anna Jameson, whom they knew to be in the city. She, of course, had known nothing of their marriage, and her astonishment at seeing them together was almost comical, or so her niece Gerardine, who was travelling with her, recalled. 'You dear, abominable poets!' she exclaimed. 'Why what a ménage you will make! – You should each have married a *petit bout de prose** to keep you reasonable.' Nevertheless, the kind-hearted, quick-witted woman welcomed the happy but emotionally and physically exhausted couple with open arms – and immediately took them under her wing, even escorting them as far as Pisa. Mrs Jameson also gave them much unwanted advice along the way. When she told the newlyweds that even in the happiest marriages passion turns to mere friendship – 'just what one might feel for an old armchair' – Robert whispered to Elizabeth that if she lived to be eighty, he could only think of loving her better.[13]

Anna Jameson had always been fond of Browning. 'His joy & delight,' she wrote to her friend Lady Byron, 'and his poetical fancies & antics, with every now & then the profoundest seriousness & tenderness interrupting the brilliant current of his imagination make him altogether a most charming companion.' Charming but hopeless: '*He* is full of spirits & good humour & his unselfishness – & his turn for making the best of every thing & his bright intelligence & his rare acquirements of every kind rendered him the very prince of travelling companions – *but* – (always *buts*!!) he is in all the common things of this life the most impractical of men – the most uncalculating – rash – in short the worst *manager* I ever met with. *She* – in her present state – & from her long seclusion almost helpless – now only conceive the ménage that is likely to ensue & without FAULT on either side!' 'With all the abundance of love, & sense & high principles,' the matron and occasional governess confessed to Lady Byron, 'I have had now & then a tremour at my heart about their future.'[14]

Despite Mrs Jameson's heart tremors, the Brownings survived and, what is more, they seemed to delight in every aspect of marriage, physical as well as spiritual. Early in their marriage, first from Pisa then Florence, Elizabeth wrote to Arabel and Henrietta that Robert would insist that he loved her more and more every day and with so much greater love. His 'dogma' was that she did not know and never would know how much he loved her. Still concerned for his wife's health, he consulted her

* 'A little bit of prose'.

sisters by letter and also Wilson, who would exclaim from time to time, 'I never saw a *man* like Mr Browning in my life.' Like most newlyweds, the couple preferred to keep to themselves. If the bell rang, how 'detestable!' Elizabeth told Arabel: 'Robert has to run away & put off his slippers, & I, to put on as goodnatured face as I can.' She said of this 'quiet yet new life' with Robert: 'it is like riding an enchanted horse .. he is *perfect.*' Elizabeth was not that fragile. If there were any awkward moments, she did not share them with her sisters, in whom she confided most things. She described for them one occasion, at breakfast, when Robert suddenly declared – in the midst of their talking and laughing – 'Now I do wish your sisters could see us through some peephole of the world!' Yes, Elizabeth agreed, 'as long as they did not HEAR us through the peep-hole!' – for, like all people in love, they talked mainly nonsense.

Browning, who described himself as a 'born, bred and bigoted hater of letter writing', gladly left Elizabeth to describe the day-to-day events for the benefit of friends and family.[15] Rather, he wove the fabric of their life together into his verse. This middle-aged couple revelled in their new-found freedom like children let out to play: 'Laughs with so little cause! / We devised games out of straws. / We would try and trace / One another's face / In the ash, as an artist draws; / Free on each other's flaws, / How we chattered like two church daws!' So Robert wrote in 'A Lovers' Quarrel'.

They loved each other for their 'flaws' as well as their virtues. Robert could be impetuous and judgmental, but these faults stemmed from that boundless energy and sense of fun which Elizabeth seemed to feast upon. She was, perhaps, too soft-hearted and impressionable, but these qualities flowed from the same tranquil source which so often cooled Robert's temper. An early Casa Guidi neighbour, Mrs David Ogilvy, who saw the Brownings in the most domestic and natural of settings, remembered Mr Browning as 'vehement, talkative, and hasty, full of gesticulation, and fond of argument'. (He mounts an argument 'just like a battery', Elizabeth told Arabel six months into married life.) Mrs Browning, on the other hand, was 'quiet, half-proud, half-humorous in her expression, as he expatiated, coming in now and then with a little deprecatory "Oh, Robert!" as a gentle drag on his impetuosity'.* A visitor to Florence, Sophia Hawthorne, concurred, describing Browning as 'very mobile'.

---

* Annie Thackeray Ritchie called Mrs Browning's voice, 'a sort of faint minor chord, as she, lisping the "r" a little, uttered her remonstrating "Robert!" '

He 'flings himself about just as he flings his thoughts on paper, and his wife is still and contemplative. Love, evidently, has saved her life.'[16]

Elizabeth enjoyed teasing the boisterous Robert, and he affectionately rose to the bait. She often found his constant concern for her health a little stifling and told him so in her droll way. Robert, feigning indignation, declared that she could not possibly love him and composed an impromptu verse to illustrate the point: 'That I only deceive / Beguile him and leave / At the treason to grieve, / While like fair mother Eve / I laugh in my sleeve!' All because, Elizabeth explained after recording these lines for Arabel, 'I object to turning him out of his chair, when my sofa is as near the fire .. or because I dont sit with a shawl over my head, or some such fantastical reason.'[17]

Browning knew that laughter was the best medicine. 'He amuses me & makes me laugh,' Elizabeth told her sisters in the early days of their marriage, 'till I refuse to laugh any more.' In early 1847, recovering after her first miscarriage, she described how Robert talked and jested, told stories, improvised verses in several different languages, sang, explained the difference between Mendelssohn and Spohr by playing on the table and, when he had thoroughly amused her, accepted it as a triumph, a pleasure of his own. On another occasion Robert had Elizabeth literally in tears of laughter while recounting his attempt to catch a lift home to Casa Guidi with a friend, Hatty Hosmer, in a vegetable cart. The donkey, when it heard the words *Andra, andra*, took off at a full gallop. The footboard began to slip from beneath the passengers' feet; the seat slid perilously backward; vegetables flew everywhere. Finally, the animal came to an abrupt stop, not in front of Casa Guidi, but before his own gate, dislodging everything and everyone in the cart. When the bedraggled pair finally reached the apartment, Robert set about dramatising the scene for Elizabeth. He rigged up a rope and a few boards, rattled the furniture and, for the full effect, produced some vegetables, which at stated intervals, Hatty Hosmer recalled, but with utter disregard of Mrs Browning's safety, were hurled about the room. 'Nothing,' Robert commented afterwards, 'does Ba so much good as a good laugh, and I will set this down as the laugh of her life.' This was only a year before she died.[18]

These and so many other memories must have flooded back to Browning as he sat alone in the tomblike silence of Casa Guidi that night after the funeral. 'The cycle is complete,' he had told William Story and his wife,

Emelyn; 'here we came fifteen years ago; here Pen was born; here Ba wrote her poems for Italy.'[19] The next day he trudged up to the hills above Florence, a journey he and Elizabeth had made a thousand times before, up the winding road, 'past the herbs in red flower & the butterflies on the top of the wall under the olive trees', to take refuge at the Villa Brichieri in Bellosguardo, the home of the Brownings' closest friend, Isa Blagden.[20] His twelve-year-old son Pen had been staying there for some days.

Browning later confided to the Storys that he had remained in his place at Casa Guidi 'like a worm-eaten piece of old furniture looking solid enough, but when I was *moved*, I began to go to pieces'. Pen tried in his childish way to comfort his father, but Robert broke down completely in front of Isa. He cried out, 'I want her, I want her!' and whispered his fear that he would not get through the night. He had several choking fits and passed out, terrifying poor Isa. She was to call this time her 'apocalyptic month'. In the weeks that followed at the Villa Brichieri, Robert tried again and again to reassure his friends – and himself – that he was not prostrated by this calamity.[21]

Browning was certain of only one thing: he could not stay in Florence. He knew the city intimately. Every sight and every sound – the blue-tinted hills by day, the twinkling of firefly lights at night, the nightingales' song, the sweet bells of Florence – would remind him of the fifty-five-year-old woman who had died in his arms looking like a young girl, free from pain at last. 'Places are ideas, and ideas can madden or kill,' Elizabeth had once remarked. Robert thought that he would never again be able to settle in any one place. He would leave Italy altogether. 'No more "housekeeping" for me, even with my family,' he told an old friend, Fanny Haworth: 'I shall grow, still, I hope – but my root is taken, remains.'[22]

Within a month of Elizabeth's death, Robert and Pen left Florence together with the ever-faithful Isa Blagden and the boy's pony. They must have made a sad, strange entourage. Browning's plans (such as they were) were to spend a few quiet months with his father and sister in France, perhaps Paris. He roamed Europe that summer a haunted man. He thought of spending a few days in London to see Elizabeth's sister Arabel, but the process of going over the old ground, stopping at the old inns was all too much, and he abandoned the idea. Paris, where he and his wife had spent their honeymoon, proved equally unbearable.[23]

In his despair Robert went out of his way to avoid greeting the friends he came across on his travels. At the train station in Amiens, and again at Boulogne, he caught sight of the Poet Laureate, Alfred Tennyson. He pointed out the great bearded man to Pen but kept well out of sight himself, pulling his hat over his face. Yet Browning knew Tennyson well. Before his marriage Robert had seen Tennyson at one or two London dinner parties, but their close friendship had begun when they met in Paris in 1851 (Tennyson had been made Poet Laureate the previous year). Elizabeth greeted Tennyson's new wife, Emily, like a sister, and Robert was touched by the invitation to stay at the Tennysons' house in Twickenham, near London. A year later Robert attended the baptism of the Tennysons' son Hallam while Elizabeth commiserated with Emily on the matter of screaming babies. The Brownings had last seen the Poet Laureate in the autumn of 1855, in London, when they had invited him to their humble lodgings in Dorset Street. Dante Gabriel Rossetti and his brother William, two of Browning's earliest admirers, were also present, as were Ford Madox Brown, William Holman Hunt, Browning's sister Sarianna, and Elizabeth's sister Arabel. Over two evenings, Elizabeth recorded, Tennyson 'dined with us, smoked with us' – Robert did not smoke,* nor did the ladies – 'opened his heart to us (and the second bottle of port), and ended by reading *Maud* through from end to end, and going away at half-past two in the morning'.[24] Browning returned the compliment by reading 'Fra Lippo Lippi' from his forthcoming volume entitled *Men and Women*. Dante Gabriel Rossetti sketched both poets.

On its publication later that same year Browning had had high hopes for *Men and Women*, the first major collection of new poems to be published since their marriage,† saying: 'They are the best of me, hitherto and for some time to come probably.' They also represented Robert's new life with Elizabeth his Muse. Her poetry had made him understand what had been lacking in his own, or so he believed. Long before their marriage, Browning confessed to Elizabeth that 'you *do* what I always wanted, hoped to do, and only seem now likely to do for the first time – you speak out, *you*, – I only make men & women speak.' Elizabeth had thought herself, as a poet, to be at a lamentable disadvantage, having been shut away from most of the outward aspects of life. Yet, in truth,

---

* Nor did he gamble or drink excessively. Elizabeth would sometimes tease him about the old Puritan blood which ran through his veins (EBB to Arabel, 12 April [1847]).
† Browning had published separately in 1850 *Christmas-Eve and Easter-Day*, and also a poem, 'The Twins', in aid of Arabel's School for Ragged Children in 1854.

Browning had had the more sheltered life. Yes, he had been places and seen things (Italy and Russia), but he had never felt genuinely isolated or hopeless; he was happy at home – even spoiled, as he admitted – and had never experienced emotional tyranny; he had never lost anyone dear to him, as had Elizabeth with the death of her mother and brother. If it had been otherwise, she told Robert, 'your step would not be "on the stair" quite so lightly.'[25]

In her poetry Elizabeth spoke from the heart, in her own voice. By contrast, Robert's poetry was at one remove from the poet. He invented dramatic situations and spoke through his characters – many of them obscure figures from the past – but always with sharp psychological insight. 'My Last Duchess' (1842) is a chilling tale of murder narrated by the perpetrator himself. Set in the Italian hill town of Asolo, 'Pippa Passes' (1841) tells the story of how the lives of four unhappy people are transformed when they chance to hear the sweet, innocent song of the little silk weaver Pippa beneath their windows. Browning's characters, friends noted, seemed to take on a life of their own, moving about in their creator's mind long after he had laid down his pen.

When in 1847 Dante Gabriel Rossetti, aged nineteen, first came across Browning's strikingly modern poems, everything else took second place, his brother William recalled. The poems 'were endless delights; endless were the readings, and endless the recitations'. The young artist imposed Browning's verse as a sort of dogmatic standard upon the nascent Pre-Raphaelite Brotherhood – 'thrust[ing] it down everybody's throat'. The early Pre-Raphaelites strove to breathe new life into their historical subjects on canvas – to depict them warts and all – just as Browning did on the page. Only a few days after that memorable evening in 1855 when Dante Gabriel Rossetti heard Browning read 'Fra Lippo Lippi', the artist visited Oxford to meet Edward Burne-Jones and other undergraduates.* One poor young man who made some disparaging remark about *Men and Women* 'was rent in pieces at once for his pains', Burne-Jones recalled, 'and was dumb for the rest of the evening'.[26]

'My Last Duchess' and 'Pippa Passes' are extraordinary poems – Eliza-

---

* Another Oxford man, Lord Carnarvon, wrote to Browning in 1883: 'I can remember when I was an undergraduate at Oxford singing or shouting out your ballad of the ride to Ghent ['How Thy Brought the Good News from Ghent to Aix'] – with poor Lothian in a midnight ride which we took – in defiance I am afraid of Collegiate discipline – one hot summer' (BL Add 60865, ff. 1–29). Henry Howard Molyneaux (Herbert), Lord Carnarvon, gained a first-class degree in 1852.

beth wished that she had written the latter – but 'these scenes and song-scraps', as Robert himself admitted before their marriage, give '*no* knowledge of me – it evidences abilities of various kinds, if you will, – and a dramatic sympathy with certain modifications of passion .. *that* I think: but I never have begun, even, what I hope I was born to begin and end, – R.B. a poem.' '*Now*' was the title of the poem that he would write, he said, returning to the subject a few weeks later: 'what is to be done *now*, believed *now*'. Browning was never to abandon the use of drama. The theatre had always been a great love of his, and he felt secure writing with a cast of characters in mind. Like his realist painter, Fra Lippo Lippi, he knew 'the value and significance of flesh'. He also understood that 'the common reader is susceptible to plot, story, and the simplest form of putting a matter "Said I," "Said he," & so on'. Nevertheless, greatly influenced by his wife's example, he began to attempt poetry without a stage setting or protagonist to hide behind. 'So into me has it gone, and part of me has it become,' Browning had told Elizabeth in that very first letter, 'this great living poetry of yours, not a flower of which but took root and grew.'

'I felt sure,' she declared, 'that as a poet you fronted the future – & that your chief works .. were yet to come.'[27]

And so it was with future glory in mind that Robert had set to work to finish *Men and Women* in the winter of 1854–5. After a breakfast of fruit and coffee he locked himself away at Casa Guidi in the small sitting room, lined with delicate frescoes, to write his lyric poetry; Elizabeth settled herself in the drawing room to compose her long novel-poem, *Aurora Leigh*. Each morning, as he got up from the table to go to his desk, he would ask Elizabeth to wish him 'good-fortune'. They both meant to 'make a success if we can', she had told Arabel. By the summer Browning's collection was complete. It contained his most personal poems to date, including 'Guardian-Angel', 'By the Fire-Side', 'In Three Days', and 'A Lovers' Quarrel'. Most afternoons Elizabeth read through the poems, offering her comments, just as when, before their marriage, Robert had asked her to look over his poems, to 'read them and heed them and end them and mend them!' Even Isa Blagden was drafted in to transcribe them for the printer, which she did every morning for four hours. As a token of his love and gratitude, he dedicated *Men and Women* to Elizabeth, 'my moon of poets'. 'There they are,' begins 'One Word More', 'my fifty men and women / Naming me the fifty poems finished! / Take them, Love, the book and me together: / Where the heart lies, let the brain lie also.' With the title of this poem Robert, who had a remarkable memory for such things, was reminding Elizabeth of her stern injunction, before their engagement, to forsake all talk of love 'without *one word more*'. She was delighted. 'After one word more,' she told Isa Blagden, 'I needn't live one day more, need I? far less write?'[28]

But *Men and Women*, published in November 1855, failed with both critics and public – 'energy wasted and powers misspent' was *The Athenaeum's* verdict. Worse, the *Sun* printed a glowing review of Mrs Browning's poetry just ten days after disparaging Mr Browning's work. 'Perhaps they praised me with the amiable motive of vexing him more,' Elizabeth told Arabel, 'but he is'nt to be vexed by such means. If a calculation, it was miscalculated.' Browning's friends had looked for great things from him. Thomas Carlyle had told Robert three years earlier, in 1852: 'I remind you what is expected; and say with what joy I, for one, will see it arrive.' But the plain-speaking Scotsman, although he had some praise to bestow on *Men and Women*, told Browning that his poetry was, in the end, unintelligible, and that was really a sin. John Ruskin, another friend, thought his poems the most extraordinary 'conundrums' he had ever come across. Browning answered Ruskin that, while in prose the meaning should be crystal clear, poetry does not work to the same rules: 'Why, you look at my little song [Ruskin had singled out the poem "Popularity" as an example of his obscurity] as if it were Hobbs' or Nobbs' lease of his house, or testament of his devisings .. Do you believe people understand *Hamlet*?'[29] Despite this spirited defence, Robert was thoroughly discouraged by the negative reaction to *Men and Women*. He published no more poetry during his marriage.*

His career moribund, Browning had professional as well as personal reasons – the recent death of his wife – to shrink from Tennyson on that train platform in 1861. Ironically, one could say that he had prophesied his own ignominy in the poem which Ruskin had found especially

---

* Browning's poems 'Ben Karshook's Wisdom' and 'May and Death', both written before 1855, appeared in *The Keepsake* for 1856 and 1857, respectively, as a favour to the editor, Marguerite Power.

At least Robert and Elizabeth had the satisfaction of reading Ruskin's praise of 'The Bishop Orders His Tomb' in *Modern Painters* (vol. IV), issued in April 1856: 'I know no other piece of modern English, prose or poetry, in which there is so much told, as in these lines, of the Renaissance spirit – its worldliness, inconsistency, pride, hypocrisy, ignorance of itself, love of art, of luxury, and of good Latin. It is nearly all that I said of the central Renaissance in thirty pages of the *Stones of Venice* put into as many lines, Browning's being also the antecedent work.'

difficult. The speaker in 'Popularity' defines a true poet as one whose full promise will only be realised in the future, not the present. 'Stand still, true poet that you are! / I know you; let me try and draw you,' the narrator declares. When, one day, you are famous, 'remember one man saw you, / Knew you, and named a star!' But 'Meantime, I'll draw you as you stand, / With few or none to watch and wonder.'

The only peace the poet found that first summer without Elizabeth was at St Egonat on the wild, primitive, and lonely coast of Brittany, where he took a house for himself, his father, sister, and son. But Browning could not hide from the world for ever. The Brittany coast was an inhospitable place in the winter months. Paris was still too full of memories, 'nothings that grew to be somethings from their first association', as he told Isa Blagden in mid-August. More importantly, there was Pen to think of, and the matter of his education became more pressing as autumn approached. Dull, dark, damp London, whose climate seemed to match Robert's mood and where tutors were easy to find, seemed the obvious choice. 'London,' he remarked to the Storys the same month, 'may suit me better than a brighter place for some time to come.' But he remained absolutely determined, as he told friends repeatedly, that he should have no ties, nothing to prevent him from wandering about, if circumstances permitted: 'I want my new life to resemble the last fifteen years as little as possible.'[30]

Robert and Pen arrived in London on 29 September 1861. For the first fortnight they stayed with Elizabeth's spinster sister, Arabel, who lived on Delamere Terrace near Paddington. Mary, Henrietta's daughter, recalled her aunt and uncle 'arm in arm walking slowly up & down the double drawing room, in speechless sorrow'.[31] The Brownings then moved into rented accommodation nearby at 1 Chichester Road, Upper Westbourne Terrace. It was a great comfort to Robert when dear Isa, who had already been in England for some months, took a house across the way, no further from his lodgings, he informed the Storys in November 1861, than 'your ball-room from the green drawing room', in the Palazzo Barberini in Rome. Nevertheless, by the next spring Browning had tired of the strange furniture, communal staircase, and all the other grim accoutrements of London digs. He finally gave in and set up housekeeping just a few streets away, at 19 Warwick Crescent.

But Browning's main reason for acting against his earlier wish to have no ties was his son. Like all children, Pen needed a stable home. He was an odd child, by all accounts. 'I never saw such a boy as this before,' remarked Nathaniel Hawthorne when he visited Florence in 1858, 'so slender, fragile, and spirit-like, – not as if he were actually in ill health, but as if he had little or nothing to do with human flesh and blood. His face is very pretty and most intelligent, and exceedingly like his mother's. He is nine years old, and seems at once less childlike and less manly than would befit that age.' Hawthorne's robust young son, Julian, put it less delicately: 'I had the contempt for him which a philistine boy feels for a creature whom he knows he can lick with one hand tied behind his back, and I had nothing whatever to say to him.'[32]

Julian's contempt was owing, in no small part, to Pen's appearance. Elizabeth had endeavoured to keep her only child in a permanent state of androgynous babyhood, 'a sort of neutral creature', as she expressed it to Arabel, with blond curls and fantastic dress. She called Pen her 'Florentine boy' and claimed that his golden hair was due to his being born under the Italian sun. She was horrified when her Casa Guidi neighbour, Eliza Ogilvy, put aside the toddler smock and dressed her five-year-old son Alexander in pants and vest 'like an American'. In such garb, Elizabeth insisted, Pen would look like a 'small angel travestied'. She took more pride in her son than in twenty *Auroras*, she told Leigh Hunt. (Elizabeth's novel-poem, *Aurora Leigh*, was published to great acclaim in 1856.) Pen, Elizabeth told Mrs Ogilvy, was much 'the fashion' in Rome, and Elizabeth was secretly pleased when strangers mistook her son for a lovely little girl. Elizabeth fervently hoped that by the time Pen was twelve years old – 'the age for entertaining the idea of cutting off ringlets' – the style for men would have reverted back to long hair parted in the middle like Milton or Goethe.[33]

The boy's upbringing was unconventional in nearly every regard. Mrs Browning had wholeheartedly adopted Italy as her native country, and she duly made her son's first language Italian. The little boy subsequently went about lisping in two languages, often within a single sentence. Robert, however, spoke English to his son, insisting, 'the child's English, & *shall* be English.' Despite his father's dictum, Elizabeth told Henrietta, Pen persisted in professing to be an Italian – 'he tells everybody he's Italian.' Hawthorne had noted that Pen 'prides himself on being a Florentine, and is indeed as un-English a production as if he were native of another planet'. Pen certainly did appear to be from another world when it came to spiritualism, a subject in which his mother had taken a keen interest. In fact, Pen lived quite happily amongst the spirits and loved to babble about them to other children. On one occasion some of the younger ones, not surprisingly, took fright at his talk of spirits and angels. Poor Isa Blagden, who had been left in charge of the nursery, tried to calm the children by declaring it was all nonsense – 'angels remain in heaven & did'nt come into houses.'[34] In regard to more earthly matters, Elizabeth, who had become a mother at the age of forty-three and had lost four other babies through miscarriages, could never bring herself to discipline or even reprimand Pen. The boy's lessons – not to mention his ability to concentrate – suffered as a consequence.

Following Elizabeth's death, Browning's first thoughts had been for their son. Pen could not know his loss yet, he confided to Fanny Haworth. 'After years, his will be more than mine, he will want what he never had – that is, for the time when he could be helped by her wisdom, and genius and piety.' 'You know, I have her dearest interest to attend to at once – her child to care for, educate, establish properly .. all, just as she would require were she here.'[35] Robert knew, as he told his brother-in-law George Barrett the day after the funeral, 'all Ba's mind as to how that should be'.

But did he? On her deathbed Elizabeth had not uttered any last-minute wishes concerning their son; she had not even whispered Pen's name. At first Robert put this down to the fact that his wife had (thankfully) seemed unaware of her impending death. But the grieving widower and anxious father soon 'construed the silence into an expression of trust, more binding upon him than the most earnest exacted promise could have been', as Alexandra Orr would remark many years later. 'I have much or everything to do as directly in my wife's interest,' Browning told the actor William Charles Macready at the time, 'as if she were enjoining it on me when we talked over our plans the last evening of all.'[36]

In truth, Elizabeth's wishes for Pen had always been at odds with Robert's own. He gravely disapproved of his wife's immersion in the spirit world and worried about the effect of such 'humbug', as he called it, on a young mind. Unlike Elizabeth, Browning believed in a strict learning regime for Pen from an early age. And he hated to see his son in frills; he was mortified when people asked whether the child was a boy or a girl. Elizabeth recorded for Arabel's benefit one quarrel they had on the matter of Pen's lace caps and ribbons while drinking coffee on a moonlit evening in Venice's Piazza San Marco. 'Oh, man's pride!' was her comment. At least Elizabeth attempted to spare her husband's feelings by keeping compliments to the 'lovely little girl' as much as possible in the background.[37]

Pen did not much like being called a girl either. He had once, aged seven, doubled his fist and threatened a boy five years his senior to stop teasing or, 'I will show you that *I'm a boy*.' Elizabeth's comment to her friend Mrs Martin: 'So you will please to observe that, in spite of being Italians and wearing curls, we can fight to the death on occasion.'[38] Pen finally turned twelve, the age for entertaining the idea of cutting off ringlets, in March 1861. But, despite his mother's promise, the curls remained, much to Pen's disgust, recalled another English boy then living in Florence, Henry (Hal) Cottrell.

Four months after Pen's twelfth birthday Elizabeth was dead; within days of her funeral, Robert decreed that his son's ringlets should go. Hal Cottrell, who had long since shed his own childish curls, escorted Pen along the cobbled streets of Florence to the barber's shop. The child who sat down in the barber's chair that day stood up a fully fledged adolescent. At long last Pen had shed the golden locks which had kept him his mother's little angel and his father a mere bystander in his life. To make him a 'common boy all at once', Browning also ensured that his son had a new wardrobe. Pen was delighted.[39]

Soon after their arrival in London in September 1861 – the velvet tunic and short trousers, the hat and feather now just a bad memory – Robert set about in earnest transforming the uprooted Pen into a perfect English gentleman. Like all fathers, Browning wanted for his son what he thought best. A member of Cavour's Italian government had expressed the hope that Elizabeth's husband would remain in Florence and continue to raise their son as a Tuscan. But Robert was adamant in a letter to his old friend John Forster: 'Of course Pen is and will be English as I am English and his Mother was pure English.' He distrusted all hybrid and ambiguous natures and nationalities, Browning told the Storys that August, and wanted to make 'something decided of the poor little fellow'.[40] He did not want Pen to end up as one of that breed of displaced persons, 'idle and dilettantish and second-rate' (Henry James's phrase for Gilbert Osmond in *Portrait of a Lady*), whom he had known so well in Florence and had himself already become – or so he perhaps feared.

But how to make Pen an Englishman? Browning himself had grown up outside the Establishment. Oxbridge had been closed to him owing to his upbringing in a Dissenting household. Robert Lytton, a young diplomat and aspiring poet whom the Brownings had known in Florence, recommended an English public school. 'I am just the sort of man,' he explained, 'to have quite unEnglish-ed myself in so long a residence abroad, but for certain Saxon foundations laid at Harrow, which never quite give way and are always satisfactory to fall back on.'[41]

Browning himself never attended public school, but he knew that institutions like Harrow and Eton conferred aristocratic connections and friendships, 'which in England is the chief end of man!' Nevertheless, he thought that the rough rules at such an establishment would be a shock to the poor little fellow.[42] Furthermore, at Eton and Harrow learning was strictly limited to Greek and Latin. If Pen were educated at home, he could continue to pursue music, French, German, Italian, and drawing; or so Browning told himself, for the truth was, he could not bear to part with the sweet, good-natured Pen who so resembled his mother. 'I see increasingly every day,' he confided to Isa in October 1862, after he had been in London a year, 'that were [Pen] not *here*, I should be *no where*.'

Elizabeth would have approved wholeheartedly of educating Pen at home, although not with the rigour which Robert sought to impose. But it was his intention to 'grind a Balliol student' out of Pen – Balliol being the most prestigious, and academic, of the Oxford colleges – and he had to make up for lost time. Pen was anxious to please his father, and in this he appeared to succeed. Pen 'has the spirit of emulation singularly strong – accompanied, as it is, by no drawback such as envy or vanity', Browning had reported to the boy's uncle George in September 1861; 'his abilities are considerable & various, and he has a happy, social temper that makes him friends everywhere.' He confided to the Storys that Pen did not display the love for lessons which '(at bottom of my heart) I should like'. Pen's tutor, Mr Gillespie, thought the boy lacking in self-confidence, and it was no wonder: his mother had been taken away from him, as had his childhood home and friends. Nevertheless, Pen could fence, row, box, ride and swim as well as any Eton boy, as Browning repeatedly boasted to his friends. The rowing, which Pen did every day in the winding canal opposite Warwick Crescent, was particularly beneficial; he cut no bad figure, Browning remarked, in his white dress, managing a boat to perfection, as if it were a feather. Compliments paid to Pen were the one pleasure the widower had.[43]

All Browning's hopes and dreams at this time seemed to revolve around his son. Isa thought that he was in danger of becoming a 'monomaniac' on the subject of Pen's education. She had good reason to worry, for Robert's feelings for his son seemed much too closely bound up with the twin emotions of love and guilt which he felt towards the boy's mother. When he looked back on his marriage amidst the turmoil of his grief and recalled every ill-judged word and thoughtless action, Robert convinced himself that he could have – should have – been a better husband. 'All I can be sure of was my entire love,' he confessed to Isa in a muddle-headed way, 'by the light of, & for the sake of which, *now*, I dare hope that all my follies, mistaken procedures & inconsequentialities are understood & forgiven; it was *so* with me *then* – I could have loved *so*, without erring *so*: *now* I know better, do not love better, but certainly know immeasurably better, and should not, or if God please, *shall* not – offend again: and I hope there will be found evidence of that in whatever I do till the end.' Even after her death, Robert continued to think of himself as Elizabeth's husband, with all the responsibilities and obligations that entailed. As for Pen, he continued in his letter to Isa of April 1863, 'I love him dearly, but if I hated him, it would be pretty much the same thing.' Browning seemed to view his duty towards Pen not so much as a labour of love as the road to salvation.

In those first six months at Warwick Crescent the widower received few visitors, nor did he call on anyone except a very few close friends, in particular, his neighbours Arabel Barrett and Isa Blagden, and anyone else who could be of use to Pen. On his daily walks, Annie Thackeray recalled, Browning ventured beyond the 'peaceful oasis' of Warwick Crescent, eastwards towards the 'despairing shrieks and whirling eddies' of Paddington. 'Whether in an unconscious hugging of his chains,' Alexandra Orr remarked, or simply 'from the desire to save time, he would drag his aching heart and reluctant body through the sordidness'. She was in no doubt that this first period of Mr Browning's widowed life 'was one of unutterable dreariness, in which the smallest and yet most unconquerable element was the prosaic ugliness of everything which surrounded him'.[44]

Nevertheless, the day-to-day running of the household as well as the reassuring sound of the innocent Pen at his lessons forced Browning to turn away from his most morbid thoughts. He soon had another distraction to help ease the grief and appease the ghosts: the safeguarding of his wife's literary reputation. He painstakingly guided her *Last Poems* and a collection of her essays* through the press in 1862 and 1863, swearing to Isa Blagden that 'nothing that ought to be published, shall be kept back.' Robert may not have seen some of these poems while Elizabeth was alive. She had firmly believed that an artist needed complete

---

* *The Greek Christian Poets and the English Poets* (1863).

solitude and was loath to show her work to Robert until it was finished. He had respected her wishes, never reading a word of hers, he once told Annie Thackeray, until it was polished and ready for publication. To read these poems, then, for the first time after her death must have been melancholy work indeed.

One poem, entitled 'My Heart and I', Robert had probably seen before: Elizabeth had sent it to Miss Marguerite Power, editor of *The Keepsake*, in August 1857 (although it seems never to have been published).[45] The speaker, a woman who had in her 'own blood drenched the pen', is leaning upon a graveyard stone. 'So tired, so tired, my heart and I!' she repeats: 'We seem of no use in the world.' Despite her melancholy, the woman understands that all that matters in life is to have been loved. 'Yet who complains? My heart and I? .. if before the days grew rough / We once were loved, used – well enough, / I think, we've fared, my heart and I.' Browning could not but have been deeply affected on (re)reading 'My Heart and I'. He would have recalled those times – which became more frequent as her health declined – when the weariness of life had overwhelmed Elizabeth. And did not his wife's words seem to resound in his own breast at that moment: 'So tired, so tired, my heart and I'? When he told the Storys in March 1862 that 'reviewers will have my heart in their rough hands for the next month or two', Browning was referring not to any work of his own, but to the posthumous publication of Elizabeth's *Last Poems*.

Elizabeth's poetry had always had a popular following during her lifetime, a fact which Robert had proudly acknowledged. 'Thus they see you, praise you, think they know you!' he proclaimed in 'One Word More': 'There, in turn I stand with them and praise you – / Out of my own self, I dare to phrase it.' Such praise for Robert's poems remained elusive. Browning had instead concentrated his energies on helping Elizabeth correct proofs and basked in her success. 'That golden-hearted Robert,' Elizabeth had remarked concerning *Aurora Leigh*'s success, 'is in ecstasies about it – far more than if it all related to a book of his own.' Browning honestly believed that Elizabeth was the better poet, and to anyone who tried to tell him otherwise, he would reply: 'You are wrong – quite wrong – she has genius; I am only a painstaking fellow.'[46]

In March 1862, the same month that *Last Poems* appeared before the public, the publisher of *Cornhill Magazine*, George Smith, asked Robert to fill the distinguished post of editor.[47] The posthumous publication of

Elizabeth's verse turned the spotlight on her husband. George Smith had known and admired Browning since before his marriage. Thackeray, who had recently resigned from the job, would have supported Smith's choice in a fit of compassion, if nothing else. Browning's despair was obvious to his literary friends. Certainly Thackeray's daughter Annie, then in her early twenties, remarked on the poet's 'blackness through the sunshine' when she and her father met him in Kensington Gardens. On subsequent occasions she noted his 'jarred and troubled state'. 'The Editorship has, under the circumstances &c &c been offered to – *me*!' Browning told the Storys. 'I really take it as a compliment because I am, by your indulgence, a bit of a poet, if you like – but a man of the world and able editor, hardly! They count on my attracting writers, – I who could never muster *English* readers enough to pay for salt & bread!'

Browning's knee jerk reaction was to flatly refuse. 'My first answer was prompt enough,' he told the Storys: 'that my life was done for & settled, that I could not change it & would not.' But George Smith would not take no for an answer and insisted that Robert have a week to consider. His being a poet did not preclude him from having the common sense and literary judgement necessary to edit a magazine. 'I can't be sure how I shall answer,' he confided to his friends, 'for I have rather an impulse – first to get the salary, which Pen might find something to do with – next to figure as a man capable of choosing better articles . ., and last, to try what the business is like.' At the end of the week, the answer was still no, but the offer had made Robert begin to look beyond the dreariness.

Smith's offer seemed to mark the beginning of a genuine turnaround in Browning's literary fortunes. He was the prodigal son returned home: 'He, of all men,' explained the critic in *The Times*, 'needed the English air, and he went away from it.' The British reading public were now prepared to welcome the poet back with open arms. 'Seriously,' Robert continued in his letter to Story, 'now that I care not one whit about what I never cared for too much, people are getting goodnatured to my poems.' John Forster and B. W. Procter were editing selections from his work, he wryly commented, 'which is to popularize my old things: & so & so means to review it, and somebody or [other] always was looking out for such an occasion, and what's his name always said he admired me, only he didn't say it, though he said something else every week of his life in some Journal. The breath of man!'

The *Selections* appeared at the end of 1862; a three-volume edition of his *Poetical Works* followed in 1863.* At the opening of the annual exhibition of the Royal Academy the following spring, Forster, Browning's earliest and staunchest supporter, his editor, and dedicatee of the *Poetical Works*, declared before the assembled dignitaries: 'I see poetry in some pleasant forms known to you all, and especially in that of Mr Browning, one of the most original thinkers as well as one of the first poets of his time.'[48]

To Browning this success was bitter-sweet, for his wife was unable to share in it. Just as he knew that she had genius, so Elizabeth had understood her husband's poetic brilliance and originality. She had thought the poems in *Men and Women* his ablest work; indeed, she had been 'ready to die for them, at the stake'. She was often heard to remark that the British public's failure to appreciate his gifts was an infamy. Robert had never stopped believing that he would only produce his very best work with his wife by his side. Of course, he would still endeavour to write if, he once told Elizabeth before their marriage, 'I were forced to "live among lions" as you once said – but I should best do this if I lived a quietly with myself and with you.'[49] Despite her ill health, he rarely dared imagine life without her. When he did, it was a life, bleak enough, without poetry – in both the literal and figurative sense: 'How well I know what I mean to do / When the long dark autumn-evenings come, / And where, my soul, is thy pleasant hue? / With the music of all thy voices, dumb / In life's November too! / I shall be found by the fire, suppose, / O'er a great wise book as beseemeth age, / While the shutters flap as the cross-wind blows / And I turn the page, and I turn the page, / Not verse now, only prose!'†

Browning knew that he should get out more, see friends, enjoy all that London had to offer now that he was, indeed, living amongst lions. 'I make up my mind from week to week, *next* Monday I will begin & call on my friends,' he had confided to the Storys in January 1862; but invariably he would find an excuse not to venture forth that day. His friends persisted, the invitations increased, and the poet steeled himself. 'I go out a little,' he wrote to Story a month later, 'have called on friends, old & recent, – mean to accept all invitations henceforth: am just made

---

* Proctor published under the pseudonym 'Barry Cornwall'. The only previous collected edition of Browning's works had appeared in 1849.
† 'By the Fire-Side'.

a member of the Athenaeum by the committee, and in short am like one of those well-appointed cockney sportsmen who are accoutred from head to heel in sporting-gear, with the primest of guns & perfectest of pointers, & who only want nerve to pull the trigger.' By April 1862 he reports that he goes out to dine, 'in a cold-blooded way'. But he swore that he would not stay in a country house if invited by the angel Gabriel himself, and, on the first anniversary of Elizabeth's death, the widower spent the evening at home alone, politely but firmly refusing the eight well-meaning invitations which he had received.

Browning's Italian friends (including Isa Blagden, who had returned to Florence after nearly a year's absence) longed to hear the London gossip – and, more importantly, how he was getting on, for they mourned his absence. 'You cannot imagine how I shall miss him,' Story wrote at the time. The sculptor had acquaintances by the hundreds, but Browning had been his only intimate companion. The poet would not – or could not – oblige. 'I can't chronicle all these people that come & go before me, and whose very names I forget the next day,' he wrote to the Storys in January 1863: 'why do I like so much to hear gossip from you and fancy that London news can no more interest you than it does me? You throw bits of porphyry & marble pavement from Rome, and I have only London mud, that's the fact.' A year and a half later Browning's mood still had not changed. 'Well, I ought to regale you with accounts of my own goings-on, the dinners and the at-homes,' he confessed to the Storys, 'only, it is so flat an affair to me, – at all events, the retelling or even remembering it, that I should not answer your benevolent purpose, which is to do *me* good, not you.'[50]

Although he had fled its borders as quickly as was decently possible after Elizabeth's death, Robert's heart still lay in Italy with all its associations. Society had been so easy in that sunny country. Every street or square became a sort of common parlour, as Hawthorne described it, where friends and acquaintances gathered to see and be seen. The poet liked to imagine his true friends in Italy 'like portraits in the one habitable room of a house'. 'I go in among them many a time,' he told the Storys in January 1862, 'in the course of the day & night.' When Annie Thackeray and her father called on Browning in Warwick Crescent, he talked on, not of the present London, but of Italy. In the spring of 1863 the poet ran into an old acquaintance from Rome, Robert Macpherson, on the Underground. 'He seemed to have much of Rome in his beard & hair,' Browning remarked to the Storys; 'I felt unwonted love for him – &

so it is with the many people I meet, – whom I knew there and fancied I never could care three straws about.'

Alone, adrift in England, Browning clung to the idea of one day returning to Italy. He told himself and his friends that the only thing keeping him in England was his duty towards his son. 'I shall not keep house when Pen is at Oxford – to what use?' he wrote to Isa in November 1864, looking ahead several years: 'He will enjoy his vacations best in travelling. I yearn for Italy again.' He had told the Storys, 'I hope to end my life in the land I love best, and what with work and troubles of great & little degree,' – referring in the main to Pen's education – 'five or six years will pass, if I don't pass them – so one day a very aged person will come knocking &c as in the story books!'[51]

The Storys lived in Rome, a place where Robert could easily imagine himself retiring to. The thought of living once more in Florence was altogether another matter. With respect to Florence, he confided to Isa, 'I cannot tell how I feel about it, so do I change in my feelings in the course of a quarter of an hour sometimes: particular incidents in the Florence way of life recur as if I could not bear a repetition of them – to find myself walking among the hills, or turning by the villas, certain doorways, old walls, points of sight, on a solitary bright summer Sunday afternoon – there, I think that would fairly choke me at once: on the other hand, beginning from another point of association, I have such yearnings to be there! Just now, at the approach of Autumn, I feel exactly like a swallow in a cage, as if I *must* go there, have no business anywhere else, with the year drawing in. – How thankful I am that all these foolish fancies never displace for a moment the solid fact that I can't go but have plain duty to do in London, – if there could be a doubt about that, I should drift about like a feather: at times (to give you a notion of what I might do if free to be foolish) I seem as if I should like, by a fascination, to try the worst at once, – to go straight to the old rooms at Casa Guidi, & there live & die! But I shake all this off – & say to myself (sometimes aloud) "Don't be afraid, my good fellow, you'll die too, all in good time." '[52] In grey, drab London Robert could imagine nothing else for himself but old age and death. Italy stood for the best years of his life.

Browning seriously considered travelling to Florence in the summer of 1863 to oversee the final stages of Elizabeth's funeral monument, which he had asked Frederic Leighton, a friend from Italian days (and Alexandra Orr's brother), to design. But, in the end, his courage failed him. He apologised to Isa, asking that she attend to the details, which included disinterring the body, for he had 'a horror of that man of the graveyard'.[53] At about this same time, a nostalgic visit from Pen's Tuscan nurse, Annunziata, brought on one of Robert's old headaches. When Isa had written in October 1862 to tell Robert of the plaque, dedicated to the memory of his wife, which the citizens of Florence had placed above the threshold of Casa Guidi, Robert replied: 'I can't tell you the thrill of pain & pleasure I feel about it: the presence of Her is now habitual to me, – I can have no doubt that it is my greatest comfort to be always remembering her, – the old books & furniture, her chair which is by mine.'

Just the month before, surrounded by the old books and furniture, Robert had begun to consider a new book of 'Men and Women' – what would eventually appear in 1864 as *Dramatis Personae*. He pulled out poems, some only half written, which he had not touched since leaving Florence. After the failure of his previous book, Robert had done his best to avoid the blank sheets of paper on his desk. Nevertheless, he had continued, fitfully, to compose poems – some Elizabeth had seen. 'Robert deserves no reproaches,' Elizabeth had written to Fanny Haworth from Rome in May 1860, 'for he has been writing a good deal this winter – working at a long poem which I have not seen a line of, and producing short lyrics which I *have* seen, and may declare worthy of him.'[54] Robert may have had the idea for one of these short lyrics, entitled 'Confessions', during the long hours he spent nursing Elizabeth, feeding her jelly and warming coffee on the bedroom stove. Husband and wife might have passed the time imagining another world below the vials of medicine on her little table, with its pretty landscape painted by her sister Arabel. 'Where the physic bottles stand,' the invalid fancies, 'On the table's edge, – is a suburb lane, / With a wall to my bedside hand.'

The long poem which Robert had been working on that winter in Rome was almost certainly 'Mr Sludge, "the Medium" ', based largely on America's spiritualist ambassador, Douglas Home. Browning had had a running feud with Home ever since 1855 when he and Elizabeth had attended one of his seances in London. With nine people gathered round the table, a clematis wreath had risen in the air and settled on Elizabeth's head – a delicate compliment to genius. The poetess asked 'the spirit' wielding the wreath to crown her husband, that he might share in the honour. It was all too much for the non-believer Robert. He tried, and failed, to grab what he thought was a flesh-and-blood hand beneath the table. Furious, he grabbed his wife instead and stormed out. The next day, when Home had the audacity to call upon the Brownings, Robert – to Elizabeth's great dismay – nearly flung him down the stairs. The medium, however, had his revenge. Home claimed ever afterwards that Browning had resented the fact that his wife, and not he, had been crowned by the spirits.

After that experience, spiritualism became a taboo subject in the Browning household, yet Elizabeth remained firm in her faith, as did most of her fellow expatriates. Indeed, in Florence in the 1850s people rarely seemed to meet except to move tables. 'Try, will our table turn?' so begins a light-hearted stanza from 'A Lovers' Quarrel', written by Browning before the Home affair and other similar incidents had pro-voked his wrath. Some, like Elizabeth, thought spiritualism a new phase of Christianity; others looked upon it as a science; a few believed it to be the Devil's work. At the very least, spiritualism was an attempt to gain some consolation and understanding in the midst of bereavement and grief. The death of a loved one back home was particularly hard on the expatriates, for not only was there no chance of a final deathbed reconciliation, but often the dreadful news did not reach them for weeks.

The rational Browning would have none of it. Although he would not do so in front of her, Robert sometimes stamped on the floor 'in a frenzy of rage at the way some believers and mediums were deceiving Mrs Browning', according to Frances Cobbe. Isa Blagden had often found herself at the receiving end of Robert's anger. Bellosguardo neighbours, like Miss Cobbe, heard the two friends quarrelling over the matter. After Elizabeth's death, the poet's scepticism might understandably have been shaken. But when he spoke to Isa of 'rejoining' his wife one day, Robert was careful to dissociate himself from spiritualism. 'The difference,' he wrote, 'between me and the stupid people who have "communications" is probably nothing more than that I don't confound the results of the natural working of what is in my mind, with vulgar external appear-ances.'[55] While she lived, Robert dared not show Elizabeth a single line of his poem ridiculing spiritualism – and those who believed in it – for fear of upsetting her.

As Browning continued to think about a new book of verse, it no longer seemed enough merely to revisit these old poems; he had some-thing new to say. London streets may have looked grim, but the city's intellectual climate was especially exciting at this time. Old orthodoxies were being challenged, in particular the authenticity of the Gospels and of the biblical story of the Creation. Controversial works such as Charles Darwin's *On the Origin of Species* (1859) and Ernest Renan's *La Vie de Jésus* (1863) fuelled the debates which were going on in London newspapers, clubs, and drawing rooms. Just as Darwin imposed the rigours of science on the natural world, so Renan applied the discipline of history to the life of Jesus. Robert, who had always possessed an inquisitive mind, was intrigued.

Neither an historian nor a scientist, Browning responded to the ideas swirling around him in his own inventive – and slightly subversive – fashion. In the poem 'Caliban upon Setebos', the creature from Shakespeare's *Tempest* contemplates the creation of his world. Browning gives a nod and a wink to Darwin by presenting Caliban as the literary precursor to evolution's 'missing link' and his island, complete with finches and fossils, as a kind of Galapagos.* Another poem, 'A Death in the Desert', purports to transcribe the last words of St John the Evangelist from an ancient parchment. Browning was as sceptical about some of Renan's statements as Renan was about St John's. He had no doubt, Browning told Isa on reading *La Vie de Jésus*, that the author imagined himself stating absolute fact, just as the Evangelist had done.[56] The poet preferred to explore a different, and for him more fundamental, issue raised by these debates: the uneasy yet inextricable relationship between doubt and faith. We know just enough to have faith, the poet suggests, but not enough to dispel doubt, for man is 'a thing nor God nor beast, / Made to know that he can know and not more'.

Although he sought to escape his grief, at least for a while, by throwing himself into these abstract arguments, Browning could not shake off the memory of what he had lost. The scene of St John the Evangelist as he lay dying is reminiscent of Elizabeth's last moments as Robert described them to his sister: 'Only, he did – not so much wake, as – turn / And smile a little, as a sleeper does / If any dear one call him, touch his face – / And smiles and loves, but will not be disturbed.' But at least Browning had begun to perceive that he might tame his grief and harness it to his poetry. 'Yes,' Robert told Isa in December 1863, when he was hard at work on *Dramatis Personae*, 'the years go – we are in the *third*: at first, when you were here, the business was of the hardest, for nothing seemed

---

* The 'missing link' was a popular phrase in the 1860s. Caliban, drunk on a potent mix of honeycomb and seed pods 'which bite like finches when they bill and kiss', describes a fossilised newt 'turned to stone, shut inside a stone'.

doing, nothing *growing*, – only the emptiness and weariness of it all: now, there seems really *use* in the process, & fruit.' Browning now knew what real despair was, and his poetry began to reflect the 'fruits' of his suffering. Although he continued to speak through strange voices from the past, his new poems were, nevertheless, more personal, more heartfelt, and more insightful than anything he had written while Elizabeth was alive.

It was as though Robert was learning how to live again through his poetry. In 'A Death in the Desert' Browning finds that love is to be treasured above all else: 'For life, with all it yields of joy and woe, / And hope and fear, – believe the aged friend, – / Is just our chance o' the prize of learning love, / How love might be, hath been indeed, and is.' Time heals, the poet realizes, not by allowing us to forget but by bringing us closer to the truth. 'Grow old along with me!' begins 'Rabbi Ben Ezra':* 'The best is yet to be, / The last of life, for which the first was made.' All will be revealed, so 'Be our joys three-parts pain!' – 'Young, all lay in dispute; I shall know, being old.' In 'Abt Vogler' the poet eavesdrops on the eponymous eighteenth-century German composer as he contemplates life's joys and sorrows while extemporising on a keyboard instrument. Robert had always loved music, but after Elizabeth's death he discovered its restorative powers. He became an avid concert-goer, telling Isa that 'the infinitely best thing in London to me is the *music* – so good and so much of it.'[57] In the poem Abt Vogler describes the notes as they soar above. Suddenly the chord resolves and the music stops, 'for my resting-place is found, / The C Major of this life: so, now I will try to sleep.'

Browning's grief had awakened something deep inside, and with these poems, published in *Dramatis Personae* in May 1864, he bared his soul before the public. Certainly, no one could have doubted the personal anguish which lay behind one in particular, 'Prospice'. Browning composed it soon after his return to London, as he sat alone in those grim rooms in Chichester Road, wondering what was to become of him. The Latin title translates as 'Look forward'.

Fear death? – to feel the fog in my throat,
   The mist in my face,
When the snows begin, and the blasts denote
   I am nearing the place,

* Ben Ezra was a twelfth-century Spanish scholar.

The power of the night, the press of the storm,
   The post of the foe;
Where he stands, the Arch Fear in a visible form,
   Yet the strong man must go:
For the journey is done and the summit attained,
   And the barriers fall,
Though a battle's to fight ere the guerdon be gained,
   The reward of it all.
I was ever a fighter, so – one fight more,
   The best and the last!
I would hate that death bandaged my eyes, and forbore,
   And bade me creep past.
No! let me taste the whole of it, fare like my peers
   The heroes of old,
Bear the brunt, in a minute pay glad life's arrears
   Of pain, darkness and cold.
For sudden the worst turns the best to the brave,
   The black minute's at end,
And the elements' rage, the fiend-voices that rave,
   Shall dwindle, shall blend,
Shall change, shall become first a peace out of pain,
   Then a light, then thy breast,
O thou soul of my soul! I shall clasp thee again,
   And with God be the rest!

In an age when bereavement was a shared experience, the public recognised Robert's courage in the midst of sorrow, and they responded to it. 'Those who know the story of the one great loss of Mr Browning's life,' *St James's Magazine* wrote of *Dramatis Personae*, 'feel *how* and *whence* has come to him the serene wisdom, the belief in things good, which is the best and most valuable characteristic of his poetry. Further, out of his great love for and belief in mankind, he takes his readers into his secret, though with a vague reticence that shows how profound and how sacred has been the man's agony.' These poems do indeed convey a kind of wisdom, but it is far from serene. Rather, Browning had come to acknowledge as noble and good man's constant struggle to understand – and 'bear the brunt' – in an ever-changing world. The critic for the *Quarterly Review* saw Browning's new collection in its wider context: 'Coming fresh from a great deal of our nineteenth-century poetry to that of Mr Browning, we are in a new world altogether, and one of the first things we are apt to do is to regret the charms of the old.' Nevertheless, he added, 'the new land is well worth exploring, .. It breathes into modern verse a breath of new life and more vigorous health, with its aroma of a newly turned and virgin soil.'

With the publication of *Dramatis Personae* Browning had redis-covered – one might almost say, reinvented – himself as a poet after nearly a decade's silence. It was his first book of poetry to reach a second edition. In December 1864 he wrote to Isa: 'I feel such comfort and delight in doing the best I can with my own object of life, – poetry, – which, I think, I never *could* have seen the good of before, – that it shows me I have taken the root I *did* take, *well.* I hope to do much more yet: and that the flower of it will be put into Her hand somehow.' He still clung to that image which had sprung to mind before his marriage: of Elizabeth's poetry taking root and flowering in his own literary imagination.

But, for the rest, as Robert wrote in this same letter, he was at best resigned. He continued going through the motions – 'dining out in a way that looks absurd enough'. 'I can never, – shall never try to go an inch below the surface,' he had once told Isa; 'but what need is there of that with you?' Although he might meet with kind acquaintances, his only true friends were those who had been part of the world he and his wife had created. Robert especially valued Isa's friendship precisely because she had been Elizabeth's closest confidante in Florence: 'no human being can give me one hand – with the feeling on my part that the other holds that of my own Ba – as you can & do': so he had written the last day of August 1861, two months after his wife's death.

But with Isa and his other close friends, the Storys, far away in Italy, Robert felt increasingly isolated and lonely in London. The company of an adolescent son was not enough, and the epistolary tittle-tattle which he exchanged with his Italian friends could not replace 'what will be lost to us for many a year', he told Isa, 'the old chats and gossips'.[58] In this state of mind, Browning had gone to dine at the home of Mr and Mrs Hensleigh Wedgwood of 1 Cumberland Place, Regent's Park, in the autumn of 1863, when he was still hard at work on *Dramatis Personae*. There he was introduced to their thirty-year-old daughter, Frances Julia ('Snow') Wedgwood, who later remembered him on that occasion as 'so ailing'. Robert found genuine warmth and sympathy amongst the Wedgwoods, and he became a frequent visitor to the house. The intel-lectual and high-minded Julia was shy and reserved. But, as one of the few early admirers of his verse, she had come to think of the poet as an 'old friend' long before they met. Moreover, Browning, who was more at ease around women than men, did not patronise Miss Wedgwood but seemed to enjoy her company and treated her as his equal.

Within a few months of that first visit to Cumberland Place, the eldest Wedgwood son had fallen ill and was not expected to live. Browning was kind and sympathetic, and Julia knew that he understood grief. 'Your own unparalleled loss,' she wrote in the first letter, dated 14 May 1864, of a revealing correspondence, 'must dwarf in comparison every other separation, but I believe it is just those who have experienced the worst of that terrible wrench, who can also feel the most for those who undergo a lighter form of it.' The Wedgwoods' affection for, and trust in, Browning was shown by the fact that he continued to be welcome in the sad house throughout the young man's illness. His first question as he crossed the threshold on each visit would no doubt have concerned the health of the patient. On departing, Browning might have squeezed Miss Wedgwood's hand to express what he could not voice: the feeling of hope tinged with pity.

James Mackintosh Wedgwood breathed his last on 24 June 1864. The family had called him 'Bro'; Elizabeth's brother, who drowned at sea, had also gone by that name. Browning must have been struck – and morbidly attracted – by this and other eerie similarities between his dead wife and Julia Wedgwood. Both women were intelligent and well educated. Like Elizabeth, Julia was a semi-invalid and an author, albeit a minor one. Their families were affluent and well-connected (Julia's great-grandfather was Josiah Wedgwood and her uncle was Charles Darwin), so unlike Browning's humble Dissenting background. His description of the heroine in the poem 'Too Late', which appears in *Dramatis Personae* (published just a month before James Wedgwood's death), bears an uncanny resemblance to the photographs of the thirty-year-old Julia: 'a funny mouth' that 'would not shut; / And the dented chin too'.* 'There were certain ways when you spoke,' the narrator adds, 'some words / That you know you never could pronounce', an observation which would have fitted Julia, for she suffered from partial deafness, condemning her, in her own words, to 'a life of silence'.

During her brother's illness, Julia had much to occupy her time and thoughts. Her world would have revolved around the sickroom: the meals to be specially prepared, the medicine administered, James's favourite books read aloud, a routine punctuated only by visits from the doctor

* Betty Miller first noted this resemblance in *Robert Browning: A Portrait* (1952).

and close friends of the family. With Bro's death, a huge void opened up in Julia's life, and her impulse was to turn to Browning. Suddenly those safe topics of conversation – the patient's care and comfort – had disappeared. The relationship took a new turn. Writing to Browning less than twenty-four hours after the sad event, 'in the awful stillness that follows that last look' of the deceased, Julia declared: 'it seems easy to go on, rather it seems impossible to stop, till I have said all I want to say.'

She knew she was defying convention writing to a middle-aged widower in this way. 'A woman who has taken the initiative in a friendship with a man, as I have done with you, has either lost all right feeling or has come to a very definite decision on the issue of all such friendships' – that is, that they be chaste and she remain a spinster. 'I have told you what your intercourse has been to me,' Julia wrote, recalling their previous meeting, 'and I am sure you hardly needed to be told, for it was sufficiently obvious.' She could not bear to forgo his company; she worried that Browning, kind, good man that he was, might decide that he could not risk compromising her good name.

Browning sat down immediately on receipt of this letter to reply by return of post. For his part, he desired human – and especially female – companionship: a kind ear to listen, a delicate hand to touch. Just at this moment he himself was in an emotional state, for 'three years ago, in this very week,' he confided to Julia, 'I lost my own soul's companion.' 'I do understand you,' he reassured her, 'and know that you understand me . . . Your friendship has been always precious to me, and that while I live it will be most precious.' He had no intention of breaking off his visits; he would call at the Wedgwoods' home the next day to ask after them all.

Julia (rather tactlessly, since James was not yet buried) showed these letters to her mother, led not so much by feelings of filial duty as by the desire to let someone in on her secret: that her friendship with Browning was special – nothing improper or scandalous, mind – just special. Poor Mrs Wedgwood was startled at her daughter's boldness towards Mr Browning. However, she must have been used to Julia's tendency to overdramatise and was satisfied that nothing was amiss.

And so, Miss Wedgwood and Mr Browning, aroused by a mutual sympathy and fascination, entered into a strange, cerebral affair. Browning's visits to 1 Cumberland Place continued, usually on Sunday afternoons. The poet asked for a photograph of Julia and presented her with several inscribed volumes of poetry, including *Dramatis Personae* when it appeared. Their correspondence began in earnest in mid-July when, after James's funeral, Julia embarked on a series of visits to aged aunts in the country where she felt 'muzzled'. Julia was thinking of Browning constantly. 'I look round me today at the shrubs and the distant hills,' she confessed, 'as if I should find some change in *them*, that I had ceased to feel "Oh Earth, release me!"' Is it possible, she asked herself, that she no longer wished for death 'because a fellow-creature – not spotlessly perfect, by any means – tells me that my absence makes a hole in his life, that I am willing, oh more than willing, to keep my foothold here, while he cares to have me?'

But Julia's happiness was tempered by fear. First there was the very real threat of scandal. She assured Browning that 'one who never *over-hears*' – referring to her partial deafness – 'cares little for and knows little of that surface current of opinion which expresses itself in slight remark.' But the fact remained: English Victorian society simply would not countenance an intimate friendship between a man and a woman that did not lead directly to marriage. Isa Blagden, who was used to the more open and relaxed ambience of Florence, had found this strait-laced attitude infuriating on her long visit to England: 'if a man talks twice to the same lady,' she declared, 'he is thought engaged to her. It makes me so mad – for of course one can talk to men all eternity without thinking or dreaming of anything but what one is saying.'[59]

Although Browning had been used to Florence's breezy society, he understood well enough that he and Miss Wedgwood had come up against 'The world, and what it fears'.* 'You know the difficulties will begin soon enough,' he told Julia; 'my visits will seem importunate, be remarked on.' He had already been the subject of gossip from another quarter. 'I thought myself too plainly a sort of tombstone,' he wrote elsewhere, 'to be scribbled over when so many blank walls spread on every side: yet a friend of yours and mine did, out of fun, write a silly name on me some months ago, which was read and repeated by various people.'

But the greatest danger, Julia knew deep down, came not from any idle gossip but from herself. 'I dread myself,' she told Browning early on in their correspondence, 'for I know there is in me an exacting spirit that dries up all the love and kindness which it needs so terribly.' Several weeks – and letters – later she admitted that 'our intercourse seems on

* 'Respectability' (*Men and Women*).

my part one perpetual farewell', but she could not help herself: 'All love has been passion with me, and it is a simple translation of that phrase to say that at one time or other, all love has proved a scourge.'

Julia was trying to tell Browning that her resolve to abandon all hope of love and remain a spinster was owing, not to any lack of passion within her, but to some terrible heartache which she had suffered in the past. She had sworn not to be hurt again. The grief and strain which accompanied her brother's death had made the normally repressed Julia emotionally vulnerable to Browning's kindness. His unaffected manners put her at ease, and his booming voice penetrated the silence. She assured herself – and Browning – that theirs would be a purely platonic affair. 'My sphere is the intercourse of spirit with spirit,' she told him, 'and this is my excuse for this fearlessness towards you.' 'Oh my friend, what unique trust is in my soul, that it can thus unveil itself to you.' But her next thought betrayed the passion within her: 'Sunday – do I wish I was back in Cumberland Place today? You shall guess ..' Perhaps this time, she hardly dared contemplate, things would be different.

When Browning had first begun to correspond with the reclusive Miss Barrett, she too had declared that she could never be happy or bring happiness to another. Like Julia, Elizabeth had insisted that she and Robert should be friends – no more. One feels that she meant it; Elizabeth had the self-confidence to consider Browning as her intellectual equal and to value that relationship above all else. Julia, however, craved affection. Robert was in love with Elizabeth and, despite her protests, eventually won her over. He had no such feelings for Julia and made no attempt to change her mind. Rather, her passionate outpourings set off gentle alarm bells; he thought he should set the record straight before matters got out of hand. Sadly, he had forgotten how it felt to be at the receiving end of an unrequited love. In his convoluted way, Browning tried to say to Julia what Elizabeth had said to him all those years ago: that they should look on each other merely as friends. 'Keep you in mind, for justice sake,' Browning urged Julia in his next letter, dated 25 July, 'exactly what my claims are – arising from your own free gift, but understood in their largest sense, – and do not let them presume to obstruct what may, ought to be claims paramount: don't cut, in that royal way, your palm-tree to the heart, that the poor traveller you delight to honour may have a draught of palm wine "after which," says Xenophon, "the whole tree withers." A better than I, God knows, should have the whole palm tree in its season. There, that's said. Meantime,' he added, 'let me sit under the branches to my day's end, come what will.'

In her reply, written the very next day from an aunt's house in Bedfordshire, Julia misconstrued Browning's meaning, perhaps deliberately so as to avoid the issue. 'Love' – love for her fellow man – 'I wanted to put that everywhere,' she confided, 'to fill every cup to the brim with it, and it was simply annoying and inconvenient to others to find them all so full .. What you charge me not to do for you, I have been trying to do for everybody (Xenophon's palm-wine) and my Ten thousand did not want my wine very often.' Julia then continued in the same ardent vein as before. When her widowed aunt spoke of her own past happiness – 'the passionate love whose embers give her all the warmth she needs' – 'With whom were my thoughts then?' she whispered into the sheet of writing paper before her.

This same aunt must have noticed something unusual in Julia's behaviour, for she decided to quiz her niece. Julia recorded the exchange for Robert's benefit.

'Well, I saw your Mr B and I don't think he looks poetical at all,' began the aunt.

'No, I don't think he does, particularly,' Julia replied, trying to propitiate her.

'Well then, why do you admire his poems? How can a man write poetry who is not poetical? I don't know how that can be.'

Her niece probably just shrugged her shoulders at this.

'But that is very foolish,' the old woman insisted. 'You confess he is not poetical, and yet you admire his poems.'

And so the conversation ended. 'I thought it hard,' Julia told Browning, 'to be called to account for your looks!'

Browning saw that Julia had not taken on board what he had said. Two days later, on 28 July, he tried again. 'I shall tell you exactly what it was I meant – not quite what you fancy – that I would not have you give away more in your generosity than you may need to account for, hereafter, in your justice, when some husbandman from a far country arrives and wants his whole palm tree: in other words, – no, there shall be other silences.' Although Browning could not bring himself to spell it out, Julia understood well enough this time. The poet had no romantic interest in her. Of course, she told herself, she would never have countenanced any such feelings on his part; but, even so, to know that she was loved in that way .. The tone of her next letter is markedly cooler. After commenting on an anecdote by Browning, Julia adds tellingly: 'I feel as if I had slipped into an improving and sermon-like vein which will of all others be the very thing to suit your taste.' If she did not want to lose him – his friendship – altogether, she would have to tread more carefully from now on.

Mercifully for Julia, there was to be no awkward meeting between them before Browning left on 3 August for his summer holiday with Pen; she made sure of it. She prolonged her stay with her friends in Falmouth, then set out on a series of 'suburban visits, where the outer world will present no temptations to me and the inner world ought to produce some crop'. She had retreated back into her shell. Over the next few months Julia wrote to Browning in Biarritz of poetry and literature generally; she told him of her mother's improving health and spirits; she even gossiped a little, repeating friends' opinions of the 'dreadful' Mrs Cameron (the photographer).* But, there were no more inward glimpses of her deepest, darkest thoughts. Before he left Warwick Crescent, Browning and Julia had been corresponding by return of post; from France the poet's letters, full of holiday news, reached Julia only every few weeks rather than every few hours.

At the end of two months, on 3 October, Browning bid Julia: 'Write and hold out a light, if I am ever to swim across the dark strait from Boulogne to the Abydos† of Warwick Crescent, which invites me very little otherwise.' She seemed the one bright spot in his otherwise drab London life, and he had no idea that he had hurt her. The poet was eager to resume his visits to 1 Cumberland Place, but Julia remained in her self-imposed exile with suburban friends and country relations. She still had not seen Browning since he had made it so plain that he did not care for her as much – or, at least, not in the same way – as she did for him. Julia had enough self-control with pen and paper to hide her true feelings from Browning, but she dare not trust herself in his presence.

In his next letter, written two weeks later, Browning happened to mention a small incident from the past, which only confirmed to Julia that the poet would never reciprocate her ardour, while also reminding

---

* When Julia Margaret Cameron took Browning's photograph, in about 1870, she draped him in a toga and left him sitting there while she sped off on some other quest (Ward, *Robert Browning and His World*, II, 123).

† Browning is referring here to the story of Hero and Leander. Hero was priestess of Aphrodite at Sestos. Leander, who lived at Abydos, fell in love with her and swam the Hellespont nightly to see her until a storm put out the light by which she guided him across. He was drowned; Hero threw herself into the sea after him.

her of what she could never have. Once, Robert told Julia, when he was suffering from a terrible headache, his wife 'took my head in her two little hands, in broad daylight, and I went to sleep at once, and woke better'. Julia would have immediately thought of Browning's very personal poem, 'The Guardian-Angel' from *Men and Women*. 'I would rest / My head beneath thine,' so the narrator explains, 'while thy healing hands / Close-covered both my eyes beside thy breast, / Pressing the brain, which too much thought expands, / Back to its proper size again, and smoothing / Distortion down till every nerve had soothing, / And all lay quiet, happy and suppressed.' Julia wrote to Browning: 'Those hands that hold the aching head are strong links here till they become strong and painfully stretched links in another direction, but even so I hope that invisible touch is felt by you still.' 'Forgive me,' she added, 'that my own thoughts lead me so much to your sacred place. I know that you are always there – but one likes to be there alone.'

Julia delayed her return to London for yet another fortnight, until mid-November. Robert's visits to Cumberland Place then resumed, but with nothing like their previous regularity. Near Christmas Browning came down with a cough; then for the best part of a week he was indisposed after over-indulging at a dinner. Early in the new year Julia went off unexpectedly to visit still more relations; in February Pen contracted measles. Finally, on 1 March 1865, Julia put an end to her suffering: 'I have been intending to write to you for several days,' she began her letter to Browning (which went through three drafts)*, 'to say – what I do not say willingly – that it would be better that we did not meet again just now, at least that you did not come here.' 'I have reason to know,' Julia explained, 'that my pleasure in your company has had an interpretation put upon it that I ought not to allow.'

The fault was hers, she confessed, 'in incautiously allowing it to be known that I made an object of your visits'. To those who knew her well, it had been obvious for some time that Julia was in love with Browning. She had not been able to hide her feelings and had even felt the need to confide in a female friend, Julia Sterling. (It was the Sterlings with whom Julia stayed in Falmouth.) Robert, on the other hand, had had no difficulty in keeping quiet about his intimacy with Julia. He seems not to have breathed a word to anyone; indeed, he even wrote to Isa Blagden,

---

* Browning's correspondence with Julia, at one time part of the Van der Poel collection, was sold at Christies, London, on 3 March 2004, and is now at the Armstrong Browning Library.

between visits to 1 Cumberland Place, that he could 'no more take root in life again, than learn some new dancing step'.[60] Julia had represented just one facet of his life; there was also Pen to think about as well as his poetry following the success of *Dramatis Personae*. But for Julia, there was nothing else. So that Browning would not guess the truth, she lied about just how much their association had meant to her: 'Do not exaggerate what it is to me. I have had your sympathy, your friendship, through the darkest part of life. You know in some degree how dark it was, in what a delirium of sorrow I turned to you; you know too, I hope, how fully you satisfied that need.'

Robert sent a gracious, heartfelt reply to Julia. 'I thought from the beginning it was too good to last,' he wrote, 'and felt as one does in a garden one has entered by an open door, – people fancy you mean to steal flowers' – an obvious, if subliminal, sexual image. Of course, he understood and would obey her wishes. Julia showed Browning's letter to her confidante in Falmouth. 'What a real effort you must have made,' Miss Sterling comments, 'in your appeal to him to conceal the fact that your heart had betrayed you. If he guesses the truth, he certainly most honourably ignores it – and makes the path easy to you which you now have chosen.'[61]

In actual fact, Julia's decision had left Browning baffled. He could not resist making the point that surely an even darker interpretation would be put upon such a sudden cessation in their relations. But if Julia had come to dread the knowing glances and pointed remarks about 'her Mr Browning' it was not because of any threat to her reputation. She dreaded them because she knew they were not true. He was not her 'Mr Browning'; he was still 'Elizabeth's poet'.

Julia had been painfully reminded of this truth only a few months earlier, when she mentioned that she had come upon Elizabeth's 'wonderfully beautiful' *Sonnets from the Portuguese*, first published in 1850. 'Generally the life and the art are two things,' she remarked; 'at least, it seems to me an exception when they are so much one as they were with her.' In reply, Browning recounted for Julia the story behind his wife's poems.[62] Several years into their marriage, in 1849, when Robert was deeply upset over the recent death of his mother, Elizabeth placed a crumpled manuscript of poems before him, saying, 'Do you know I once wrote some poems about *you*?' She had composed them shortly before their marriage, Browning explained, but had kept them hidden, thinking that he disapproved of putting one's love into verse. As he read the

Sonnets, Robert's mind would have wandered back to their courtship. So many of the words, the images, even the moments they shared – as well as her secret thoughts – had found an echo in Elizabeth's verse: 'I never gave a lock of hair away / To a man, Dearest, except this to thee' (XVIII); 'Yes, call me by my pet-name! let me hear / The name I used to run at, when a child' (XXXIII); 'First time he kissed me, he but only kissed / The fingers of this hand wherewith I write' (XXXVIII); 'My letters! all dead paper, . . mute and white! / And yet they seem alive and quivering / Against my tremulous hands which loose the string / And let them drop down on my knee to-night' (XXVIII); 'I lived with visions for all my company / Instead of men and women, years ago, . . Then THOU didst come' (XXVI).

Robert had been greatly moved at the time and was able to recall the moment with startling clarity: his wife's expressions, her voice, even the tall mimosa at the window where he was standing. But, in describing the scene this time to Julia, Browning was to put a new gloss on Elizabeth's tender gesture. With the publication of *Sonnets from the Portuguese* in 1850, the Brownings' life together had entered the realm of popular folklore, a fact which Julia had made the poet all too aware of throughout her correspondence. Robert had assured Elizabeth, when she insisted that he was not to feel entangled by their engagement: 'my crown is loose on my head, not nailed there.' But the crown had grown tighter over time. The myth of their marriage, which had hitherto been a comfort to the grieving widower, was now threatening to ensnare him.

'Yes,' he told Julia, 'that was a strange, heavy crown, that wreath of Sonnets, put on me one morning unawares, three years after it had been twined.'

'And, if God choose,' so wrote Elizabeth in *Sonnets from the Portuguese*, 'I shall but love thee better after death.'

CHAPTER TWO

Fathers and Sons,
1865–8

'I only breathe freelier since we arrived at this wild, primitive & lonely place,' Browning said of Brittany, where he had first taken refuge with his son, father and sister in 1861, six weeks after Elizabeth's death. The isolated and bleak landscape of the French coastal province drew him, in the years that followed, during every month of August and September; it provided a welcome and much needed contrast to the hustle and bustle of London streets. The primeval feel of the place, the weather-beaten faces of the Bretons and their old ways, stirred something deep within the poet. 'I feel out of the very earth sometimes, as I sit here at the window – with the little church, a field, a few houses, and the sea,' he wrote to Isa Blagden from Ste Marie, near Pornic: 'Such a soft sea & such a mournful wind!' After sitting with Pen during his lessons. Robert would leave the boy in the care of his grandfather and aunt, and embark on solitary walks, either along the rocks on the sea's edge or beyond the fields. That first unhappy summer he would stay away for three or four hours at a time, trying to walk the despondency, as he put it, out of his head.[1]

It was amongst the 'hay-stacks, cows and fowls' of Ste Marie in 1862 that Browning had first resolved to gather together his new book of 'Men and Women', *Dramatis Personae*. The sea air invigorated the poet, and the wildness of the coastline kindled his imagination. 'The place is much to my mind,' he had remarked to Isa that August; 'I have brought books, & write: I wanted a change.' As company for Pen, Willy Bracken and his mother (relations of Isa Blagden who also lived in Florence) usually joined the Brownings for part of the holiday. Apart from the boys' noisy games – and occasionally Mrs Bracken's 'mild mournful voice' competing with the wind[2] – Robert suffered few distractions.* He continued in his letter to Isa: 'I wrote a poem of 120 lines – & mean to keep writing, whether I like it or no.'

As Browning sat in his room upstairs, pen in hand, looking out across the Atlantic, the seascape, local stories, and personal broodings seemed to fuse in his mind. Those 120 lines (slightly extended) would eventually appear in *Dramatis Personae* under the title 'Gold Hair'. It recounts the strange legend of a 'beautiful girl, too white, / Who lived at Pornic, down by the sea, / Just where the sea and the Loire unite'. On her deathbed, the only request from this virtuous young girl was that she be buried with her crowning glory, 'her great gold hair', left undisturbed. Years afterwards, when a loose coin is found near her grave, the priest orders that her coffin be dug up: 'And lo, when they came to the coffin-lid, / Or rotten planks which composed it once, / Why, there lay the girl's skull wedged amid / A mint of money,' which she had hoarded in life and coveted in death. The saintly maiden had not been so snow-white after all.

This legend, which Browning had picked up in a local guide book, struck a chilling chord with the poet. He had recently been corresponding with Frederic Leighton about the sarcophagus which was to be erected on the site of Elizabeth's grave in the Piazzale Donatello. In the same letter to Isa, which tells of his 120-line poem, Robert admits to being anxious about the monument – not least because, in order to put it in place, the body would have to be disturbed. He clearly could not shake off the macabre image of unearthing a bare skull where once there had been flesh and blood. The poet must also have had in mind Dante Gabriel Rossetti's ghoulish act on the death (by suicide) of his wife at the beginning of that year, February 1862. Laid in her grave was, not a 'mint of money', but something equally precious to the distraught Rossetti: his unpublished poems – the only copy. Small wonder that Browning developed a 'horror of that man of the graveyard'.

The legend of Pornic had also struck a chord with Browning for a different reason. He was determined to protect his dead wife's posthumous reputation against would-be biographers. 'Ever since I set foot

* Willy and Pen were like brothers. Browning did not particularly like Mrs Bracken – Isa's step-aunt – but he felt sorry for her as she had lost a daughter in the same year he lost his wife. Yet 'Mrs B. is curious to me, with her intense appreciation of trifles – you'd suppose she had no other object in the world than to get thro' the day pleasantly: how can people who have known real grief *stop* to notice the darkness of the sky, the ill-manners of the passers-by .. and so on?' (RB to Isa Blagden, 19 November 1863).

in England,' he told Isa in January 1863, 'I have been pestered with applications for leave to write the Life of my wife.' 'What I suffer in feeling the hands of these blackguards'; he confided, 'what I undergo with their paws in my very bowels, you can guess & God knows!' Elizabeth had been more sanguine on the subject of biography, believing only that one '*ought* to be let alone while one's alive'.[3] She was past caring now – but Robert was not. He dreaded the idea of some grave-robber digging up his wife's secrets (such as her reliance on morphine) or uncovering her foibles (her passion for spiritualism, for example) just as the villagers of Pornic had exposed the beautiful young girl's miserly ways. 'Saints tumble to earth with so slight a tilt!' so the verse goes.

Yet Robert had himself been excavating the past that same year, 1862, as he watched summer turn into autumn on the Brittany coast. September was an especially reflective time for the widower. Not only did it herald the onset of winter cares, as he told the Storys,[4] but it also marked two important anniversaries: his wedding day and the day, exactly one week later, that he and Elizabeth had fled England together. Robert and Isa agreed to write every month, she on the 12th, and he on the 19th, to commemorate these events. The poet insisted on more than one occasion that he was not superstitious, but the smallest things clearly had significance for him – those 'nothings that grew to be somethings from their first association'.

'The sun's away, / And the bird estranged, .. Summer has stopped,' begins the poem 'James Lee's Wife', which Browning wrote around this time. A winter chill is in the air; the eponymous narrator fears that her husband's love for her has also cooled. This richly complex piece shifts, like the sand beneath the waves at Pornic, from scene to scene – 'Along the Beach', 'Among the Rocks', 'On Deck' – and back and forth in time. There are echoes of Browning's earlier verse, such as the section entitled 'By the Fireside', clearly a reference to his poem in *Men and Women* in which the narrator, sitting by the fire, wonders what he means to do when the autumn evenings come. 'Is all our fire of shipwreck wood?' asks James Lee's wife. Yet, she already knows the answer. In 'Reading a Book, Under the Cliff', she loses patience with the hopelessly naive verses of a young man – verses actually written by the twenty-three-year-old Browning* – enquiring of the wind why it sighs and moans so. The poet must learn by experience, as she has learned, that 'nothing endures' – the

---

* Published in *The Monthly Relpository* in May 1836 under the title 'Lines' and signed 'Z'.

wind says so. 'Nothing can be as it has been before; / Better, so call it, only not the same.' Browning was here voicing his fear that the intense love which he had felt for Elizabeth during their life together would eventually slip away, until 'death's wave' should overcome him too: 'time first washes – ah, the sting! – O'er all he'd sink to save.' He did not want to let go. How bitter it was, the section concludes, for man to lose 'one fair good wise thing / Just as he grasped it!'

Julia Wedgwood, who read 'James Lee's Wife' when it appeared in *Dramatis Personae*, was puzzled by the couple's apparently 'proletarian' background. She felt these were not the feelings of people who earned their own bread. Browning explained that the man and wife were meant to be newly married, 'trying to realize a dream of being sufficient to each other, in a foreign land (where you can try such an experiment)', but failing when the man tired of their love. He and Elizabeth had been such a couple, unworldy newlyweds imagining a new life for themselves in Italy. Despite the scepticism of their friends – Mrs Jameson had not held out much hope for the 'dear, abominable poets' and Mary Russell Mitford had never thought Elizabeth would reach Pisa alive – both the bride and the marriage had survived. With 'James Lee's Wife', Browning was exploring an alternative version of his own story – one which Mrs Jameson and others would have thought more likely.

That summer in Brittany, Robert could only look back on their life together with feelings of wonder and some disbelief. It was stranger still to think that he and Elizabeth might never have married. Robert used gently to chide Elizabeth about her original wish that they should be friends, not lovers. 'Had she willed it, still had stood the screen / So slight, so sure, 'twixt my love and her,' so Browning had teased his wife in 'By the Fire-Side' – 'Friends – lovers that might have been'.* He had sworn, Elizabeth once told a friend, that 'he would wait twenty years if I pleased, and then, if life lasted so long for both of us, then, when it was ending, perhaps, I might understand him and feel that I might have trusted him.'[5] Might Elizabeth have persuaded Robert that his marriage proposal was an attempt, albeit an unconscious one, to relieve the tedium of his bachelor life? – 'a yawning-fit o'er books and men', as he put it in 'Dîs Aliter Visum', a companion piece to 'James Lee's Wife' in *Dramatis Personae*.

---

* This sentiment echoes Robert's first letter to Elizabeth (10 January 1845), when he recounts how he had once nearly met her, 'only a screen to push and I might have entered – but there was some slight . . and just-sufficient bar to admission'.

'Dîs Aliter Visum', in which two former lovers recount their last meeting against a backdrop of baths and bay, sands and seagulls, explores the notion of missed opportunity and unrequited love. Its Latin title, taken from Virgil, translates as 'To the gods it seemed otherwise'. His marriage appeared all the more precious to Browning, knowing as he did that it might never have succeeded. The gods had, after all, been good to him. 'I sometimes see a light at the end of this dark tunnel of life, which was one blackness at the beginning,' he had told Isa in December 1864, just at the time that he was enlightening Julia Wedgwood on the finer points of 'James Lee's Wife'. 'In many ways,' he continued in his letter to Isa, 'I can see with my human eyes why this has been right & good for me – as I never doubted it was for Her.' Elizabeth was out of pain; he now understood how fortunate he had been in his love. 'If we do but re-join one day, – the break will be better than forgotten, remembered for its uses.'

While the poet mulled over the past alone in his French garret, life was going on downstairs amongst the rest of the family. Pen adored his summer holidays in Brittany. Even in that first year, 1861, only a month or two after his mother's death, Browning noted that the boy '*never* was so happy & so cheerful. He amuses himself with my father, whose kindness & simplicity make him a wonderful child's friend certainly, – they sketch together, go home & paint &c. and Pen's loud merry laugh is never out of my ears.'[6] Pen swam in the ocean each day, taught his father how to swim, scrambled on the rocks with Willy Bracken, and was by the end of every holiday 'brick-coloured and broad-shouldered'. In the summer of 1863, Pen had pleased – but somewhat surprised – his father when he helped to save the life of a bather dragged unconscious from the water. 'He ran into a house,' Browning told Isa in August, 'got brandy & vinegar, and on being directed by somebody to do some stupidity or other, bade him "Allez au diable" – So, you see, he *promises.*' Pen, then aged fourteen, was beginning to have a mind of his own.

By 1865 Pen was forced to eschew the pleasures of the beach to devote part of each day to the *Aeneid* as well as to produce Greek translations, which his father then diligently corrected. Around the time of his son's sixteenth birthday earlier that year, Robert had written to the Storys, saying: 'Pen is a great fellow now, with incipient moustaches.' The young man had even appeared at a party one evening in coat and white tie – 'inevitable but bitter!' No doubt Pen's coming of age seemed bitter to Browning because Elizabeth was not there to share it with him. But his words also betray a feeling of unease; perhaps there would not be time enough to refashion (or, in Browning's own words, 'grind') the once velvet-clad Pen into a Balliol scholar. Pen's 'whole great soul was wrapped up in the Boatraces last Saturday', Browning continued in his letter to the Storys, 'when Oxford again beat Cambridge, the cool long & strong stroke against the spurt and spasmodic dip: the English do best by sticking to the English way'. It was looking as though Pen, in his studies if not his rowing stroke, tended towards the more Italianate 'spurt and spasmodic dip'.[7]

There seemed to be a general air of gloom that summer (1865) on the Brittany coast. While the fun-loving, mustachioed Pen was locked up with Virgil, his antiquarian grandfather sketched 'groaningly' the exquisite ornaments of Ste Marie's Norman church, which lay scattered by the roadside. The villagers had torn them down to make smooth the walls and whitewash the building. If that were not enough, he told Isa in September, the old Pornic church was being demolished by the local Bretons who were 'without a touch of the sense of the picturesqueness in their clodpoles'.

Nevertheless Browning had by this time, a full four years after Elizabeth's death (and several months after his break with Julia Wedgwood), regained a certain light-heartedness. In October, back at Warwick Crescent, Robert attempted to describe Pornic's earthy charms to Isa, with a decided twinkle in his eye: '*fancy* (. . shall I be cruel enough to bid you? . . yes, I will –) fancy the buxom servant girl, aged some 20, washing clothes before my window (on the pianterreno), dressed in a blue gown & nothing else, I can see, just covering the naked legs below the knees – and so kilted, turning her back to me and burying herself with linen she has to stoop for on the ground!'

Even before he had left London for his French holiday that year, Browning had shown sure signs of recovering his spirits. He and Tennyson had begun to correspond again and exchange their published volumes. Robert must have even plucked up the courage to confess to hiding his face from the Poet Laureate that time in the Boulogne railway station, a month or so after Elizabeth's death. 'Ever yours,' so he ended a letter to Tennyson around this time, 'on the various stations of this life's *line*'.[8]

Robert's newly found fame ensured that his social calendar was crammed with dinners, musical evenings, and balls (although he stubbornly refused to dance) hosted by Lady Westmorland, Lady de Grey,

Lady Colvile, the Duchess of Cleveland, Lady Salisbury, Lady Palmerston, so on and so forth. In May 1865 we find a jovial Robert, 'jammed between two ladies' on the crowded landing of a fashionable staircase, laughing at his friends below. Women practically threw themselves at the widower, but he was not attracted to the archetypal English beauty – an 'aquiline nose between two pudding cheeks with lightish hair & eyes, & "fine" complexion', as he once told Isa.[9]

Inevitably rumours began to circulate in many a London drawing room that the eligible widower was about to remarry, although the name of the lucky lady varied from day to day. Two such candidates were Miss Gabriel, a composer of drawing-room ballads who set 'James Lee's Wife' to music, and, of course, the serious-minded Miss Wedgwood. Most people, however – Charles Dickens included – subscribed to the hearsay concerning Mr Browning and Miss Ingelow, the poetess. This report even found its way to Isa Blagden in her Italian villa. Robert insisted that he had only ever seen Miss Ingelow once, at a morning gathering. He managed to upset yet another contender, Miss Bonham Carter, the sculptress. Browning told Julia Wedgwood, who knew her slightly, that he liked the sculptress, 'though she don't believe it, on account of a failure on my part of going to some party to which she invited me'. The next time he met Miss Bonham Carter, he was not so much cut, Robert told the Storys, as fiercely abused by the lady as 'wanting in the attributes of a poet – *gentleman*, she would not say'. In September 1865, when Browning heard of her untimely demise, the only words he could find to describe the dead woman to Isa were 'a lying tittle-tattle'.[10]

Poor Browning could do little to end the gossip, which, as far as he was concerned, ranged from the nonsensical to the impertinent and downright spiteful. It was an inevitable consequence of going out into society and, as he remarked wryly to Isa in August 1865, 'showing myself to be alive'. He was only looking forward to the day, he kept assuring Isa and the Storys, when he would return to Italy. But Isa, who knew him better than anyone, had begun to have her doubts. Each new letter from Robert led her to believe that London best suited his temperament; Italian society was so sluggish by comparison. Shelley had described Italy as 'the paradise of exiles and the retreat of Pariahs', and these were just the people who had constituted the Brownings' world. The expatriates in Florence, one transient artist observed, lived 'a little, fussy, literary life, filled with their sayings and doings'. During the day, the 'Inglese' (the Florentines' term for all foreigners) drove about in the Cascine, a lush green oasis on the Arno, where, according to the writer Charles Lever, scandal held its festival. At night they attended lavish receptions at the Pitti Palace where the Duke (affectionately known as 'Grand Ciuco' or Grand Ass) boasted of having the worst drawing room in Europe – open to anyone and everyone.[11]

Owing to Elizabeth's delicate health, the Brownings' society had been of a more intimate nature. Their especial friends were, of course, Isa Blagden and William Story along with Hiram Powers, who like Story was an American sculptor. Powers' ego was larger than any statue he ever conceived but he was in reality a disappointed man, neglected by his own countrymen across the Atlantic. Story also had his limitations. One Yankee visitor, Mrs Henry Adams, remarked after a visit to his studio: 'Oh! How he does spoil nice blocks of white marble. Nothing but Sibyls on all sides, sitting, standing, legs crossed, legs uncrossed, and all with the same expression as if they smelt something wrong.' Henry James, in his memoir of the sculptor, was later to describe Story's career as 'a sort of beautiful sacrifice to a noble mistake'. Story had begun life as a promising young Boston lawyer; his father was Associate Justice of the Supreme Court and a founder of Harvard Law School. But the young man had artistic leanings, and he was utterly charmed by Italy on his first visit there. For ten years he sailed back and forth between Rome and Boston in a state of indecision, dragging his wife and children with him. It was only in 1856, when he was thirty-seven, that he chose the life of a sculptor in Italy, although he also dabbled in poetry, prose, and drama. Both Story and Powers wished – and firmly believed – that they would end their lives in the land of their birth. Neither did. Nathaniel Hawthorne, a temporary exile who found Italy as uncomfortable as it was charming, was struck by his countrymen's dilemma.[12] 'It makes a very unsatisfactory life, thus to spend the greater part of it in exile. In such a case, we are always deferring the reality of life till there are no future moments.'*

One feels that Browning was slowly coming to the same conclusion. Certainly Hawthorne, who met the poet for the first time in Florence, thought that he was a cut above the other expatriates. Browning, he later recalled, 'seemed to be in all parts of the room and in every group at the

---

* Hawthorne, who had rented a house on Bellosguardo, was impatient to return home, 'for, taking no root, I soon weary of any soil in which I may be temporarily deposited'. As Henry James later observed, by delving into its Puritan ancestry Hawthorne bequeathed to America its own Gothic landscape and haunted past. He did not need Italy's antiquity for inspiration.

same moment' with his 'effervescent' conversation. Tom Trollope, the novelist Anthony Trollope's older brother and a fixture of Florentine society, concurred. He recalled that the 'tag-rag and bob-tail' of the men 'who mainly constituted that very pleasant but not very intellectual society, were not likely to be such as Mr Browning would readily make intimates of'. He was never discourteous to an out-and-out fool, Trollope added, 'but there was a quiet, lurking smile', which did not fail to make the fool aware of his mistake. Even Elizabeth had realised that Florence and its milieu, which suited her perfectly, were for Robert 'dead & dull'.[13]

In any case, the Florence of Browning's remembrance was fast disappearing. In 1865 it became the capital of the newly united Italy and rebuilding had begun apace. 'Yes, Florence will never be *my* Florence again,' Robert wistfully remarked to Isa in January 1865. If he were free to run away one day, it would not be to Florence. As an old man once said to him of Jerusalem: 'No, I don't want to go there – I can see it in my head.' Browning learned by degrees to regard London as a home, Mrs Orr explained, 'the only fitting centre for the varied energies which were reviving in him'. Although she had first met him in Paris in 1855, it was in London that Alexandra Orr came to know Browning well. He even learned to appreciate the outlook from his house, she added, despite the rough neighbourhood thugs who would sometimes yell at the street corner, or fling stones at his plate-glass. After five years in 'dear ugly old England', as he called it, the poet was beginning to see that the life of an exile was indeed, as Hawthorne said, a very unsatisfactory existence.[14] Although Browning did not realise it then, Story would end up – as does Gilbert Osmond in James's *Portrait of a Lady* – 'dilettantish and second-rate'. Story himself knew it, or so Hawthorne thought. He saw in his uprooted compatriot 'a pain and care, bred, it may be, out of the very richness of his gifts'; he was doomed to be good at many things but never great. Browning had had a lucky escape.

Moreover, for the first time since his marriage, Alexandra Orr wrote, Browning was able to enjoy an 'unshackled' social life. He could attend the myriad dinners, recitals, and balls – all that London society had to offer – without having to wonder whether he was keeping his invalid wife out too late or, more likely, if he should be getting back to her. The poet brought to these occasions, she added, 'a kind of freshness which a man of fifty has not generally preserved'. The poet came to be regarded as one of the great diners-out in London, cordial and hearty, who shook people's hands as if he were genuinely glad to see them. With this new lease of life, Robert braved the 'double current', as he put it, of both people and gossip which flowed up and down the staircases of London's most exclusive homes.[15]

Nevertheless, as Browning confided to the Storys around this time, after first satisfying people outside he would return to Warwick Crescent and sit down quietly 'with the inmates of my soul's little house'. 'In this House of Life,' he had written to Elizabeth during their courtship, 'where I go, you go, – where I ascend, you run before, – where I descend, it is after you.' He had fancied himself meeting Elizabeth on the stairs, 'stairs and passages generally, and galleries (ah, those indeed! –) all, with their picturesque *accidents*, of landing-places, and spiral heights & depths', but above all, '*landing-places* – they are my heart's delight – I would come upon you unaware on a landing-place in my next dream!'[16] In the autumn and winter of 1865 Robert was putting together a new selection of Elizabeth's poems for publication; her verse was as popular as ever. As he stood on those fashionable landings, overlooking *la crème* of British society, Robert would have, if only for a split second, looked around the room below for Elizabeth. 'Room after room, / I hunt the house through / We inhabit together. / Heart, fear nothing for, heart, thou shalt find her,' so Browning had begun his poem 'Love in a Life', published in *Men and Women*.

The dizzying whirl of social engagements ceased, however, when on 12 June 1866 Robert received a telegram from Paris informing him that his eighty-five-year-old father was dying. He left for France immediately. Pen wanted to go with him to see his beloved 'Nonno' one last time, but Browning thought it best that the seventeen-year-old should not see his grandfather suffer; the internal haemorrhaging was very painful. 'Let me have the comfort of knowing, dearest,' he bade Pen, 'that you do your work well – and act like a man in my absence.'[17]

Robert arrived in Paris early the next day and found Sarianna waiting for him on the staircase of their humble lodgings. She had delayed in sending for her brother, hoping that the dreadful ordeal would be over by the time he reached them. But the old man was still clinging to life. Robert kept vigil by his bedside for the whole of that day and through the long night, doing everything he could – which was very little – to make the invalid more comfortable. Despite the intense pain, Mr Browning appeared so utterly indifferent to death that the attending doctor asked Sarianna if the gentleman knew that he was dying. Robert persuaded Sarianna, who had been up for two nights running, to get some sleep.

At long last the end came – 'to my infinite joy, for the suffering was terrible to see', Robert wrote to his son on 14 June: 'this morning at 8.25 dearest Nonno died.' He was alone (with only a female attendant to help) when, as he put it, 'Nonno was simply *overcome* by death.' Robert had persuaded his sister not to witness the last struggle; he was as keen to protect her from the distress and trauma as she had been to shield him. In his next letter to Pen, Robert bade his son read St John's Gospel 14 to 17, those chapters which his grandfather had asked to hear just a few hours before his death. 'Let not your heart be troubled,' the passage begins: 'I am the way, the truth, and the life.' Browning wrote to Isa, 'So passed away this good, unworldly, kind hearted, religious man, whose powers natural & acquired would have so easily made him a notable man, had he known what vanity or ambition or the love of money or social influence meant.' He followed his father's coffin to its resting place in the Cimitière du Nord in Paris.

Through the long hours that his father lay half sensible and breathing heavily, memories of his childhood and of his parents would have come flooding back to Robert: the love they bore him and the sacrifices they made. As a young man, Robert Senior had been sent to manage the West Indies plantation which he was in line to inherit. He was so horrified by what he saw – the injustice and cruelty meted out to the slaves – that he willingly forfeited his right to the property and returned to England. His father (the poet's grandfather), an uncomplicated, inflexible, and self-righteous man who reread *Tom Jones* and the Bible – and only these two books – every year, refused to support his son's dream of becoming an artist. Robert had no choice but to follow in his father's footsteps and become a clerk in the Bank of England – and not a very effective one at that, 'consuming his life after a fashion he always detested', his son said.[18]

The artist manqué found happiness instead in his home life. At the age of twenty-nine he married Sarah Anna Wiedemann of Dundee, then aged thirty-eight. Their two children, Robert and Sarianna, arrived within the next three years, and the family settled down to domestic bliss in leafy Camberwell, a suburb of South London. The elder Browning would have travelled six mornings a week to his humdrum job in the City, returning home each evening to those domestic affections and endearments mentioned by Macaulay in his account of the rise of the suburbs: the fireside, the nursery, the social table, the quiet bed and, in the bank clerk's case, the library. Old books were his delight, his half-brother Reuben Browning remarked, and by his continual search after them he came to know not only all the old bookstalls in London but their contents too. He had 'the scent of a hound and the snap of a bull-dog' for an old or rare volume, as one acquaintance put it. His house overflowed with books – some six thousand volumes – although his generosity towards friends who made the trip to Camberwell meant that there was always room for a few more volumes to replace the ones he had just given away. He collected books on every subject, but his special interests were art, history, and murder cases.[19]

Blessed with a remarkable memory (which he passed on to his son), Robert Senior absorbed everything he read. Reuben called him 'a living encyclopaedia'. As a boy, he memorised the first book of the *Iliad* and organised Homeric battles in the schoolyard 'with mock sword, and slate, our mimic shield', as his childhood friend John Kenyon later recalled.* The young Greeks and Trojans drove each other into the fray with insulting speeches lifted from Homer. Twenty-five years later Robert Senior soothed his infant son to sleep by humming an ode of Anacreon to the tune of a lullaby.[20] Within a few years the bank clerk was once more staging the siege of Troy, this time in his own front room. Robert Junior described just such a scene in verse when he himself was an old man: 'My father .. piled up chairs and tables for a town, / Set me a-top for Priam,' King of Troy, 'called our cat / – Helen, enticed away from home (he said) / By wicked Paris, who couched somewhere close / Under the footstool, being cowardly.'† The family dogs, Towzer and Tray, as Agamemnon and Menelaus, laid siege to the furniture (that is, Troy), and Achilles '(My pony in the stable) – forth would prance / And put to flight Hector – our page-boy's self'.

Robert Senior had, according to Dante Gabriel Rossetti, a real genius for drawing, and he loved to delight children with his caricatures. Annie Thackeray, when she was a child living in Paris, used to look with a 'certain mingled terror and fascination at various pages of grim heads drawn in black and red chalk' in the gentle Mr Browning's sketchbook. 'Masks and faces were depicted,' she later recalled, 'crowding together with malevolent or agonised or terrific expressions. There were the

---

* John Kenyon, *A Rhymed Plea for Tolerance* (1833).
† 'Development'.

suggestions of a hundred weird stories on the pages at which one gazed with creeping alarm.' Reuben told how his half-brother, with slips of paper and pencil to hand, would at social gatherings dash off a satirical sketch illustrating any topic under discussion to the assembled crowd's amusement. Robert Junior was reminded of his own happy childhood in Camberwell when he watched Pen and the boy's grandfather sketch together for hours on end during the summer holidays. Such weird and wonderful faces had once haunted his own imagination, as had the contents of his father's books, which he perused, read, and treasured from a very early age.

This had been the young poet's education, spending hours on end in the library at home, pulling down from the shelf whichever books struck his fancy and were within reach: the great poets – Shakespeare, Milton, Pope and Byron – treatises on painting and music, dictionaries of biography, encyclopaedias, famous murder trials, and tomes of strange lore, such as Quarles' *Emblems* (1777), which had been his 'childhood's pet book'. The precocious young Robert's more formal schooling had not been a great success. From the age of eight to fourteen he boarded weekly at a school in nearby Peckham run by the Reverend Thomas Ready and his two spinster sisters. Browning's impression was that he had learned nothing at this worthy establishment. He spent his schooldays longing for the weekend, when he might be back home amongst his father's books. The little boy was so homesick and miserable in Peckham – although only a mile or so from his parents – he thought he was going to die. He even transformed an upturned cistern in the schoolyard into his private burial place where he would go after lessons to sigh aloud, 'In memory of unhappy Browning'.[21]

For Robert Junior, no book was too great or too humble, too sophisticated or too childish. And this was to be true of his poetry: no subject was too large or too small, too ambitious or too trifling. He had never learned to discriminate. Moreover, he was fascinated by the notion of the unsung hero and the neglected artist, and many of his works explore historical figures long forgotten whose stories had been left to gather dust on old library shelves. During his long exile in Italy, when popularity continued to elude him, Browning could have been forgiven for thinking that one of his early poems, 'Pictor Ignotus', had become a self-fulfilling prophecy. Written before he had ever met Elizabeth, the title translates either as 'painter unknown' or, more pointedly, 'artist overlooked'.

In some sense the poet never really left that book-laden house in

Camberwell. His mind would revert to the nursery rhymes and fairy tales read to him and often illustrated by his father. 'Higgledy piggledy, packed we lie, / Rats in a hamper, swine in a stye,' begins the third stanza of Browning's 'Holy-Cross Day', one of Robert Senior's favourite poems. So it was that in 1842 both had been drawn to that most anarchic of children's stories, the Pied Piper of Hamelin. Robert Senior abandoned his own attempt to put it into verse when he discovered that his son had already done so for his friend William Macready's bedridden little boy. Browning *père et fils* derived a strange sort of comfort from these silly children's fables and their topsy-turvy world, where successes look like failures and failures like successes.

The world had seemed topsy-turvy indeed when good, kind Mr Browning Senior became embroiled in scandal. In October 1851 the old man had arrived on his son's doorstep in Paris (where Robert and Elizabeth were spending the winter) with a distressing tale to tell. Like all good fairy stories, it featured an enchantress – a potential wicked stepmother – with the suitably evil-sounding name of Mrs Von Müller.

After the death, in 1849, of his wife of nearly forty years, Mr Browning had continued to go to his desk in the City every day. As he set out each morning, the lonely widower began to notice an attractive woman sitting at her window. He waved to her; she waved back. Before long he was offering to accompany the twice-widowed Mrs Von Müller home when they met in the street. All this was innocent enough, but at some point there had been a proposal of marriage. The widow, in a fit of honesty, had confided to her fiancé that she might – unwittingly, or so she claimed – have married her second husband before the first was dead. No sooner had this confession left her lips than poor Mr Browning wished to extricate himself from the woman's clutches. Perhaps he had begun to feel that he had been not only imprudent but also disloyal to the memory of his beloved wife. Not knowing what else to do, he fled to Paris that autumn of 1851 to beg his son to rescue him from the enchantress's evil spell.

Robert composed a very stern and self righteous letter to Mrs Von Müller, declaring that his father had explained the manner in which she had annoyed him and the persecution he had undergone. Mr Browning himself then wrote to her, withdrawing his offer of marriage; the reason given was her misconduct from the time she was a girl. The widow, and her son-in-law, were furious. They determined to use the old man's letters to her – awkward, gushing, and incriminating letters – to sue him for breach of promise and defamation of character. For the next six weeks or so, until Mr Browning and Sarianna returned to London, Robert was, Elizabeth noted, 'absorbed between his father & sister (whom he had to carry about Paris from morning till night when they were here)'.[22]

The case went to the High Court on the first day of July 1852. It was awful. Counsel for the prosecution said that, whereas there was usually more or less romance involved in breach of promise cases, there was none at all in this one. He then recounted Mr Browning's pursuit of Mrs Von Müller, producing letters to illustrate the sad tale. 'My dearest, dearest, dearest, dearest, dearest, dearest much-loved Minny,' and suchlike the attorney solemnly read out loud, sending the entire court into fits of laughter. The widow's character and conduct were wholly vindicated: her first husband's death certificate proved that he had been in the ground for a full two months before she remarried. Mr Browning's counsel had no defence other than to argue that his client was 'a poor old dotard in love'. Lord Campbell, the judge, showed little mercy, declaring that the defendant had conducted himself in a most cowardly manner and that 'his folly was his own folly'. Damages of £800 were awarded to Mrs Von Müller and her name cleared.

Robert and Elizabeth, who had stayed on in Paris through the early summer of 1852, arrived in London five days or so after the trial. They did not have to be told what had occurred in the court room; the whole sordid business had been reported in *The Times*. Not only had the old man been publicly humiliated, but he could not even afford the £800 damages. 'It is enough to make one both smile & sigh,' Elizabeth told her sister. There was only one course of action: to flee Britain – and debtors' prison – and take up permanent residence abroad. Robert escorted his father and sister to Paris. It was the first time he had been parted from Elizabeth since they themselves had first crossed the Channel to begin their married life in exile. Robert returned to London, and to Elizabeth, physically exhausted and emotionally drained. She later confessed to a friend: 'If you knew how, at that time, Robert was vexed and worn! – why, he was not the same even to *me*!'[23]

Nor was he the same to his father. In October, Robert returned to Paris with Elizabeth. He did all he could for his father and sister in the few weeks before starting for Florence. He settled them into comfortable lodgings and tried (through John Frazer Corkran, Paris correspondent for the *Morning Herald*) to keep the sordid Von Müller story out of the

French newspapers – or at least the one that expatriates read, *Galignani*. But every now and then Robert's anger and frustration would surface. One day, Elizabeth told Arabel, old Mr Browning turned to her and said dolefully that he knew it had been a trouble to her – '*Of course*, it *has*,' said Robert – '*What did you imagine?*' – at which the poor man looked utterly miserable.[24]

'Dost thou call me fool, boy?' So King Lear addresses his court clown. Shakespeare's drama about an old man's descent into madness was very much on Browning's mind at this time. At the start of the new year, on 16 January 1853, he reassured John Kenyon that his father was content, filling his days in Paris sketching at the Louvre and book-hunting along the quays, 'shaping his old course in a country new', like Lear's Kent. In fact, he was 'well as ever, – of all his old spirits – strange, in one sense, not in another'.[25]

It was Sarianna who suffered. Her pride had been hurt, and Paris seemed scarcely much better to her than a penal settlement, so Elizabeth observed to Arabel. Sarianna carried a heavy burden. She no doubt tried to hide from her father the fact that, six months after the trial, Mrs Von Müller was still trying to get hold of her money by petitioning the Bank of England. With very little to live on, Sarianna allowed the old man only a few coins daily for pocket money. He would disappear to buy books in obscure corners of Paris, often missing trains and getting lost, causing his daughter even more worry, so recalled the Corkrans' young daughter, Henriette. Henriette also remembered Sarianna glancing severely at her father or treading on his toes if he began a story with 'when I was clerk in the Bank of England'.[26] Some accused the ever-watchful daughter of snobbery, but perhaps she feared that the old man would be driven mad if he revisited the past. 'O! that way madness lies; let me shun that,' cries Lear.

It was two weeks before his letter to Kenyon, on 3 January 1853 – his head full of his father's plight and King Lear – that the poem 'Childe Roland to the Dark Tower Came' appeared to Browning 'as a kind of dream'. 'Child Rowland to the dark tower came,' sings Poor Tom in Shakespeare's tragedy, 'His word was still, Fie, foh, and fum, / I smell the blood of a British man.' Robert wrote to George (the only Barrett brother to whom he was close) a few months later, in July, referring to his father's troubles: 'These horrible nightmares slip off one's breast at last, and become a laughing matter – while they hold us, they are formidable enough.' In Browning's poem, despite the obstacles in his path – both real and imagined – Childe Roland finally reaches the Dark Tower. As he sounds the slug-horn* to signal his approach, the dreamer wakes and the poem ends. 'He that endureth to the end shall be saved': was this what Browning meant by the poem, someone once asked him. 'Yes,' he replied, 'just about that.'[27]

They had got through the crisis, but Robert Senior's foolishness led his son to question the nature of love and marriage. Mr Browning had adored his wife, yet when left alone he seemed to succumb so easily to another woman's charms. 'Is the remainder of the way so long,' the woman asks in 'Any Wife to Any Husband', which Browning composed at about this time, 'Thou need'st the little solace, thou the strong?' It was an issue which was all too real for Robert, especially as his own peculiar fairy tale was by this time (1853) coming to an end. During those first few years in Italy Elizabeth's health had improved dramatically – even miraculously. With Robert's encouragement, she took less and less morphine, especially during her third (and only successful) pregnancy for fear of its effects on the unborn child.† She looked back on the house in Wimpole Street and her life there with 'the sort of horror with which one would look to one's graveclothes, if one had been clothed in them by mistake during a trance' – 'I was buried, and that was the whole.' Browning had fought his way into that dark and dusty bedroom, which had been to her a tomb and, just as Prince Charming awakened Sleeping Beauty with a kiss, so the poet – her 'New Cross Knight' – liberated Elizabeth from her self-confessed morbid and desolate state. If he was vain about anything in the world, Elizabeth said of her husband regarding those first years of marriage, it was her new-found, nearly drug-free vitality. 'You need'nt talk so much to people, of how your wife walked here with you & there with you, as if a wife with a pair of feet was a miracle of nature,' she chided him.[28]

But during the winter of 1851–2, in Paris, Elizabeth's health had begun to slip back into what would turn out to be its inexorable decline. Browning exclaimed repeatedly – and, no doubt, more loudly after the Von Müller affair – that he would never marry another woman. But

---

* A phrase coined by Thomas Chatterton, one of Browning's unsung heroes, a young poet who died penniless. Browning wrote an anonymous article on him that was published in the *Foreign Quarterly Review* for July 1842.
† Elizabeth suffered two miscarriages in March 1847 and March 1848; after Pen's birth in March 1849, she had two more miscarriages, in November–December 1849 and July 1850.

Elizabeth's was a sensible, unselfish love. 'I've stopped him twenty times in such vows as never to take another wife, & the like,' she wrote to her sister Arabel in April 1854: 'I've held his lips together with both hands .. I would'nt have it!' Elizabeth did not fear her own death; she had lived beneath its shadow for too long. Such forthrightness and courage would have come as no surprise to Robert, for in his world women were stronger than men (and considerably older than their husbands).

Robert's mother, Sarah Anna Browning, a woman of Scottish-German extraction, had not been particularly clever, nor was she much of a beauty. According to a boyhood friend of Robert, she had 'the *squarest* head & forehead' he had ever seen, which put him in mind of 'a tea-chest or tea-caddy'. Yet she clearly had a strong character. Thomas Carlyle, who sometimes visited the Brownings at home, called her 'the true type of a Scottish gentlewoman'. She would 'talk Scotch' with Carlyle and play Gaelic laments on the piano. Some of Robert's earliest – and fondest – reminiscences were of his mother playing that instrument, alone, in the twilight.[29]

Sarah Anna passed on to Robert her great love of music and of animals. The house in Camberwell (and later nearby New Cross) hosted not only Mr Browning's collection of books but also the family menagerie, which included (besides the canines Towzer and Tray) owls, monkeys, magpies, hedgehogs, snakes, even an eagle. Young Robert was constantly bringing home in his pockets small creatures, ugly and slimy as well as cute and furry, which he would hand over to his mother for immediate attention. One of Browning's abiding memories, Alexandra Orr noted, was of 'the maternal parasol, hovering above the strawberry bed', as his mother searched for a speckled frog with which to bribe her son to take his medicine. She knew to avoid bedtime stories in which any animal met an unhappy end, as it upset the boy so.[30]

Mrs Browning, who was a deeply religious woman, chose instead to read Robert stories from the Bible – stories which the poet would treasure throughout his life. She had been brought up in the Kirk of Scotland and, although he had been born into the Church of England, her accommodating husband also became a Dissenter. The Browning family attended Chapel together every Sunday to hear the Reverend George Clayton, a preacher of the old school. From his high pulpit it was said that he 'stiffened and starched' those who sat under him. As a very young child Robert was for a time caught up in his mother's passion for religion. Once he preached to his little sister such a powerful sermon that she burst into tears; whereupon, turning to an imaginary usher, he declared solemnly, 'Pew opener, remove that child.'

But these Sunday services began to try Robert's patience as he grew older. Clayton's long prayers put a fellow parishioner, Edward White, in mind of a newspaper being read aloud, filled as they were with notices and local events. On at least one occasion his obvious indifference to Clayton's sermons provoked the awesome preacher to rebuke young Browning openly in the middle of a church service. The sermons preached by Robert's headmaster, the Reverend Thomas Ready, were no better. '.. A *Heavy* Sermon! – Sure the error's great – / For not a word Tom uttered *had its weight*' was the poet's pronouncement.[31]

Mrs Browning sometimes smiled, despite herself, at her son's irreverent attitude towards his elders, as when he mimicked the Misses Ready ferociously brushing the hair of the smaller boys while singing the hymn: 'Fools never raise their thoughts to high, like *brutes* they live, like BRUTES they die.' But this precociousness was more than just childish fun; Robert was by nature a rebel. As he grew older, he showed that he cared little for the opinion of others. It distressed his mother.[32] At the age of fourteen, inspired by Shelley's *Queen Mab*, Robert declared himself to be a vegetarian and, for a short while, an atheist. (Ironically, Mrs Browning had gone to some trouble to procure Shelley's poems for her son, who had requested them for his birthday.) Mealtimes, as the Brownings prayed over the family roast, must have been awkward, not to mention Sunday mornings, when they set off for church leaving Robert, proud and defiant, behind.

Robert, however, remained in awe of his mother, with her unerring ability to discern right from wrong. She instilled in Robert this same moral sense, but along with it came feelings of guilt, for he believed early on that he could never live up to his mother's strict code. Whenever the impatient young Robert called someone a fool his mother would declare, 'whoso calleth his brother "fool" is in danger .. for he hath committed murder in his heart already.' 'In short,' Robert told Elizabeth before their marriage, 'I stood there a convicted *murderer* .. to which I was forced penitently to agree.' Nevertheless, Robert was never in any doubt that he was, as Carlyle noted, the very apple of his parents' eyes. 'Since I was a child,' he once confided to Elizabeth, 'I never asked for the least or greatest thing within the compass of their means to give, but given it was, – nor for liberty but it was conceded, nor confidence but it was bestowed.'[33] Thus it was that Robert continued to live at home, pursuing his career as a penniless poet while continuing to kiss his mother good-night every evening, until the age of thirty-four, when he eloped with a woman whom his parents had never met.

Browning was never to see his mother again. He learned of her death only a few weeks after the birth of Pen in Florence in the spring of 1849. He had never wanted a child, not after the anguish of Elizabeth's first two miscarriages. He told his wife that he could never love a child the way he loved her, and had repeatedly denied that he had any paternal instinct. As the pregnancy went into its ninth month, Robert wished the unborn child would somehow magically disappear so that their lives could go back to the way they were. But on 9 March a son was born – a fine, strong boy 'with the voice of three' – and Browning's relief turned to joy. He did not walk but danced about the streets of Florence delivering the good news, as one maidservant observed. He rocked and cradled the child, made funny faces, and thought the boy a genius at nine days old: 'he follows lights or noises,' Robert noted, 'with his little great eyes and even hands – and, when I make a chirrup to him with my lips, fairly takes hold of my nose!'[34]

The proud parents clipped a strand of hair to send to Mrs Browning to announce the birth of her first grandson. When it arrived at New Cross a week or so later,* she was lying desperately ill in bed, 'in the insensibility precursive of the grave's', Elizabeth told Mary Russell Mitford. Although Sarianna was certain that the news would have made her heart bound, the wise doctors thought it would all be too much for the invalid. As far as Elizabeth knew, her mother-in-law never heard the contents of that letter before her death a few days later, on 18 March 1849. The woman who had been the mainstay of family life in Camberwell and then New Cross was now gone. It must have been a dreadful shock to her husband and daughter. The capable Sarianna, so like her mother, would have taken charge of the burial arrangements while the childlike Mr Browning looked on sadly.

Despite her own grief – not to mention exhaustion – Sarianna had sought to soften the blow which their mother's death would surely deal Robert. Her first thought always was to protect those whom she loved, especially her brother. To this end, Sarianna composed a succession of heart-wrenching letters to Robert over three days. The tears must have

* Post could travel between England and Italy in as few as six days if it went by steamer, otherwise in nine days.

welled up in her eyes as she wrote the first note, on 17 March, conveying the family's congratulations on the news of the birth, joyous news which was being needlessly – and cruelly – withheld from their mother.* She followed this the next day with another letter, 'written when all was over', but saying nothing more than that their mother was very ill and promising to write tomorrow.[35]

When Robert received Sarianna's third and final letter, telling him of their bereavement, his grief – and guilt – were profound. Sarah Anna Browning had died without her beloved son by her side because he had chosen to live with Elizabeth as a voluntary exile in Italy. She never had the chance to meet her daughter-in-law. If Mrs Browning could hate anybody, Elizabeth had told Arabel only the year before, 'she must hate *me*, for taking him away from her.'[36] Robert, for his part, had been denied the chance to sit by her deathbed and express those things that so often remain unsaid between a mother and child.

Elizabeth was all too aware of the thoughts torturing her husband. 'I never saw a *man* so overcome & wrung to the soul,' she confided to Arabel. 'The bursts of convulsive weeping, the recapitulation of all her goodness & tenderness in words that made the heart ache, & then the recovery of composure with such a ghastly violence, that you wished the agitation back again – these things, I shall not try to describe.' Worse, Robert shrank from the infant whose birth he had celebrated so recently. 'While he was full of joy for the child, his mother was dying at a distance,' Elizabeth tried to explain to her friend Mrs Martin; 'the very thought of accepting that new affection for the old became a thing to recoil from – do you not see?'[37]

Three months later, in June, it was still a melancholy scene in Casa Guidi. Elizabeth was desperate to get Robert away from Florence, but he seemed incapable of movement. She resorted to subterfuge, swearing that she and the baby could not bear the heat. Browning responded to her plea. They temporarily left the three-month-old bundle of joy behind in Florence while they scoured Tuscany looking for a suitably cool retreat. An ill-advised visit to Shelley's house at Lerici, near the bay of Spezia, made them both melancholy. Shelley's death by drowning reminded Elizabeth of her brother's fate; Robert cannot but have recalled his

* Years later Sarianna claimed that she had defied the doctors and told her mother about the birth of her grandchild; both she and Robert certainly would have preferred to remember this version of events (Domett, *Diary*, 30 April 1878).

mother's gift of Shelley's poetry and how he had repaid her by turning to atheism. As they each stood, lost in thought, near the spot where Shelley's body had washed up on the shore, Robert and Elizabeth must have felt dreadfully isolated not only from the rest of the world but also from one another.

It was then, at the end of June, that the Brownings first discovered the resort of Bagni di Lucca, tucked away in a steep, wooded gorge which provided plenty of cool shade. The 'Bagni' actually comprise three separate villages, very different in character as well as altitude, which hosted annual summer gatherings of expatriates and tourists. Elizabeth and Robert avoided the lower resorts, thinking them a 'wasp's nest of scandal & gaming'. They made the fifty-mile journey back to Florence to collect the baby and the rest of the household before settling into their summer quarters, 'a sort of eagle's nest in this place', Elizabeth remarked. But still Robert's mind was on his mother's death. 'I have been thinking over nothing else,' he confessed to Sarianna at the beginning of July, 'than Mama and all about her, and catching at any little fancy of finding something which it would have pleased her I should do.' It was Elizabeth who had thought to christen the infant Wiedeman, his grandmother's maiden name.* They went to some trouble to arrange a baptism (at the French Evangelical Protestant Church in the Prussian Legation in Florence), which was 'very simple and evangelical – just the same as at Mr Clayton's', Robert told his sister. Bagni di Lucca suited the Brownings perfectly. The little boy was 'always merry and laughing' – all of which, Robert wrote in this same letter, 'ought to be unmixed pleasure to me, but is very far from it'.[38]

Elizabeth perceived that his mother's death affected Robert 'not only acutely for the time but deeply and permanently'. He could think of nothing else but that insolent, selfish boy – 'the wise person of my perfect remembrance and particular dislike', as he would describe his youthful self to Julia Wedgwood years later. 'Very bitter has it been to me,' Elizabeth confided to Sarianna, 'to have interposed unconsciously as I have done and deprived him of her last words and kisses – very bitter.' She convinced herself that Robert was repenting 'in the secrecy of his heart, having called it happiness to be with *me*' rather than his mother.

---

* The full name given to the baby was Robert Wiedeman Barrett Browning (Elizabeth dropped the second 'n' in Wiedemann). When a toddler, the boy took to calling himself Wiedeman, which, Elizabeth explained to her sister, he 'turned into Peninny – by an extraordinary resolution of syllables' (EBB to Arabel Barrett, [12–14 October 1851]).

She could not find the words to console him. Once, when Robert let slip that the sadness only seemed to sink deeper and deeper, Elizabeth answered lamely that he would feel better when the weather was a little brighter. That reminded him, he commented wryly, of the bishop's advice to a man who had serious doubts about the Christian religion: to 'take horse-exercise'.[39]

What was to be done? It was then, in Bagni di Lucca, that Elizabeth, with some trepidation, presented Robert with *Sonnets from the Portuguese*, those love poems which she had composed not long before their marriage. He had so often snarled at effusive love poetry that Elizabeth had never dared show Robert her sonnets. But there in Bagni di Lucca, with the tall mimosa beside the balcony, he needed to read those words: 'I love thee to the depth and breadth and height / My soul can reach.' He had to be reminded that one person at least thought he was still worthy to be loved even if he himself did not. Elizabeth's gamble paid off; her gift of poetry had brought Robert back to her and to their son.* 'Ba must have told you about our babe,' Robert wrote to Mrs Jameson from their mountain retreat that August, 'and the little else there is to tell – that is for *her* to tell, for she is not likely to encroach upon *my* story which I *could* tell of her entirely angelic nature, as divine a heart as God ever made; I know more of her every day; I, who thought I knew something of her five years ago!'[40]

By the time they left Bagni di Lucca in October, Elizabeth had helped Robert to reaffirm not only his love for her and for their child but also, for a time at least, that faith in God which his mother had desired above all else to instil in her son but which her death had so badly shaken. Robert had always drawn strength from Elizabeth's simple yet devout belief. In July 1845, when they were still getting to know one another, Elizabeth had admitted that, when it came to religion, she cared very little for most 'dogmas & doxies in themselves'. 'I used to go with my father always,' she explained, 'when I was able, to the nearest dissenting chapel of the congregationalists – from liking the simplicity of that praying and speaking without books.' She then added rather wickedly, 'There is a narrowness among the dissenters which is wonderful, – an arid, grey Puritanism in the clefts of their souls.'

---

* Elizabeth had not intended to publish these love poems, but Robert insisted, and they duly appeared in her two-volume *Poems* (1850). To mask their personal nature, the Brownings called them *Sonnets from the Portuguese*, 'Portuguese' referring to the heroine of Elizabeth's poem 'Catarina to Camoëns'.

Browning was delighted. 'Can it be you .. *you* are a schismatic and frequenter of Independent Dissenting Chapels? And you confess this to *me* – whose father and mother went this morning to the very Independent Chapel where they took me, all those years back, to be baptized!' Robert divined that Elizabeth's religious views were very close to his own: profound but occasionally irreverent. 'I believe in what is divine & floats at highest, in all these different theologies,' she wrote some months later; '& because the really Divine draws together souls, & tends so to a unity, I could pray anywhere & with all sorts of worshippers .. In all religious societies, there is a little to revolt, & a good deal to bear with,' she added; 'Still you go quickest there, where your sympathies are least ruffled & disturbed – & I like, beyond comparison best, the simplicity of the dissenters.'[41]

Elizabeth's religious views had continued to influence Browning's own, and never more so than in the months following his mother's death, when she would have spoken to him of God's mercy.* On returning from Bagni di Lucca that summer of 1849, Robert sat down at his desk at Casa Guidi to begin a new poem (only his second since his marriage), a Christmas story in verse.† *Christmas-Eve* charts the spiritual journey of a man who is driven by the rain into a Dissenting Chapel, 'to wit, in Zion Chapel Meeting, / On the Christmas-Eve of 'Forty-nine, / Which, calling its flock to their special clover, / Found all assembled and one sheep over.' He has escaped the rain but is subjected instead to 'the hot smell and the human noises', not to mention 'the preaching man's immense stupidity'. Suddenly a ghostly vision appears clothed in a 'sweepy garment, vast and white', much like the ghost in Dickens' *A Christmas Carol*, published six years earlier. The frightened man takes hold of the flying robe and, like Ebenezer Scrooge, is magically transported: first to St Peter's in Rome, then to a German university where a 'hawk-nosed high-cheek-boned Professor' is lecturing on the Christian myth.

Eventually the man finds himself back in the crowded chapel, certain that he has experienced a vision, although from his neighbours' angry looks he admits that 'a spectator might have fancied / That I had nodded,

---

* It was not until later, in the 1850s, that Elizabeth's openness to whatever 'floats highest' led her to see spiritualism as part of Christianity – an aspect of her belief which, of course, Robert vehemently disagreed with.
† Browning followed it with a companion piece, *Easter-Day*. The two poems were published together in the spring of 1850.

betrayed by slumber' during the sermon. No matter – he had come to realise, as Elizabeth had remarked, that there was a little to revolt against and a good deal to bear with in religion; you go where your sympathies are least ruffled and disturbed. At that moment, the narrator 'does best to receive in meekness' the Dissenting faith wherein God 'appears serene / With the thinnest human veil between'. But, whereas Elizabeth had easily (but not complacently) embraced her faith, Robert would continue to wrestle with his. 'All we have gained then by our unbelief,' so declares the speaker in 'Bishop Blougram's Apology' – written within a few years of *Christmas-Eve* – 'Is a life of doubt diversified by faith, / For one of faith diversified by doubt: / We called the chess-board white, – we call it black.'

One awful irony surrounding his mother's death in 1849 was that Robert and Elizabeth had been planning a visit to England to see family and friends that very summer. His mother had been so anxious to have them back home, Elizabeth told Arabel in 1848. But after what had passed, Robert could not even think of returning to London, to his parents' house. It would break his heart, he told Elizabeth, 'to see his mother's roses over the wall, and the place where she used to lay her scissors and gloves'.[42] They urged Mr Browning and Sarianna to come to them in Florence or, better still, meet them in Paris; but for one reason or another it never happened. It was another two years before Robert was able to consider a visit to London, and even then, in the summer of 1851, he dreaded it. His dread was so great that Elizabeth worried about his health, both mental and physical. She suggested that they cancel, or at least postpone, the journey. Relief instantly swept over Robert. But then he thought of Arabel's disappointment at not seeing her sister, and he resolved to travel with his wife and son to London.

They decided not to stay with Browning's father and sister – the house held too many memories – and instead rented rather ugly rooms (as it turned out) in Devonshire Street, around the corner from Wimpole Street. Robert proceeded alone to New Cross to face his personal demons amongst his mother's roses. However, the joy in seeing his father and sister after so long soon overtook his grief and anxiety. A few weeks into their visit, Robert was thoroughly enjoying London, especially the evenings spent with various shining lights and old friends such as Carlyle, Macready, and Forster. 'I felt all those spark-like hours in London struck out of the black element I was beset with, all the brighter for it,' Browning afterwards wrote to John Kenyon.[43]

Elizabeth could see that their time in London was pure joy to Robert: 'I do believe,' she told Mrs Jameson, 'he would have been capable of never leaving England again.' But this was not practicable nor, as far as Elizabeth was concerned, was it desirable. Her relations – or lack thereof – with her father, the weather (her first step on English ground was into a puddle), and their miserable lodgings all conspired to make her wish she was somewhere else – preferably Paris. They duly retreated to the French capital, from where a lately jealous Elizabeth wrote to Arabel: 'our divorce is at [an] end .. I mean the divorce which London dissipations made necessary for the time.'[44] She and Robert were constantly together, both day and night, once more.

Within a year the Von Müller affair had made exiles of all the Brownings. It was another cruel irony that, just when Robert had rediscovered the pleasures and advantages of London society, his father and sister were forced to uproot themselves from Mrs Browning's rose garden. 'Oh, to be in England / Now that April's there': so Robert had written presciently in 'Home-Thoughts, from Abroad' before he had ever met Elizabeth.

At least Robert had been able to be by the side of his dying father that June of 1866, adjusting the invalid's pillows, reading aloud and, no doubt, recounting Pen's latest exploits. Robert was fully aware of what he owed to this remarkable man, who had gladly paid for the publication of his son's early works and who took the reviews very much to heart. Browning can only have been thankful that his father, who had been so supportive of his literary efforts, lived long enough to see him beginning to succeed as a poet.

Yet one senses that Robert had not always been able to look after the old man as he would have wanted. In 1851 – even before the Von Müller affair – the idea had been mooted that Robert's father and sister might move to Paris* to be near Elizabeth and Robert, who were considering Paris as a possible permanent residence. Sarianna certainly believed that such was her brother's earnest wish. Their father doted on his grandchild so, drawing him soldiers and swans from morning to night. As for Sarianna herself, she would infinitely prefer it to her 'solitary life' in New Cross, so far from London. Elizabeth thought differently. Robert told his father and sister that he 'did not bind himself at all' to staying in Paris; he might even go to Italy for a year. 'So this is understood,'

---

* The lease on the New Cross house was due to expire.

Elizabeth explained to Arabel. One suspects that this escape clause was added at Elizabeth's suggestion.[45]

Within three months of Sarianna and her father moving to Paris, in October 1852, Robert and Elizabeth did indeed return to Italy, and in Italy they remained. As her health – and her ability to travel – steadily declined, he was torn between attending his wife and visiting his father in the French capital. Elizabeth felt it a duty to go to see Robert's father, but it was a burdensome one. 'If it were not for the Brownings I would sulk on this side of the Alps,' she confided to her sister.[46] More than once she admitted to being the cause of Robert's not seeing his father. After Elizabeth's death, Robert's feeling of duty towards Pen had compelled him to settle in London, not Paris. The summer holidays in Brittany which he had shared with his father and sister held, therefore, a special significance for Robert.

At the time of his father's death, Robert deemed Sarianna, his fifty-two-year-old spinster sister, to be the lucky one. He acknowledged that she had long ago sacrificed any hope of a family of her own. Elizabeth once hinted to Arabel that her sister-in-law might have married but had turned down the chance.* 'You see what she loses,' Browning told Isa a week after the sad event; 'all her life has been spent in caring for my mother, and, seventeen years after that, my father.' Yet 'you may be sure she does not rave and rend her hair like people who have plenty to atone for in the past,' the poet added, clearly racked with guilt. At least it was in Robert's power to care for Sarianna as he felt he ought. 'My sister will come & live with me henceforth,' he informed Isa.

Sarianna was no retiring old maid; she was, by all accounts, clever, talkative, and animated. Henriette Corkran had never heard anyone relate an anecdote so well and with so much verve. Her lisp (she pronounced her brother's name 'Wobert') must have made her stories all the more singular and amusing. Sarianna, like her Scottish mother, was more prosaic than poetic, and said what she thought. She tended to make fun of Elizabeth's zeal for the Risorgimento, telling the diarist William Allingham that her brother and his wife had remained too long in Florence in the summer heat, 'being unable to tear themselves away from a place where they could get two bulletins of the war a day'. As for the

---

* Tantalisingly, Elizabeth mentioned the man's name in her letter, but the name has since been obliterated (EBB to Arabel, 4 April [1853]). Years later, Browning told Daniel Sargent Curtis that 'his sister might have married, but devoted her life to her parents and to her brother' (Curtis, 'Robert Browning,' in Meredith (ed.), *More than Friend*, Appendix C).

political storm over Elizabeth's pro-Italian and anti-British *Poems before Congress* (1860), Sarianna remarked, 'I am wicked enough to suspect she rather enjoys it.' For her part, Elizabeth deplored her sister-in-law's 'excessive scepticism' in regards to table-rapping. 'I hope when I leave this world,' Sarianna once declared, 'I shall not be doomed to take up my abode in the leg of a table, answering silly questions.'[47] Nevertheless, Elizabeth had fully appreciated the wisdom and love – not to mention courage – shown by Sarianna when she had thought to soften the impact of their mother's death on Robert.

On taking up residence at Warwick Crescent, Sarianna – or 'Sis', as Robert called her – continued to brandish her good sense. She saw to the linen, the servants, and the larder. Elizabeth, by her own admission, had been a terrible housekeeper, serving her guests half-cups of tea and measly dinner portions when she – inevitably – found there was not enough to go round. After one such 'make-believe' dinner in Paris, she apologised to William Allingham, a charming Irishman who had attached himself to the Pre-Raphaelites and was something of a literary habitué: 'in spite of your good nature, you must have softly moralized on a certain friend's unfortunate destiny in having married a mere rhyming woman instead of an "angel in the house" capable of looking to the chops.' Sarianna also took charge of her brother's menagerie which came to include two geese called Edinburgh and Quarterly (which, like the periodicals, always greeted their master hissing and fluttering), and an owl: 'The light of our house,' Browning called this creature, 'for his tameness and engaging ways.' Allingham, always assured of a good meal with Miss Browning in charge of the kitchen, observed the poet during one Sunday lunch in April 1867 petting and stroking the bird, all the while calling him 'a good man'. Sarianna added to the menagerie, taking pity on a tortoise for sale on a wheelbarrow in the street. 'Our owl is well in body,' she reported two years later to Annie Smith, Willy Bracken's aunt, 'and somewhat acid in temper – the tortoise is quite rampant with to-day's warmth, and has almost crawled an inch!'[48]

In fact, from 1866 onwards the household at Warwick Crescent, overflowing with books (many of them his father's) and overrun by animals, mirrored the family homes in Camberwell and New Cross. Sarianna inevitably became privy to the tittle-tattle associated with her brother and various women. While she was still living in Paris, one old lady regularly came to condole with her about Pen's 'approaching change of circumstances' under a new stepmother. One of his tutors even asked

Pen if it was true that his father was intending to remarry. 'It is funny,' Browning told Isa, 'people think I am likely to do nothing naughty in the world, neither rob nor kill, seduce nor ravish, – only honestly *marry* – which I should consider the two last, – and perhaps two first, – naughtinesses united, together with the grace of perjury.' The practical Sarianna, however, did not see it this way and told her brother on at least one occasion, as reported by his valet: 'Why don't you mawwy one of these ladies who is so fond of you?'[49]

The Brownings did not forgo their Breton holiday that first summer after his father's death. However, Robert had been resolute that he would not return to Pornic, 'full of my dear old Papa'; they lighted instead on the even more wild and primitive Le Croisic. When the threesome returned to London at the end of September (1866), Robert redoubled his efforts to tutor Pen in Greek and Latin. Pen was scheduled to sit the Balliol entrance examination soon after Easter, Robert told George Barrett in October: 'I hope – earnestly pray, he may be successful, but am not sure. They require real proficiency in Greek & Latin at Balliol, and the examination is in no sense a sham.' 'I don't in the least know how he will turn out *eventually*,' the poet had written to Isa from Le Croisic; 'I want him to be what I think he may be: next year or two will decide perhaps if I shall be disappointed or no.' Alarm bells must have gone off in Isa's mind on reading this. She already thought him a 'monomaniac' in regard to Pen, and other of his friends were starting to agree. Benjamin Jowett, Regius Professor of Greek at Oxford and Fellow of Balliol College, commented that 'of personal objects he seems to have none except the education of his son.' George Smith, his publisher from 1867, remarked that the poet's affection – or was it ambition (Browning himself had used the word) – for his son 'was almost painful in its intensity and absorption'.[50]

Doubtless the level-headed Sarianna remonstrated with her brother not to be too hard on the boy. She knew well enough that her nephew had 'a wholesome love of play and horror of lessons'. But one gets the sense that, with Pen, Browning was still desperately trying to make up for lost time. The anguish which the poet had felt on his mother's death, occurring so soon after Pen's birth, had set up a barrier between father and son. His son's birthday never passed without his thinking back to that terrible time.* The bond had been – and continued to be – strongest

* In 1883 Browning wrote to a friend on Pen's birthday: 'That event was a joy soon enough

between Pen and Elizabeth; indeed, Robert still sometimes thought of him as her son, not his. 'Here was her child entering his eighteenth year this month,' Robert had remarked to Isa in March 1866. 'I hope he does well: I want a good deal, for him – & her.' On another occasion he observed to Isa, who had seen a recent photograph of Pen, 'he ought to be somebody above nobody by virtue of the likeness you perceive, which gets stronger & stronger: but his development has been very gradual, indeed.'[51]

Pen had inherited Elizabeth's big black eyes, not her sharp intellect – but then she had pampered him so. Once, when the Brownings were travelling together by train to England, someone in the carriage, seeing Pen asleep on his father's lap, remarked, 'I think papa spoils you.' Pen opened his eyes, Elizabeth noted, and gravely explained, 'no, it isn't papa: it's mama.' The boy was probably repeating, as children do, a conversation he had overheard between his parents. In his mother's eyes, Pen could do no wrong. He was a 'saint of a child', so witty, sociable, irresistible and, yes, spoiled, Elizabeth admitted to Henrietta. The doting mother thought it delightful when on one occasion Pen went up to a church altar in Florence and began to sing aloud the ditty 'Margery Daw'. She had been equally amused when, before Pen's birth, her spaniel Flush had walked straight up to the high altar and performed 'his devotions thereat'. On the latter occasion – and no doubt the former also – Robert was 'in an agony the whole time'.[52]

Robert loved his son. He would have given his life for him, as he swore to Elizabeth at Pen's birth. Once he spent an entire Sunday morning trying to teach the toddler to spin a top. He considered it, Elizabeth repeated to Henrietta, a 'religious duty'. One suspects that, joking aside, Browning took the duty of educating his son – and instilling discipline – very seriously indeed. He was determined not to indulge the boy, especially as he grew older. There was quite enough of that from Elizabeth. Although it dismayed her when Pen was inattentive at lessons, 'talking nonsense, dawdling in finding his books, .. & kissing me instead of pleasing me', she would not teach a child against his will – it was against her principles.[53] If Robert, on the other hand, ever fashioned ancient Troy out of tables and chairs for the young Pen, it would have been for

dashed with grief, for, one week after, my mother died suddenly: and the news, she had been anxious to learn, reached England when she was just passing away' (T. J. Collins (ed.), 'Letters from Robert Browning to the Rev. J. D. Williams, 1874–1889', *Browning Institute Studies*, 4 (1976), 1–56).

the sole purpose of instructing him in Homeric verse. Unlike his own father, he did not then know 'better than turn straight / Learning's full flare on weak-eyed ignorance'.*

In fact, as regarded the conduct of a father towards his only son, the contrast between the Browning household in Camberwell and that in Warwick Crescent could not have been more different. Robert's parents had had great faith in their son and had invested much, both emotionally and financially, in his genius. The poet, although he continued to have high hopes for his own child, still did not give the boy much credit beyond being a good fellow – and a good oarsman. Robert even betrayed a streak of competitiveness. One summer's day at Warwick Crescent, William Allingham heard Pen, then fifteen, play Chopin. 'Did you ever play as well as that?' he asked Browning. 'A thousand times as well!' was the reply.[54]

Yet Pen adored his father; he always had. Elizabeth once confessed that she was 'rather jealous' of Robert who was Pen's favourite. When she wanted more kisses, she wrote to her sister Henrietta, she was told, 'No – no more! All mine oller kisses are Papa's.' By the time Pen was nine and too old for kisses, he tried instead to earn his father's approval and would burst into tears if Robert found fault with him. Elizabeth remarked a little sourly to Arabel, 'Pen does'nt care as much for *my* displeasure, I observe.'[55] The small boy's finite number of kisses and attempts to please would have been wasted on his mother, who loved him unconditionally; his father's affection, however, was harder to come by and, therefore, more dear.

In October 1866, at least, Pen stood in good stead with his father. The poet was feeling cautiously optimistic about the future, his own as well as Pen's. 'Pen working hard,' Browning informed Isa, 'and I have my poem to mend and end in the gaps between Greek and Latin' – the poem that would become *The Ring and the Book*. Robert had begun serious work on this, his magnum opus, shortly after the publication of *Dramatis Personae* in 1864; two years later the poem, which Browning felt was nearly complete (although nowhere near ready for publication), comprised 16,000 lines.

Browning had never worked so hard – certainly not so diligently – as

* 'Development', written at the very end of Browning's life, when Pen was already in middle age.

during the composition of *The Ring and the Book*. He thoroughly researched the story, based on an actual Roman murder trial of 1698, reading everything he could find on the subject. His starting point had been a contemporary account discovered at a pedlar's stall in Florence. Robert also recruited others to the cause. He sent Frederic Leighton to visit the Church of San Lorenzo in Lucina to verify certain facts. He consulted a Catholic lawyer at Middle Temple about a point of law and quizzed Antony Panizzi, Librarian of the British Museum (and Italian refugee), about historical sources. He co-opted George Barrett: 'any old postal map of the road between Arezzo and Rome, via Perugia, – containing the names of *all* the little villages by the way, – of the year 1700, a little earlier or later, – I should be glad to have such a thing.' Robert even asked his father about one or two details of medieval history. Old Mr Browning, who was as fascinated as his son by it all, put together – just a few months before his death – a book full of detailed research together with a narrative of his own. Indeed, everyone he knew, both in England and in Italy, was on the lookout for anything to do with Browning's 'murder-case', so often had the poet told the story to friends. He later told Allingham that a builder will tell you sometimes of a house: 'There's twice as much work underground as above,' and thus it was with his poem.[56]

Browning lost himself in his work, so absorbing was it. He told William Rossetti that he was no longer working by 'the inspiring impulse', as in Florence, but according to 'a regular systematic plan', sitting down at his desk in Warwick Crescent for three hours every day. There were, of course, times when he threw down his pen, 'after hours and hours of writing, sick of the sight of paper and ink', the poet confided to a friend in early 1865. Nevertheless, he stuck to it. Browning had once preferred solitude to society owing to his grief over Elizabeth's death; by 1865 it had become part of the discipline of writing. He refused to be drawn out into the light, whether the invitation be to a garden party or regatta, with the ready excuse, 'I never accept such.' He told the Storys' daughter Edith, 'What has a grey owl like me to do with Regattas & the lovers of the same? No, no! the dark for me!'[57]

His confidence in the future was given a further boost in January 1867 when Jowett suggested that Browning be put forward as a candidate for the Professorship of Poetry at Oxford, recently vacated by Matthew Arnold. 'A body of the young men actually came and declared they wanted me in that capacity,' Robert told a friend.[58] A petition was sent round, declaring that the poet should receive an honorary MA so that he might qualify for the post. The council, however, denied the request on the grounds that it would be unfair to the other candidates. Browning agreed; in any case, he was not keen to spend his precious time slaving over lectures. Yet, he admitted to Isa the following month, 'I should have accepted it – simply on account of the wish I have to stand well with, – and, above all, near to – the University where Pen will spend the next three or four years.' 'Had they wished me to blacken their boots instead of polish their heads, I should not have demurred, you understand, in the prospect of possible advantage to Pen.'

The offer, although withdrawn almost as soon as it was made, had meant all the world to Browning. Of course, he viewed it as a good omen for Pen's Oxford career, but his appreciation sprang from an even deeper source. Robert, whose Dissenting background had kept him from entering the hallowed halls of Oxford and Cambridge, had always felt himself to be on the outside looking in. Mr Browning Senior had anticipated his young son's dilemma. In 1825, when Robert was still only thirteen, he contributed £100 to the foundation of a new non-sectarian institution, University College, London; in return, a nominee of his choice would be eligible to receive a free place. Three years later he duly wrote to the university concerning the boy, saying that he 'so earnestly desires I would interest myself in procuring his admittance, that I should feel myself wanting, as a Parent, were I to neglect any step to procure what he deems so essential to his future happiness'.

Robert was duly admitted. (He was one of the first students to register at the newly established university.) The excited sixteen-year-old, accompanied (one supposes) by his father and clutching the bag carefully packed by his mother, entered the precincts of University College in October 1828. He took a room in nearby Bedford Square with one Mr Hughes and signed up for classes in German, Greek, and Latin. But within a week Robert had abandoned his student digs and fled back to the comforts of Camberwell. Six months later, in May 1829, poor Mr Browning wrote to the College Warden: 'I am very sorry to communicate my son's determination to withdraw from the London University (an event as painful as it was unexpected).' He could only assure them that he was 'entirely satisfied with every thing that has been done on your part, and make my grateful acknowledgments for the kind and affectionate treatment with which you have always behaved to him'.[59]

Robert had offered no satisfactory explanation to his parents at the time, nor would they have pressed him for one. Yet he had not put the unhappy episode out of his mind entirely. Five years later a friend suggested that Browning, still only in his early twenties, take as the subject of his next poem the Renaissance physician and alchemist Paracelsus. Paracelsus was one of those neglected figures of history, found buried amongst his father's books, whom Robert so loved to resurrect. 'To crown your dearest wish, / With a tumultuous heart, you left with me / Our childhood's home to join the favoured few' – so Browning has the fatherly Festus tell Paracelsus, a flawed genius who had also gone to university, only to abandon his studies. 'Not one youth,' he continues, 'Of those so favoured, whom you now despise, / Came earnest as you came, resolved, like you, / To grasp all, and retain all.' But Festus, like poor Mr Browning, had witnessed a 'sudden pause, the total change' in Paracelsus, 'From pressing onward as his fellows pressed, / To a blank idleness', which appeared to be 'free from all pretence', but which gave way to 'rare outbreaks, fierce and brief'.

This was Browning's portrait of the artist as a young man – intellectually arrogant, ambitious, and homesick. The sixteen-year-old clearly felt that his professors and fellow students had nothing to offer. Moreover, he must have been painfully aware of the fact that University College, London, was not Oxbridge, at least not in those days. Thus, nearly forty years on, Browning regarded the mere idea that he might be considered for the Professorship of Poetry at Oxford as a compliment to an outsider, as he thought himself to be. Just at this time he was revising *Paracelsus* and other works for a new collected edition of his poetry. He must have smiled to himself (or moaned aloud) when he reread Paracelsus' words to Festus: 'Surely you know I am engaged to fill / The chair here [at Basle]? – that 'tis part of my proud fate / To lecture to as many thick-skulled youths / As please, each day, to throng the theatre, / To my great reputation.' The fifty-four-year-old Robert had left behind that disdainful youth – 'the wise person of my perfect remembrance and particular dislike'.

Jowett's recognition of Browning's stature as a poet had indeed been gratifying; equally, if not more, important to him was the enthusiasm which the Oxford undergraduates had shown for his poetry. 'The orders come from Oxford and Cambridge,' Browning's publisher had told him; 'all my new cultivators are young men: more than that,' he remarked somewhat wryly to Isa in August 1865, 'I observe that some of my old friends don't like at all the irruption of *outsiders* who rescue me from their sober and private approval and take those words out of their mouths "which they always meant to say," and never *did*.'

Most Victorians believed that green grass, verdant meadows, tall pines, and vineyards were the 'essentials of poetry', but Browning eschewed this aspect of Romanticism, so observed F. G. Stephens, one of the Pre-Raphaelite Brotherhood, which had kept a small candle burning for Browning's poetry in Oxford's hallowed halls since the 1850s. Browning looked instead, Stephens continued, 'into the heart of man', and revealed 'its pulsations, fears, self doubts, hates, goodness, devotedness, and noble world-love . . with the firm knowing hand of the anatomist'. The strangeness of his poetry – jarring syntax and obscure vocabulary, unreliable narrators and open endings, ambiguity and complexity – raised puzzled eyebrows amongst the public. But in the mid-1860s, these same qualities began to appeal ever more widely to a new generation who were seeing the old certainties crumble before the forces of industrialisation and science. William Rossetti admired, as had Elizabeth also, the masculine quality of Browning's poetry: 'He is thoroughly a *man*.' Browning 'never thinks but at full speed', Swinburne remarked, comparing the poet's rate of thought to the speed of a railway train. His verse was as new and different, as exciting and immediate, as the art of photography or locomotion. Browning approached his verse, as he himself once explained, 'just as if the experiment of expression were being tried for the first time'. Henry James pronounced him 'a tremendous and incomparable modern'. Perhaps it was this combination of modernity and manliness which appealed to Americans,* amongst whom Browning was 'a power, a writer, a poet', as Elizabeth told Sarianna.[60]

'I was much struck by the kind ways, and interest in me shown by the Oxford undergraduates,' Robert continued in his letter to Isa that August; 'I am sure they would be the more helpful to my son.' (Always his thoughts reverted to Pen.) 'So,' Browning ends, 'good luck to my great venture, the murder-poem, which I do hope will strike you and all good lovers of mine.' He sensed that *The Ring and the Book* would be something remarkable, pushing the poetic boundaries even further.

In June 1867 the council relented and bestowed upon the poet an Oxford MA by diploma 'before the assembled universe' at Convocation:

---

* The American critic, G. W. Curtis, writing in 1888, also thought that for Americans, 'the very fact of the obscurity of Browning's verse is an allurement, because it gives them a reason for devoted study and comparative interpretation' (*Critical Heritage*, 503).

'a very rare distinction said to have only happened in Dr Johnson's case!' Robert observed to Isa. 'Of course, it is purely for Pen's sake – ' (one can almost picture Miss Blagden throwing up her hands in exasperation as she read this) 'though I am not insensible to the strange liking for me that young & old Oxford seem to have.' On a more sombre note he added, 'Poor Papa was buried last year about this time: I should have enjoyed the thing for his sake.' Degree in hand, Browning was then elected an Honorary Fellow of Balliol College the following October. He was as thrilled as a schoolboy. 'This is a very pretty compliment to me, – Pen at the College of which I am Fellow, is it not?' Robert gleefully told Isa. 'I really don't know what makes folk so kind all at once!'

Would the poet's honours, however, really blaze a trail for Pen's entrance to Balliol? In March 1867, a few months before Browning was due to receive his MA, Jowett had invited the young man up to Oxford to see how he was getting on with his studies. After putting him through his paces for a week, the Professor of Greek tactfully suggested that Pen's matriculation be delayed until the autumn. There had been warning signs. A month before Pen was due to meet Jowett in Oxford, Robert had observed to Isa that his son '*boats* – cares more for that than aught else, – unless perhaps for shooting and breech-loaders: but he is a good fellow all the same, and may wake up ambitious one day'. That November, after a few months' holiday in Le Croisic, Browning sent Pen back to Oxford to revise under the watchful eye of his tutor. The poet was confident. 'The impulse gained by a glimpse, or rather good gaze into the life of young men with a purpose to study,' Robert told Isa, 'has done him great good. He writes me often, – enjoys himself much, having his own boat there. Indeed, people are only too kind to him, & the magnates have him to breakfast &c in an unusual way.' To Pen, those few weeks at Oxford must have felt like a holiday camp compared to the strict regime imposed at Warwick Crescent.

Always the gentleman, never the scholar. Jowett heartily liked young Browning and deemed his Latin up to the mark – but not his Greek. More worryingly, he seemed to have a remarkably bad memory and was clearly unused to writing in English. The examination was once more postponed, this time until the following spring. Browning nevertheless thought Pen's future secure and wrote to Isa on the last day of 1867: 'Pen is back for the holidays, having done very well indeed at Oxford: he will matriculate next Term & reside forthwith.' It simply had to be – it was all so perfect: Pen at the same college where his father was an Honorary

Fellow. After yet more intensive revision, Pen sat and failed the examination in April 1868. But the increasingly anxious father did not give up, although it seems his son already had. Browning arranged for Pen to go into the country for two months with a tutor before joining Mr Jowett's reading party in Scotland during the long vacation.

In the early summer of 1868 Browning was beginning to have doubts not only about Pen's future but also about the public's reception of his bold epic, *The Ring and the Book*. Although he had often discussed the plot with friends, he had let no one read the work, which had grown to over 20,000 lines. (Allingham was allowed only a 'bird's-eye view' of the manuscript.) Robert had begun to rise at 5 a.m. to finish the final draft. It must have occurred to him, as it did to George Eliot when she learned how long the poem was to be: 'Who will read it all in these busy days?' Browning was not sure what form it should take when published. 'I want people not to turn to the end,' he told Allingham, 'but to read through in proper order. Magazine, you'll say: but no, I don't like the notion of being sandwiched between Politics and Deer-Stalking, say.' He was thinking of four monthly volumes, but the final decision lay with the publisher. The poet did not even have a title for the work; he had thought 'the Book & the Ring' (*sic*) too 'pretty-fairy-story-like',* but could come up with nothing better than 'The Franceschini'.[61]

Amidst all the uncertainty concerning both Pen and his poem, an event occurred which threw Browning further off-balance. When he called on Arabel Barrett early one evening in June 1868, he found her very poorly. He was more anxious than the doctor for the patient's welfare and called in a second 'wise man'. The second opinion being no graver than the first, Browning left Arabel in the care of her servants and went to hear the pianist Anton Rubinstein play at a party. But at six o'clock the next morning Robert was summoned across the road by one of Miss Barrett's maids; her mistress was in a bad way. The doctor again came – and went, still insisting there was no danger. Five minutes later Arabel died in Robert's arms, just as his wife had seven years before. Both sisters passed away in the month of June, the same accursed month in which his father had breathed his last. It was left to Robert to take care of the funeral arrangements since George, the only 'useful' Barrett brother (the Barretts were not the most practical family), was away touring in Ireland. 'I am as full as a sponge of vinegar & gall just now,' Browning confided to Isa. It was a

---

* Thinking, no doubt, of Thackeray's fairy tale, *The Rose and the Ring* (1855).

nightmare repeating itself. Worse still, someone had to meet George at the train station and break the news that she was dead and buried.

For Robert, Arabel's death marked an abrupt and all too real break with the past. Elizabeth had introduced Robert to her two sisters even before their marriage, and Robert always looked upon Arabel, Elizabeth's closest confidante, as a great ally. She was the one who kept the family together, the only daughter to remain a spinster, dividing her time between caring for her father and charity work: the proverbial angel in the house. Elizabeth and those other siblings who had been cast out by the demonic Mr Barrett were drawn back to Wimpole Street – if only for fleeting afternoon visits – by Arabel's kindly spirit. Robert once told Elizabeth, no doubt as a means of chiding her, that Arabel suited him as a wife better than she did. 'I upbraid him for it!' Elizabeth declared to her sister, 'at intervals'.[62]

When Robert first returned to London after Elizabeth's death, he chose to live in the less than desirable Paddington area, first in Chichester Place then Warwick Crescent, in order to be near Arabel. He called on his sister-in-law every evening, when Pen would sometimes meet and play with his cousins, Mary and Charlie (the children of Elizabeth's siblings Henrietta and Ocky), who were motherless too. On Sundays Browning accompanied Arabel to the Bedford Street Chapel. The poet, who was not usually such a regular churchgoer, respected – even envied – Arabel's unshakeable faith just as he had respected the deep religious feelings of his mother and his wife. After her death, he could not bear to pass in front of Arabel's house on Delamere Terrace, although it was only across the way from his own. On 16 June Robert told Isa, quoting a line from one of Elizabeth's poems, that Arabel's death deprived him of the one 'steadfast friend who never did my heart or life misknow'.

His sister-in-law's presence so near to Robert had made the widower feel that much closer to his wife's memory. Arabel was said to be very like her sister, and she and Robert would have spoken of Elizabeth often. As they strolled to church, Miss Barrett might have remarked on the uncanny resemblance between Pen and his mother when the boy spoke a certain phrase or tilted his head in a particular way. Robert would have mentioned to Arabel the selection of her sister's poems which he was preparing for the press in the autumn of 1865. Perhaps the poet confided to her, as he did to Isa, 'how I have done it, I can hardly say: it is one dear delight to know that the work of her goes on more effectively than ever – her books are more & more read – certainly sold.'[63]

Browning was reminded of one such conversation when, around the time of Arabel's funeral, he took from the bookshelf his copy of Elizabeth's *Poems before Congress*.[64] He saw that in it he had recorded on 21 July 1863 a dream which Arabel, 'much agitated', had described to him that same day. 'She saw Her,' meaning, of course, Elizabeth, 'and asked "When shall I be with you?" The reply was "Dearest, in five years," whereupon Arabel woke.'

'You know I am not superstitious,' Robert insisted to Isa on 19 June 1868, almost exactly five years later, but the coincidence made him introspective. 'And this is the 19th once again,' the poet's appointed day to write to Isa, 'and in ten days will be the 29th' – the anniversary of Elizabeth's passing.

With Arabel gone, it would become increasingly difficult for Browning to keep Elizabeth – or, rather, the saintly creature which he had fashioned – on her pedestal. Nor was it right that he should try, if he was ever to accept his loss and live his life. There had already been signs in the year before Arabel's death that Browning's perception of the past had become unstable, veering between blissful and bitter-sweet. In June 1867, somewhat to Browning's surprise, Isa wrote from Bagni di Lucca, where he and Elizabeth had fled in 1849, and again in 1853 and 1857, to escape the summer heat in Florence. Isa was at the Bagni with her cousin (Willy Bracken's older stepsister) Annette, who had joined the Brownings there ten years before. 'If you have Annette,' he told Isa, 'give her my best love and tell her I never forget our old rides and walks and talks: I have plenty of new lady-acquaintances, some of them attractive enough, but I don't get intimate with any of them.'

Robert then went on to describe in this same letter one of his more recent 'female encounters'. Two weeks before, when he mentioned at a morning party that Rubinstein would be playing 'quite alone' that afternoon, a lady leaped to her feet and asked, 'Will you take me?' 'And me,' said one sister, 'And me,' said a third. The pianist was a little surprised, Robert remarked, when the three loveliest women in London sailed into the private recital. 'Now, they all pet me, you must know,' Robert continued his tale of the three sirens; 'and yet, when I handed them into their carriage again, I made an excuse about wanting to go elsewhere, rather than accompany them farther. Yet,' he confessed to Isa, 'I would gladly ride with Annette once more up to the little old ruined chapel, by the bridge, – she may remember, – where we took shelter from a thunderstorm. This is because she is part of the Past, while Ladies This, That and the Other are of this present time which wearies me.'

However, not-so-pleasant memories of the resort had also begun to surface. 'I think you said the place was little changed,' Robert replied two months later, in September 1867, to another letter from Isa post-marked Bagni di Lucca; 'I was there three times. α β γ δ ε ζ ι There! Those letters indicate seven distinct issues to which I came with Ba, in our profoundly different estimates of thing and person.' Browning does not specify what they were, but in April 1861, a few months before Elizabeth's death, he had confided to her brother George: 'Ba and I know each other for time and, I dare trust, eternity: – We differ *toto coelo* (or rather, *inferno*) as to spirit-rapping, we quarrel sometimes about politics, and estimate people's characters with enormous difference, but, in the main, we *know* each other, I say.'[65] The more divisive issues which would forever be associated in Robert's mind with Lucca were Pen's education and Elizabeth's faith in spiritualism and its purveyors.

The event which – besides the heat – had first made the Brownings seek out Bagni di Lucca in 1849 was the death of Robert's mother; in 1853 it was the Von Müller affair. That first summer was redeemed in Robert's eyes by Elizabeth's gift of *Sonnets from the Portuguese*; four years later it was the presence of the Storys who, by a happy coincidence, had taken a villa at the top of the hill. There were visits back and forth by donkey, much tea-drinking and gossiping, as well as mandatory picnics at the most scenic – and remote – spots. Near the end of one such marathon outing, to Prato Fiorito, Elizabeth yelled from the back of a donkey to another friend present, Robert Lytton, 'I am dying. How are you?' (He was about the same.)[66] It had been a perfect day, one that inspired Robert to capture the moment in his poem, 'By the Fire-Side', composed soon afterwards.

In this most personal of poems Robert was recalling not only the scenery of Prato Fiorito – the ruined chapel and the woods round them 'heaped and dim' – but also the intense love he had felt for Elizabeth during their courtship, when he had declared in a letter 'that I may forever . . certainly during our mortal "forever" – mix my love for you, and . . your love for me'. 'A bar was broken between / Life and life,' so Robert addresses 'my perfect wife' in 'By the Fire-Side': 'we were mixed at last / In spite of the mortal screen.' On their honeymoon he was still insisting to Elizabeth, as she confided to her sisters, that 'no two persons could have one soul between them so much as we.'[67]

However 'By the Fire-Side' is not a poem merely about love; it is about marriage, and marriage is far from simple. In the early days of their courtship, Robert and Elizabeth had called each other 'dear' and 'dearest' friends. Once he had declared his love, he liked to joke that he had lost his friend Miss Barrett – 'gone, the friendship, so gone!'[68] It is a thought which Browning returns to in 'By the Fire-Side': 'To gain a lover and lose a friend'. Moreover, in the seven years since their wedding day – as the quarrels increased in frequency and intensity – Browning had come to realise that 'If two lives join, there is oft a scar, / They are one and one, with a shadowy third; / One near one is too far.' By a 'shadowy third' the poet meant not just one thing but everything, both trivial and profound, that comes between two people. On this, their second visit to Lucca, the matter of Pen's lessons had begun to cast a shadow over his relationship with Elizabeth.

Pen, then four years old, wanted to learn to read that summer. He solemnly promised his parents that he would do 'mine lessons evelly day'. But the little boy soon decided that the Brownings' new manservant, Ferdinando, was much more interesting than the written word. He had fought for the unification of Italy in 1848 and had the gun to prove it. Pen preferred to tag along after his hero on the wooded hillsides rather than spell out over and over again 'D-O-G, dog' on his mother's knee. (Robert, listening in, certainly found it 'a slow business' and even Elizabeth thought it dull.) What the boy needed, Browning declared, was a little discipline. When Pen was naughty his father shut him in a room by himself or deprived him of something nice. But the four-year-old always seemed to have a smart remark in his defence which invariably caused Elizabeth to stop the proceedings. She was secretly pleased that Robert 'suffered in his soul', she told her Casa Guidi neighbour Eliza Ogilvy, for seeking to impose any sort of punishment.[69] It was then, in Bagni di Lucca, that Robert realised there was nothing he could do to dissuade Elizabeth; their son was to be raised strictly (or rather, not so strictly) in accordance with her views on the matter.

After another four-year interval, the Brownings set out for Bagni di Lucca for the third and last time, propelled as before by personal tragedy which, like the stifling summer heat, seemed to drive them to the mountain resort. In April 1857 Mr Barrett had died. Even at the end, he had not thought to leave his eldest and once favourite daughter with some sign of his love. The news left Elizabeth prostrate; she lay on the sofa, she told her sisters, and neither stirred nor spoke. They needed to get away from the Florentine heat and Mr Barrett's portrait, which stared down at Elizabeth from the bedroom wall. Robert suggested the sea – somewhere different – but to please Elizabeth he agreed to return to Bagni di Lucca. With Elizabeth in much the same condition as he had been after his mother's death, Robert could only hope that Bagni di Lucca would work its magic once more. But his wife was in such a fragile state that he did not feel he could cope with her depression alone. He therefore pleaded with Annette Bracken, and also Isa Blagden and Robert Lytton, to join them; he had, he assured them, looked into all the necessary arrangements. They obeyed the summons and arrived at the beginning of August. Elizabeth was especially partial to the young diplomat and poet Lytton, whom they had first met in Florence five years before, as he shared her enthusiasm for table-rapping. The Brownings had not seen much of him since their last visit to Bagni di Lucca together, after which he had been posted to The Hague.

Elizabeth no doubt enjoyed the company. She was amongst kindred spirits who, unlike Robert, shared her views on Italian politics (husband and wife disagreed about Napoleon III) as well as spiritualism. Within a few days, however, it all began to go terribly wrong. Lytton became deathly ill with a fever (probably typhoid). Isa, who was a little in love with the young poet, insisted that she alone should nurse him; Robert might help. He agreed, although he thought it an absurd arrangement. Lytton lay at death's door for more than two weeks, during which time Isa and Browning, with his impeccable bedside manner, alternated in sitting up with him through the long nights. Elizabeth did not like any of it, and told her sisters so. Why could not a trained nurse have been called? What if Robert – or, God forbid, Pen – were to contract the illness? Lytton should have known better than to return to Florence at the hottest time of year. There was more: both her maids had fallen ill (Wilson was pregnant). 'It has been a summer to me full of blots, vexations, anxieties,' she confided to Fanny Haworth.[70]

Elizabeth was no Florence Nightingale, as Robert well knew.* Four years before (1853), when the Brownings were wintering in Rome, the Storys' young son Joe had fallen ill. Robert went to lend what help he

---

* Nor was Elizabeth an uncritical admirer of Florence Nightingale: 'Every man is on his knees before ladies carrying lint, calling them "angelic she's," whereas, if they stir an inch as thinkers or artists from the beaten line (involving more good to general humanity than is involved in lint), the very same men would curse the impudence of the very same women and stop there' (EBB to Mrs Jameson, 24 February 1855: Kenyon).

could. He was present when the boy died, attended to the body – yielding to the mother's 'pathetic fancies in the arrangements of this & that', Elizabeth wrote – and chose the gravesite near to Shelley's.* Elizabeth fell into a selfish panic, as she later confessed, especially when the Storys' daughter Edith took ill. She was afraid of infection; she dreaded having to see little Joe's body. Robert managed to spare her that, but she felt sick accompanying Mrs Story to Joe's grave a few weeks later. Elizabeth's 'old natural horror of grave-yards, the earth-side of death', and her worries for Pen's welfare, stifled any sympathy she might have felt for the bereaved parents. She wanted to flee back to Florence. She and Robert had had words then; it would have been no different this time, especially when he returned, drained and exhausted, from his all-night vigil at Lytton's bedside only to face Elizabeth's fretfulness. To make matters worse, Pen contracted gastric fever towards the end of September, confirming his mother's darkest fears. 'Little Joseph Story died of it before our eyes in Rome,' she reminded her sister Henrietta.[71]

Happily, Pen was never seriously ill, but they thought it best to delay the strenuous journey back to Florence until the second week in October. Bagni di Lucca is a strange place, wrapped by a forest and nestled in a gorge so narrow that the sun barely touches the treetops. This makes the place beautifully cool in summer, but rather gloomy and confining the rest of the year. The Brownings' last impression of the Bagni, as their carriage rattled along the road at the bottom of the gorge, when the summer was well past, would not have been a cheerful one. Isa Blagden had, apparently, felt the same. A year later Elizabeth told Fanny Haworth that 'Isa Blagden would never go to the Bagni – never. She suffered too much last time – and she hates the place besides.'[72]

One of the few things that had redeemed that summer of 1857 in Elizabeth's eyes was meeting Mrs David Eckley of Boston, an attractive woman of means in her early thirties (a cousin of Louisa May Alcott), who was also staying at Bagni di Lucca. Feeling neglected during Lytton's long illness – and with an active eight-year-old to entertain (before he too fell sick) – Elizabeth spent more and more time with Sophie Eckley and her son, who happened to be the same age as Pen. The ladies' main

* He had also performed this sad duty for the Cottrells in 1849 when their baby daughter died and the father was 'unmanned'. Robert 'managed the whole melancholy business, selecting the ground for the small grave', Elizabeth wrote, '& officiating as chief mourner' (EBB to Mary Russell Mitford, 1 December [1849]). This incident was the inspiration for Elizabeth's poem 'A Child's Grave at Florence'.

form of amusement, besides watching the boys at play, was attempting to lift the veil between this world and the next, for Elizabeth's new friend was a self-declared medium. Perhaps it was through Sophie that Elizabeth would find the forgiveness she had so desperately sought from her father over the past eleven years and still sought now, after his death. Robert did not trust the woman and said so. 'I cried "poison" at first sniff,' he later claimed, 'and suffered more, from maintaining it, than from any incident in my whole life.'[73] He took consolation in the rides and walks and talks with Annette Bracken between nursing shifts.

For the next three years Sophie stuck to Elizabeth 'like treacle'. Mrs Eckley had 'taken it into her enthusiastic head to fall into a sort of love with *me*', the poetess told Arabel. She commissioned the Italian artist Michele Gordigiani to paint the Brownings' portraits and showered Elizabeth with gifts. 'You have done too much for me, thought too much of me,' Elizabeth protested at one point; 'I have had to be on guard against your kindness, as I might be against other people's malice.' Sophie was determined to keep the invalid under her spell. With her devoted husband and son in tow, she followed the poets to Florence, then to Rome and back again, all the while acting as Elizabeth's guide through 'the vast spiritual sea'.[74]

Yet, by the beginning of 1860, only a year before her death, Elizabeth had broken off all relations with Sophie. It was not her skills as a medium that Elizabeth began to doubt, although Americanisms did tend to creep into Sophie's communications with her English spirits. Nor had she personally injured Elizabeth; that would have been easier to forgive. 'What was impossible,' Elizabeth explained to Arabel, 'was to feel the same to a person in whom one had lost faith.' Elizabeth had, it seems, caught her friend out in a lie regarding her marriage. Sophie had been playing the role of 'the injured wife' for some time, but it became clear that it was she who was cheating on her poor, devoted husband. 'Those inventions about spirits &c were not at all more prodigious,' Robert later said of Mrs Eckley, 'than the daily sprouting toadstools of that dunghill of a soul, – lies about this, that & the other.'[75] There is certainly a whiff of sexual indiscretion in Elizabeth's exposé of Sophie's betrayal, 'Where's Agnes': 'Corrupted thus and lost .. / She, my white rose, dropping off / The high rose-tree branch!'*

---

* Robert might also have written a poem with this incident in mind. In 'The Worst of It' (*Dramatis Personae*) a foolishly devoted husband tries to prove that it was his fault, not his

The Eckleys lingered in Florence for a time. In a desperate attempt to keep up appearances, Sophie went about as if nothing had happened. She hoped to pass still for being Elizabeth's friend, but the latter was as cold as ice towards her. In the autumn of 1860 they finally left Florence for good, owing to Sophie's 'health'. She told everyone that the doctor could find no pulse; 'but,' Elizabeth dryly remarked, '*she knew*'.[76] The poetess was crushed then horrified by the betrayal. What if Mrs Eckley were to 'make a show' of her letters – letters of the most intimate nature? 'It is a punishment you must bear – that of having her name associated with yours,' so Robert recalled his conversation with Elizabeth at the time; 'you should have believed *me* so far at least as to use your own faculties and so get to believe for yourself' in that woman's duplicity.

'So I say still,' he declared to Isa in March 1868, seven years after his wife's death.

It was only a few months before this, in September 1867, that Robert had alluded to those seven areas of disagreement between husband and wife, insisting: 'I go over them one by one, and must deliberately inevitably say, on each of these points I was, am proved to be, right and she wrong.'* Despite the sharp words spoken, Browning was glad, he told Isa, that he had maintained the truth on each of these points, and had not said, 'What matter whether they be true or no? – Let us only care to love each other.' These sentiments echoed Elizabeth's own, which she often expressed. She too had believed that she was always in the right. 'Oh Arabel,' she wrote in answer to her sister's questions regarding the couple's quarrels, 'we are famous for quarrelling – are we not? That is, because we love one another too much to be contented with temporizing.' When Robert became too bumptious and the argument too heated, Elizabeth would take up a book and observe in a provoking way: 'I wont dispute a moment longer – you say things that you dont mean ... Only, I protest against all you have been saying .. & there's my last word.'[77]

---

wife's, that she could not keep her marriage vows: 'Would it were I had been false, not you! / I that am nothing, not you that are all.' It may have been one of the lyrics which Elizabeth saw in May 1861. Two years later, when discussing Mrs Eckley, Browning confided to the Storys: 'I had reasons of my own for studying that very peculiar mind' (27 March 1863). My thanks to William Askins for this point.

* The other contentious issues, besides politics, people's characters, spiritualism, and Pen's upbringing, were almost certainly money, Elizabeth's morphine habit, and Robert's reluctance to write any more poetry after the failure of *Men and Women*.

Browning knew that he could be overzealous when preaching his version of the truth. (One thinks of the time, years before, when he made his little sister burst into tears.) 'If I ever seem too authoritative or disputative to you, dearest Isa,' he stated in his defence that September of 1867, 'you must remember this, and that only to those I love very much do I feel at all inclined to lay down what I think to be the law, and speak the truth.' 'As for *seeing* the truth,' he went on, 'it seems to me such angelic natures don't – and such devilish ones *do*.' Robert was still casting himself as the devil and Elizabeth as an angel. 'If I could ever have such things out of my thoughts,' Robert remarked, 'it would not be to-day – the day, twenty years ago [actually twenty-one], that we left England to-gether.'

But by this time Browning did not need an anniversary to remind him of such things, for he had daily reminders of (as he saw it) Elizabeth's blindness to the truth. 'Speckly Eckley', as Browning took to calling her, continued to haunt the poet. The Eckleys had soon divorced after leaving Florence. The husband returned to America; Sophie continued to roam through Europe and eventually published a book of poems. She claimed that Elizabeth Barrett Browning had betrayed her and penned a riposte to 'Where's Agnes', entitled, 'The Lyre': 'In the heart of my lyre, which had once seem'd divine, / A snake was coil'd up in the treacherous shrine.' Even more irritating to Robert, Sophie took to showing his wife's letters about and threatened to publish them. It had also become painfully obvious to Browning that Elizabeth's indulgence of Pen's whims, in the face of his objections, had contributed to the teenager's poor academic performance. The 'shadowy third' – those niggling matters, both large and small, which had come between the Brownings – had begun to return with a vengeance, reviving those unpleasant memories which Robert, in his grief, had suppressed after his wife's death.

When, in the spring of 1867, Isa first told him that she was planning to return to the resort that summer, Browning had responded: 'So you go to Lucca. I don't in the least know – or rather in my fancies I change continually as to how I should feel on seeing old sights again.' 'The general impression of the past,' he then added, 'is as if it had been pain. I would not live it over again, not one day of it. Yet all that seems my real *life*, – and before and after, nothing at all: I look back on my life, when I look *there*: and life is painful. I always think of this when I read the Odyssey – Homer makes the surviving Greeks, whenever they refer to Troy, just say of it "At Troy, where the Greeks suffered so." Yet all their life was in that ten years at Troy. "*Lucca, where I suffered so.*" *

At the time of Arabel's death, in June 1868, Browning still believed that all his life was in the fifteen years he had spent with Elizabeth. Although her memory was at times a crown of thorns around his head, it was also a comfort, a refuge as well as a prison, and he clung to it. Before he could look to the future, he would have to continue to excavate and reinterpret the past – a past which was looking increasingly murky. 'Saints tumble to earth with so slight a tilt!'

* My italics.

CHAPTER THREE

'Some Faint Show of Bigamy',
1868–72

One night in November 1868, on the eve of publication of *The Ring and the Book*, Robert Browning arrived on the doorstep of the architect James Knowles' house on Clapham Common where Alfred Tennyson was a guest. The night before, the select group had assembled to listen to the Poet Laureate read aloud his latest work, *The Holy Grail*. Now it was Browning's turn. Much had happened since the last such gathering, fourteen years earlier, when the Brownings had invited Tennyson to their modest London lodgings to read his poem *Maud* and to hear Robert's 'Fra Lippo Lippi'. Then the forty-two-year-old Robert had been full of optimism about the reception of *Men and Women*, composed with his Muse Elizabeth by his side.

However, in 1868 the fifty-six-year-old widower, his hair now streaked with grey and his figure a little stouter, was in a very different frame of mind, standing on that South London doorstep with the first volume of *The Ring and the Book* tucked under his arm.* It was a poem of over 21,000 lines to which he had devoted himself for the last three years, in the gaps between Pen's Greek and Latin tutorials, having only twice put it to one side, on the deaths of his father and his dear friend Arabel Barrett; three years 'without an eye over my shoulder to read, much less, whisper in my ear to counsel & criticize'. Browning could not guess how the work would strike people, for was he not (as he had declared two years earlier) 'the most unpopular poet that ever was'?[1] The 'British Public', so he read aloud from the first volume of *The Ring and the Book*, 'ye who like me not, / (God love you!) – whom I yet have laboured for'.

That night in Clapham, the Poet Laureate listened to Browning's

---

* *The Ring and the Book* was published in four volumes between 21 November 1868 and 27 February 1869.

piercing voice as it recounted – in the style of a courtroom drama – the story of the child-bride Pompilia who, mistreated by her husband Count Guido Franceschini, escaped to her parents' house with the help of a young priest. To reclaim her dowry, Pompilia's parents confessed that they had secretly procured her as a baby to defraud their rightful heirs. This deception drove the enraged and dishonoured count, along with a gang of cut-throats, to kill Pompilia and her parents. 'Full of strange vigour and remarkable in many ways,' Tennyson noted in his letter-diary the next day; 'doubtful whether it can ever be popular.' The Poet Laureate persisted with the poem, however, for in February 1869, when the fourth and final volume of *The Ring and the Book* was published, Mrs Tennyson recorded in her diary that her husband was reading Browning's poem to her at night. On the whole, Robert's friends seemed to agree with the Poet Laureate's initial verdict. 'In reading *The Ring and the Book* I felt,' Allingham told Carlyle, 'like a creature with one leg and one wing, half hopping, half flying.' Carlyle agreed, telling Rossetti that the poem was 'all made out of an Old Bailey story that might have been told in ten lines'.[2]

But the reviewers, who like insects swarm together in strange and unexpected formations, deemed otherwise. 'The newspaper critics have I see got it into their heads that it looks intellectual to admire or rather to praise Browning,' John Blackwood wrote to George Eliot in December 1868, a few days after the publication of the second volume of *The Ring and the Book*. Blackwood would have had *Vanity Fair*, amongst others, in mind. The periodical had always stood 'aghast' at Browning's 'enigmatical' poetry. Having had a sneak preview of *The Ring and the Book*, its critic 'Richelieu' was 'quite prepared for a repetition of the old verdict of *Vanity Fair* upon [the poet's] choice of a subject and his treatment of it'. After all, how extraordinary to put into verse a murder trial as seen through the eyes of nine different people: the defendant Count Guido, the victim Pompilia (speaking from her deathbed), the young priest Caponsacchi with whom she fled, the two lawyers arguing for and against, three onlookers from the street, and the Pope, the final arbiter in the case. Yet, the anonymous 'Richelieu' found the poem so powerful and compelling he generously conceded that, although still enigmatical, Browning was 'the spiritual athlete of poetry, descending into the arena as did the Roman gladiator of old, to grapple with terrible realities, and hold death itself in his strong grip'.

Of course, not all the critics liked *The Ring and the Book*; some agreed with Carlyle, calling it the newspaper in blank verse. Nevertheless, by January 1869 Browning was sufficiently gratified by the favourable reviews – and sales – to revise the last volume shortly before publication, giving an appreciative, if still tentative, nod and a wink to that same 'British Public, who may like me yet'. But he remained sceptical. Robert told a friend, whom he ran into at the Athenaeum in April, that, yes, 'he had at last secured the ear of the public, but that he had done it by vigorously assaulting it, and by telling his story four times over.' He added, Sir Frederick Pollock recalled, 'that he had perhaps after all failed in making himself intelligible, and said it was like bawling into a deaf man's trumpet, and then being asked not to speak so loud, but more distinctly'.

Robert did not believe that the public had at last begun to understand his poetry; it was merely that, confronted by such a tour de force as his 'murder-poem', they felt obliged to reappraise their opinion of him. In one sense he was right. After *The Ring and the Book* Browning could no longer be called a minor poet; nor was he a mere one-poem wonder, as his six-volume *Poetical Works*, also published in 1868, so clearly demonstrated. But he was not giving his readers – or himself – enough credit. He 'had never designedly tried to puzzle people', the poet once remarked; but nor did he pretend 'to offer such literature as should be a substitute for a cigar, or a game of dominoes, to an idle man'.[3] 'People must take me as they find me,' he would often tell Tennyson and others. By the late 1860s, the reading public were beginning to do just that. They recognised, appreciated, and even craved that same intensity and vitality in Browning's poetry which had first struck the Pre-Raphaelites and, later, the young men of Oxford and Cambridge. 'Everywhere there is life, sense, motion – the flash of real faces, the warmth of real breath,' wrote *The Athenaeum*, reviewing *The Ring and the Book*. Today one might describe Browning's use of shifting perspectives in his 'murder-poem' in terms of the film-maker's art.

The Ring and the Book had secured Browning's reputation as one of the great poets of his age, along with Tennyson; yet he nearly did not write this magnum opus. On 'that memorable day / (June was the month, Lorenzo the Square)' – 1860 the year – while rummaging through the stalls, ''mongst odds and ends of ravage, picture-frames / White through the worn gilt, mirror-sconces chipped, / Bronze angel-heads once knobs attached to chests,' Robert spied an old vellum-bound book. 'A *lira* made it mine,' the poet tells his listeners. He began to read the book as he walked, 'from written title-page, / To written index, on, through street and street, / At the Strozzi, at the Pillar, at the Bridge; / Till, by the time I stood at home again / In Casa Guidi by Felice Church, / .. I had mastered the contents, knew the whole truth / Gathered together, bound up in this book .. "*Romana Homicidiorum*" – nay, / Better translate – "A Roman murder-case."' The 'truth thus grasped and gained', Browning laid the book on the mantelpiece in the drawing room – that 'cream-coloured massive agate, broad / 'Neath the twin cherubs in the tarnished frame / O' the mirror' – and stepped out on to the narrow terrace. As he paced up and down, listening to the monks' chant and observing the passers-by in the street below, the poet imagined himself back in time, the tragedy of Pompilia unfolding before him.

The murder case as set out in the various pamphlets and letters – some printed, some handwritten – bound together in the 'Old Yellow Book' (as he liked to call it), had ignited the creative spark in Robert. At some point, perhaps later that evening when he stepped down from the terrace to join Elizabeth in the drawing room, he told her of his great find; he may well have mentioned his idea of forging a poem out of the crude elements of the story. Elizabeth took an instant dislike to the whole business. She was repelled by the sordidness of the tale and refused even to leaf through the papers. Bowing to the judgement of his flesh-and-blood Muse, Browning put aside his own ambitions for the Old Yellow Book, yet surely someone could do something with his 'Roman murder case'. He invited Tom Trollope's brother, Anthony, who paid them a visit at Casa Guidi in 1860, to base a novel on the story; he suggested to Tennyson that it might make a poem; he even approached a minor author, Miss Ogle, with the idea, but she could make 'nothing of it'. Only after Elizabeth's death did Robert take the creased vellum binding from its drawer and consider, as he told Isa in October 1862, making a 'regular poem of it'.

Elizabeth's offhanded reaction to the Old Yellow Book and its treasures within must have been hurtful to Robert at the time. Little else had inspired him to write; in fact, he seemed to be doing everything in his power to avoid pen and paper. It had been nearly fifteen years since he had declared that Elizabeth's love, and her good example, would inspire him 'to write more, and very likely be praised more'; 'but still more', he wrote to his wife-to-be, do 'I look to have you ever before me, in your place, and with more poetry and praise still'. Not only was she to be his inspiration but also his judge and jury, for he really believed her to be his superior. As for Elizabeth, she informed a friend after their elopement: 'My husband's name will prove to you that I have not left my vocation to the rhyming art, in order to marry: on the contrary, we mean, both of us, to do a great deal of work, besides surprising the world by the spectacle of two poets coming together without quarrelling, wrangling, and calling names in lyrical measures.'[4]

But things did not turn out as they had planned. Elizabeth did churn out 'more poetry and praise still', but Robert's own poetic font seemed to dry up in the course of their life together. In the beginning, there had always been a good excuse. The honeymoon period had not been conducive to work. 'Being too happy,' Elizabeth confessed at the time, 'doesn't agree with literary activity.' Nevertheless, almost from day one of their marriage, Elizabeth produced a stream of poems, which were published in *Blackwood's Edinburgh Magazine* and elsewhere. Apologising to James Russell Lowell in December 1846 for her delay in sending the poem 'The Runaway Slave at Pilgrim's Point' for publication in *The Liberty Bell*, Elizabeth explained that she had recently been distracted from work, 'only three months married & in this sudden glare of light & happiness, here in Italy, after my long years of imprisonment in sickness & depression'.[5]

As for Robert, he put his literary langour down to the 'lazy Italian air', so he told his (and Elizabeth's) publisher, Edward Moxon. Well, perhaps it was a change of publisher rather than a change of air that was needed. Browning had been unhappy with Moxon for some time, and in 1848 Elizabeth called him a 'shabby man' for not properly valuing her husband's worth.[6] The poet first approached George Smith, who had expressed the greatest admiration for his work, but Smith turned him down. Robert was hurt and angry. (He did not know that at that time Smith's business partner had just brought the firm to the brink of bankruptcy by stealing £30,000.) Browning then took himself and his wife to Chapman & Hall. He worked hard to revise his poems for the two-volume collected edition which Chapman & Hall had agreed to publish – and to pay for – in 1849.

But then came the death of Robert's mother in March of that year, soon after which they retreated to Bagni di Lucca. Elizabeth had hoped that the peace and quiet – not to mention the pure mountain air – might motivate her husband. Surely, poetry was the therapy Robert needed to help recover from his recent loss. Elizabeth was all too aware of the fact that, except for 'The Guardian-Angel' written a year earlier, in 1848, Robert had not composed any new poems since they had left England together as man and wife.*

But their 'eagle's nest' above Bagni di Lucca did not provide the necessary inspiration, nor had even her gift of *Sonnets from the Portuguese*. 'My poet,' Elizabeth addresses Robert in Sonnet XVII: 'How, Dearest, wilt thou have me for most use? / A hope, to sing by gladly? .. or a fine / Sad memory, with thy songs to interfuse?' Yet no verses had flowed from Robert's pen that summer. 'What am I to say about Robert's idleness and mine? I scold him about it in a most anti-conjugal manner,' Elizabeth confided to Mrs Jameson in October 1849, shortly before they were due to return to Florence. It appears from Elizabeth's reply to her sister's enquiries – 'Henrietta is not right – there is no "hen-pecking" ' – that the invalid had been rather exacting at times in Wimpole Street. In any case, it must have pained Robert to see the disappointment on Elizabeth's face as the weeks flew by without a single new poem from his pen. Then at last, that winter back in Florence, he began *Christmas-Eve*. 'I hope to be able for some time to come to write regularly now,' he wrote to a friend on the poem's completion, 'and so "fulfil my destiny," as they say, for good or bad – & this is the beginning.'[7]

Christmas-Eve, and its companion piece *Easter-Day*, were a critical and commercial failure. Robert was downhearted. He worried that the publisher would set his losses against his wife's profits. In early 1852 he wrote to Chapman & Hall – who were proving no better than Moxon – asking for the money owed to Elizabeth while pointing out that their publications were wholly separate concerns. 'You will not,' he pleaded, 'be accessory to making her repent that she married me, *poems and all!*'[8] Browning was referring to Elizabeth's *Poems*, including *Sonnets from the Portuguese*, published by Chapman & Hall in the same year as *Christmas-Eve and Easter-Day*, 1850. Did it ever cross Browning's mind that Chapman & Hall had agreed to take him on in order to secure the name of his more saleable wife?

Elizabeth remained determined that he should carry on writing. To this end, whether they were in Paris lodgings, a hillside villa in Bagni di Lucca or at home in Casa Guidi, Elizabeth made certain that her husband had a room – a room of his own – consecrated to his work. But Browning

---

* Browning did not believe in publishing his poems in periodicals, only in separate volumes, so his work was not before the public as often as Elizabeth's.

had always found composition to be a slow and painful process. His heart would sink, so he once said, when he opened his desk to write, only to rise when he shut it.[9] He was more inclined to help Elizabeth correct the proofs for the third edition of her *Poems*, which appeared in 1853. 'I often am much wearier than you think, / This evening more than usual,' Robert might have pleaded with Elizabeth, as the painter Andrea del Sarto does with his wife: 'and it seems / As if – forgive now – should you let me sit / Here by the window with your hand in mine / And look a half-hour forth on Fiesole, / Both of one mind, as married people use, / Quietly, quietly the evening through, / I might get up tomorrow to my work / Cheerful and fresh as ever.' Browning eventually managed, after much beating of the breast and pulling of hair, to produce the fifty-one poems (including 'Andrea del Sarto') which made up *Men and Women*. But after that book's equally unenthusiastic reception in 1855, he seemed to give up nearly altogether.

By contrast, people (especially men) marvelled at the ease with which Elizabeth, who had no private study, was able to churn out verse in the drawing room as she sat curled up on the sofa looking like a King Charles spaniel. Elizabeth would put down her sheet of paper to hear Pen spell, Robert told Leigh Hunt, or thrust it under a cushion if a visitor arrived, to be taken up again just as easily after his or her departure. When he was still working on *Men and Women*, Elizabeth was carefully going over Robert's poems in addition to her own writing and Pen's lessons. On receiving his copy of Elizabeth's masterpiece *Aurora Leigh* (1856), Robert Lytton wrote to Elizabeth, 'How often, in reading *Aurora*, did I recall the many times when I found you on that same little sofa, book in hand; and you let me (so quietly and kindly) interrupt you (perhaps in the break of a six line cadence!), and put away the book to talk to me, instead of sending me away as – had you been less great an Artist – you would have done.' Alexandra Orr would later remark that Browning always regarded his wife's 'genius as greater, because more spontaneous, than his own'.[10]

Although Robert was genuinely delighted by *Aurora Leigh*'s success – the edition had sold out within two weeks – it cannot have inspired much confidence in his own genius, application, or subject matter. A poet's sole work, Elizabeth's contemporary heroine Aurora Leigh pleads with those, like Tennyson and her own husband, steeped in medieval lore, 'is to represent the age, / Their age, not Charlemagne's – this live, throbbing age, / That brawls, cheats, maddens, calculates, aspires, / And spends more passion, more heroic heat, / Betwixt the mirrors of its drawing-rooms, / Than Roland with his knights.' 'Darling' Robert had been twice moved to tears, Elizabeth confided to Arabel, when he sat down to tell her what he thought of her masterpiece.[11]

Around this time Robert began to experience violent headaches. Homoeopathy offered some relief, but he felt best when he threw himself into some new activity – riding for three or four hours every day and attending the artist George Mignaty's life-drawing classes. Elizabeth was heartily glad of Robert's drawing, for she knew that he could not relax, as she did, by reading light literature. So, of an evening, while Elizabeth lay on the sofa and rested in a novel, Robert had a resource in his sketchbook.[12] His artistic efforts seemed to have inspired him to write an exquisite little poem, 'Study of a Hand, by Lionard'. As the speaker 'learned and drew' the woman's hand, 'Drew and learned, and looked again, / While fast the happy minutes flew, / Its beauty mounted into my brain, / And a fancy seized me; I was fain / To efface my work, begin again, / Kiss what before I only drew.' This poem was sent to Marguerite Power for *The Keepsake*, along with Elizabeth's 'My Heart and I'. 'I have begun to write poetry again,' Robert wrote to Isa optimistically in August 1857 from Bagni di Lucca, '& shall send Miss Power her portion this very day.' However, neither poem was published, and Robert's pen again fell silent.*

A complete change of scene – new sights, sounds, and colours – that is what Robert needed to inspire his imagination, for his poetry always had such a strong sense of place. He and Elizabeth had first toyed with the idea of travelling to the Holy Land in 1853 after meeting the American diplomat George Perkins Marsh and his wife Caroline in Florence. Mrs Marsh, Elizabeth told Mary Russell Mitford, 'is pretty & interesting – a great invalid & almost blind, . . yet she has lately been to Jerusalem, & insisted on being carried to the top of mount Horeb. After which I certainly should have the courage to attempt the journey myself, if we had money enough.' 'Perhaps,' she added a few weeks later, 'it is as well that we have not.' In 1856, after the failure of *Men and Women*, Robert returned to the subject. Elizabeth suggested that he travel to the Holy Land on his own for a few months, but, of course, she knew that he would not leave her if it were merely for pleasure. Robert was still

---

* Browning incorporated 'Study of a Hand' into 'James Lee's Wife' seven years later, followed by the line: "'Tis a clay cast, the perfect thing, / From Hand live once, dead long ago.' One can imagine the poet musing on the old poem while looking at the cast which Hatty Hosmer took of the couple's clasped hands in 1853 (*Reconstruction*, H538).

thinking of it in the spring of 1858. 'I have sworn to Robert to go with him,' Elizabeth told Arabel – not to Jerusalem (she was not up to the camels) but to Egypt. What is more, 'Robert made me *swear* because he distrusted my wishes & intentions, I think – However, plans make me sick – & it is too early for planning – The winter just over.' Robert had longed to travel, not only to the East, but to parts of Italy that for them were hitherto unexplored. But somehow Elizabeth's health always made it impossible. 'In all my journeyings in Italy,' Browning later confided to Isa, 'I could never venture to leave the straight line of obligation to get from such a place, in such a time, to such another, – thus I never saw (after fourteen years of intention to see) – Volterra, St Gimignano, or Certaldo, Pistoja, and other points of great interest to me, – Ba could never go, I could not leave her.'[13]

In 1859–60, when all hopes for the Holy Land and other points of interest had been abandoned owing to Elizabeth's fragile state, the Brownings wintered in Rome. Robert was plunged into gaieties of all sorts by night, and by day he took to modelling clay in William Story's studio. Anything to do with more intellectual pursuits, whether reading or writing – even letter-writing – seemed too difficult. 'I have got stiff at a distance,' Browning wrote to a friend in 1860, 'with daily nothings to do and chronicle (in head at least), and my words do not fly out as promptly as I could wish and as once may have been the case.' As for composing verse, he had confessed to Isa in September 1858, 'it's of no use now: nor will the world very greatly care.' For the first ten years of their marriage, Browning had been concerned to earn an income from his pen; otherwise they sometimes went without, not only luxuries such as a trip to the Holy Land, but also a haircut for himself, a new pair of shoes for Elizabeth, or riding lessons for Pen. But all that changed when John Kenyon bequeathed to them, on his death in 1856, a combined legacy worth £11,000. 'So plenty of distraction,' Elizabeth now observed, 'and no Men and Women. Men and women from without instead!'[14]

Elizabeth was in two minds about Robert's modelling, his latest displacement activity. For one thing, there was nothing to show for all the hard work since, as soon as he completed the sculptures, he broke them up. Moreover, she 'grudged a little the time from his own particular art', poetry, so she confided to Sarianna.[15] Hadn't Robert declared to her in 'One Word More' – the dedicatory poem in *Men and Women* – that 'I shall never, in the years remaining, / Paint you pictures, no, nor carve you statues, / . . verse alone, one life allows me; / Verse and nothing else have I to give you'?

Elizabeth was delighted when, early in 1859, Robert suggested that they both write on the 'Italian question' and publish jointly. Once before, they had thought of collaborating on a book of poems about Italy, in the heady days of their 'honeymoon' in Pisa. 'Such planners & dreamers we are,' Elizabeth had told her sisters, but nothing came of it.[16] However, when on 11 July 1859 at Villafranca Napoleon III reneged on his promise to help liberate Italy and made a separate peace – one that was to Italy's disadvantage – without informing Cavour, Robert destroyed his poem, thinking it no longer suited the moment. If he was disheartened, Elizabeth was distraught over events. For weeks afterwards she was deathly ill, unable to move from her bed. Robert, for the sake of her health, tried to reassure his wife that Napoleon was not necessarily a traitor. He alone, from amongst the great powers of Europe, had stood against the Austrians. One leader, one nation, could only do so much. Italy might yet be unified.

Once Elizabeth had regained her strength – and her faith in the Emperor – the worldly-wise Browning left his wife to carry on the poetical fight alone. If Robert had not approved, Elizabeth swore to her brother George, she would have torn up her political poems too. But in this she was being disingenuous. It was Robert who sought approbation for his work, not Elizabeth. She was the genius, after all; certainly, she was older, more well known, more self-assured. He never had anything but praise for her work. Her poetic justification of the Emperor's actions, 'A Tale of Villafranca', appeared in *Poems before Congress* in 1860, together with its companion piece, 'Napoleon III in Italy'. Browning must have felt, as did Gilbert Osmond in James's *Portrait of a Lady*, 'I could do nothing in Italy – I couldn't even be an Italian patriot.' The truth was he did not think of man in terms of mankind. In Elizabeth's poetry, especially her later verse, mankind and particular causes appear more alive than any individual.* The same was true of Tennyson's gloriously inaccurate

---

* The contrast in their approach is glaringly obvious in the poems each wrote in 1854 to benefit Arabel's charitable work (their only joint publication). In 'A Plea for the Ragged Schools of London', Elizabeth chastised the 'lordly English' who have free parliaments, princes' parks and merchants' homes, 'but ruins worse than Rome's / In your pauper men and women'. Robert took as the starting-point for his poem 'The Twins', a story which he found in an old book (Martin Luther's *Table-Talk*). It begins: 'Grand rough old Martin Luther / Bloomed fables – flowers on furze, / The better the uncouther: / Do roses stick like burrs? / A beggar asked an alms / One day at an abbey-door, / Said Luther, but; seized with qualms, / The abbot replied, "We're poor!" '

and misguided 'The Charge of the Light Brigade'.* Robert had cared desperately about the Crimean conflict, but, far from wanting to write some jingoistic verse, he wished only that the incompetent British ministry 'be torn to pieces in the streets, limb from limb'.[17]

Although clearly frustrated by Robert's literary langour – and 'a little jealous for the poems' – Elizabeth was astute enough to realise that it did not do to dishearten him about his modelling. Robert, she explained to Sarianna in March 1861, 'waits for an inclination – works by fits and starts – he can't do otherwise he says'. Elizabeth confessed that she struggled with him a little on this point, for she did not think him right – at least, it would not be right for her. Although he had declared before their marriage that he took no pleasure in the act of writing except in the sense of fulfilling a duty, Elizabeth could not believe that Robert did not feel, deep down, as she did: 'I seem to live while I write – it is life, for me.' She '*could not live* the sort of desultory meaningless life which so many others are contented with – or appear contented with', she told a friend; 'a little reading, a little drawing, a little playing on the piano perhaps.' She was speaking here of 'the common woman's life' but her comments described her husband's existence just as aptly. Apparently Elizabeth was not as discreet in the matter as she might have been, for the Brownings' friends, such as Lilian Whiting, were aware that she 'gently wrangled' with her husband 'to give more attention to his art, and held before him the alluring example of the Laureate [Tennyson] who shut himself up daily for prescribed work'.[18]

'Nothing but clay does he care for, poor, lost soul,' so Miss Whiting records Mrs Browning laughing among friends. But in private Elizabeth revealed her growing concern for Robert's peace of mind. 'An active occupation,' she went on in her letter to his sister, 'is salvation to him with his irritable nerves, saves him from ruminating bitter cud, and from the process which I call beating his dear head against the wall till it is bruised, simply because he sees a fly there, magnified by his own two eyes almost indefinitely into some Saurian monster. He has an enormous superfluity of vital energy, and if it isn't employed, it strikes fangs into him.' At least, she comments, 'the modelling combines body-work and soul-work, and the more tired he has been, and the more his back ached,

---

* Tennyson, infected by battle fever, hailed war and disparaged peace in *Maud*, the poem which he had read aloud to the Brownings in 1855, while the conflict was still raging in the Crimea. Why, he demands, 'do they prate of the blessings of peace?' If the choice was between war and peace, 'better, war! Loud war by land and by sea.'

poor fellow, the more he has exulted and been happy – *no, nothing ever made him so happy before.'*

The most obvious reason for Robert's long-term depression was the British public's indifference to his poetry: 'his treatment in England affects him naturally,' Elizabeth told Sarianna; 'for my part I set it down as an infamy of that public – no other word.' Then there was his wife's increasing ill health and its effect on their life together. Writing in 1866, Browning recalled one evening fifteen years earlier when he and Elizabeth had walked from Isa Blagden's villa on Bellosguardo back to Casa Guidi, a long, winding descent. That was at the very peak of his wife's health, he told Isa. But, following their return to England in the summer of 1851, she began to suffer severe coughing spells, fatigue, and breathlessness. The English climate had never agreed with her. Robert worried about Elizabeth's health and, increasingly, her state of mind. She returned to her old habit of taking morphine in larger doses until it again became 'second nature', so she told Arabel in 1858.[19]

Browning began to witness moments when his wife's mind was clearly wandering. One such episode occurred in Florence in the spring of 1855. Harriet Hosmer, the American sculptress who defied convention in everything she did, thought up a scheme whereby she, Elizabeth, and Mrs Kinney, wife of the former American chargé d'affaires in Turin, would dress as boys in order to gain admittance to a monastery with particularly fine paintings, which was closed to women. Hiram Powers helped with the disguises. When the day came, Elizabeth was the first one ready in her garb of 'loose trousers *à la Turque*'. Rather than wait discreetly inside the gates of Casa Guidi until the others came down, she paraded herself around the square in full view. Catching sight of Elizabeth from the window, Mrs Kinney and Hattie rushed to the rescue before anyone could recognise her. 'Our strange appearance,' Mrs Kinney recalled, 'began to attract attention, when all at once Mrs Browning, seeming conscious of the situation, began to cry, and whispered in my ear, "Oh, Mrs Kinney, we shall be in the Bargello!" '* The other two women thought the situation so ludicrous they burst out laughing, as did Mr Kinney. Robert, however, turned 'pale as death'. The diplomat's wife reckoned that 'it had been an extra dose of opium' – to steady her nerves – 'that pushed [the poetess] to such a wild step!'[20] Elizabeth's subsequent remorse – and Robert's distress – suggest that this had indeed

---

* The prison in Florence.

been the case, and the incident gave them both a terrible scare.

People other than close friends soon began to notice Elizabeth's drug habit. The old American battleaxe Julia Ward Howe (author of 'Battle Hymn of the Republic') claimed, in a poem published in 1857, that some artists relied on 'the nameless draught' for inspiration – not she. The title, 'One Word More with E.B.B.', left no one in any doubt as to her intended target. Robert was furious. When in Rome, he made a special point of telling Mrs Howe's sibling, wife of the sculptor Thomas Crawford, how much he despised her sister. Elizabeth was more sanguine, admitting to Sophie Eckley that it was 'perfectly true, so far, that life is necessary to writing, & that I should not be alive except by help of my morphine'.

Elizabeth's illness and its remedy took its toll. By 1858 she was describing herself to her sister Henrietta as a 'rag of a woman', and Nathaniel Hawthorne, when he visited Italy that same year, thought her to be an unearthly, 'elfin' creature. She had gone through a terrible time, both physically and emotionally, following her father's death in 1857; there was still worse to come with Henrietta's bout with cancer in 1860. Robert spent more and more of his time nursing his wife (he could not have been more kind and gentle, as Elizabeth testified again and again in her letters), and he took care to shield her whenever possible from emotional upset. She beseeched him to read first the family letters addressed to her which spoke of Henrietta's condition. It then fell to him, of course, to break the news to Elizabeth of her sister's death. Browning also took to inspecting – and sometimes censoring – the Italian and English papers. Elizabeth had begun to identify herself so closely with the cause of Italian independence that the latest war bulletin became a more reliable predictor of her health than the doctor's stethoscope. 'I am scarcely of sane mind about Italy,' so Elizabeth described her symptoms to Isa; 'I pass through cold stages of anxiety, and white heats of rage.'[21] She lived to see Victor Emmanuel proclaimed King of Italy in March 1861, but the unexpected death in June of the great Italian statesman Cavour anticipated her own, which was equally unexpected, despite her weakness, only three weeks later.

Elizabeth's growing infirmity must have left Browning not only emotionally drained but also sexually frustrated. It had begun as far back as July 1850, when his wife suffered her fourth and final miscarriage. The haemorrhaging – she lost over a hundred ounces of blood in twenty-four hours – made this by far the worst. 'Dr Harding,' she confided to Arabel, 'means to set to with all force of his will to prevent its happening again, he says – because four times in less than four years, to say nothing of Wiedeman, is exhausting to the constitution.' Elizabeth could not risk another pregnancy, and Robert would have taken the only means open to him to comply: at least partial abstinence. The certainty – and the bitterness – with which Elizabeth refuted the gossip, two years later, concerning another Browning bundle suggests that this was indeed the case. (She had longed for a second child, a little girl – and Pen had begged for a brother.) '*Bosh*,' she told Mary Russell Mitford, 'I have not any prospects, nor have had since the bad illness in Florence nearly two years ago.' Four years later, in 1856, the seven-year-old Pen was banished from the newlywed Wilson's room and moved into his parents' bedroom to sleep. The little boy took to fastening his bed by a string to his parents' bedpost just before he went to sleep in order to be 'tied tight to mama', so Elizabeth told Arabel in 1859.²² This arrangement would certainly have stifled the couple's love life, but by this point it was no longer an issue owing to Elizabeth's deteriorating health.

Elizabeth understood Robert's sexual frustration and its side effects: his passion first for riding, then life drawing, and finally sculpture. Did she not know his extraordinarily sensual poem, 'Women and Roses', written in 1853, three years after that last miscarriage, and published in *Men and Women*? The narrator dreams of a red rose-tree. Just as the bee 'is sucked in' deep 'by the hyacinth, / So will I bury me while burning, / Quench like him at a plunge my yearning, / Eyes in your eyes, lips on your lips! / Fold me fast where the cincture slips, / Prison all my soul in eternities of pleasure, / Girdle me for once! But no – the old measure' – such euphoria continues to elude the narrator. If Elizabeth was a saint, it was the down-to-earth kind. 'So I couldn't be much in opposition against the sculpture,' she concluded in that letter to Sarianna written in March 1861; 'I couldn't, in fact, at all.'

When a wife or husband becomes a permanent invalid, the relationship changes; the intimacies of the bedroom are no longer those between lovers but between patient and carer. Such a dramatic transition often creates a rift in the marriage; certainly it has an impact, and so it had on the Brownings. As Elizabeth grew weaker and more dependent, her power over Robert grew stronger. He held back from doing or saying anything that might upset her. His nursing duties proved to be as good a distraction as riding, drawing, and sculpting – better, even, for at least he was doing something useful for the person he loved. But it is hard to be with someone who is 'always dying' (as she once described herself): the feelings of responsibility and helplessness; the need to escape, if only for a few hours; the guilt for doing so. Nevertheless, the Brownings' marriage remained solid. Although physical gratification was limited, the physical attraction between them remained. Just a few months before her death, Elizabeth had expressed the opinion that Robert was 'infinitely handsomer and more attractive' than when she first saw him sixteen years before.[23] Robert was furious with Mrs Kinney after she published a letter in 1854 describing his wife as a woman whose looks were 'shattered by disease' (although imbued with 'a moral beauty').* 'I see well enough yet .. without spectacles,' he fumed, '& yet see nothing of the matter.'[24]

Husband and wife also believed – much of the time – that they could divine each other's thoughts. Elizabeth once confided to Sarianna that she was 'in the inside' of Robert and could 'hear him breathe', for 'he thinks aloud with me and can't stop himself' – no matter what role he was playing: friend, lover or protector. 'Ba and I know each other for time and, I dare trust, eternity,' Robert had told George. But, as he had intimated in 'By the Fire-Side', the poet was also aware that between any two people, no matter how close, there was always a 'shadowy third'. He had developed this thought in another poem included in *Men and Women*, 'Two in the Campagna'. In the spring of 1854, the Brownings had gone on a number of picnics to explore the Roman countryside together with two sisters, Mrs Adelaide Sartoris and Fanny Kemble Butler. Once, when Robert forfeited an expedition to some ruin or other near Tivoli in order to stay behind with Elizabeth, who was too tired to move, Fanny Butler (the victim of a disastrous marriage†) remarked, 'You are the only man I ever knew who behaved like a Christian to his wife.' It may have been on such an occasion, sitting beside Elizabeth as he watched the rest of the party go, that Robert conceived of 'Two in the Campagna'. 'I would I could adopt your will,' the man muses, 'See with your eyes, and set my heart / Beating by yours, and drink my fill / At your soul's springs, – your part my part / In life, for good and ill.' He thinks it possible, but 'then the good minute goes.' He can discern only 'infinite

---

* Mrs Kinney had, in fact, published her letter in defence of Mrs Browning after reading a disparaging article about the poetess in the *Newark Daily Advertiser.*
† In 1834 Fanny Kemble had married Pierce Butler, an American slave owner. When they divorced in 1848, she was separated from her two children. Fanny 'talked of her children in such an agony of sorrow that no one could sit by & see that face, & hear that voice without tears of sympathy' (EBB to Arabel Barrett, 16–19 December 1853).

passion, and the pain / Of finite hearts that yearn'. Robert saw not only love but also poetry in these same terms. 'I *know* that I don't make out my conception by my language,' he had replied to Ruskin's complaints about the obscurity of *Men and Women*, 'all poetry being a putting the infinite within the finite.'[25]

There was a side to Robert which his wife did not see and could not adopt. Before their marriage, he had tried to tell Elizabeth that she 'knew nothing' of him. 'For every poor speck of a Vesuvius or a Stromboli in my microcosm,' he wrote, 'there are huge layers of ice and pits of black cold water.' Yet 'this last' – what one might call his dark side, which delighted in the strange and macabre, feeding his imagination – 'is a true part of me, most characteristic part, *best* part perhaps'. Elizabeth made light of Robert's confession. 'I was certainly innocent,' she replied, 'of the "ice & cold water" you introduce me to, and am only just shaking my head, as Flush w^d, after a first wholesome plunge – Well – if I do not know you, I shall learn, I suppose, in time.'[26] But she never did learn to recognise or acknowledge that cold, dark place which lay at the very core of Robert's art.

Early in their marriage, when they were still in Pisa, Robert had been fascinated by the elaborate funeral processions, with open caskets and a cortège of monks, which passed beneath their windows. Elizabeth grew to hate the very sound of the monks' horrible hoarse chanting. She would plead with Robert not to look outside, but he could not help himself – the sound drew him, he said. Later, when he began attending drawing classes, Browning brought back to Casa Guidi a skeleton of his own to study and sketch. The mere sight of it made Elizabeth feel sick and dizzy, yet Robert insisted on telling her how beautifully the bones fitted together and demonstrating the ease with which the head came off. She declared that if she was expected to put up with Robert's bones, he could tolerate her spirits.[27] The Old Yellow Book, with its story of a grotesque murder, had had a similar effect on Elizabeth. No wonder Browning had taken the book down from the agate mantelpiece and thrown it into the proverbial closet along with the skeleton.

Yet, Elizabeth was not prudish, certainly not in the sense that she thought the English prudish who so disapproved of French novels. She liked books such as Eugène Sue's *Mystères de Paris* (1842–3) not only for their reforming zeal but also for the new worlds they opened up to her (usually populated by the criminal and underclasses). When the Brownings first arrived in Italy, Elizabeth had begged her husband to take out a more expensive library subscription so that she could get hold of these naughty, wicked books, as she called them – the Italian ones were so dull. She did not like novels to be dull, but neither did she like them to be too unsavoury. 'I don't like coarse subjects, or the coarse treatment of any subject,' so Elizabeth had defended her poem 'Lord Walter's Wife' (1861), which Thackeray thought unsuitable for the *Cornhill Magazine* owing to its account of unlawful passion. 'But,' she told Thackeray, 'I am deeply convinced that the corruption of our society requires not shut doors and windows, but light and air.'[28]

Such had been Elizabeth's justification five years earlier for describing the plight of destitute women in *Aurora Leigh* (a poem clearly influenced by *Mystères de Paris*). 'Oh – I think it very likely that the poem will be shoved away from the reading of young girls,' she told her brother George, 'but if it stoops low on certain dunghills, *that* is in order that it may leap high to the most skyey significances.' Yet, she had worried that she had been too 'plain' in *Aurora Leigh*. Robert had assured her again and again that she couldn't be coarse if she tried. Her nature, like her poetry as described by Ruskin, belonged in a 'golden binding'.[29] Browning, however, fitted most comfortably between soiled, aged, and wrinkled covers like those of the Old Yellow Book.

It was Julia Wedgwood who, inadvertently, forced the poet to confront the fact that his career had been bedevilled not only by Elizabeth's ill health and its effects on the marriage but also by his angelic wife's acute sensibilities. Browning had respected Julia's wishes; for two years he had refrained from either writing to or visiting her. Then, in May 1867, an awkward dinner invitation arrived from her mother, which he felt obliged to turn down. However, Robert used the opportunity to ask Miss Wedgwood if she still cared to see 'the Poem' – *The Ring and the Book*, which he had begun work on not long after their first meeting. Julia answered Browning's letter by return of post. No, she knew nothing about her mother's invitation; yes, she would very much like to cast her critical eye over the proofs. 'I have often longed since our last meeting,' she teased, 'for opportunity and sarcasm to remark on the long delay of the appearance of your Italian.'

Julia had, in fact, to wait another year and a half before Browning brought the poem to a halt. Still, he was as good as his word, and she was able to read *The Ring and the Book* in proof. She did not like it. Painfully honest as ever, she wrote that she could not contemplate it without a sort of a squint. There was too much about the despicable husband, the vulgar parents, the brutal cut-throats – not to mention the scene where onlookers crowd around the dead bodies laid out in the church, ghoulishly trying to count the number of stab wounds. 'Do you remember,' Julia wrote, 'once saying to me that your Wife was quite wanting in .. the scientific interest in evil? .. I feel as if that interest were in you unduly predominant.' Returning to the matter in another letter, she remarked: 'I felt as if I were reading what you had lost in your wife. The sense of good seemed dimmed.'

Perhaps, Browning suggested to Julia, she simply could not bring herself to like a poem, no matter how well executed, about vengeance, duplicity, and triple murder. He had a point; no, she could not sympathise with his choice of subject. But 'surely,' Julia confessed, 'I must be wrong here, you cannot have spent all these years on a mistake.' Up until this point Browning had taken Miss Wedgwood's criticism in his stride. He respected her opinion, even when it differed from his own. However, to refer to *The Ring and the Book* as a 'mistake' was too much for the poet. 'I have given four full years to this "mistake",' Browning croaked on 22 February 1869 just a few days before the last volume of the work was due to appear before the public, 'but what did I do with my fourteen years in Italy?'

Browning's bitter tone betrays the fact Julia had exposed a raw nerve. He had never stopped thinking of Elizabeth as his model and his inspiration. 'Do you see this Ring? / 'T is Rome-work, made to match / (By Castellani's imitative craft) / Etrurian circles.' One can imagine Robert sitting at his desk, clutching Elizabeth's delicate gold ring, as he scrawled these opening lines to *The Ring and the Book*. Since her death, he had worn this gift from Isa Blagden to his wife (inscribed AEI, 'always' in Greek) on his watch chain.* The 'ring' of the title is not an exact description of Elizabeth's ring; the poet also had in mind some fanciful object from Castellani's Roman workshop, which the Brownings had visited together. It might have struck Robert at the time, with Elizabeth standing beside him, that the jeweller's craft, the mingling of 'gold / With gold's alloy, and, duly tempering both', reflects the poetic process; it also mirrors the art of memory. Just as he extracted and shaped 'the pure crude fact' that lay buried in the Old Yellow Book to create his

---

* Isa Blagden gave rings to both the Brownings; Robert's was inscribed VIS MEA ('my strength' in Latin). For both rings, see *Reconstruction*, H462, 472.

masterful poem, so he had worked the raw material of his own memory –
smoothing over the rough elements – to forge an idealised image of the
past. Thus there is a striking resemblance (which Julia Wedgwood was
quick to note) between Pompilia, the one pure, unsullied thing in *The
Ring and the Book*, and Elizabeth Barrett Browning. Pompilia's dark
beauty and sweet nature, her house-arrest and eventual rescue: these were
the very elements which had fuelled the myth surrounding Elizabeth.
Mrs Browning's spiritual presence 'was more than a presiding memory
of the heart', remarked Alexandra Orr; 'it entered largely into the conception of *Pompilia*.'[30]

With the completion of the poem – the story come full circle –
Browning again recalls Castellani's craftsmanship, 'the rough ore ..
rounded to a ring'. He had already invoked Elizabeth as his Muse: 'O
lyric Love, half-angel and half-bird / And all a wonder and a wild desire.'
He ends by proffering *The Ring and the Book* as a symbolic guard ring to
his wife's poetry: 'Might mine but lie outside thine, Lyric Love, / Thy
rare gold ring of verse (the poet praised) / Linking our England to his
Italy.'* So Robert had felt on the eve of publication. But Julia Wedgwood's dislike of the poem – Julia who was so much like his wife – made
Robert admit what he must have known in his heart of hearts. Elizabeth,
in actual fact, would have been deeply disturbed by the predominance
of evil – 'the morbid psychology of the soul', as he himself put it – in
The Ring and the Book. Indeed, he conceded to Julia that 'my wife would
have subscribed to every one of your bad opinions of the book; she never
took the least interest in the story, so much as to wish to inspect the
papers.' Yet, all the time that he was slaving over the Old Yellow Book,
studying its contents and fashioning a poem, Robert had believed that
he was doing what would have pleased and gratified Elizabeth. Now he
saw that he had been deluding himself.

It must have suddenly become clear to Browning why his fourteen
years in Italy, nearly the whole of his marriage, had enveloped him in
silence when he should have been so prolific; why that time had been –
perhaps 'mistake' was too harsh a word – such a disappointment, at least
poetically. Elizabeth's sensibilities, so different from his own, had acted
to rein in Robert's vivid imagination, and he was too much in awe of her

---

* Browning is here referring to the tablet above the entrance to Casa Guidi inscribed by the
poet Niccolò Tommaseo who spoke of Elizabeth Barrett Browning as having 'made with her
verse a golden ring between Italy and England' ('e fece del suo verso aureo anello fra Italia e
Inghilterra').

to rebel. The contrast between the poet's present literary fecundity and past impotence was striking. 'I used to be idle enough in Italy,' Browning told the Storys in April 1865, when he first began work on *The Ring and the Book*, 'but here [in London] I stick to my business honestly.' There had been other instances besides the Old Yellow Book when Robert had put to one side the idea for a poem – sometimes one that lay half written on his desk – because it did not accord with Elizabeth's tender feelings. During the winter of 1859–60 Robert had not dared show Elizabeth his work-in-progress ridiculing spiritualism, 'Mr Sludge, "the Medium" ', for fear of upsetting her. He published it only after her death.

The poet Walter Savage Landor had once hailed the young Browning as another Chaucer: 'The Siren waits thee singing song for song.' Landor had in mind the sirens of Plato, who make the music of the spheres. 'You ARE the veritable Siren,' Browning declared to Miss Barrett, who had seen Landor's poetic tribute to him, ' – and you "wait me", and will sing "song for song" ' – 'Ba, my dearest siren, and muse, and Mistress'. However, Elizabeth had turned out to be the Siren, not of Platonic thought, but of Homeric myth, disabling men with her song. 'Can I be as good for you as morphine is for me,' Elizabeth had asked Robert just a few weeks before their wedding, 'even at the cost of being as bad also? .. I wonder.'[31]

Julia had thought that the morbid tone of *The Ring and the Book*, 'this diminished seventh', as she put it, was a sign of Browning's unabated grief. His vision of the soul may indeed have become bleaker following his wife's death (just as Elizabeth probably became less tolerant as her illness progressed), but it had always been present in his work, from the chilling 'My Last Duchess' and 'Porphyria's Lover'* (who strangles his mistress with her own golden hair) to the nightmarish 'Childe Roland'. Julia, like Elizabeth before her, could not see that it was this dark side, nurtured amongst the weird and wonderful books in his father's library, which aroused the poet's creativity. Browning felt he had to write about life around him as he saw it, the sordidness as well as the beauty. He believed, as he told Julia, that cultivated men were capable of the 'grossest' wickedness; the more cultivated the mind, the more repressed the individual; and the greater the self-denial, the greater the wickedness. Three years after Elizabeth's death, at just about the time that he began to work in earnest on *The Ring and the Book*, Browning had expressed to Isa

* *Dramatic Lyrics* (1842).

Blagden the hope that 'the flower' of his poetry – taken, as he liked to say, from Elizabeth's nourishing root – would 'be put into Her hand somehow'. Browning would have had in mind the last of the *Sonnets from the Portuguese*: 'Belovèd, thou hast brought me many flowers / Plucked in the garden all the summer through ... Instruct thine eyes to keep their colours true, / And tell thy soul, their roots are left in mine.' However, Julia Wedgwood's reaction to the 'murder-poem' must have made him think that Elizabeth saw lying in her ghostly hand not a beautiful flower but some hideous weed. 'Thus old memories mar the actual triumph.'*

The very act of writing *The Ring and the Book* had – at long last – broken the soporific, opiate spell which Elizabeth had, unwittingly, cast over Robert's own poetic genius. It also went some way towards purging his remaining desire to return to Italy – certainly to Florence. His great 'Italian' poem sounded a long, fond and final farewell to the principal scenes – and some of the key figures – in his marriage. Browning had described it all in loving detail. Guido lives in Arezzo (Florence's Tuscan neighbour) beyond the carved 'archway's grin' of Porta S. Spirito. Pompilia and Caponsacchi stop and consume bread and wine at a certain 'post-house and a hovel or two' on their way to Rome, along the same road that the Brownings had travelled many times; the parents' bodies are laid out in S. Lorenzo in Rome, with its 'marble lion, / With half of his body rushing from the wall, / Eating the figure of a prostrate man – / (To the right, it is, of entry by the door)'. The Swiss Guards, in their 'wasp-like black and yellow foolery', patrol the Vatican.[32]

One also catches a glimpse of the Brownings' fellow expatriates behind the seventeenth-century faces. The two opposing lawyers, the short, podgy and clownish 'Archangelis' and the tall, thin and pompous 'Bottinius', are very like William Story (who had, after all, once practised law) and his rival sculptor, Hiram Powers. According to Hawthorne, Story, small and round in stature, bubbled and brimmed over with fun,† while the lofty and rather elegant Powers was always ready with a dissertation on any subject, from the common cold to blood transfusions.

* 'One Word More'.
† Typical of Story was the moment when, as Browning read aloud 'The Pied Piper of Hamelin' at a children's party in Rome, the sculptor burst in, dressed as the piper and playing the flute ('"Come in!" – the Mayor cried, looking bigger: / And in did come the strangest figure!'). 'We had a great romp .. all the children flocked screaming & laughing after me' (Story to C. Sumner, 13 May 1861: Houghton Library, Harvard University). Hans Christian Andersen, who was also present, read his story, 'The Ugly Duckling', rather badly in English (EBB to Arabel Barrett, [25 May 1861].)

Elizabeth described him as 'a cautious, reasoning man, rather calculating than otherwise'. The chivalrous but flawed priest Caponsacchi is all too like the poet-diplomat Robert Lytton whose infatuation with the beautiful young wife of a retired British captain scandalised polite society in Florence. Finally, with the 'ring' itself the poet was tipping his hat to dear Isa and her gift to Elizabeth. Just as Browning had in 1863 set up a little sculpture studio in Warwick Crescent, 'letting the memories curl round me while I preposterously meddle and make', so he had steeped himself in these same recollections of people and places as he sat at his desk scribbling *The Ring and the Book*. 'Poets are apt to be most present with the distant,' Elizabeth had once remarked to Mrs Jameson, apologising for the fact that there was 'nothing *Italian* in Robert's poems *Christmas-Eve* and *Easter-Day*.[33]

'How will it be, my four years' intimate,' Browning muses at the end of *The Ring and the Book*; 'When thou and I part company anon?'

Not as he had hoped was the answer – certainly not as far as his plans for Pen were concerned. The previous summer Browning had arranged for his son to join Benjamin Jowett's reading party in Scotland. He was confident that Pen would then be ready to resit the Balliol entrance examination in the autumn. But in October 1868 Jowett wrote Browning a letter that began politely but ominously: 'We were very glad to have him with us.' The anxious father read on. 'I wish I could say that he was quite certain of getting through. But I see that to accomplish that is a more difficult matter than I supposed.' It seems that Pen was just too careless. 'I have scolded him a little,' Jowett confessed, 'but only to impress on his memory that $\lambda\acute{v}\pi\eta$ does not mean a wolf.'[34] (Pen was confusing the Greek word with the Latin *lupus*.) The poor Oxford don, delicately perched on a windy crag, must have trembled with frustration as he found himself telling Pen for the tenth time that $\lambda\acute{v}\pi\eta$ meant 'sad plight', not 'wolf'. Surely the irony was not lost on Jowett that it would be his sad plight to have to inform Robert Browning that his son was not – and never would be – Balliol material.

Browning was forced to lower his sights. Ten days after receiving Jowett's learned opinion, he wrote to the Dean of Christ Church (H. G. Liddell, father of 'Alice'),* asking him to permit Pen to matriculate 'with

---

* Charles Dodgson was a tutor at Christ Church at this time. *Alice's Adventures in Wonderland* had been published just three years before, in 1865.

as little delay as possible'. 'I had hoped he would enter Balliol,' the poet confessed; 'but, at the last moment, and however reluctantly, I seem to perceive that my choice of a College has been a wrong one, and that his qualifications would serve him in better stead elsewhere.' Certainly with his qualification as a bon viveur, Pen would fit in perfectly at the 'more congenial' (as he described it to Julia Wedgwood) Christ Church. Indeed, it was so 'congenial', states one contemporary handbook, that 'a large number of undergraduates do not, and perhaps do not intend to, take their degree or even pass any examination'. The father could not hide his disappointment. 'The first twelve years of his life were spent abroad,' Browning felt obliged to explain to the Dean, 'and it could hardly be helped that his early studies were too many and too varied.' He had wanted to give his son a broader education, to include not only Greek and Latin but also music and modern languages, but it had become obvious in the last few months that this had not been the best course.[35] Although Robert reproached himself for so badly misjudging Pen's requirements, he clearly believed that those first twelve years in Italy under Elizabeth's lax tutelage had done irreparable damage.

Disappointment and bitterness were evident too in his New Year epistle to Isa, written soon after Pen had matriculated at Christ Church on 15 January 1869. 'He did it easily & creditably, just because he fancied the thing would be as easy as he fancied the Balliol business an awful affair.' It did not seem to occur to Robert – although surely Isa realised – that his high hopes for his son would have only added to Pen's jitters. 'He consequently read Greek till they bade him stop,' he continued rather tetchily in his letter to Isa, '& wrote Latin so that they never told him to translate at all, – solved every problem proposed to him and, in short, did all he ought to have done at Balliol.' Did Browning share these thoughts with Pen when, hoping to impress his father, the poor boy described how he had sailed through the examination?

Still, Pen was at Oxford; Browning could at least take comfort in that. 'They have given him good rooms,' he told Isa, 'and he is enjoying himself immensely. I chose my own rooms at Balliol – side by side with Jowett's – it will be pleasant, won't it? I enter them at June, – waiting till then, for those particular rooms: so when you come to England and want to see Pen, I shall entertain you!'

Back in London, life was not so bad. That spring Browning, together with Carlyle, the historian George Grote, and the geologist Sir Charles Lyell, had been summoned to meet Queen Victoria, take tea and 'pretend' to converse for an hour and twenty minutes. 'This eventful incident in my life,' so the poet told Julia Wedgwood, 'seems to have opened people's minds at last: and provided the Queen don't sent for the Siamese Twins, the Beautiful Circassian Lady, and Miss Saurin as her next quartette-party, I am in a way to rise.'[36]

Meanwhile in Oxford, Pen was excelling himself – on the water. One Saturday in May, Robert and Sarianna made the journey to Oxford and stood on the banks of the Isis to watch Pen steer the Christ Church boat to glory on the last day of the week-long Bumps competition. 'Pen was never seen by either of us to such advantage,' he wrote to Isa that same month, 'at least in his *manly* character.' He proudly boasted that in the course of the week their boat had bumped* five times. 'He was most affectionate and assiduous in his attention,' Browning added. Pen was still seeking to procure his father's love, much like the little boy who had kept back all his 'oller kisses' for Papa.

As summer approached, Browning was looking forward to spending the next few months with his family in Brittany. However, soon after Pen's arrival home from Oxford, something happened to make him cancel the holiday. 'An extraordinary press of matters, – if I dare not call them "business," – matters for consideration, fell on me at the end of June,' he told Thomas Kelsall, without further explanation.[37] It had something to do with Pen. Perhaps Browning had by this time received the report from Pen's tutor indicating that, although he was a credit to the Christ Church boathouse, he was not helping to improve the college's academic reputation. But Pen was not simply delivered into the hands of yet another reading party, and such was the poet's evident consternation over the next few months that the matter seems to have been far more serious.

London society was, as always, awash with tittle-tattle, much of it about Browning. 'There is a curious lie flying about *here*,' he had warned Isa the previous February, 'concerning poor me, – I am going to marry Miss A. daughter of L^y B. mother also of L^y C. &c. &c. I heard of it three times last week. I never even heard there was such a person as any one of the three, – never heard their names even. You,' he added wryly, 'will soon have it retailed you as indubitable fact.' But this time the gossip may have been about Pen. Certainly a rumour circulated – and persisted years later – that the young man had fathered two daughters

---

* When a boat 'bumps', that is touches, the one in front, it takes over the lead position.

by different Breton 'peasant girls' the previous summer (1868), or even the summer before that. How Browning might have found out is not known.[38] Perhaps Willy Bracken let slip the secret to his mother, who then felt obliged to inform Sarianna.

'Pen & Willy swim & shoot & enjoy themselves,' so Browning had written from Le Croisic two years earlier, in September 1867. Enjoy themselves, indeed. If such a rumour had reached the father's ears, we can only imagine the stern words which he reserved for Pen. But he would have been most angry with himself. How could he not have guessed, when he himself had been mesmerised by wild, strange, romantic Le Croisic? He may even have described to Pen and Willy, over a crackling fire one chilly summer's evening, how Le Croisic was 'the old head-seat of Druidism in France, probably mentioned by Strabo'. 'The people,' so he had written to his old Florentine friend Seymour Kirkup, 'were still Pagan a couple of hundred years ago, despite the priests' teaching and preaching, and the women used to dance round a phallic stone still upright there with obscene circumstances enough, – till the general civilization got too strong for this.'[39] 'Really, Mr Browning,' one can just hear Mrs Bracken whimper as she looked towards Sarianna for moral support, 'you shouldn't fill the boys' heads with such nonsense.'

That summer of 1869 Browning was facing a personal crisis. Whether or not Pen denied the allegation, whether or not his father believed him, if such a rumour was abroad it would have persisted. Enquiries would probably have had to be made. Browning's recent good health began to deteriorate. He was 'frightened a little at all this bad luck', he confessed to his good friend Mrs Frederick Lehmann at the end of July, when he backed out of a dinner invitation; 'I was unwell – having been so for some time – and felt the grasshopper a burden all day long* in the house from which I never stirred.'[40] The poet needed to get away from London, but Brittany was now out of the question. The Storys were in London en route to Scotland. They persuaded Browning to join them on their holiday. The poet looked so 'thoroughly worn out & unwell' when he boarded the northbound train, he told Isa in August, that a stranger thought him 'dying'. Little did he know, as the engine slowly pulled out of the station, that he was only heading for more trouble: of the female variety.

---

* 'When . . the grasshopper shall be a burden, and desire shall fail . . then shall the dust return to the earth as it was: and the spirit shall return unto God who gave it. Vanity of vanities, saith the preacher; all is vanity' (Eccles. 12: 5–8).

'When you have your autumn holiday in hand to dispose of it,' Browning's friend Anthony Trollope observed in *The Eustace Diamonds* (1873), 'there is nothing more aristocratic that you can do than go to Scotland. Dukes are more plentiful there than in Pall Mall, and you will meet an earl or at least a lord on every mountain. Of course, if you merely travel about from inn to inn, and neither have a moor of your own or stay with any great friend, you don't quite enjoy the cream of it; but to go to Scotland in August and stay there, perhaps, till the end of September, is about the most certain step you can take towards autumnal fashion.' The small holiday party that autumn of 1869, comprising Browning, Sarianna, and a closely guarded Pen, together with William Story, his wife, and twenty-five-year-old daughter Edith, did the rounds of fashionable hotels. They sought quiet lodgings in village inns. But the hotels were soulless, and the inns proved uncomfortable. And, naturally, the weather was miserable. They certainly were not enjoying 'the cream' of Scotland.

However, they did have at least one 'great friend' with a great house in the Scottish Highlands. Before they left London, Browning and his friends had been invited by Louisa, Lady Ashburton, to stay at her estate, Loch Luichart, in Ross-shire. Browning and his wife had first met Lady Ashburton – then Miss Louisa ('Loo') Stewart-Mackenzie – eighteen years earlier, in December 1851, at the Paris salon of Mme Mohl. (To Elizabeth's delight, the twenty-four-year-old had asked Robert if the Portuguese sonnets were really Portuguese!) Louisa was tall and dark – handsome rather than pretty – and the Brownings were quite taken with her, especially after they discovered they had a close mutual friend, Mrs Jameson. Anna Jameson, who had taken the newlywed poets under her wing in that same city seven years earlier, had been Miss Stewart-Mackenzie's governess. Louisa and her mother were also staying the winter in Paris. Robert accompanied the young Louisa to the Louvre at least once and went to music recitals hosted by Mrs Stewart-Mackenzie in her apartment close by the Brownings. Elizabeth wrote to Louisa after she had returned to England: 'We have not it is true, met very often – but there are instincts are there not? – and when my instincts tell me, I am apt to be forward in love. My husband and I have felt a warm interest in you from the beginning, and shall to the end.'[41]

Despite these sentiments, the Brownings lost touch with Louisa. However, their clutch of close mutual friends – which came to include Thomas Carlyle and William Story, to mention just a few – meant that, after his return to England, Browning came across the sociable Louisa, now Lady Ashburton, at the usual London gatherings.* When he and Elizabeth had first known her in Paris, Louisa was desperately but hopelessly in love. But the years passed, and with them her prospects for a suitable husband. Carlyle's impression of Louisa at around this time was of a 'bright vivacious damsel, struggling fitfully about, like a sweet-briar, and with hooks under her flowers, too, I understand; for they say she is much of a coquette, and fond of doing a stroke of "artful dodging" '. Her marriage at the age of thirty-one to Lord Ashburton, a widower twenty-eight years her senior and in poor health, was born of self-preservation not passion. Yet they were not unhappy together, even though the difference in character was as great as in age. Whereas Lord Ashburton was shy, staid, and stately, Louisa was all contradictions: generous, violent, rash, and impulsive. Despite his barbed comments – born out of loyalty to the first Lady Ashburton – Carlyle was soon charmed by her winsome ways: 'Lady Ashburton is too absurd,' he tut-tutted, 'a perfect "*dingle* dousie" ' – a term of endearment in his book. Admirers and detractors alike agreed that Louisa was a handful. 'Most capital is your description of L^y A. whom I exactly fancy!' Browning replied to a letter of 1863 from Mrs Story regarding the Ashburtons' unlikely union: 'He [Lord Ashburton] *would* have it so, & has got it: I always liked him much, & liked his wife much.' The very next year Lord Ashburton was dead, leaving Louisa a very rich widow of thirty-seven with several country houses and a young daughter, Maysie.

Lady Ashburton had issued at least one invitation to Browning soon after her marriage, but he declined on that occasion.[42] After reading of Browning's great triumph with *The Ring and the Book*, she was prompted to try again. In April 1869 she asked the poet to dine at her fashionable London house in Knightsbridge. 'Indeed I do "remember you",' his reply began; 'I shall be changed miraculously when I cease to do *that*! It is very pleasant to find that you remember *me* – not that I ever doubted it.' However, he had to say no for he was just about to leave for Paris. A few months later, in July, the invitation was repeated, and on this occasion Robert was happy to accept. Louisa clearly enjoyed his company, for three weeks later, on 29 July, Browning was obliged to decline yet another invitation. 'I leave town next Saturday with the Storys for – Scotland,'

---

* Browning inscribed a copy of his wife's *Last Poems* to Lady Ashburton 'London, Apr. 11, '62' (*Reconstruction*, C44).

he explained; 'what a delight it has been to me to find that the best thing in the world does not change and that your friendship remains as of old for Yours ever most truly and, – may I say in right of those old days, – affectionately Robert Browning.' But that was perfect, Lady Ashburton replied within a day or two; they all must come and stay at Loch Luichart. She would be there from the middle of August; they had only to name the day.

Browning, however, turned down the offer. He was not used to house parties. A wholly English institution, they had not been a feature of society in Italy, and his desire to lead a quiet life on his return to England led Robert to eschew all such invitations. One also suspects that he disliked the idea of having to breakfast, dine, and sup with the other guests who might be, for all he knew, complete fools. In any case, on this particular occasion he was determined to be miserable. 'I go simply to Scotland – to North Berwick, and there an end,' Robert had insisted to John Forster a few days before boarding the train; 'all I agree to, is company for a month or so, at the roughest place discoverable – afterward, they will make visits, I dare say, but I mean to return.'

The Storys, intending to stay on in Scotland, had apparently accepted Lady Ashburton's invitation. After 'the hideous confusion of three weeks' constant inconstancy' (as Browning told Isa on 28 August) '& flitting from bad place to worse', his friends were looking forward, no doubt, to hot water and other home comforts at Loch Luichart. But the Storys arrived there on the appointed day only to discover that 'the lady of the Lake was far from home', as Story's biographer, Henry James, put it. Baffled, the wayward travellers were reunited with the Brownings and 'made merry' as best they could at yet another squalid little inn near by, punctuating the long days with picnics amongst the heather while Browning read *Rob Roy* in a loud voice. Louisa finally returned to Loch Luichart to find, as she later told Carlyle, a reproachful note from Story. 'There was nothing for me to do,' she later wrote to Carlyle, 'but have them all here – so here they came the *lendemain*' (the next day). Sarianna was merely grateful that Lady Ashburton had 'by main force compelled' her and her brother to leave the dreary inn and partake of her hospitality.

James's epithet for Lady Ashburton, 'the Lady of the Lake', was an especially apt one. Her mother had been the model for Ellen Douglas, the heroine in Sir Walter Scott's poem, *The Lady of the Lake*. Louisa herself was closer to the enigmatic figure of Arthurian legend, at one time a benevolent, at another a mischievous, if not malicious, being.

The charms of the magnificent estate and its hostess worked their magic on all concerned, and within hours Lady Ashburton's guests – a cross Story and reluctant Browning included – firmly believed they had stumbled into a sort of paradise. 'The place is most beautiful,' Sarianna commented: 'Lake and mountains, moorland and waterfall, everything is here; with abundance of books, newspapers, magazines and periodicals.'[43] Pen, Robert told Isa that August with a touch of annoyance in his voice, 'has got what he wanted – shooting & deer-stalking'. The first day out he shot a royal stag, 'the head of which will glorify his rooms at Ch Ch'. Nevertheless, Browning regained his health and his composure. 'All goes well in this beautiful place,' he assured Isa. 'Through circumstances unforeseen & quite out of my control I am not in Brittany but here: having been bothered in the last three weeks beyond most folks' bearing: never mind, the worst is over & here, at an old friend's I am comfortable altogether: Sarianna & Pen (for whose sake I came) are here.' His 'tallowy hue' had grown 'russet' in the fresh air, and he added, 'I am bound to confess that, – whether travel in Scotland *please* me or no, – it does me more good in one week than Brittany in eight.'

As for Lady Ashburton, she found her guests 'very pleasant' and 'Browning a *delightful man*'. He read aloud 'all day and nearly all night', she told Carlyle, 'Shakespeare, Keats etc. etc.', and one day he set in motion a round robin, to which everyone contributed a verse, addressed to Harriet Hosmer. Within the last two years Lady Ashburton had become a patron of the sculptress who counted the Brownings amongst her oldest friends. Hattie had been Robert's companion in the runaway vegetable cart episode and, before that, Elizabeth's co-conspirator in the cross-dressing scheme. It was the forthright and slightly odd Hattie – 'our great pet, Robert's & mine', as Elizabeth put it – who created one of the most enduring images of the Brownings' marriage: a bronze cast of the poets' clasped hands. 'Dear Hosmer; or still dearer Hatty – / Mixture of *miele* and of *latte*, / So good and sweet and – somewhat fatty,' so Robert started off the round robin.[44]

At some point during the visit – perhaps on the eve of her guests' departure – a strange interview occurred between Browning and Lady Ashburton. The exact circumstances are not known. She may have invited her distinguished guest to inspect the garden one last time, or perhaps he asked his charming hostess to show him the Rubens again before he left (she had an exquisite art collection). In any case, Robert and Louisa found themselves alone together. The conversation would have easily drifted to more personal matters. After all, they had so much in common – shared memories, mutual friends. They had both experienced loss and loneliness. Louisa had the education of her nine-year-old daughter, Maysie, to consider; Robert was sick with worry about Pen's prospects. It may have been during such an intimate moment that Louisa declared her love for Browning. There may even have been a passionate embrace. 'I wrap me round with love of your black hair, / Black eyes, black every wicked inch of those / Limbs' war-tower tallness' – so Browning would recall their encounter years later.* If Louisa did not ask Browning to marry her outright, she at least posed the question: why should they not join their lives together? The poet was caught off-guard. He probably pleaded for some more time to think about it; then again, he may have just muttered something incoherent before escaping the room as quickly as possible. In any case, Browning gave no clear answer and, as she waved goodbye to her departing guests on or around 10 September, Lady Ashburton believed that her proposal of marriage still hung in the air. A few days later she wrote to Lord Houghton of the visit. 'I cannot say what delightful guests I found them. Mr Browning I think a charming man. Is he a friend of yours?' she casually enquired, savouring the idea that Mr Browning might soon become a permanent fixture in her life.

Still reeling from his interview with Lady Ashburton, Browning proceeded to Naworth Castle, the Cumberland home of the young couple George Howard and his wife Rosalind. The Storys were still with him, but Pen had gone to Hampshire and Sarianna back to London. 'My "worry" is increased to pretty nearly the last degree,' Browning wrote to Isa from Naworth Castle on 19 September. The worry over Pen's future had been compounded by his brief but nerve-racking encounter with Lady Ashburton. 'There is no need to put it on paper yet, – or perhaps ever'; time would tell. Just to be on the safe side, he added: 'Of course, that I have been, or am, – "worried" is, as usual, wholly between me & your dear self.'

It was in this emotional state that Browning had been speaking to the twenty-five-year-old Edith Story. Two days before his letter to Isa, and a week into his visit to Naworth Castle, Rosalind Howard – who was no older than Edith – wrote in her diary: 'We think Edy is in love with Browning and he with her.' Rosalind probably added this last part – 'and

* 'With Daniel Bartoli' in *Parleyings with Certain People of Importance in Their Day* (1887).

he with her' – after confronting her guest with the first conjecture during a late-night chat in her room. 'She says he is in love with her but that she will never marry him – that he is her best & greatest & oldest friend but that she is not in love with him': so Edith defended herself to Rosalind that night. 'She is very unhappy for him .. She never knew his love for her till they went together to Scotland this year. He has been in love with her for years.' 'Poor Edy,' Rosalind sighed into her diary, 'it is terrible trouble for her because everyone will fall in love with her & not the right people.'[45]

Or, was it that *Edith* would fall in love with the wrong people? Did she also tell Rosalind that night of her passion for the charming English diplomat Odo Russell who had spurned her only the year before to marry another? That autumn in Scotland the broken-hearted Edith was in as much of an emotional state as Browning. Rosalind, observing the two alone in conversation, thought Browning 'seemed very miserable & desperate'. Perhaps Browning, still worried sick about Pen's alleged peccadilloes, was at that moment trying to explain to Edith about male desires and high spirits without being too explicit. Who better to talk to about Pen than Edith, who had always been like a sister to him? When they were little, Edith had been Pen's special friend. At Bagni di Lucca they had had their own tea parties and had always sat close to each other, exchanging great secrets. When the Brownings wintered in Rome, the two children took lessons together from a rather ineffectual priest who indulged Pen's lazy study habits. Browning no doubt hoped that Edith might be able to offer comforting words – assuring him that he had always been a good father, or, perhaps, that Pen was a good boy, really. But Browning was incoherent when talking about his feelings at the best of times, and the unhappy young woman completely misunderstood.

Rather curiously, Edith also told Rosalind how 'Lady Ashburton had declared herself to be in love with Browning & showed it to everyone' at Loch Luichart. Perhaps Edith was just a little jealous. One morning the poet spent an hour in the library at Naworth Castle discussing 'the Lady Ashburton matter' with Mrs Story and Edith. Rosalind overheard through the open door that Mr Browning had got a letter from Lady Ashburton in which she expressed a wish 'to clinch the matter one way or another'. No, he did not love her, the poet assured the two ladies. But should he marry her for Pen's sake – to raise his position in the world and give his life some stability? Browning finally decided, on the advice of Mrs Story, 'to write to say *no*'. And all the while, Rosalind added, Mrs Story knew nothing of Browning's passion for her daughter! Then came a 'queer', 'very curious and dramatic' turn of events. Edith received a 'most gushing' letter from Lady Ashburton, who 'thinks Edy speaks in her favour to R. B.'. Just wait, Rosalind whispered into her diary, until Mr Browning's letter reached Loch Luichart.

Rosalind reported that Browning had appeared much more 'light hearted' after that enclave in the library. He was naturally relieved that a decision had been taken. And yet, to refuse Louisa's offer of marriage was, in his own words, 'an exercise of self-denial'. If there had been rumours of Pen's trysts with Breton peasant girls, these would have made the widower confront what must have been his own very real sexual frustration. Robert had suppressed his libido for the last ten years of his marriage, and his grief following Elizabeth's death had driven away all thoughts of physical passion. But eight long, lonely years had passed, and that autumn in Scotland Lady Ashburton saw in Browning a fifty-seven-year-old man in his prime – healthy, attractive, and extremely eligible. Like his father before him, Robert had proven himself weak and helpless before a seductress's charms. Elizabeth had anticipated her husband's predicament. Shortly before her death, she had written to her brother regarding her will: 'Agreed that Robert will probably survive me, – agreed even, on my side, that he may remarry .. being a man .. nay, "being subject to like passions" as other men, he *may* commit some faint show of bigamy – who knows?'[46] Browning felt he had been tested by the Lady of the Lake and had failed in thought if not in deed. He was racked with guilt.

Browning got back to Warwick Crescent on 27 September. He confessed to Edith Story, who had asked for a 'special word' from the poet on his return home, that he was 'tired and out of sorts on my arrival at 10 o'clock; and, having somehow got out of my good old habit of soundly and expeditiously sleeping, I continued to weary myself in bed, – but in the end the sleep came, and I woke aware of the accustomed curtains and furniture' – so full of memories of Elizabeth and Casa Guidi – 'and none the worse for a little tossing and tumbling .. You seemed,' he added, addressing Edith, 'nervous and fatigued – take care of yourself, will you?' By November, Browning was trying to put his Highland fling with Lady Ashburton behind him. 'The fact is,' he told the Storys, 'the holidays are over, with (for me) an end of boys'-play, which, – it is said, – men ought to know when to leave off: and "left off" it all is, I very sincerely assure you.' He had behaved no better than Pen; at least Pen had the excuse of youth. 'I am seeing all my sober friends,' he continued, 'and still have visits to pay before I settle down to my work at London, – whatever that work is to be.' But Louisa had other ideas. As Robert later explained to the sculptor, she began to launch a series of 'cajoleries and pathetic appeals', as well as 'teazing with her invitations' to entice him back and to ensnare him.[47] She was not prepared to give up just yet.

Browning was annoyed with Lady Ashburton, with Pen, but most of all with himself, and he took it out on everything and everyone around him. He was 'ill-natured', 'bilious and out of sorts', as he explained to Isa over and over again. If the ink he used was half as acidic as the remarks he made in the months that followed, his words would have burned through the paper. He called Mary Russell Mitford's letters, recently published, 'sad twaddle'. Annie Thackeray's book was even poorer than Miss Mitford's efforts. Browning's old arch-enemy, the poet Alfred Austin, was a 'filthy little snob'. The Pre-Raphaelites' paintings were full of 'girlish boys and boyish girls', and their verse was equally effeminate. Nearly a year after the Ashburton affair he decried the Brotherhood's notion of 'love' as a 'lubberly naked young man putting his arms here & his wings there, about a pair of lovers, – a fellow they would kick away, in the reality'. He did not even have a kind word for *The Holy Grail*, the poem which Tennyson had read aloud not so long ago to an appreciative Browning on Clapham Common. 'I should judge the conflict in the knight's soul the proper subject to describe,' he told Isa. 'Tennyson thinks he should describe the castle, and effect of the moon on its towers, and anything *but* the soul.' Browning was hardest on himself, with talk of washing himself 'with divine salt-water, "which cures all pollution" says the ancient'.[48]

His relations with Pen went from bad to worse. Their quarrels must have continued. 'I shall best "shut up," as Pen would say' – so Browning had written to the Storys in November 1869. The poet's tone of voice was light-hearted enough, but these words surely echoed many an unpleasant scene at 19 Warwick Crescent, especially after Pen performed badly yet again. Altham (the son of Elizabeth's sister Henrietta) was also at Christ Church. 'Our darling Altham, this day,' his father recorded in his diary for 25 November 1869, 'passed his preliminary exam for "smalls" (as they call it) at Ch. Ch. Oxford. Thank God. His cousin Pen .. also of "the House" ploughed* poor fellow the same time.'[49] Certainly, Browning would have found all this very upsetting. At least he was beginning to

---

* That is, failed.

realise that the last few years had been 'a sort of battle' on Pen's part 'for his own individuality'. But, Browning told Isa in February 1870, when Pen had returned to Oxford for the winter term, just as 'I was fairly giving up on my part of the strife, – *what* do you suppose? – What that should, most of all things imaginable, stupefy me? Why .. he has once more broken out in violent poetry! He wrote, a few weeks ago,' Robert explained, 'a poem in some six hundred lines about an adventure he had at Croisic.' (One wonders if this 'violent' burst of poetry had anything to do with the young man's amorous exploits in Brittany.) He would not give much for it, Browning added, 'but considering the boy's all but absolute ignorance of poetry, it was a very welcome proof indeed of what may be still in him'. There had once been a time when Robert thought his son's poems were works of genius – for an eight-year-old.

Whatever talent lay within Pen, he was not to find it at Oxford. On 17 June Robert wrote to George Barrett that he had failed again. Two months of labour revising for his Part One examination were not enough to overcome 'nine years of idleness'. In the opinion of his tutor, the boy 'has been helped too much, and done too little for himself'. Browning was at his wits' end. Pen was obliged, he went on in his letter to George, 'to take his name off the books at Ch. Ch., – and, though I might possibly get him yet another respite, I shall not dream of doing so'. Despite his protestations, the boy had continued to run up huge bills each term. 'He cannot be made to see that he should follow any other rule than that of living like the richest and idlest young men of his acquaintance, or that there is any use in being at the University than to do so.' 'You see,' Browning groaned, 'that all my plans are destroyed by this double evil – the utmost self-indulgence joined to the greatest contempt of work and its fruits: how should I be justified in proposing to introduce him to a diplomatic career' – something which the poet had long been considering for Pen – 'wherein his temptations to spend would be far more numerous, and his incitements to study infinitely less?

'So, dear George,' Browning cried out, '*what do you advise?*'

He was ready to do anything, make any sacrifice, he pleaded to the boy's uncle. 'I can hardly make a greater [sacrifice] than I have done – of the last nine years of my life, which have been as thoroughly wasted as if they were passed in playing at chuck-farthing. All I can do, – except to give money, – is *done* & done in vain. What do you think of the army? Or will it all end in my pensioning off the poor fellow to go & rot in the country?' Worse, the father felt he had no sort of influence over his son.

'But something must be decided on at once for a young man in his twenty-second year, who told me just now, in Ocky's presence [another Barrett uncle], that he would not have consented to be at Ch. Ch. at any less expense than he had been incurring, and that he considered getting a first class no brilliant thing at all.' One can almost hear a door slam behind the young man following this angry exchange.

George Barrett did not receive this first letter for some time, owing to postal delays. In the meantime, Robert sat down to write again on 1 July; his rage had abated – only to be replaced by despair. A career as a cavalry officer was, on closer consideration, not an option. 'I will not hear of a life,' he told George, 'first of all, hateful to his Mother: next, as hateful to me, – finally, involving all the worst temptations to every sort of weakness. It is all miserable to contemplate. The poor boy is simply WEAK – not bad in any way, .. singularly engaging to his friends with whom he is as popular as possible, and quite docile and amenable to reason with a comparative stranger' – that is, anyone but his own father. Relations between father and son had, in fact, completely broken down. 'I am merely the manger at which he feeds,' Browning went on, 'and nothing is more certain than that I could do him no greater good than by dying to-night and leaving him just enough to keep him from starving .. There is something infinitely pitiable in this butterfly-nature with no fault in it but what practically is the worst of all faults, – weakness.' A restive horse may be broken of his vice and made to win a race against his will, the poet concluded, but how can you make a butterfly cross the room to save his life, much less yours? For the time being, Pen was being made to cross yet another tutor's chambers to read law, a profession particularly unsuited to a butterfly.

That June of 1870 Browning was at a particularly low point. He could not face sitting down to write to Isa on the appointed day, the 19th of the month. 'My excuse,' he pleaded two weeks later, 'must be the very real one that I was quite unfit for writing from various causes: the time of the year always weighs upon me, – most of my troubles happen in June' – the deaths of his wife, father, and sister-in-law, the 'worry' of the previous year, and now Pen's utter and complete failure at Oxford. Unusually, Robert did not tell Isa of Pen's disgrace; the feelings of disappointment and heartache were probably still too great.* He chose

---

* Edward C. McAleer, editor of the correspondence between Browning and Isa Blagden, suggests that Pen, who was in possession of the letters after his father's death, might have

instead to look back to the day of Elizabeth's death, 'nine years ago, completed on the 29th. The years they come and go – The races drop in the grave – But never the love doth so': so Browning quoted from his wife's translation of Heinrich Heine. (This line became a sort of mantra, which Robert chanted to Isa every June.) 'It was *this* day' – that is, the day on which he was writing, 2 July – 'that I went to your house in the evening: how utterly good and kind you were, and always have been, before and since.' He conceded that he and Isa had had their differences over the years, 'yet so are we made that I suppose we should teaze each other again if the seas and lands did not separate us'. His brush with Lady Ashburton had made the widower – who had been so safe and snug, wrapped up in his grief – wake up to the fact that he desperately missed the sort of intimacy which female companionship provided. 'Whom *does* one care to teaze,' he asked Isa, 'that one does not also care to kiss? "Love both ways, kiss & teaze." It is a bad sign that I teaze nobody now, nor let them teaze me in the rare cases when they are able.'

Robert had no special female friend whom he could 'kiss & teaze' – with impunity. Isa was too far away, and Lady Ashburton was proving too dangerous. As for Julia Wedgwood, Browning had finally ended that difficult – not to say, tortuous – friendship only weeks before, on 14 June 1870. Although they had not been in touch for the two years prior to the publication of *The Ring and the Book*, Browning and Julia had been able to pick up where they had left off. Their letters convey the same level of intensity, intimacy, and mutual attraction as before. Julia may not have been beautiful, but Browning had always been drawn to her intellect and integrity, qualities which he had treasured in his wife. Julia alone had had the privilege of reading *The Ring and the Book* in its entirety before publication. She was perhaps the only woman of Browning's acquaintance who was able to give constructive criticism and not merely flatter, something that he had missed since Elizabeth's death.

Robert had clearly hoped that he might renew his visits to Cumberland Place. Even better, he wrote on Guy Fawkes' night 1868, 'my sister keeps house here and people come to see her sometimes, – women-people: is the notion that I might see *you*, so – a birth of this memorable Gunpowder-

---

destroyed the account of his failure at Oxford. However, the sequence of Browning's monthly letters is complete, without any gaps, although not always written punctually on the 19th.

treason-and-plot-day – fraught with fire and brimstone?' Apparently it was. As far as Julia was concerned, the spark was still there, and she dared not trust herself to meet Browning again face to face. She even confessed that she had seen the poet in the street twice since they last parted but had crossed the road to avoid an encounter. Of course, Julia's reticence only added an air of mystery – if not romance – to it all, which Browning got caught up in. 'I was startled the other day,' Browning confided to Julia, 'at a house where I dined for the first time, – the Spottiswoodes, – by hearing that "the Wedgwoods" were expected afterward: I had to go away elsewhere, and don't know what came true of the promise: I should not like to meet you that way, however.'

Browning seemed more than willing to agree to Julia's terms. Even after her harsh criticism of *The Ring and the Book*, the poet happily imagined that 'whatever I write, I will always send you, and you will always like to see it, will always speak your mind about it, and will always be exactly in the relation that you are now to – R. B.' 'You are not really so arrogant,' Julia lashed out in reply a few weeks later, on 5 March 1869, 'with all your arrogance, as to think that our shares were equal?' – that 'it was a loss to *you*' when all communication between them ceased. She had suffered; he had not. Even after all this time – five long years – Browning still did not have a clue. 'Honestly, I do not understand what you mean,' he wrote a few days later. 'There was certainly as great a loss to me as to you .. in the cessation of our intercourse.' Yes, he conceded, it was true; whereas he used to lament that the British public did not understand his poetry, he was now being fêted and honoured by that same fickle body. Nevertheless, 'I lost something peculiar in you, which I shall not see replaced – is that stated soberly enough?'

Julia then let slip what she had concealed from Browning five years before. 'I was the seeker, you know,' she wrote on Good Friday 1869. 'I think every step in our intercourse was initiated by me. My friendship with you was – is – the great blessing of my life, but it was impossible to me to carry on that outward indulgence of it after it had been implied to me "He feels it a gêne [embarrassment]." But why do I go back to this?' Why go back to this? repeated Robert. 'Ask rather – or I ask – what is this going forward to a quite new piece of information?' Friends had misread him, he insisted, thinking his silence at the mention of Miss Wedgwood was prompted by embarrassment when in fact he was just being discreet. In reply Julia further admitted that the reasons which 'impelled me to the surrender of the most prized possession of my life' were 'multiform and complex', but she did not elaborate. Browning was still in the dark. She merely left him with a teasing remark: 'I wish you would let me copy for you [as Elizabeth once did], you see how beautifully I can write. Perhaps you would be afraid of any interpolating moral sentiments? – and it might be a danger.'

They did not correspond again for over a year – during which time Lady Ashburton had entered Browning's small world and turned it upside down. Then, in June 1870, it was Julia who made the first move. 'I cannot help writing to try to pass on the impression made by Pompilia on a beautiful soul, among my friends'; this friend had spoken of it to Miss Wedgwood in terms of an exquisite sunset. 'You know,' Julia added, 'you owe us an adequate translation of what your wife was to you.' The poet was defensive. 'Why or how do I owe you,' he declared, '– or whomsoever is included in "us" – any "adequate translation of what my wife was to me"?' He resented Julia for calling upon him to 'step up on to some pretty sort of pedestal' in order to keep sacred the past – that strange, heavy crown – and he hated himself for being caught off-guard at Loch Luichart.

Yet the Ashburton episode, which had reawakened Browning's deep-seated sensuality, seems to have given the poet at least an inkling of how blind he had been to Julia's feelings. Julia, like Louisa, had sought the poet out. The same sort of intimate words and gestures which Louisa had employed to show the depth of her feelings, Browning would have recognised from his visits to Cumberland Place all those years ago. But he had been so self-absorbed back then that it had never crossed his mind that Julia might be in love with him. When he did not reciprocate, she had devoted herself to the memory of Elizabeth in the same way that some women, disappointed in love, devote themselves to God. Julia had even grown to enjoy the role of martyr. But Browning finally now understood the increasingly bitter tone of her letters; he also understood that he could never return her love. Robert was 'subject to like passions as other men', as Elizabeth had noted, but he simply was not drawn to Julia in the same way that he had been drawn to Elizabeth and, if only for a brief instant, to Louisa. To prolong their intercourse would only increase Julia's feelings of heartache and his sense of loneliness. No, the best thing for both of them was to say goodbye – once and for all. 'Come,' he gently beckoned in his last letter to her, dated 14 June (his month of troubles) 1870, 'let us go back to the quiet place, where we "do not forget each other." Goodbye, dear friend; it was very pleasant to hear your voice in the dark – though I see no face since years now. R. B.'

When the summer holidays arrived that year (1870), Browning found himself in a bit of a quandary. He still swore off country-house parties. 'I shall escape if I can all visits in England this year,' he told Isa; 'the country-life does not suit me' and – what he did not say – leads to mischief. Nor would he return to Le Croisic, which had led Pen into trouble. Rather, Browning found an even wilder retreat than Le Croisic: St Aubin-sur-Mer, which suited him perfectly. 'I prefer the utter rough-ness of this hamlet,' he declared, 'to the finery of . . the other great place where I might be,' that is, Loch Luichart, where he had again been invited. Pen was safely lodged with his law tutor back in England. Robert and Sarianna inhabited a cottage of the most primitive kind on the seashore, he gleefully wrote to Isa; 'I don't think we were ever quite so thoroughly washed by the sea air from all quarters as here.' Perhaps at St Aubin he would find the 'divine salt-water' with which to wash away all his sins, as the poet had mused six months before.

Each night, as he looked out of his window at the beam from the Le Havre lighthouse shining across the inlet, Browning was reminded of Elizabeth, for they had once spent the summer at Le Havre. 'It always gives me a thrill as I see, afar, *exactly* a particular spot which I was at, along with her. At this moment, I see the white streak of the phare [that is, lighthouse] in the sun from the window where I write and *think*.' He may have thought of how he had once, before their marriage, described his poetry to Elizabeth. It 'lives in me', he wrote, 'like the light in those crazy Mediterranean phares I have watched at sea – wherein the light is ever revolving in a dark gallery, bright and alive, and only after a weary interval leaps out, for a moment, from the one narrow chink, and then goes on with the blind wall between it and you'. The young Robert felt he had yet to fulfil his potential – to 'bring forth "R. B. a poem" '.[50] *The Ring and the Book* was that poem. As he sat looking out at the Le Havre lighthouse, the fifty-eight-year-old widower cannot but have been struck by the fact that it had taken him nearly twenty-five years – eight years after the death of Elizabeth – to produce it.

Although nearly two years had gone by since the publication of *The Ring and the Book*, Browning had yet to begin his next work. He was still preoccupied. Lady Ashburton's cajolings continued. His anger over Pen's academic failure had been replaced by his concern for the young man's health. Pen had been ill, at times quite seriously, on and off since around the time of his disastrous Christ Church examination. Nerves obviously played a part, but there was more to it than that. He had come home from the Oxford spring term, in April 1870, very unwell; that summer he contracted measles, unusually, for the second time. He always seemed to have a cold (which he would inevitably pass on to his father). The young man was eventually diagnosed with rheumatism and confined to bed for five weeks.

But Pen's most serious underlying malady seems to have been depression, and no wonder. He must have dreaded the inevitable discussions with his father about the future. And Pen had his own spirits – or 'spillets', as he used to lisp – to deal with. Browning had always been amazed at how well the twelve-year-old Pen had coped with his mother's death. Yet, she had not said goodbye to her beloved son, nor had she left any message for him. Pen must have missed her terribly, especially at such a difficult time as this. When Isa Blagden learned of Pen's attack of rheumatism, the kind spinster thought that he might like to spend some time with her in Florence. She of all people knew the pressure Pen had been under. Perhaps sunnier climes and memories of happier days would help to revive him. 'How good you were to wish to have Pen!' Browning wrote some time later, thanking Isa. 'It would have been an unsuitable place, under the circumstances' – circumstances which he does not explain – 'I can only hope that *one day* . .'[51]

Did Browning fear that Pen's return to Florence would draw him back also, against his will? Only five months earlier he had told Isa – who wondered when he would ever see her garden – that all he could do for Pen now was to 'watch him & watch for him – which to do with effect, one must keep quietly at home'. Surely, it might have done both father and son a world of good to visit Isa in her Bellosguardo villa. One feels that Browning was not being honest with himself. But there was perhaps another, more particular, reason for not letting Pen go to Florence: the presence of that selfish 'young piece of worthlessness', Willy Bracken, Pen's best friend who had married the daughter of a French painter, M. Desboutin, against his mother's wishes. It might have crossed Browning's mind, thinking back to those summers in Brittany, that Willy was a thoroughly bad influence on his son. He could at least take comfort in the fact that, as he said to Isa, 'Pen, with plenty of faults, is altogether of another sort than Willy – is not cold bloodedly selfish.' No, he would never do such a thing against his father's wishes. As for Willy, 'the sooner *he* breaks his neck, the better.'[52]

Pen's travels then, since being sent down from Oxford, had been restricted to long stays in the country with his law tutor. When the festive holidays came at the end of 1870, he returned to Warwick Crescent only long enough to pack his riding breeches and dinner jacket before setting off on a succession of country-house visits. Browning preferred to stay behind in London. He wrote to his friend Richard Monckton Milnes that Pen 'will enjoy Christmas nowhere better than with you; and I rather wish him enjoyment, that he has been doing well, and working hard, – lately,' he added. 'Don't trouble yourself about any thought of a youth quite able and willing to amuse himself – make him play to the young ladies if they like music, for one thing.' After the new year Pen went on to spend a week or so at Melchet Court, Lady Ashburton's estate in the South of England, bordering the New Forest. Browning had, of course, been invited too. He chose to stay away. Louisa knew she had to tread carefully. The best way to reach the father, she calculated, was through the son.

With Pen at Melchet Court, Louisa addressed a pretty little note to the poet, full of the young man's praises. How she wished Mr Browning were with them. That same day Pen dutifully sat down in the drawing room to write to his father, describing a picture of domestic bliss: Lady Ashburton, who was kindness itself, drawing from a cast, Maysie playing the piano, and Miss Ronan, the governess, reading aloud from a French book. 'So I see you,' Browning replied to Lady Ashburton, after quoting from his son's letter, ' – and am prepared for "kindness itself" speaking so kindly of Pen to me .. Thank you for that and all else; most of all for what I dare not doubt is true, – since you again assure me of it – that you have "wished for me much".' He felt he should say more – she had been so good to Pen – and proceeded to babble on about his feelings. What could Louisa possibly have thought when she read about his 'self-denial'; how 'the right course' – to remain a widower – is 'never very attractive you know!'? Perhaps, she mused, Mr Browning was slowly coming round to the realisation that he had been too faint-hearted and that a second marriage, although a huge step, had its appeal. The poet then returned to the pretty scene in his mind's eye, which had clearly charmed him: 'But you are copying your cast, and Maysie is playing and both are listening to the French book, and I confess I feel I am best here, now – however I may feel one day, what cast I wonder!' His prose was more obscure than his poetry. Elizabeth had sometimes thought it harder to understand than Greek, and a friend once swore that the poet managed to be obscure even in a telegram. 'Remember me whenever you come to town,' Browning ended, 'and, if it can be without inconvenience, apprise me and let me see you for a few minutes. God bless you ever. R. B.'[53]

Louisa reckoned that the poet was still open to the possibility of marriage. The following March he very kindly but rather stupidly, perhaps, sent her daughter Maysie a book inscribed: 'The gift is small, / The love is all.' She renewed her campaign: if only she could tempt him back to Loch Luichart, where she could ensure the perfect setting .. Browning did his best to resist the continued teasing that accompanied her invitations. (It was not the sort of teasing he liked.) However, in August–September 1871 he found himself again in Scotland. One suspects that Pen was behind it. Pen loved nothing better than the shooting season in Scotland, and when friends in Perthshire, Ernest Benzon and his wife Elizabeth, invited the Brownings, father and son, to stay at their hunting lodge (three miles from the main house) above Loch Tummel, Browning felt he could hardly say no, especially since Pen had again been in rather poor health.

Once in the Highlands, the young man's condition quickly improved. 'He has been assiduously labouring,' Browning wryly informed Isa that August, 'in that occupation to which Providence apparently hath pleased to call him, – that is shooting, idling and diverting himself.' In one day, he had shot fourteen and a half brace of grouse, four hares, and a plover. 'A poor business,' the poet commented, '& one I could wish him to hate as much as I do .. To a certain degree, I am relieved about Pen by knowing the very worst of the poor boy' – besides his love of slaughter – 'to-wit that he won't work, or perhaps can't.' Pen was indeed on his way to becoming an English gentleman – the sort who exuded charm, excelled in grouse-shooting, billiards, and after-dinner charades, and so drifted from house to house, scrounging off friends. At least Browning had escaped the strain of London life, as he put it, as well as the August heat. He consoled himself by remaining blessedly alone all day in the hunting lodge with his books and a piano. An added benefit was Benjamin Jowett so close by; he was in the Highlands with yet another of his reading parties. Lady Ashburton had, of course, invited the Brownings to Loch Luichart; Pen would so enjoy the deerstalking. Pen might do as he wished but, Browning stated firmly to Isa – and presumably to Lady Ashburton: 'I shall not accompany him.' A few weeks later, however, Browning found himself once more at the wild and grandiose Loch Luichart.

'Circumstances,' as he told Isa on 1 October had made it 'impossible' to return straight to London.

On 8 August, just before leaving London – when he still thought he would not be seeing Lady Ashburton – Browning had asked George Smith to send a copy of his newly published poem, *Balaustion's Adventure*, to Loch Luichart.[54] Although Robert called it 'the most delightful of May-month amusements', *Balaustion's Adventure: Including a Transcript from Euripides* was, in fact, the poet's oath of loyalty to Elizabeth's memory, which he had composed one month short of the tenth anniversary of her death, in May 1871. It was the first thing of any substance that he had published since *The Ring and the Book*.* In his dedication, Browning states that it was Countess Cowper who imposed on him 'as a task' this poem, a creative rendering of Euripides' drama, *Alcestis*. But there was much more to it. Robert needed to take stock of his life – his success and Pen's failure, his too-discreet friendship with Julia Wedgwood and his indiscreet relations with Lady Ashburton – and he did it the only way he knew how, through poetry.

To employ Euripides' *Alcestis*, which tells the story of a wife who dies that her husband might live, as a vehicle for his poetry was a brilliant stroke.† 'You owe us an adequate translation of what your wife was to you.' Browning had taken offence at Julia Wedgwood's remark at the time, but it was as though the idea had continued to gnaw away at him. The widower would be able to convey – and to purge – his own inner turmoil while hiding behind the dramatic mask of Euripides. Yet, it is not just Browning's voice which we hear, but also that of Elizabeth in the guise of Balaustion, the young maiden of the title. Thus, the poem begins with the story of Balaustion, a refugee from war, whose ship, pursued by pirates, is forced to seek shelter in the hostile waters of Syracuse. (The basis of the story appears in Plutarch.) To placate the enemy, Balaustion offers to recite Euripides' play *Alcestis*, which she has recently seen performed, and this is the version which Browning puts before the reader. Balaustion – idealistic, passionate – is very like Elizabeth (both were exiles from their native land, in company with the men they loved). Balaustion proceeds to win over the Syracusans with the beauty of her speech just as Elizabeth had won over the Italians with her 'golden verse'.

---

* He published a short poem, 'Hervé Riel', in *Cornhill Magazine* in March 1871, the proceeds of which he donated to the starving French during the siege of Paris.
† Interestingly, Ted Hughes, another poet who married a famous poetess (Sylvia Plath) and outlived her, also chose to translate Euripides' *Alcestis* (2000).

Balaustion's recitation (which includes her own running commentary) begins after Alcestis has declared to the god Apollo that she alone from amongst friends and family is willing to take the place of her husband, King Admetos, in Hades – to exchange her life for his. The king is torn apart by sorrow after her death from a wasting disease. He too wishes to die, now that he realises 'how dear death is, / How lovable the dead are'.

But Admetos had to think of the living – the children who were now made orphans. Tellingly, Browning chose not to include the heart-wrenching scene in Euripides where Alcestis' young son cries out, 'Oh, what has happened? Mummy has gone away, / And left me and will not come back any more! / Father, I shall be lonely all the day .. Mother! Oh, speak a word! / Answer me, answer me, Mother! It is I. / I am touching your face. It is I, your little bird.'[55] Memories of the sad but stoic twelve-year-old Pen were too painful. However, Browning did not flinch from translating Admetos' argument with his father, Pheres, who had refused to give his life for his son and thus save Alcestis. One feels that the poet had some sympathy with the old man when he declares: ' "Too arrogant art thou; and, youngster words / Casting against me, having had thy fling, / Thou goest not off as all were ended so! / I gave thee birth indeed and mastership / I' the mansion, brought thee up to boot: there ends / My owing" .. And so died out the wrangle by degrees / In wretched bickering.'

Admetos feels deep remorse; his wife died so that he might continue to live and rule his people. Browning is remorseful, too, not only because he had been unfaithful to Elizabeth's memory but also because her death had somehow enabled his life – his poetry – to flourish. Admetos is given that which is so rare in life; a second chance. Heracles, the son of Zeus, to whom Admetos has shown hospitality, wrestles with Death to bring Alcestis back from Hades and presents her, hidden behind a veil, to the king. Admetos, determined to remain loyal to the memory of his wife, bids Heracles send away this strange, haunting figure, for 'Her, wherever she abide, / My duty is to honour'. The veil then lifts to reveal the flesh-and-blood Alcestis. But will they live happily ever after? Euripides does not tell us, nor does he pass judgement. Browning's Balaustion, although she does not condone Admetos' conduct, suggests that the king finds redemption and self-knowledge.

When Balaustion has finished her recitation of *Alcestis*, she invokes the poet's privilege, to 'bring forth new good, new beauty, from the old' in order to come up with a completely different, and more compassionate, version. With this departure from Euripides' text, Robert is reflecting not only Elizabeth's sensibilities but also her sentiments. Poets should look to create something new, she believed, not merely copy the old. And so, Balaustion moulds 'a new Admetos, new Alkestis'. Admetos, fully aware that his life would be nothing without Alcestis, refuses her offer to die for him. Despite his protestations, such is her love for her husband – and her belief in his duty to rule – that she descends into Hades. 'This is not to die, / If, by the very death which mocks me now, / The life, that's left behind and past my power, / Is formidably doubled,' cries Death on beholding Alcestis. 'Two souls in one were formidable odds: / Admetos must not be himself and thou!' Love has triumphed over death; Alcestis rejoins her husband.

Browning, of course, could not bring Elizabeth back from the dead – there could be no new ending, no deus ex machina for him. However, it was in his power to make certain that her poetry lived on. Just the year before, on the publication of the eighth edition of Elizabeth's *Poetical Works*, he had told an American publisher, 'I should greatly like that wherever my poems are published, those of my Wife should be obtainable also.'[56] Moreover, Robert could ensure that she lived on in his poetry, and in *Balaustion's Adventure* he makes the link explicit. 'I know the poetess who graved in gold,' the Greek girl proclaims, referring to Elizabeth: 'Among her glories that shall never fade, / This style and title for Euripides, / *The Human with his droppings of warm tears*' – a line from Elizabeth's 'Wine of Cyprus'. Browning prefaced *Balaustion's Adventure* with four lines from this same poem, written in 1844. Is it not extraordinary, Balaustion asks, that when *Alcestis* was first performed at the Athens festival (438 BC), the judges chose Sophocles over Euripides as the greater dramatist?* 'All cannot love two great names; yet,' she suggests, 'some do.' Just as, in Balaustion's version, the reunited Admetos and Alcestis live happily together, so Browning's poetry and that of his wife should be able to co-exist and flourish side by side.

'They are one, the same, and indivisible,' explains Wallachia Petrie, one of Anthony Trollope's characters in *He Knew He Was Right* (1868– 9), to an Englishman who assumes the Yankee poetess† does not know

---

* Balaustion declares that she also knows 'a great Kaunian painter who made a picture of it all', referring to *Hercules Wrestling with Death for the Body of Alcestis* (1871) by Frederic Leighton, another source of inspiration for Balaustion. 'And just think,' Balaustion notes, 'it all came of this play that gained no prize!'
† Miss Petrie is known as 'the American Browning'.

the difference between Mr and Mrs Browning. 'The spirit and germ of each is so reflected in the outcome of the other,' she continues, 'that one sees only the result of so perfect a combination, and one is tempted to acknowledge that here and there a marriage may have been arranged in heaven. I don't think that in your country you have perceived this.' Browning was trying his best to convince the British public.

'Fool call me – only one name call me not! / Bridegroom!' Browning has Admetos declare before Heracles. Alcestis' dying wish was that her husband be both mother and father to their children, that he never bring a 'hostile new-comer, the step-dame .. a very viper' to rule over her children. 'Fear not!' Admetos assures her. 'Alone wilt thou be called my wife .. No woman, be she of such lofty line / Or such surpassing beauty otherwise!' This, Browning's coded message to the handsome, aristocratic Lady Ashburton, had reached Loch Luichart by the time the poet himself arrived on 2 October 1871. In spite – or because – of this, Louisa made him promise to visit her for that one day in order to 'get handsomely done with it all', he told his young confidante Edith Story (who by this time was over her girlish misapprehension regarding the poet).

The house was overflowing with guests, some of whom, Browning included, had to lodge at Brahan Castle, the Stewart-Mackenzie family seat near by. Despite this added complication, Louisa managed to take the poet to one side so that they might have a chance to talk. She was probably the first to mention the dreaded M-word. An extremely tense and uncomfortable Browning blurted out that his 'heart was buried in Florence, and the attractiveness of a marriage with her lay in its advantage to Pen: two simple facts, – as I told her', he informed Edith, 'which I have never left her in ignorance about, for a moment', or so he had thought. Possibly it was the tone in which he spoke as much as the actual words that upset and humiliated Louisa. She 'exploded', he told Edith's father, 'in all the madness of her wounded vanity'. Rather than show her disappointment, she lashed out. She wanted 'to have the air of shutting the door in my face with a final bang' – to give the impression that it was she who had rejected Mr Browning.[57]

A shaken Browning left Loch Luichart the next day. As far as he was concerned, that meeting with Lady Ashburton would always be a 'nauseating remembrance', and she was for evermore the 'black beetle' – the 'bold she-shape'. He returned to the Benzons' isolated hunting lodge to put the finishing touches on the poem, entitled *Prince Hohenstiel-*

Schwangau, which he had begun there in August. This long dramatic monologue portrays an exiled ruler – a thinly disguised Napoleon III – in a run-down hotel room in Leicester Square, apparently alone with a prostitute, a cigar, and his thoughts. (Napoleon, in actual fact, had been living as a refugee in Kent since March 1871.) The Prince is a deeply flawed man who must struggle against his own faults and weaknesses, 'and when that is the case, depend on it, in a soliloquy, a man makes the most of his good intentions and sees great excuse in them': so Browning told Edith Story.

'Won't you just dislike it!' Browning told Isa regarding *Prince Hohenstiel-Schwangau.* She, like Elizabeth and most of the other English women in Italy, had 'silver-electroplated' Louis Napoleon.* He could do no wrong in their eyes, and they were not alone. In the 1830s and early 1840s, Louis Napoleon was admired as a revolutionary and socialist; created Emperor in 1852, he was widely regarded as the 'arbiter of Europe', especially after the Crimean War. The English men, however, thought differently. Whenever Tom Trollope entered Isa's Bellosguardo villa, he turned her portrait of Napoleon III to the wall. The Emperor was one of those topics on which the Brownings often disagreed. Robert explained to Edith Story that he actually wrote, 'that is, conceived the poem [*Prince Hohenstiel-Schwangau*], twelve years ago in the Via del Tritone – in a little handbreath of prose, – now yellow with age and Italian ink, – which I breathed out into this full-blown bubble in a couple of months this autumn that is gone'.[58] It may well have been the poem that Robert had originally intended to publish alongside Elizabeth's 'Napoleon III in Italy' but had torn up instead. 'Oh, oh, Ba,' he had expostulated in a letter to Isa the day France declared war on Prussia in July 1870, 'put not your trust in princes neither in the sons of men, – Emperors, Popes, Garibaldis, or Mazzinis, – the *plating* wears through, and out comes the copperhead of human nature & weakness and falseness too!'† *Prince Hohenstiel-Schwangau* – or at least its seed – was yet another work, like 'Mr Sludge, "the Medium"' and *The Ring and the Book,* which Robert had first envisaged while Elizabeth was alive but had put to one side so as not to upset her.

Like his flawed protagonists, Admetos and the Prince, Browning had had to face up to and wrestle with his faults and weaknesses. Ten long

---

* Silver-electroplating is an industrial process which deposits a thin layer of silver on a base metal object, thereby making an inexpensive item seem more valuable than it really is.
† In fact, Elizabeth was not that naive, for she admitted to Arabel that Napoleon III, 'being a man, after all, may be a cheat like the rest' (EBB to Arabel Barrett, 7–8 February [1860]).

years after his wife's death, this inner struggle was to mark a turning point in his life as a man and as a poet. He resolved never again to commit even the faintest 'show of bigamy', as Elizabeth had put it. She would always be his wife, in death as in life. They may have disagreed – even argued – about certain subjects, but she had never misunderstood Robert's feelings for her as had Lady Ashburton. Yet even Elizabeth, he knew now, had not been perfect. The success of *The Ring and the Book* made him realise that his angelic, impressionable wife had to some extent stifled his poetic imagination.

Just at the time in August 1871 when he sat down in the Benzons' hunting lodge to return to the poem which had first occurred to him all those years ago in Rome, Browning insisted to Isa, who had praised his verse: 'But, NO, dearest Isa, – the simple truth is that *she* [Elizabeth] was the poet, and I the clever person by comparison: remember her limited experience of all kinds, and what she made of it – remember, on the other hand, how my uninterrupted health & strength, & practice with the world have helped me.' His thoughts then turned to Julia Wedgwood's observation concerning *The Ring and the Book*: that the scientific interest in evil, which was wanting in Elizabeth, was unduly predominant in him. '*One* such intimate knowledge as I have had with many a person,' Robert continued in his letter to Isa, 'would have taught her, – had she been inclined to learn: though I doubt if she would have dirtied her hands for any scientific purpose.' He, on the other hand, not only understood evil but was somehow drawn to it. What is more, it informed his art; Elizabeth's poetic genius had needed no such sullied inspiration. 'All is best as it was – for her, & me too. I shall wash my hands clean in a minute, before I see her, as I trust to do.' But, first, Robert had to carry on with his life and write the poetry that was within him. In doing so, he would be forging a new relationship with Elizabeth. She would be his ghostly consort for ever but never again his Muse.

CHAPTER FOUR

Kid Gloves

1872–7

By November 1872, Browning had returned from Scotland and was once more safely entombed in Warwick Crescent amongst the Casa Guidi furnishings. Nevertheless, he continued to brood over his encounter with Louisa at Loch Luichart. Lust and loneliness had driven him, first to engage in a seemingly innocent flirtation, then to entertain the possibility of taking the handsome Lady Ashburton as his wife. But what had he been thinking? To remarry would be – to his mind – tantamount to banishing Elizabeth's memory, already fading, to oblivion. Were his earthly passions stronger than the love he felt for his dead wife?

Browning took up his pen, letting his mind wander back to scenes in Brittany which had earlier begun to rekindle his sexual desire: the buxom peasant girl of Ste Marie bending over her washing, Le Croisic's phallic stone monument, an enchanting gypsy dancer at St Gilles Fair in Pornic. He decided to make Pornic the setting for a new poem, *Fifine at the Fair*, and the gypsy girl its focal point. Lust and infidelity are its themes. The poem's anti-hero, the urbane Don Juan, is another one of Browning's flawed characters, like Napoleon III and Admetos, but one who was closer to home.

As Don Juan and his wife Elvire walk through the fairgrounds of Pornic, Don Juan falls for the dark charms of Fifine, who 'Points toe, imposes haunch, and pleads with tambourine!' He tries to justify his attraction, demonstrating the value of Fifine to his long-suffering wife. The gypsy girl seems to have a heavenly spark about her, some virtue – no, well then, at the very least she is something new, different. Elvire's silence throughout this monologue frightens her husband. 'Suppose you are a ghost!' he cries out. 'A memory, a hope, / A fear, a conscience!' He will resist temptation, Don Juan assures Elvire, and return home with her, never to wander more. No sooner has he said this than Fifine slips a note – an invitation to a tryst – inside the gentleman's glove. It seems that Don Juan had inadvertently thrown a gold coin in her tambourine. 'Five minutes shall suffice / To clear the matter up. I go, and in a trice / Return; five minutes past, expect me! If in vain – / Why, slip from flesh and blood, and play the ghost again!'

These prove to be ominous words. In the Epilogue, entitled 'The Householder', a widower addresses his dead wife, implying that Elvire has indeed slipped away to become, as Alexandra Orr observed, the mere 'phantom of conscience', which, in one sense, she is always felt to be. So Elizabeth had often appeared to Browning, and never more so than during the Ashburton affair. The Householder, who could just as easily represent Browning as Don Juan, pleads with his wife's ghost, 'Ah, but if you knew how time has dragged, days, nights! / All the neighbour-talk with man and maid – such men! / . . Who were they had leave, dared try / Darker arts that almost struck despair in me? / If you knew but how I dwelt down here!'

In the course of writing *Fifine at the Fair*, the gossip and 'neighbour-talk' surrounding Browning's disloyalty (as he perceived it) had indeed gained momentum, owing to the 'darker arts' of Lady Ashburton. At the end of March 1872 he was, Robert told Isa, 'very tired & bilious – & have accepted (quite against my habit) an invitation to spend a week in the country' with Lord Brownlow at Belton House, Lincolnshire. He had only been there a few days when Louisa swept in to join the house party. The poet fled as soon as was decent – the very next day. He 'felt excused from even looking at – much less, speaking to her', so Browning scrawled in a note to Edith before leaving Lincolnshire. Louisa used the poet's abrupt departure to her advantage, deftly orchestrating the rumours which flew about the corridors of Belton House. 'We all supposed he [Browning] was proposing to Lady Ashburton,' reported another house guest, Mary Gladstone, daughter of the Prime Minister; 'at least she let it be thought so.'[1]

That Robert had his dead wife's memory very much in mind as he worked at *Fifine at the Fair* is made clear by the poem's Prologue, entitled 'Amphibian'. In it a man bathing in the sea catches sight of a strange butterfly, a kind of spirit creature hovering above. Just as he seems to become part of the sky by floating, weightless, on the water, so the man hopes to be borne up to heaven – within reach of that certain soul above – through 'the passion and thought' of poetry. But what is she (the female butterfly) thinking as she hovers over him: 'Does she look, pity, wonder / At one who mimics flight, / Swims – heaven above, sea under, / Yet always earth in sight?'* It is a peaceful scene. But, by the end of Don Juan's misadventures, the impression of sunshine and fresh air has completely vanished; the holiday is over. In the Epilogue, the guilt-ridden Householder is once more ensconced in his claustrophobic dwelling, 'Every crumbling brick embrowned with sin and shame!' He is not certain if his ethereal visitor has come to haunt him or to comfort him. The tormented man pleads for death: 'Help and get it over!' he cries. But the ghost only answers, 'Love is all and Death is nought!' – words of comfort, or admonishment?

On the publication, two months later, in June 1872 of *Fifine at the Fair*, Browning's contemporaries were disturbed by the fact that, as Alexandra Orr remarked, it was impossible to see 'where Mr Browning ends and where Don Juan begins'. 'The speaker's tone,' she mused, 'has often the tenderness of one who, with all his inconstancy, has loved deeply and long.' Browning was aware of just how bold *Fifine* was; he was very doubtful as to its reception by the public. Its readers detected, as did Mrs Orr, a 'leaven of bitterness' in the poem – and, by implication, the poet.² Don Juan's unfaithfulness, together with the Householder's despair, threatened to defile the sacred myth of the Brownings' marriage – love and devotion in this world and the next – a myth which Robert had helped to perpetuate. Typical of the public's reaction to *Fifine at the Fair* was the *Westminster Review*, which thought the work 'an apology for himself and his poetry' and 'utterly unworthy of Browning'. There was something 'akin to profanation' about it.

Even more unsettling, Browning's Don Juan is not just a melding together of the anti-hero and his creator; he is also Everyman. Dante Gabriel Rossetti identified so closely with the poem that he thought Browning meant it as a personal attack. In October 1871 an article entitled 'The Fleshly School of Poetry – Mr D. G. Rossetti' had appeared in *The Contemporary Review*, savaging the 'fleshly' excesses – not to say, obscenity – of the artist's *Poems* (1870). Although published under a pseudonym, its author was soon revealed to be Robert Buchanan, a minor literary figure whom Browning knew. Rossetti was unnerved by the criticism, in part because it rang true. He was as much a sensualist as

---

* Julia Wedgwood may have suggested the image of sea and sky to Browning when she wrote to him on 10 February 1865: 'I know that your past is mirrored in your future, and the mere edge of land that divides the blue sky from the blue sea is small.'

an idealist in his art. In any case, he was already in a morbid state of mind, for several of these poems had only recently been exhumed, at his request, from his wife's grave, where they had lain since 1862. Moreover, when the 'Fleshly School' article appeared, the widower was deeply involved in an affair with the wife of his friend and fellow artist, William Morris.

In the December issue of *The Athenaeum*, Rossetti attempted to vindicate his work with a riposte, 'The Stealthy School of Criticism'; Buchanan fuelled the controversy the following May (1872) with a separately printed pamphlet, an expanded version of his previous piece. Rossetti, high on chloral and whisky, became convinced that there was a conspiracy against him. When, in June, he received a copy of *Fifine at the Fair* personally – and affectionately – inscribed by Browning, Rossetti was at first 'touched even to tears' at this sign of support from an old friend. But, as he read on, the poem seemed to turn hostile. It appeared to be mocking his own recently published *Jenny*, in which a chaste night spent with a prostitute leads the young hero to ponder her beauty and hidden virtues. (*Jenny* was one of the poems rescued from the worm-eaten manuscript.) Certain passages even seemed to be sneering at Rossetti's personal life: his (in his own eyes) disregard for his wife while she was alive and the desperate attempts to reach her after her death through seances and table-turnings. What else, the unhappy man thought, could Browning mean by those lines in the Epilogue – Browning who detested table-rapping and seances: 'Savage I was sitting in my house, late, lone .. / When, in a moment, just a knock, call, cry, / Half a pang and all a rapture, there again were we! – / "What, and is it really you again?" quoth I: / "I again, what else did you expect?" quoth She.'

Browning was, Rossetti concluded, 'his greatest enemy, determined to hunt him to death'.

Of course, Browning was not at the head of any conspiracy against Rossetti, but there may have been some truth to the latter's suspicion that *Fifine at the Fair* was conceived, at least in part, in reaction to *Jenny*. Browning had fallen out of sympathy with Rossetti, the scented quality of his poems and the effeminacy of his school, as he explained Isa Blagden. The critics, many of whom had also come to view the Pre-Raphaelites' art as emasculated, increasingly praised Browning's poetry for its manliness – its energy and vigour. Although sometimes unnerving, it never succumbed to sentimentality. Robert had told Isa, anticipating her adverse reaction to *Prince Hohenstiel-Schwangau*, that he was 'helpless against all sympathies I have to hurt, when once I begin quill-driving';

but Browning never meant *Fifine* as a personal attack on Rossetti. If this had been his intention, he would not have been so duplicitous – or so cruel – as to send his old friend and protégé an inscribed copy. Rossetti was at this point too unhinged, too paranoid, to consider the possibility that Browning had also felt sexually frustrated, that he too suffered from a guilty conscience towards his own wife. Rossetti refused ever to speak to Browning again.[3]

In 1871–2 Browning was, indeed, in the midst of an emotional crisis. At the front of the manuscript of *Fifine at the Fair*, he neatly penned a fragment from Pindar (in Greek), which translates as: 'Fair is the tale I have to tell, and courage that maketh straight for the mark prompteth my tongue to speak; it is a hard struggle to quell one's inborn nature.' This poem of some 2,500 lines was Browning's attempt to understand – and to quell – his sexual desires. There is also, scrawled in large Greek letters diagonally across the page, an exhortation from Aristophanes: 'Take courage! Forward! March! Oh well done, heart!'[4] – sentiments which closely echo those voiced in 'Prospice', the poem with which Browning had steeled himself to face the world following Elizabeth's death. Ten years on, life without her was not proving any easier.

The image of the fair in his Don Juan tale did not owe its whole inspiration to Browning's holidays in Brittany. As a small boy, Robert had been fascinated by the gypsies and travelling players who gathered on Camberwell Green for its own St Giles summer fête. Early in 1871 the poet – when first thinking, perhaps, of writing *Fifine* – had occasion to recall that same fair of his young days and, in particular, Richardson the showman. If, he explained in a letter to Isa Blagden, Richardson found that the action on stage had come to a halt, 'he set the blue fire burning, and ended the scene with éclat.'* The young Browning would wander amongst the gypsy caravans together with his wild cousins, the three Silverthorne boys. Their mother, Sarah Anna Browning's sister, had married a brewer from Peckham, which lies between Camberwell and New Cross. Of her three sons, James Silverthorne, three years Robert's senior, was his closest boyhood companion and mentor. They shared many of the same artistic passions, subscribing (along with their mothers)

---

* By the 1850s Victorian sensibilities had come to consider Richardson's itinerant group as an 'abomination' which 'tended to contaminate the youth of the district and annoy the more staid and respectable residents'. When the shows ceased, John Ruskin called it – not progress – but the triumph of 'our precious gentilities here at Camberwell' (Maynard, *Browning's Youth* 82).

to a new volume of poetry by 'a Young Lady',* venturing into London to watch Beethoven's *Fidelio* from the gallery, walking together over the fields to Dulwich Gallery or to Richmond to see Edmund Kean play Shakespeare's Richard III, returning on foot through the country lanes in the early hours of the morning. They were the sort of friends, Robert recalled in a poem following James's death in 1852, 'Who, arm in arm, deserve the warm / Moon-births and the long evening-ends'.†

As Browning approached his sixtieth birthday, in 1872, scenes of childhood, like Richardson's blue fire, were beginning suddenly – and vividly – to flash before him. This is a common experience amongst people as they grow older, but for Robert it was a two-edged sword. Although the past might serve as a blessed escape from present worries – Lady Ashburton's intrigues, the critics' indifference, Pen's academic failure – it was also a stick with which to beat himself, for, as Alexandra Orr noted, he always insisted that he had been 'worth little' in his young days.[5]

This ambivalence about the past was evident when, in 1870, Browning read William Rossetti's memoir of Shelley, appended to a new edition of his works. 'When I think,' he told Isa Blagden that January, 'how utterly different was the fancy I had of him forty years ago from the facts as they front one to-day' – by which time it was common knowledge that Shelley had cruelly abandoned his wife and children – 'I can only avoid despising myself by remembering that I judged in pure ignorance.' It was absolutely characteristic of Browning to be so hard on himself when, aged eighteen, he could not possibly have known or even suspected the unsavoury truth. Browning had learned of Shelley's infidelity in the late 1850s, only after he had written a preface, full of praise for Shelley, the man and the poet, to accompany a collection of newly discovered letters.‡ (To make matters worse, most of the letters turned out to be forgeries.)

Nevertheless Browning could not wholly obliterate the happy memories associated with Shelley, nor the poet's profound influence on his own life and work. In 1878 he would take the trouble to note in his copy of Shelley's *Miscellaneous Poems* that it had been given to him by his

---

* Unidentified.

† 'May and Death', written in 1853, first published in *The Keepsake* for 1857 and collected in *Dramatis Personae* in 1864. Sarianna had thought it would show proper respect for the family if Robert travelled from Paris to London for the funeral; but, when Elizabeth took fright at the idea of being left alone, Robert decided not to go (EBB to Arabel Barrett, 25 May [1852]).

‡ *Letters of Percy Bysshe Shelley: With an Introduction by R. Browning* (1852).

cousin, James Silverthorne, in 1826.* James's gift – a small duodecimo volume bound in plain calf – had been Robert's first taste of Shelley, who had drowned in Italy only four years earlier and copies of whose poems were then very scarce. Browning remembered how on that May evening he had sat in the family's Camberwell garden, listening to the night-ingales' song while poring over *Miscellaneous Poems* and Shelley's other works, which he had requested from his mother for his fourteenth birthday. Up until that point Robert had been besotted with the romantic adventurer Lord Byron; so much so that his death, in 1824, inspired the fledgling poet to compose Byronic verse. Over the next few years he collected them into a volume entitled *Incondita*. His parents, full of pride and wonder at their son's achievement, took the manuscript from publisher to publisher without success. But with James's gift of *Miscellaneous Poems* Shelley became Browning's God.

Robert preached his Shelley-inspired atheism to whoever would listen. He made a convert of Sarah Flower – a young woman seven years his senior – when he went with his parents to visit her family who lived near Hackney, in North London.† Sarah, who described herself as frank, unworldly, even a little dull and very deaf, confessed to a friend, the Unitarian minister W. J. Fox, that after talking to young Browning she 'turned recreant, and sided with the enemy'. She dared not let her father – despite his being a radical printer-journalist – 'have a glimpse at the infatuation that possesses me'. In May 1827 Sarah sent two of Robert's poems from *Incondita* to Fox, who was a literary editor as well as a minister, with a note explaining that 'the boy' Browning – just turned fifteen – was 'mad' to publish them. When he heard Fox's sober verdict, Robert promptly threw his juvenile poems in the fire.[6]

Nevertheless, Robert must have been gratified by Sarah Flower's genuine enthusiasm for his literary efforts. He shared with both Sarah and her sister Eliza not only a love of poetry but also a passion for the theatre and especially music. (Eliza compiled *Hymns and Anthems* and composed the tune of 'Nearer my God to Thee'; Sarah, something of a poet as well as an actress, wrote the words of the familiar hymn.) They also played a little at falling in love. Sarah might have bestowed favours on the young poet, but it was the pretty Eliza – two years older than

* At the same time, Browning rubbed and snipped out most of his juvenile markings (*Reconstruction*, A2109).
† The Flowers, who had known the Brownings for some time, moved to North London from Essex in 1827.

Sarah – with her dark eyes, dark ringlets, and 'a fragile sylph-like figure', who captured his heart.* They talked of Shelley on woodland picnics; the besotted youth watched Eliza perform her own compositions on the drawing-room piano; and it was for her that he 'played at verses and letters, instead of cricket and trapball', as he later admitted.[7]

But Robert's relations with the two sisters were to come to an abrupt end all too soon. On Benjamin Flower's death in February 1829, the terms of his will made Eliza and Sarah wards of his friend Fox. This was, in fact, a most awkward arrangement, for the forty-year-old minister, married with three children, was in love with his twenty-six-year-old ward, Eliza Flower. If Mrs Fox, a cold, extravagant woman, was not already aware of the situation, she certainly became so once they were all living under the same roof in Stamford Grove West. The seventeen-year-old Robert, a little in love with Eliza himself, may have guessed the truth; certainly he would have heard the rumours. In any case, he must have felt hurt and confused, if not somewhat foolish. Within a few months, in May 1829, the young man had abandoned not only his visits to the Flower sisters but also his studies at University College, London, preferring to remain in the relative safety and comfort of Camberwell.

Robert turned to his faithful Shelley for consolation, if consolation were needed. He continued to read and absorb the poet's works until, in 1833, he emerged from his teenage years with his first great poem in hand, *Pauline*, a confessional work in the Romantic tradition. It is particularly indebted to Shelley's *Epipsychidion*; but, whereas Shelley was inspired by his passion for a flesh-and-blood woman, the imaginary Pauline's only function is to listen patiently to the poet's extended monologue. Alexandra Orr thought that Eliza Flower might have been the model for Pauline. She has Eliza's gift for music; she indulges the young poet's feelings just as Eliza had done. But the inspiration behind *Pauline* was as much Browning's passion for poetry as his love for a woman. Nevertheless, there are autobiographical elements. An early friend, Joseph Arnould, was quite right to call it a 'poet-biography', Robert's 'own early life as it presented itself to his own soul viewed poetically'.[8] The

---

* Browning once confessed that it had been an earlier infatuation with a married woman fifteen years his senior which had prompted his very first attempt at Byronic verse. In an effusion of poetry the young Robert 'yearned for wastes of ocean and illimitable sands, for dark eyes and burning caresses, for despair that nothing could quench but the silent grave, and, in particular, for hollow mocking laughter'. It was then that his father thought of sending him away to school in Peckham (Sharp, *Life*, 27).

poet-narrator is the same age as Browning and, like Browning, is a gifted but rebellious young man who reveres Shelley ('Sun-treader') and has dabbled in atheism; his 'first dawn of life' was 'passed alone with wisest ancient books' (his father's library); the further search for knowledge only left him 'lonely, far from woods and fields, / And amid dullest sights, who should be loose / As a stag' (clearly a reference to his brief university career).

This poem of just over 1,000 lines was intended as the first in a medley of works from Robert's pen – not only verse but also prose and music – and the world was never to guess there was but one person behind it all. This 'childish scheme', as he called it,[9] which never got further than *Pauline*, had first occurred to Browning the night he saw Edmund Kean in *Richard III*; to mark its significance, he noted the place and date of the performance at the end of the poem: '*Richmond: October 22, 1832*'.* By the time Robert had seen him on stage, Kean, weak and bloated with age, was a shadow of his former self. Yet there were still flashes of brilliance: 'and there shall come / A time requiring youth's best energies': so Browning captured the mood in *Pauline*; 'And lo, I fling age, sorrow, sickness off, / And rise triumphant, triumph through decay.' The contrast between the actor's once-youthful brilliance and his sad decline fascinated Browning. He felt that he had himself undergone a transformation during his late teens, having 'too trusted my own lawless wants, / Too trusted my vain self, vague intuition', and it is the changes wrought in each stage of a poet's life which comprise the central theme of *Pauline*. 'I am no longer what I was / And I know I never shall be again': so reads the motto (in French) at the front of the poem.†

Browning published *Pauline* anonymously not only to fool the public but also to create a loophole in case the thing should prove a failure. His aunt, Mrs Silverthorne, was in on the secret as it was she who paid for its publication; so too were Sarianna and, presumably, his cousin James.‡

---

* Years later Browning dreamed that he was watching Kean in *Richard III* when the actor, in the scene where the ghosts rise, uttered a brilliant line which was not Shakespeare's but his own: 'And when I wake my dreams are madness – Damn me' (Allingham, *Diary*, 6 April 1876).
† From the poem *De lui-même*, wrongly attributed to the sixteenth-century French court poet Clément Marot.
‡ One of Mrs Silverthorne's grandchildren later claimed that Browning turned his back on the woman who paid for the publication of *Pauline* when she got into financial difficulties and had to leave England in around 1856, only a few years after her son James's death (BL Add 45563, ff. 204–5). The two families might have drifted apart for several reasons: Robert not attending James's funeral in 1851 and, around the same time, Mr Browning's involvement with Mrs Von Müller.

Robert sent a review copy – in strictest confidence – to William Fox in the hope that he might recollect meeting 'an oddish sort of boy' some years ago at the Flowers' Hackney home.[10] Fox responded more positively to *Pauline* than he had to *Incondita*. He wrote an article full of praise for *Pauline* in the *Monthly Repository*. It was also a very personal review. Only a few would have understood the reference to 'L—' dropping a poem of Shelley's in the wood from which sprang a delicate, exotic-looking plant 'with *Pauline* hanging from its slender stalk'. Eliza (or 'Lizzie') Flower had indeed lost Browning's copy of Shelley's *Rosalind and Helen* in Barnet woods.

Fox ensured that *Pauline* was noticed elsewhere. Robert soon confessed to his parents that he was the author, and together they pored over the review pages. A few critics were dismissive, but *The Athenaeum's* praise for 'the nature, and passion, and fancy of the poem' gave Robert and his parents particular pleasure and satisfaction. Despite the one or two positive column inches, not a single copy of the anonymous *Pauline* found a buyer. At least its publication had put Browning back in touch with Fox, whom the poet was to call his 'literary father', and also with Eliza and Sarah Flower. William Fox had finally separated from his wife and moved, with his two wards, to a cottage in Bayswater where Browning mixed with London's literary elite.

Fox had given the poem to John Stuart Mill to read and review. His comments were not printed at the time, but Robert read them in the margins of the philosopher's copy, which had soon found its way back to him. The young poet believed that he had already faced his demons – his lawless wants, vain self, and vague intuition – but Mill thought otherwise. 'This writer seems to me,' he noted, 'possessed with a more intense and morbid self-consciousness than I ever knew in any sane human being.' But he seems, Mill continued, to have gone straight from 'the self-seeking & self-worshipping state' to 'only the next step, .. despising his own state'. The fact that 'Pauline' is a 'mere phantom' – and a very long-suffering one at that – particularly annoyed Mill. The utilitarian ended his comments with the sound advice: 'I know not what to wish for him but that he may meet with a *real* Pauline.'[11]

Browning once told Miss Barrett that he invariably forgot his own verses after they were once on paper. In the case of *Pauline*, not only did he forget the poem, but he also thought it best left forgotten, which was not a problem as far as the reading public were concerned. *Pauline* was, he wrote in 1837, 'a poem not forgotten because never remembered'.

Browning did not like to admit that he was its author';* he was loath to show the poem to Miss Barrett twelve years later, calling it 'foolish', 'ambiguous', and 'feverish'. He also refused successive publishers permission to reprint it. The poem finally reappeared thirty-five years later, in the 1868 edition of his works, but only under duress and 'with extreme repugnance', as he made clear in the preface. Even more than half a century later, in 1888, Browning spoke of that 'unlucky' *Pauline*.[12]

As much as he admired Shelley, Robert determined to eschew the Romantics' subjective style of poetry. The subject of his next literary endeavour was a character firmly rooted in history, the sixteenth-century alchemist Paracelsus. Nevertheless, the depiction of a man, clever, ambitious, arrogant, something of a loner and impatient to know all, has elements of the young Browning's personality. He read the poem of over 4,000 lines aloud to Fox, who then found him a publisher. *Paracelsus* duly appeared before the public in August 1835, at the expense of the author's father. The adoption of the dramatic principle suited Browning, and the poem was very favourably reviewed. In *The London Journal*, Leigh Hunt – a friend and supporter of Shelley and Keats – admired its startling yet exquisite constructions. John Forster declared in *The New Monthly Magazine* that 'without the slightest hesitation we name Mr Browning at once with Shelley, Coleridge, Wordsworth'.†

Young Robert transformed not just his style of writing but also the cut of his cloth, for he was determined to present such a figure to the world as would render his heart impenetrable. The loose blouse and boyish impetuosity were replaced by a turn-down shirt collar, riding coat, and a self-possessed manner; neatly trimmed whiskers and lemon-coloured kid gloves enhanced the effect. The Romantic youth had, in a word, grown into 'a trifle of a dandy', quite 'the glass of fashion and the mould of form' – the phrases used by Fox's young daughter Tottie when, in about 1836, Robert paid a visit to the Bayswater cottage. Thomas Carlyle thought Browning, who first appeared before him at this time sporting a fashionable green coat, full of 'Cockney gracefulness, Cockney banter and logic'. 'Cockney' at this time signified a lower- or, in Brown-

---

* Dante Gabriel Rossetti guessed the truth early on when he came across a copy of *Pauline* in the British Library.

† In 1847 Browning's father wrote asking for a reader's ticket to the British Museum: 'I can procure the most satisfactory reference if required, but I think that the circumstance of my having been 44 years in the Bank, & being the father of R. Browning, author of *Paracelsus*, will be deemed sufficient.' It was not (BL Add 48340, ff. 91–2).

ing's case, middle-class Londoner. (The 'Cockney School' was a nickname given by the critic John Lockhart to Leigh Hunt and other London-based writers.) So successful was Browning's metamorphosis that the Flower sisters were hard pressed to see the poet boy of old in this young man, then in his early twenties. 'He has twisted the old-young shoot off by the neck,' the elder Miss Flower remarked rather wistfully: 'If he had not got into the habit of talking of head and heart as two separate existences, one would say that he was born without a heart.' Eliza was the first but certainly not the last to observe, as Henry James put it years later, 'two Brownings': the wholly original, passionate poet and the fashionable, practical man about town.[13]

Alfred Domett, another Camberwell lad who aspired to poetry, saw nothing disjointed or odd in Browning – except that he was particularly neat in his dress. These two young men, only a year apart (Domett being the older), were from the same mould, and they quickly came to share each other's hopes and dreams. Whereas Benjamin Flower had been a radical and bohemian, the Dometts were, like the Brownings, solidly middle class. Mr Domett had been adventurous, even daring, in his youth. (He ran away to sea when a boy and fought against the Dutch in 1781.) But, just as Mr Browning had traded a career as an artist for family life, so Alfred's father married, had nine children, became a shipowner, and swapped the sea for leafy Camberwell. Their sons yearned for something more. In 1829, at the age of eighteen, Alfred went off to St John's, Cambridge. Having, however, inherited his father's youthful restlessness, he left after four years – without a degree, brought out a small volume of poems in 1833 (under his own name), and travelled to Canada and North America. He had hoped that the New World might dispel the ennui he felt in the Old, but, as he confided to his journal, 'there is ennui in the backwoods as well as everywhere else.' His friendship with Browning probably dates from soon after his return to Camberwell in 1835, when Robert presented a copy of *Paracelsus* to him.[14]

Robert, too, had recently returned from foreign lands. In February 1834, probably through family connections at the Rothschild bank in Paris, Browning seized the chance to attend the Russian consul general on an embassy to St Petersburg. The twenty-two-year-old was entranced by this strange and wondrous city, its winter fair on the frozen Neva, the 'booths and droshkies and fish-pies' and 'the Palaces in the background', as he later recalled. He remained long enough to witness the colourful festivities which marked the breaking up of the ice and the arrival of spring. Robert thought he might combine his career as a poet with the diplomatic service, like Chaucer or Sir Philip Sidney. His subsequent application to accompany a British mission to Persia was, however, rejected. He was clearly disappointed. 'I don't go to Persia, & the Right Hon. Henry Ellis &c. &c. may go to a hotter climate for a perfect fool – (Heat at Bagdad in October, 124 Fahren. in the shade),' he growled at Sarah Flower (by this time wife of the journalist William Bridges Adams).[15] Thus, in 1835, ended Browning's diplomatic career.*

Robert and Alfred – both already published and well travelled – pictured themselves as brother-poets whose plan it was, in lieu of a university degree, to 'look on real life, / The life all new to me ... to look and learn / Mankind, its cares, hopes, fears, its woes and joys.'† Robert looked out for Alfred's 'hat above the holly hedge' from his bedroom window, and it was also to Alfred that Browning looked for constructive criticism of his poetry. 'Now this is what one wants,' Robert said of Domett's comments on his language and rhythm; 'how few men there are who will give you this.' Alfred thought his friend suffered from an overly reclusive and brooding personality. 'More exercise', he advised, along with more society 'and more cold water'.[16]

Robert took his advice, at least about getting out more. He had grown up surrounded by strong-minded, intelligent women – his mother, his sister, the Flower girls. Now, for the first time, he had the opportunity to fraternise with other like-minded young men, including Domett, who formed 'the set', or 'The Colloquials', as they often referred to themselves. Joseph Arnould, another Camberwell neighbour and old friend of Domett, was also of their number. He too dabbled in verse and in 1834 had won the distinguished Newdigate Prize for poetry at Oxford. Arnould, although the youngest (b. 1814), was the most sensible and level-headed of the three friends; an admirable dear good fellow, Browning said of him again and again; 'a prince', Domett called him.

The set frequently met in Limehouse, east of the City, where Domett's uncle George Frederick Young, a prosperous merchant and MP, had a solid-looking detached house. Other venues included the British

---

* In any case, diplomacy was a rich person's profession as young men invariably started out as unpaid attachés. For the first eight years of his embassy career, Robert Lytton, the Brownings' friend, had been expected to pay his own way. Browning wrote two poems while in Russia, 'Porphyria's Lover' and 'Johannes Agricola in Meditation' – both published in *Dramatic Lyrics* (1842).
† *Pauline.*

Coffeehouse in Central London, the Star and Garter in Richmond, and the Artichoke at Blackwall, which had a bow window over the Thames that looked out on to a forest of masts. The conversation on these occasions was joyous, if a little boisterous, mixing London gossip with literary subjects – Browning and Domett always backing Shelley, Arnould defending Byron. As to what else the young men got up to .. 'I gain the cove with pushing prow, / And quench its speed i' the slushy sand': so the young Browning's narrator describes an adventure under cover of darkness, which ends with 'two hearts beating each to each!' Yet, the morning after, it is 'the need of a world of men for me' ('Meeting at Night' and 'Parting at Morning', *Dramatic Romances and Lyrics*, 1845).

Perhaps it was at the British Coffeehouse, not too far from the theatre, that Browning told his friends about the opening night of T. N. Talfourd's *Ion* at Covent Garden on 26 May 1836. After the curtain came down, Browning, along with actor-manager William Charles Macready, critic John Forster, playwright and author Mary Russell Mitford, and poets Walter Savage Landor and Wordsworth, was invited back to Talfourd's house in Russell Square for a late supper. Browning had first been introduced to Macready at Fox's Bayswater cottage in 1835; through Macready he came to know Forster, and through Forster he met just about everyone else in the literary world. Soon he was to be seen at literary soirées, mixing with Anna Jameson, Fanny Kemble, Harriet Martineau, Charles Dickens, Leigh Hunt, Talfourd, B. W. Procter, Landor, Thomas Carlyle, Edward Bulwer-Lytton, Alfred Tennyson, and John Kenyon. Talfourd, Procter, and Landor all wrote poems addressed to the promising young poet, and Macready practically forced *Paracelsus* on his friends, amongst them Lady Pollock. When she confessed she had not read that work, 'he lifted his eyebrows; he muttered expressions of wonder; he once or twice said, "Oh, good God!"' The lady pleaded that her babies left her little time, to which he replied: 'Hand over the babies to the nurse, and read *Paracelsus*.'[17]

Thus it was that Browning found himself sitting down to dinner with such distinguished company after Talfourd's triumph at the theatre that May evening in 1836. The interminable toasts began, and Talfourd himself proposed Robert Browning, 'the youngest poet of England'. Wordsworth then leaned across the table, so the story goes, and said, 'I am proud to drink to your health, Mr Browning.' (Henry Crabb Robinson, also at Talfourd's that night, claimed that the white-haired

Wordsworth left long before the toasts began.) Before the whole – and very inebriated – company had dispersed, Macready whispered in his ear: 'Write a play, Browning, and keep me from going to America' – on tour. It was the best night of Robert's life, and Domett & Co. must have been dumbstruck and just a little envious.[18]

Browning duly wrote *Strafford* (a verse drama set in Stuart England), and Macready agreed to produce it the following year, in 1837. The late-night script meetings, the painful rewrites, the tedious rehearsals, the tantrums – the stupidity of the actors who thought 'impeachment' a synonym for poaching – Browning eagerly shared all this with his fellow Colloquials. And, of course, the young men were there amongst the 'clappers' (as one of them put it) – along with the playwright's proud father – on *Strafford*'s opening night, 1 May 1837, at Covent Garden. Macready had intended *Strafford* to run for a month; but the public had other ideas, and it closed after only five performances.[19]

This setback did not stop Browning. Domett and Arnould knew him to be a man driven by his own creativity. 'I am greatly afraid you overwork that brain of yours,' Alfred scolded him more than once, 'which is absurd, besides a shame; for a thing of such fine material is not for drudgery, even at Poetry.' Arnould thought that, whether Robert failed or succeeded, the effect would be the same, to make him 'work, work, work'. Certainly he had worn down the strength and spirits of Macready with endless talk of major rewrites as well as minor alterations to *Strafford*, even after the play had closed. The work did not come easily to Robert, as chronic headaches during this period show. But he continued to write, for, as he told a friend, 'I cannot remember the time when I did not make verses and think verse-making the finest thing in the world.'[20]

In a discarded preface to *Strafford* (the text was published in 1837, to coincide with the opening performance), Browning had admitted that he had turned to the play in an effort 'to freshen a jaded mind' which had been too hard at work on another project, an epic poem entitled *Sordello*. Browning had first begun to compose *Sordello* in 1833, following *Pauline*. He was to struggle with it over seven long years, putting it down to travel to Russia and begin work on *Paracelsus*, then to try his hand as a playwright with *Strafford*. He again took up *Sordello* only to find that a Mrs Busk had published a long poem on exactly the same subject in 1837; stirred but not shaken, Browning travelled to Italy in April 1838 'intending to finish my poem among the scenes it describes', as he told a friend. As with *Paracelsus*, Robert had chosen an historical figure as the subject of his drama, another mask to hide behind. Sordello was a thirteenth-century Provençal poet, mentioned by Dante in his *Purgatorio*, who became caught up in the Guelf–Ghibelline wars of northern Italy. The plot of Browning's poem (such as it is) forces Sordello to choose between poetry and politics.[21]

Throughout the period that he was writing *Sordello*, Browning had continued his struggle to throw off Shelley's influence. He was not always successful, but the exertion helped to define him as a poet. *The Athenaeum* had called *Paracelsus* an imitation of Shelley. Elizabeth Barrett knew better. 'If *Paracelsus* was anything,' she later declared, 'it was the expression of a new mind, as all might see – as *I* saw.'[22] Yet the similarities are there, for Browning was invariably drawn to classic Romantic heroes – in particular, Shelley's Prometheus and Alastor – who strive for perfection but ultimately fail or are punished for their hubris. Paracelsus is just such a one, as is Sordello.

Choosing the dramatic (that is, objective) over Shelley's subjective style, therefore, was not enough; Browning was also determined to turn a deaf ear to the Romantic's mellifluous voice. 'The fact is,' he told Domett in 1843, 'in my youth (*i.e.* childhood) I wrote *only* musically – and after stopped all that so effectually that I even now catch myself grudging my men and women their half-lines.' At the start of *Sordello* the poet pleads with Shelley's ghost, 'come not near / Now – not this time desert thy cloudy place / To scare me, thus employed, with that pure face .. this is no place for thee!' The poet Sordello, like the young Browning, intends to be one of the 'setters-forth of unexampled themes'. He wrestles with his craft, 'slow re-wrought / That Language, – welding words into the crude / Mass from the new speech round him, till a rude / Armour was hammered out.'* Reading *Sordello*, a fellow Colloquial despaired that the craftsman Browning had omitted essential words while 'jamming together' the rest, causing them to 'gleam and sparkle' so intensely 'the mind is at once dazzled and fatigued'. Here is that striking and innovative voice which Leigh Hunt had glimpsed in *Paracelsus* and which Elizabeth Barrett characterised as 'language cut into bits', which one has to piece together, but with depth and power enough to glorify the puzzle.[23]

Yet, the portrayal of Sordello is not a wholly objective one; the young Browning identified with the Provençal poet even more than with the

---

* The image of forging language is one to which Browning would return in *The Ring and the Book*.

German alchemist. His interest in *Sordello*, as he confessed in a later preface to the work, lay in 'the development of a soul' – the soul of a poet, a subject which *Pauline* had also explored. We see Sordello develop from a young age, reflecting that same crucial period in Browning's own artistic life. While wandering through the 'drowsy' wooded paradise that is his home (not unlike Robert's romanticised view of Camberwell), the young Sordello discovers 'verse, the gift': 'Then how he loved that art! / The calling marking him a man apart / From men.' And yet, he yearns to be a man of the world, a man of his time. Sordello is 'Sundered in twain; each spectral part at strife / With each; one jarred against another life; / The Poet thwarting hopelessly the Man.' Browning, similarly torn apart, put on a public face to shield his creative spirit, although there would be those, like Eliza Flower, who consequently thought him without a heart. For Sordello, the exertion in choosing between his poetic ideal and a more pragmatic course finally proves too much, and he dies in the prime of life (unlike the real-life Sordello who lived to a ripe old age): 'what he should have been, / Could be, and was not'. Even more than fame, fear of failure is what often drives ambition, and so it was with the young Browning as he agonised over *Sordello*.

'Out of that aching brain, a very stone, / Song must be struck.' *Sordello* was a daring enterprise for any young poet. Nevertheless, Robert had high hopes for it. He burst in upon Macready, the actor quipped, 'before I had finished my bath, and really *wearied* me with his obstinate faith in his poem of *Sordello*, and of his eventual celebrity'. To Eliza Flower, Robert wrote unashamedly: 'Do me all the good you can, you and Mr Fox.' But the difficulties Browning experienced, the false starts and the rewrites, the headaches, all told on the epic poem. (At nearly 6,000 lines it was half as long again as *Paracelsus*.) The work which might – should – have served as his poetical manifesto was generally believed to be unintelligible. Tennyson remarked that he understood only two lines of *Sordello*, the first and the last – 'Who will, may hear Sordello's story told' and 'Who would has heard Sordello's story told' – and they were both lies. Thomas Carlyle's wife Jane declared that she had read it through without discovering whether Sordello was a man, a city, or a book. Dante Gabriel Rossetti, although he would read fifty pages at a time from *Sordello* to the Brotherhood, conceded that there were some eccentricities in the text. He attributed these to Sarianna, who had performed the singular female feat of copying *Sordello* for her brother.[24]

Following the publication of *Sordello*, a blight fell upon his very admirers, Robert later told Edmund Gosse. The critics had a field day, calling the poem 'trash, of the worst kind' and 'unreadable'. For his part, Browning lost all faith in the critics. He took offence at the silence of his two staunchest allies, John Forster and William Fox, refusing to talk to the one and speaking very unkindly of the other, according to Macready. Yet, through it all, Browning never stopped believing in himself as a poet. How else could the twenty-eight-year-old justify living at home, being supported by his parents? He had had to fight too many battles against well-meaning friends and devoted parents to give up now. One can just hear the well-wishers: 'Your uncle's brewery is so close to home – your cousin James has already started there';* 'Your father could find you a good position in the bank'; 'Look at those nice young men, Mr Arnould and Mr Domett – they seem to enjoy the law.' (Joseph and Alfred had entered Middle Temple together.) Even Anne Procter, B. W. Procter's wife, ventured to remark to John Kenyon that it was a pity that young Browning had not 'seven or eight hours a day of occupation'.[25] The poet's wry comment on it all: he would rather spend his days grooming horses.

Robert drove himself as hard as ever. Despite *Strafford*'s short run, he had not turned his back on the theatre, far from it. Macready lost all patience with the young man who – insolent puppy – positively plagued him with play after play, all historical verse dramas. In 1839, before *Sordello* had even been published, Browning turned up with *King Victor and King Charles*, which Macready thought a '*great mistake*' and told him so. In 1840 it was *The Return of the Druses*, prompting the actor to think the poet's intellect 'not quite clear'. Neither was produced. His publisher, Moxon, then suggested Browning publish his plays and shorter poems in a series of inexpensive pamphlets in an attempt to woo back the public. The result, *Bells and Pomegranates* (1841–6), met with some success; however, the critics could not resist commenting anew on *Sordello* and Browning's obscurity. In such a vein, one reviewer queried the significance of the title of *Pippa Passes*, the first in the *Bells and Pomegranates* series: 'Passes what? – The critic's comprehension.'

Domett, acting as his friend's warm advocate and champion, composed a savage riposte, *On a Certain Critique on 'Pippa Passes'*. Robert still looked on Domett as his fellow poet. On its publication, he had sent Alfred a copy of *Sordello* with the enclosed note: 'I hope you will like it

---

* James Silverthorne eventually took over the family brewery but did not make a success of it.

a little, and beat it famously yourself ere the season is out.'[26] Domett had continued to write and to publish. Prompted, perhaps, by Robert's enthusiasm for Italy, Alfred had followed in his footsteps the following year and produced a poem on his return, entitled *Venice* (1839). However, when it made little impact on the literary world, his parents no doubt urged Alfred to take his law studies more seriously. With other sons to worry about, they simply could not afford to be as indulgent as the Brownings, who not only covered the living and travel expenses of their only son, but also paid his publication costs up to and including the last number of *Bells and Pomegranates*.*

Domett and Arnould were called to the bar in 1841; Arnould married the same year. Arnould was lucky – or sensible. He had decided quite early on to give up his 'deviation into rhyme', having 'such a just appreciation of what poetry is and requires that I shall be saved from the ridicule of adding another to the metrical posers of the day'. With typical bonhomie, he added that he would still have as great an interest as ever in 'all that concerns the tuneful tribe'.[27] Arnould positively enjoyed the law; Domett did not. He wanted something more out of life, and his friends seemed to expect it of him. An opportunity then presented itself; Alfred's cousin William Young had recently gone out to New Zealand. (William's father, whose house in Limehouse the Colloquials had occasionally commandeered, was active in the New Zealand Company.) Domett hastily decided to follow his cousin. 'Are there not .. two points in the adventure of the diver,' Paracelsus declares in a passage marked out by Domett, 'One – when, a beggar, he prepares to plunge, / One – when, a prince, he rises with his pearl?' With nothing to lose and everything to gain, Alfred took the plunge into uncharted waters. He borrowed £70 from Arnould and wrote a hurried note to Robert, returning some books and explaining that he had no time to call to say goodbye to Mr and Mrs Browning. He then boarded ship for New Zealand on 30 April 1842, just before his thirty-first birthday. He was hoping to find not only financial security but also poetic inspiration on the other side of the world.

Robert's first letter to Alfred, written a few weeks after his friend's departure, was heartfelt and spoke of 'my real love for you – better love than I had supposed I was fit for'. 'Begin at the beginning,' he enquired eagerly; 'tell me how you are, where you are, what you do and mean to

---

* The exception was *Strafford*, which the publisher subsidised.

do – and to do in our way, for live properly you cannot without writing.' As for himself, 'the true best of me is to come, and you shall have it.' Browning lent his friend's departure a decided air of romance in the poem 'Waring', begun almost as soon as the ship had set sail for New Zealand. The fanciful figure of the title has given all his friends 'the slip', leaving behind him 'sundry jottings, / Stray-leaves, fragments, blurrs and blottings, / Certain first steps', which had already 'borne out whoe'er believed / In more to come!' 'Puppies that we were,' the narrator laments; 'Oh, could I have him back once more, / This Waring, but one half-day more!'

But what had seemed poetic quickly turned prosaic. 'At nine-and-twenty,' Arnould solemnly reflected, 'one does not swear eternal friendship so easily as at nineteen.' Browning echoed this same sentiment when he wrote to Domett in October 1843, 'I make no new friends, which sometimes seems a pity – but I strengthen myself with the old.' The Colloquials still met, but Domett had clearly been the glue that held them together, and they missed his more practical sense. '*You* will come back again, I know,' Robert told Alfred, 'having set my heart on it, but *do* come back safely and soundly, in limb as well as life!' Browning continued to write, sending the poems intended for *Bells and Pomegranates* to the one person whose judgement he trusted. But, more often than not, the poem in question was already in print before Domett's comments came back. 'The five-months' inevitable voyage is bad enough,' Robert complained once, 'without these stoppages and delays meantime and before.' The time and distance seemed to try their patience, and the more Alfred criticised the obscurity of his verse, the less Robert listened.[28]

Perhaps because Arnould was the more faithful and even-tempered correspondent, Domett came to confide in him more and more. He was having a hard time of it. He learned on his arrival in New Zealand that his cousin William, who had preceded him, was dead – a drowning accident. Not only the farming venture but also the locals were proving desperately disappointing: 'the lounging shooting-jacket existence', Alfred moaned, Mrs Wray's aesthetic tea, Miss Essex's piano, the brandy and whist-cum-cigar evenings. New Zealand was, in fact, 'Camberwell with a dash of the Coal-Hole': so Arnould agreed with Domett's descriptions of the place; ''tis the effigy of the place in its totality of seediness, stale tobaccoism, & attorney clerkdom.'[29]

At least Arnould could report that Browning was doing splendidly, from one height scaling another, like his own 'gier-eagle strenuously beating the silent, boundless regions of the sky' (quoting from *Paracelsus*). In 1843 he wrote to Domett of Browning's new play, *A Blot in the 'Scutcheon* (a tragedy set in the eighteenth century), that it would certainly produce 'a higher opinion than ever of Browning's genius and the great things he is yet to do'. The truth was, Macready had only agreed to produce it at Drury Lane Theatre after much hesitation and delay. (Robert's gift of *The Pied Piper of Hamelin* to Macready's bedridden son, Willie, the previous year may have helped sway the actor.) When the prompter, a grotesque person with a red nose and wooden leg, did the first read-through of the play, the actors laughed from beginning to end; Macready prevaricated as to whether or not he would take the leading part; and not a shilling was spent on scenery or costumes, so Browning recalled years later.[30] After many arguments, misunderstandings, and tantrums, he and Macready fell out completely. Robert would not even allow his sister Sarianna to attend the opening night. Suffice it to say, *A Blot* ran in February for three nights only.* Arnould always did tend towards optimism when it came to his friends' affairs.

Browning appreciated his friends' zealous support, but he was becoming increasingly cynical, especially when it came to the critics. 'They take to criticising me a little more, in the Reviews,' he reported to Domett in May 1843, ' – and God send I be not too proud of their abuse! For there is no hiding the fact that it is of the proper old drivelling virulence with which God's Elect have in all ages been regaled. One poor bedevilling idiot, whose performance reached me last night only, told a friend of mine, the night before that, "how *in reality* he admired beyond measure this and the other book of Mr B.'s, but that *in the review,* he thought it best to," &c. &c.' And this man 'boasted that he got £400 a year by his practices! But New Zealand is still left me!' Yet still Robert did not despair. 'I feel myself so much stronger, if flattery not deceive,' he confided to Alfred in July 1844; 'I really seem to have something fresh to say.'

Browning was determined to move on, but it was a journey which was to take him beyond his old friendships. His correspondence with Domett began to peter out. Nor did Arnould have much communication with Robert. Their paths did not seem to cross any more; in any case, Arnould wrote to Domett, he was so engrossed in the law nowadays that he felt less equal to converse with Browning on their old topics.[31] Robert,

---

* Later performances of *A Blot* took place in London in 1848 and 1849.

for his part, had found a new interest and, he hoped, a new direction in his life. He hinted as much to Domett in a letter dated 13 July 1846: 'I have some important objects in view with respect to my future life – which I will acquaint you with next time I write, when they will be proved attainable or no.'

But no other letter followed. Rather, Robert left it to Arnould to inform Domett of his elopement with Miss Elizabeth Barrett of Wimpole Street that September. As far as Arnould could see, the rather old but gifted invalid Miss Barrett, with 'one of those tyrannical, arbitrary, puritanical rascals' for a father, had first fallen for their dashing and talented friend Browning; his love had then followed 'as by contagion or electricity'.[32] From where the young lawyer – and the rest of the world – stood, she was the one who had everything to gain by the romance. But Robert knew it to be otherwise; Elizabeth, sickly, housebound creature that she was, had a large and loving family around her (even if her father's love proved stifling). She had the time and leisure to carry on a lively correspondence with friends and, more importantly, to write poetry that was much admired by critics and public alike. Although her life had comprised so many sadnesses and so few pleasures, still she was content with her lot, or until she knew otherwise. No, it was the restless, searching Robert who first fell in love with Elizabeth – at least, the idea of her – before they had ever met.

Elizabeth was puzzled by Robert's ardour to begin with. She was a sickly, frail creature who saw very few people. Robert, on the other hand, lived close to the great social vortex and was, by his own admission, entangled with invitations. He had learned, as young men in their twenties do, how to be a man about town, talking, posturing a little, dancing the polka – and putting up with 'one lady whose *head* could not, and another whose *feet* could not, dance!' In 1843 Arnould had informed Domett that 'from the habit of good and extensive society he has improved in this respect wonderfully. We remember him as hardly doing justice to himself in society; now it is quite the reverse .. in fact, altogether I look upon him as *to be* our foremost literary man.' Although his poems and plays were neither as popular nor did they sell as well as Browning would have liked, his literary friends stuck by him. He had always been, so Elizabeth told him, a chief favourite with his cousin, John Kenyon.* She had also heard from an unnamed source that he was

---

* Elizabeth perhaps did not tell Robert that when John Kenyon first proposed introducing

to be married to a Miss Campbell! No, he did not know a Miss Campbell; the gossiper might have meant Miss Fanny Haworth (or a lady he did not mention, the lead actress in his plays, Helen Faucit), but that was not true either. Yet he confessed to Elizabeth that he had always hated society; he had only put up with it for the past six or seven years so as not to let any possible advantage pass him by. One day when he called at Wimpole Street Robert complained of being weary in his soul. Elizabeth asked, was he 'tired of a same life & want change?'³³ She could see that he felt dissatisfied.

Robert cannot but have been flattered by Miss Barrett's genuine appreciation of his work, which dated back to *Paracelsus*. She even had kind – and encouraging – words to say for *Sordello*. 'It is like a noble picture with its face to the wall just now – or at least, in the shadow,' she told him.* Moreover, Browning found Elizabeth's critical comments not only more tender and perceptive than Domett's but also more immediate, for they arrived by return of post rather than many months later by packet from New Zealand. She also steered him away from the theatre, thinking his work merely 'ground to pieces between the teeth of vulgar actors and actresses'. 'I have been guilty of wishing, before this hour,' Elizabeth wrote in January 1845, 'that you would give the public a poem unassociated directly or indirectly with the stage, for a trial on the popular heart. I reverence the drama, but – .'† Her attentions, her praise, her advice, even her teasing – his love letters, she claimed, were full of 'Sordelloisms' – all helped to sustain Robert's confidence in his ability.³⁴

Moreover, Miss Barrett stood for everything that Browning – and his friends – were not. They were middle class and of limited means; she was aristocratic and wealthy. Elizabeth understood the difference and

---

him, he explained that the poet was discouraged by his reception with the public: 'Poor Browning,' Mr Kenyon said.

'And why poor Browning?' Elizabeth asked. 'Because nobody reads him,' 'Rather then, poor readers!' (EBB to George Barrett, 30 March 1842.)

* Neither *Pauline* nor *Sordello* appeared in the 1849 edition of Browning's collected works. After their marriage, Elizabeth encouraged him to revise *Sordello*, which he thought his best performance, even after the publication of *Men and Women*. However, when the latter also failed with critics and public alike, he abandoned his efforts.

† Browning had written three more plays since *A Blot*: *Colombe's Birthday*, *A Soul's Tragedy* and *Luria*. In February 1845 he told Elizabeth that *Luria* would be his last play. None was performed at the time, but all were published. When *Colombe's Birthday* was eventually staged in London, in 1853, Elizabeth asked Arabel to tell George and her other siblings that 'if they go to anybody's play, they are to go to ours, & clap & shout & save us from damnation' (EBB to Arabel Barrett, 12 April 1853).

loved Robert for – or in spite of – it. The young Browning liked to fancy South London as a sort of pastoral idyll. 'Our little hills are stiff and springy underfoot with the frozen grass,' he had written once to Domett from New Cross, 'and you crunch the thin-white ice on the holes the cattle have made – hedge & tree are glazed bright with rime – (to speak Bucolically).'

'So you really have *hills* at New Cross, & not hills by courtesy?' was Elizabeth's riposte to this and other such pretensions. Sometimes, in jest, she called Robert an aristocrat, she told her sister Henrietta early in their marriage; 'I cry out "*à bas les aristocrats*" – because he really cares a good deal about external things,' such as houses and furniture, horses and carriages. Perhaps he had an artist's sense of grace, she admitted, but she chose to make fun of it.[35]

Elizabeth, however, had twice the share of artistic temperament when it came to the family finances, for she never fretted about money matters. She thought the fuss Robert made over pounds, shillings, and pence morbid and unpoetical – he even had an account book. He claimed he worried for *her* sake, not his, 'but of what consequence is it, *whom* one is anxious for,' she appealed to Arabel after one of the couple's many wrangles over money, 'when the anxiety is perfectly unnecessary? You ought to hear me scold sometimes.'[36] Her own casual disregard for 'external things' – and the tradesmen's bills – betrayed her privileged background. Robert thought a great deal about such things for, as the son of a humble Camberwell clerk, he understood all too well their value in other people's eyes. He was also aware of exactly how much they cost, unlike his wife.*

But all this was in the future. In 1845 Miss Barrett was, like Eliza Flower, an older, intellectually independent woman, who opened up a whole new world to the ambitious young poet. She even resembled Eliza a little, with her dark ringlets and fragile physique. Alfred Domett and 'the set' had also helped to expand his horizons, but, with Domett gone, Browning found that he preferred female society to male, after all.

---

* 'Here lies Browning,' he penned one day during their marriage, 'In bile he lived frowning / With bile he died drowning – / And the worst of his ill / Was not bile so much as a bill' (M. Stone, 'Bile and the Brownings'). The poet inscribed Pen's first account book with the following lines: "'Twas a saying of might with the great Mr Lowndes / Take care of the Pence and not care of the Pounds! / For the Pence may escape you, – light volatile elves: / But the full-bodied Pounds can take care of themselves' (ABL). Needless to say, Pen took after Elizabeth in his attitude to money.

Elizabeth quickly usurped Domett's place as Robert's fellow poet, friend and critic;* and, of course, she was eventually to become 'more than friend' to him. In February 1845, only a month after they had begun to correspond – and before they had met face to face, Browning told Miss Barrett that 'I had rather hear from you than see anybody else .. never you care, dear noble Carlyle, nor you, my own friend Alfred over the sea, nor a troop of true lovers!' And yet Browning admired Carlyle enormously for his radicalism and his doctrine of perseverance and endurance; he had hung on the Scotsman's every word in his lectures on *Heroes and Hero-Worship* (1840). 'I never was without good, kind, generous friends and lovers,' he tried to explain to Elizabeth two weeks later, 'perhaps they came at the wrong time – I never wanted them.'[37]

Although he refused to admit it, happiness had made Robert giddy, ungrateful, and ever more disdainful of the past. The good-natured Arnould noticed only the change for the better which had come over his friend. In November 1845 he wrote to Domett that 'Glorious Browning is as ever, but more genial, more brilliant.' Robert, however, had begun to think of his old friendships as a burden. 'But a word to-night, my love – for my head aches a little,' he wrote to Elizabeth that same November. 'I had to write a long letter to my friend at New Zealand, and now I want to sit and think of you and get well.'[38] In 'Waring' the speaker clearly envies his friend the possibility of travelling east, to Spain, Russia, even India. Now it was Browning's chance to weigh anchor and sail into uncharted waters.

And he never looked back, nor did he again direct a letter to Alfred in New Zealand. Two years into his marriage – not long after Elizabeth had suffered a second miscarriage – he did wistfully recall the companion of his youth in 'The Guardian-Angel': 'My love is here. Where are you, dear old friend? / How rolls the Wairoa at your world's far end? / This is Ancona, yonder is the sea.' Yet, even as he wrote these words, Browning was in the midst of trying to recover, and properly dispose of, reminders of the past, especially the, as he put it, 'boyish rubbish' – verses and letters – which he had sent to Eliza Flower when he was an awkward adolescent. Before he left for Italy, he had asked if he might see her and

---

* When in early 1846 Domett urged Browning yet again to write more intelligibly, the poet told Elizabeth that his comments were not to be taken seriously. For her part, Elizabeth had damned Domett's poetry with faint praise: 'As to the *Venice* it gives proof (does it not?) rather of poetical sensibility than of poetical faculty? Or did you expect me to say more?' (RB to EBB, [20 July 1846]; EBB to RB, [7–8 December 1845].

take her hand, knowing that she was dying of consumption. He was certain she would allow such a visit, 'remembering what is now very old friendship'.[39] Yet, after he learned of Eliza's death in 1846, he longed to pitch all tangible evidence of his feelings for her into the fireplace.* Browning wanted nothing to remind him of his former life, nor did he want anyone else to know anything about it. He had done with all that, having reinvented himself yet again. He had indeed taken to heart the motto at the front of *Pauline*: 'I am no longer what I was / And I know I never shall be again.' 'O dearest, if indeed I tell the past,' Robert may have urged a naturally curious Elizabeth as the poet does Pauline, 'May'st thou forget it as a sad sick dream!'

That blue blaze of the old Camberwell showman Richardson flashed before Browning with startling éclat one Friday afternoon, the last day of February 1872, when he walked into Warwick Crescent to be greeted by Sarianna, breathless with the news that an old friend had turned up on the doorstep from the other side of the world.

Alfred Domett had returned from New Zealand. Not knowing Browning's address – or even whether the poet lived in London or abroad – Domett had looked him up in the Directory. When he knocked at the door of 19 Warwick Crescent, he asked the servant if Mr Browning once lived there. 'He *does* live here Sir.' He was not at home, but Miss Browning was. Alfred sent up his card and soon saw Sarianna – really not much altered, he thought, considering thirty years had passed – coming down the stairs. 'Mr Domett!' Miss Browning warmly greeted her old Camberwell neighbour, assuring him that her brother would be delighted to see him.[40]

When, later that afternoon, Sarianna told him of Alfred's visit, Browning did indeed wish to see his old friend as soon as could be arranged.

---

* Browning first tried, and failed, to get his letters and verses back in 1846 by writing to Sarah Flower Adams, but to no avail. On the news of Mrs Adams' death in 1848, he wrote to R. H. Horne; he petitioned Fox himself and, after his death in 1864, he asked his daughter, Tottie Bridell-Fox, for any juvenile thing of his she could lay hands on. Browning duly burned it all, although two early poems from *Incondita* have survived: 'The Dance of Death' and 'The First-Born of Egypt'. Robert Browning Senior had long bemoaned his son's habit of destroying old poems and letters.

Eliza Flower's spirit 'appeared' to Browning during a seance in 1853. It was this incident which sparked the first serious disagreement between husband and wife on the subject of spiritualism. 'If those are spirits,' Robert told Elizabeth, 'they are *evil* spirits' (EBB to Arabel Barrett, [28–9 November 1853]).

He enclosed a note with Sarianna's invitation for Monday; there was something he needed to say – to clear the air – before they met. Having turned the matter over in his mind the rest of the evening, Browning sat down at his desk the following morning, took up pen and paper and began: 'Dear Domett, How very happy I am that I shall see you again!' He then blurted out: 'I never could bear to answer the letter you wrote to me years ago, though I carried it always about with me abroad in order to muster up courage some day which never came: it was too hard to begin and end with all that happened during the last thirty years. But come and let us begin all over again.'[41]

Domett read these words with a tremendous sense of relief, for he had not known how to interpret Browning's failure to reply to his letter of condolence (on the death of Mrs Browning) sent from New Zealand in 1864. It had begun, 'My dear friend of old days,' and went on to tell of the delight – all those years ago – when he realised that 'The Guardian-Angel' was an 'apostrophe' to himself. 'It was like a flash of light,' Domett had confided, 'piercing from the upper world down into the God-abandoned glooms of our infernal "bolge" where one lay lost for ever in a life-in-death or a death-in-life worse than death itself.' 'What a loss,' he bemoaned, 'has the breaking of our acquaintance and communion been to me.'[42]

Several years later, when he was thinking of returning to England, Domett confided to Joseph Arnould his concerns about Browning's silence. Arnould, whose law career had eventually taken him to Bombay in 1859 as Chief Justice, assured him that 'Browning could never have received the letter you spoke of: had he done so he would have answered it.' Mind you, he had heard that the poet was in all the grand houses in London and made a god of, but Browning 'has not, and never had, any of the English hard and brusque arrogance about him'. Sadly, he himself had lost touch with the poet since his wife's death – he was a trustee of their marriage settlement – but, really, it was 'quite as much through my fault as his'. 'I am sure,' Arnould ended with characteristic good humour, 'you will find he will be delighted to see you when you go back.' And so, on that February day Domett knocked at 19 Warwick Crescent and encountered Sarianna, just as lively and friendly as ever, amidst the dark, heavy Italian furniture – a strange contrast.[43]

Sitting together in front of the fire the next Monday afternoon, Browning and Domett might have recalled the reunion scene in *Paracelsus* – the poem which had marked the beginning of their friendship nearly forty years earlier – when Paracelsus cries, 'Heap logs and let the blaze laugh out!' His long-lost friend Festus replies, ''Tis very fit all, time and chance and change / Have wrought since last we sat thus, face to face / And soul to soul – all cares, far-looking fears, / Vague apprehensions, all vain fancies bred / By your long absence, should be cast away, / Forgotten in this glad unhoped renewal / Of our affections.' After lunch the two old friends took a walk through Kensington Gardens. If not on this occasion, then on their next meeting Browning would have wanted to hear about New Zealand, its politics and prospects; his old friend had risen to become Prime Minister of the country, after all.* He had tried, he told Browning, 'sticking your poems "into the entrails" of the *better* sort of *folk*' out there. He read *Paracelsus* to his son Alfred when a boy – just a year younger than Pen – he had even named a street in Napier after Browning.[44]

Browning must at some point have asked the inevitable question: 'Well, Domett, how does it feel to be back home?' Alfred found the weather, in Hamlet's words, 'O *horrible, horrible*, most *horrible*,' as he told a New Zealand correspondent, 'Arcturus'. And the English themselves were 'as thick-skinned and fashion-driven or nose-led as ever' – fatuous and self-satisfied to a degree that was 'truly irritating if not disgusting'. He was, by the way, surprised to see a '*liveried*' servant at the door of 19 Warwick Crescent; so, at least, Domett wrote to Arcturus. If he repeated any of this to Browning, the latter might have taken Alfred to task (as he did in a letter of 1843) for his old 'habit of painting everything *en noir*'.[45]

Domett mentioned, of course, that he had been following Browning's career with interest and had read all his poetry. Robert confessed that the poem he was just then trying to finish, *Fifine at the Fair*, was 'the most metaphysical and boldest' he had written since *Sordello*. Perhaps it was the mention of *Sordello* that prompted Alfred to remind the poet of that festering sore, 'his obscurity'. Browning's books sold pretty well, Domett explained to Arcturus, but nothing like what they ought to if his old friend would only '*condescend* to be a little more clear'. Within a week of their first meeting Domett had presented Browning with a large, heavy,

---

* Domett had made his reputation, first as a journalist then as a government official, defending the settlers' right to acquire Maori land – by whatever means – in direct opposition to the Treaty of Waitangi (1840). Bad feeling between the two groups had led to the First Maori War in 1843, in which Domett lost many friends and colleagues. His time as Prime Minister (1862–3) coincided with the Second Maori War, really a series of guerrilla attacks.

and well-travelled manuscript; it was a 14,000-line poem on New Zealand entitled *Ranolf and Amohia*.* Might his old friend advise him about publishers or, better yet, speak to his own publisher about it? Browning received such requests all the time from would-be authors and cherished friends (Isa Blagden, for one, who hoped to earn something from novel-writing); but, of course, he would do what he could. He knew how much it would mean to Domett to see in print 'the work of your life (in a sort)'.

'*Waring* came back the other day, after thirty years absence,' Browning informed Isa a month later, in March 1872, 'the same as ever – nearly: he has been prime minister in New Zealand for a year and a half, but gets tired, and returns home with a poem.' Alfred Domett was the same person who had boarded ship all those years ago, still restless, still painting everything black, still scolding his friends. But he had not lived up to his old friend's expectations. 'Waring' had not progressed beyond those 'certain first steps' towards poetic brilliance – at least, the London pub-lishers did not think so. After months of negotiations, none was willing to take on *Ranolf and Amohia* except Browning's own publisher, George Smith, and only then if the author covered the costs.

Domett had also found Robert just as of old. The public face – the young man from Camberwell, happy to mix literary chat with a little gossip, careful in his dress and with his money – was perhaps more polished, but the creative spirit it concealed was as ambitious, innovative, and uncompromising as ever. He was even still addicted to kid gloves, as young Tottie Fox had noted all those years ago; it was one of Browning's 'peculiarities', Alexandra Orr remarked of the grey-haired poet, that he could never endure to be out of doors with uncovered hands.[46]

Yet to those who had only known him since he came to prominence with *Dramatis Personae* and *The Ring and the Book*, Browning was a complete mystery. Julia Wedgwood's old aunt was not alone in thinking that he did not look at all poetical. Mary Gladstone, a young woman Pen's age, was positively horrified when she realised that the loud man puffing and blowing and spitting in her face at dinner was the poet Browning. 'I tried to think of Abt Vogler,' she confessed, 'but it was no use – he couldn't ever have written it.'† Mrs Thomas Aldrich, an Ameri-can woman, was reduced to tears when she saw Browning, her girlhood

---

* Domett's *Ranolf and Amohia* throws a veil of romance over Maori life during the early part of the century. It is far removed from Domett's own experiences in New Zealand.
† Mary Gladstone eventually came to regard Browning as a friend and called his death 'an unget-overable loss'.

idol, carefully remove the collapsible top hat from under his arm and sit upon it through a fashionable London dinner, just like a banker might. 'The words I had longed to say,' poor Mrs Aldrich recalled, 'all the things I had ached to say – vanished.'[47]

Some people, like the barrister Rudolf Chambers Lehmann, thought it a great virtue that Browning was 'free from bardic pose'. Benjamin Jowett had no idea there was such a thing as a 'perfectly sensible poet in the world' until he met Browning. But these two men were in the minority. By the mid-1870s it had become almost a cliché to declare that the urbane, polished Browning was, in Julian Hawthorne's words, 'a rich banker, .. a perfected butler, no one would have suspected him of poetry'.* *The World* described people's surprise on discovering 'that the crabbed and mystical poet is identical with the possessor of the compact little figure, the urbane and genial bearing, the well-made clothes'; something of a dandy, in fact. 'Well-dressed you *are*, Sir,' Browning's tailor told him, 'but "almost a dandy" – *no*!' 'Tennyson hides behind his laurels, and Browning behind the man of the world,' was one bon mot recorded by Lilian Whiting. Thomas Hardy called him '*the* literary puzzle of the 19th century'.[48]

It was at this period, in the 1870s, that Henry James first met Browning. Like so many others, James could not reconcile the author of *Men and Women* with the 'loud, sound, normal, hearty' presence, 'bustling with prompt responses and expected opinions and usual views'. He was a great chatterer, 'but no Sordello at all'.[49] The novelist reckoned that there were two Brownings and explored the idea in the short story 'The Private Life' (written after the poet's death). The narrator inadvertently discovers that there are, literally, two Vawdreys (as the Browning figure is called); one goes out, the other stays at home, slaving away in the dark.† One is the genius, the other is the bourgeois, and it is only the bourgeois who talks, circulates, and is so popular.

But, it was the Anglo-American community in Florence who were most surprised to discover that the famous poet Robert Browning was, in fact, that same Mr Browning they had known in Italy. As far as his fellow expatriates were concerned, Browning had simply been the husband – a very good husband, too – of Mrs Browning, the celebrated

---

* Nathaniel Hawthorne was more down to earth than his son Julian, thinking Browning 'logical and common-sensible, as, I presume, poets generally are in their daily talk'.
† Browning sometimes described himself, when working hard, as keeping to 'the dark'.

poetess. At that time, Frances Cobbe wrote of her life in Italy, 'I do not think that any one, certainly no one of the society which surrounded him, thought of Mr Browning as a great poet, or as an equal one to his wife .. The utter unselfishness and generosity wherewith he gloried in his wife's fame, – bringing us up constantly good reviews of her poems and eagerly recounting how many editions had been called for, – perhaps helped to blind us, stupid that we were! to his own claims.' Mrs Kinney of the cross-dressing escapade echoed this view of Browning: 'no one would have taken *him* for a poet.'[50]

Browning had indeed been a different person in Italy. He had lost all faith in himself as a poet. Although he had had setbacks before, the failure of *Men and Women* – the volume which, he believed, represented his new life with Elizabeth and the best of him for some time to come – proved too much for Robert. But if the marriage had stifled him as a poet, Elizabeth had brought out the best in him as a man, and he knew it. He was no longer the one looked after by family and friends; it was his turn to look after someone else. His duty was, not to write, but to take care of Elizabeth. He ceased to think about his own career and took pride in another's success. As Fanny Kemble said, Browning behaved like a Christian to his wife. He had written in 'One Word More': 'God be thanked, the meanest of his creatures / Boasts two soul-sides, one to face the world with, / One to show a woman when he loves her!' Robert never suffered fools gladly and was always quick to anger, but Elizabeth was usually able to coax him out of his black moods, sometimes resorting to a bit of gentle scolding and teasing. Thus it was that, as his wife's body lay in the next room in Casa Guidi, Browning had vowed to live out the years left to him in her 'direct influence, endeavoring to complete mine, miserably imperfect now, but so as to take the good she was meant to give me'. He withdrew from society for a time, but eventually he had put his kid gloves back on, adopted the urbane and genial bearing to match, and faced the world again.

But Domett, who until early March 1872 had not heard from Browning since before his marriage to Elizabeth, knew nothing of all this. At the beginning of April that year, Browning solemnly ushered Domett into his study in Warwick Crescent where he kept his most treasured keepsakes. It was only the previous week that he had encountered Lady Ashburton at Lord Brownlow's country estate in Lincolnshire. The poet must have been feeling particularly fragile that day of Domett's visit, imagining – like the Householder in the Epilogue of *Fifine at the Fair* – 'every crumbling brick embrowned with sin and shame!' Alfred described the scene in Browning's study for his New Zealand friend Arcturus: 'There was a little desk at wh. Mrs. B. wrote all her poems (you know she has been dead 11 years) – he showed me her classical books with her own *annotations* in *Greek* etc. on their margins – he and "Sarianna" always speaking of her as if she were something almost supernatural in excellence – talent – and modest unconsciousness, etc. etc.' It was almost as though Browning were trying to conjure up Elizabeth's spirit to soothe his own, as does the Householder: 'just a knock, call, cry, / Half a pang and all a rapture, there again were we!'

It was all lost on Domett; Elizabeth Barrett Browning meant nothing to him. Did Robert see from the blank, even bored, expression on his face that to Alfred the little desk, the annotated books, all these were nothing more than curiosities, museum pieces? Even as he held her books in his hand, Elizabeth's memory seemed to be slipping through Robert's fingers as relentlessly as sand in an hourglass. Her good, calming influence was also starting to fade. Browning's moods became more black and his poetic vision darker, as is clear from his next poem, *Red Cotton Night-Cap Country*, and the circumstances surrounding it.

Robert was still out of sorts and cranky owing to the Ashburton business. When he heard that Annie Thackeray, whom he had known since she was a girl, had (allegedly) begun a rumour about his remarrying, he cut her dead in public. Even when they found themselves neighbours on the Normandy coast that summer of 1872 (the poet had returned to St Aubin for his holiday), he refused to have anything to do with her. Happily his friend, the French critic Joseph Milsand, was also there and had the good sense to tell him (as Elizabeth surely would have done) that he was acting foolishly, *comme un enfant*. The Brownings had first met Milsand in Paris in 1851, shortly after his glowing review of Browning's poetry appeared in the *Revue des Deux Mondes*. Elizabeth had never seen 'more reverence for the truth', she told Arabel, 'more patience in seeking the truth, & more steadfastness in holding by it. We value him deeply. I would trust that man in any contingency of life, & Robert says he feels just as I do.'[51] Patience Milsand certainly had. Owing to his mother's disapproval, he had waited twelve years, until her death, to marry the woman he loved. When Sarianna and her father were forced to leave England in 1852, Milsand helped them settle in Paris, and on his deathbed old Mr Browning asked to see him one last time to shake hands. In the same letter (March 1872) in which Browning described 'Waring's' return, he wrote to Isa regarding Milsand: 'no words can express the love I have for him, you know – he is increasingly precious to me.'

Thus it was that Milsand was able to convince Browning to swallow his pride and apologise – after a fashion – to Annie Thackeray. The poet marched over to Annie's cottage and blurted out in his characteristic manner: 'Don't ask. The facts are not worth inquiring into; people make mischief without even meaning it. It is all over now.' Thereafter the old friends met up often, sometimes strolling together on the beach, and Browning told Annie of the poem he had in mind. Like *The Ring and the Book*, *Red Cotton Night-Cap Country* was based on an actual event – a particularly grim suicide near St Aubin – and he was excited by its dramatic possibilities. Milsand had given him the facts of the case. A profligate man (whom Browning calls Léonce Miranda), living with his mistress on the family estate, had incurred the anger of his mother. Her reproaches – and later her death – so affected him that he attempted suicide several times by throwing himself in the Seine, plunging his hands into the fire, and finally leaping off a tower. In his will, Miranda left everything to the Church, reserving a life interest for his mistress who had remained by his side throughout his ordeal. His relations contested the will, questioning his sanity. Browning has it that when Miranda threw himself from the tower he intended, not to commit suicide, but to test his new-found faith – a faith which, he prayed, would not let him fall.

Annie Thackeray suggested that Browning call the tale 'White Cotton Night-Cap Country', after the peculiar headdress worn by the local Normandy peasants. Browning snatched at the idea, replacing 'white' with 'red' to reflect the gruesome nature of the story, and dedicated the work – just over 4,000 lines long – to Miss Thackeray. 'And so, here happily we meet, fair friend!' begins the poet, celebrating their rapprochement, 'Again once more, as if the years rolled back / And this our meeting-place were just that Rome / Out in the champaign .. Or on the Paris Boulevard.'* Annie was delighted by its publication in May 1873 – until she read the very moral Mrs Trimmer's disapproving review in the *Daily News*. She must then have wondered what had come over her in Normandy – had she had too much sun? Mr Browning could be so persuasive but how could she have thought a story of suicide and

---

* Browning also paid tribute to Milsand in *Red Cotton Night-Cap Country*: 'Milsand who makest warm my wintry world / And wise my heaven, if there we consort too'.

madness suitable material for a poem? Carlyle remarked to William Allingham that 'nobody out of Bedlam ever before thought of choosing such a theme.'[52] 'Remember,' Browning tried to comfort Annie, 'that everybody this thirty years has given me his kick and gone his way.'*

'This thirty years' .. Robert was clearly thinking back to *Sordello* and its hostile reception – and so were the critics. In her review of Browning's next poem, *Aristophanes' Apology*, Mrs Oliphant asked: 'What has come to [Mr Browning] in these latter days? What bewildering spirit has carried him round the fatal circle and landed him once more in those wilds of confused wordiness which made *Sordello* the wonder and the fear of all readers?' And she was not the only critic to imagine that Sordello's demon had returned to haunt Browning; *The Athenaeum*, too, made the comparison between *Sordello* and his latest work. Ironically, with *Aristophanes' Apology* (1875) Browning was seeking to explain and justify his view of poetry to critics and public alike. Although he told Domett around this time that there was not a single living critic whose opinion he valued 'a snuff', he still huffed and puffed at their reviews.[53]

To help him in his poetical defence, Browning resurrected the popular heroine of *Balaustion's Adventure*. 'When we meet Balaustion again, in *Aristophanes' Apology*,' Alexandra Orr remarks in her Browning handbook, 'many things have happened': the death of Euripides, the fall of her adoptive city, Athens. So too had many things happened in Browning's life since Balaustion's first appearance before the public four years earlier: his clash with Lady Ashburton, Domett's return and, in January 1873, the sudden death of Isa Blagden. Her death must have come as a terrible shock to Browning. He always said that he would return to Italy and spend the rest of his days basking in the sun with Isa, like the 'two bright and aged snakes' in Matthew Arnold's poem *Empedocles on Etna*; he made a great joke of it in his letters to her. But now she was gone, his dearest friend, faithful correspondent, and close confidante. She had been the only person who, Robert once wrote, could 'give me one hand – with the feeling on my part that the other holds that of my own Ba'.

---

* In 1882, as Browning solemnly sat in the crowded Sheldonian Theatre, waiting to receive an honorary DCL from Oxford University, a red cotton nightcap was lowered from the upper gallery. It alighted on the wrong head, that of a Professor of Divinity, before it found its way to the poet's white hair. Browning thought it was good fun, but the authorities did not and proceeded to discipline the prankster until the poet intervened, exclaiming, 'Let that poor boy off!' (Irvine and Honan, 474–5).

Henry James, who visited 'Our Lady of Bellosguardo' (as Isa's friends called her) not long before her death, saw her as the last link to a 'vanished society' – one of 'friendships and generosities, in a setting of Florentine villas and views, of overhanging terraces and arched *pianterreni*, of Italian loyalties and English longings'.[54] Perhaps the return of Balaustion, so like Elizabeth, helped to console Robert as he sat down to begin his new poem just months after Isa's death. At 5,705 lines, *Aristophanes' Apology* is, apart from *The Ring and the Book*, Browning's longest poem.

In *Aristophanes' Apology* Balaustion is called upon by a drunken Aristophanes to defend Euripides. The objection is that Euripides, seeking only truth, shaped his characters out of 'earth's dung' in the belief that 'what's most ugly proves most beautiful'. Browning also searched for truth amongst the filth – the human mire which the middle classes, thinking they had escaped, tried so hard either to ignore or to reform. It is this 'morbid psychology of the soul' (in the poet's words) which makes both Euripides and Browning seem so modern to us – but which denied them easy popularity in their own time. 'He spoke quite o'er the heads of Kleon's crown / To a dim future,' Balaustion says of Euripides; how is one to know 'the fate of wise words launched / By music on their voyage', a voyage that extends beyond the life of a poet? But the vessel carrying *Aristophanes' Apology* was as weighed down by erudition as *Sordello's* had been, and people could not fathom it.

As he looked for the subject of his next poem, *Sordello's* demon still lay hold of Browning, forcing his thoughts to linger around that same painful period of his life, thirty years before. It was then, so Robert told Domett, that he had first heard the story of an unscrupulous gambler, the Baron de Ros, on which *The Inn Album* (1875) is based. In Browning's version, the old roué, having lost a large sum at cards to a younger man, offers him – to defer payment – the woman (now married) whom he once seduced and whom, by extraordinary coincidence, the younger man once loved. The lady, in horror and desperation, commits suicide. The younger man, when he realises the full extent of the gambler's wickedness, attacks and kills him.

The young Browning probably knew the story through Fanny Kemble's play, *An English Tragedy*, based on de Ros. In 1838 she had sent the manuscript to Macready from the United States, where she was then living with her husband. Perhaps Macready waved Kemble's script in Browning's face – after he had burst into the actor-manager's dressing room with yet another historical verse drama – as if to say, 'Now this,

even if it is too shocking to stage, at least has power, poetry, and pathos.'*
It is more likely, however, that Fanny Kemble discussed the story with
Browning in 1845 (by which time she had left her husband) when they
met at the Procters' house in London. Browning confided to Domett
that he had originally intended to make *The Inn Album* a tragedy for the
stage, something he had not attempted since his marriage to Elizabeth.
However, he gave up the idea on learning that Tennyson had, albeit late
in life, joined the list of poets turned playwright (which included Southey,
Byron, and Wordsworth) with *Queen Mary*. Tennyson's play had a
successful theatre run; *The Inn Album* was not so well received. Swinburne
praised the poem, comparing it favourably to the novels of Balzac. More
typical, however, were the reviewers, like J. A. Symonds in *The Academy*,
who declared *The Inn Album* nothing more than a 'penny dreadful' in
which 'we dislike the victim almost as keenly as we dislike the betrayer
of his story.' Privately, Symonds confessed that it was impossible to like
the poem: 'one feels so injured by its base negativeness.'[55]

Friends and critics alike thought that Browning was writing at unpardonable length and with indecent haste. He completed *The Inn Album*,
a poem of over 3,000 lines, in just two months, June and July 1875. It
was as if he were trying desperately to make himself forget the world
around him. A world of troubles had indeed come down on Browning
just at this time, involving himself and most especially Pen.

Browning had been going out of his way to avoid his old friend Carlyle
'for a reason' – this was all the explanation he gave to Domett in February
1874. Nearly two years later, in December 1875, he went as far as to say
that he had kept away from Chelsea on account 'of some one who visited'
Carlyle. 'Did not say who,' Domett confided to his diary, 'nor did I care
to ask.' That 'some one' was the Scotsman's close friend, Lady Ashburton,
and the 'bold she-shape' now had a familiar.

To Browning's great relief, there had not been another encounter with
Louisa since Lord Brownlow's house party in March 1872. However, in
August of that year one of Louisa's beloved country estates, Melchet,
nearly burned to the ground while she was in residence. Browning,
knowing how much the house meant to her, wrote her a brief note,
ending: 'Pray return no answer: I know you will accept the sympathy I

---

* Although Macready found *An English Tragedy* 'full of power, poetry, and pathos', he thought
it too 'immoral' to stage; moreover, it might also have been awkward as de Ros was still alive
at the time (J. H. Baker, 'The Poet, the Actress, and the Shifty Peer: Another Look at the
Origins of Browning's *The Inn Album*', *Browning Society Notes*, 24 (1997), 54–70).

should be too pained in attempting to stifle altogether. God bless you ever, dear friend, above the chances and changes of this life!' The tragedy had subdued the poet's anger, but not Louisa's – nor Hatty Hosmer's on her behalf, for the sculptress had fallen passionately in love with her patroness and, according to Browning, had become her 'cat's paw'.[56]

Hatty sent Louisa declarations of love addressed to 'my sposa' followed by further allegations of the poet's shameful character. The two women circulated these 'calumnies' (Browning's word) amongst their friends, many of whom, such as Adelaide Sartoris, were also his friends. Hatty even tried to turn the Storys against Browning by showing a letter to Louisa in which he disparages his old friends, thus revealing 'what a double dealer he is'. On reading the offending passage Mrs Story exclaimed, 'Well, I never,' and William Story remarked, 'That is not the best of letters I should expect a man who calls himself my friend to write.' At least, this was Hatty's version of events. However, no rift seems to have appeared between Browning and the Storys; indeed, the rift, although temporary, was between the Storys and Lady Ashburton.* In Roman days Browning had once called Hatty 'a darling', but now, he told Edith Story, 'I have done with Hatty, for once & always. Had I believed stories about *her*,† many a long year ago, and ordered her away from people's houses on the strength of them, I should have lost a friendship I used to value highly: but I have gained some pleasant memories by being less ready than she to believe slanderous gossip.'[57]

The social atmosphere must have seemed like pure poison to Browning – worse than the thickest, most noxious London fog – for the slanderous gossip linked his name not only to Lady Ashburton but also to another lady. Pen had been staying with the Benzons at their house above Loch Tummel, Perthshire, in September 1873 when Ernest Benzon suddenly took ill and died. On the widow's return to London, Browning

---

* It seems that Browning had been annoyed with the Storys – perhaps he blamed them for dragging him to Scotland in 1869, when all the trouble began. Rosalind Howard wrote in her diary that autumn that the poet was 'terribly irritable with the Storys & spoke rather unkindly of them to me' (Surtees, 'Browning's Last Duchess').

† The Brownings knew of Hatty's sexual proclivities, although Elizabeth had been a little naive at first. One day Elizabeth and Mrs Corkran were discussing the fact that the actress Charlotte Cushman and the translator of George Sand, Mathilda Hayes, had 'made vows of celibacy & of eternal attachment to each other' in a sort of 'female marriage'; they lived together and even dressed alike. Elizabeth happened to say, 'Well, I never heard of such a thing before.'

'Have'nt you?' said Mrs Corkran. 'Oh, it is by no means uncommon' (EBB to Arabel Barrett, [22 October 1852]).

père went to see her almost daily at her magnificent house in Kensington Palace Gardens where he had enjoyed many a musical soirée featuring such guest performers as Joachim, Mendelssohn, Clara Schumann, and Rubinstein. Elizabeth Benzon, besides having been very kind to Pen, was the sister of Frederick and Rudolf Lehmann, both good friends of the poet. John Forster and his wife, aided and abetted by Charles Dickens' daughter, Mary, began to circulate rumours as to the forthcoming marriage of Browning and Mrs Benzon, adding maliciously that the Benzons' adopted daughter, Lily, had been driven from the house by the conduct of Mrs Benzon and Mr Browning. Robert Lytton, the Brownings' friend from Florence days, told Forster in June 1874, nine months after Benzon's death: 'If the marriage ever *does* take place, I shall write the epitaph on a lost belief.' Suffice it to say, no marriage took place, nor did Lily leave home.[58]

Forster and Browning had always had a volatile relationship, ever since the days of *Sordello* and *Strafford*. The former was either a supreme hypocrite or a man with a bad conscience, for just a year later, in 1875, he wrote to congratulate Browning on *The Inn Album*. Browning replied: 'I am happy you recall our old days and conversancy – my own friendship was too vital to succumb at the interruption of *that*. Nor have I at all doubted of your good will to me.'[59] If the poet ever came to hear of the rumour concerning Mrs Benzon and himself, he cannot have known its source. Two months later Forster was dead.

And then there was Pen. The young man did not know what to do with himself. Although he snapped at his father, it was evident that he still desperately wanted to please him. Perhaps marriage would suit. Sometime in early 1873 Pen asked Miss Fannie Coddington to be his wife. Browning had known the Coddingtons, a wealthy New York family, since 1866 when they went through London on the Grand Tour. In 1868 the family moved to England; they were Alexandra Orr's neighbours in Kensington Park Gardens. Although Pen was at Oxford and Fannie at boarding school in the Isle of Wight for the first few years, the two young people met each other during the holidays – certainly at the Benzons' magnificent Christmas parties, for Ernest Benzon's sister-in-law, Mrs Henry Schlesinger, was a cousin of the Coddingtons. Fannie completed her education in 1872 and returned to live in London where she came across Pen at many a London gathering. Afternoon calls were exchanged between Warwick Crescent and Kensington Park Gardens, and Fannie met Pen on at least one visit to the Benzons' house in Scotland. However, when Pen asked her to marry him, the nineteen-year-old girl said no. Perhaps she did not fancy the young Mr Browning. In any case, she probably did not want to leave her family, especially as her parents might one day return to New York, which they did in 1875. Pen did not tell his father of the proposal. From Pen's point of view, Browning would either have disapproved – how could he think of marrying without a pro-fession? – or been disappointed when Pen failed yet again to attain his end; Miss Coddington came from such a good family, after all.

The unsuccessful suitor went to Scotland at the Benzons' invitation to take solace in his favourite pastimes, shooting grouse, stalking deer, and fishing. However, when his host took ill that September and the house was overflowing with doctors and nurses, Pen went to stay at Birnam, near by in Perthshire, with the artist John Everett Millais, who shared his enthusiasm for outdoor sports. Millais, one of the founding members of the Pre-Raphaelites, had first met the Brownings in London in 1852, when a three-year-old Pen solemnly presented one of his own drawings to the artist.* More than twenty years later, perhaps recalling the boy's pride in those childish drawings, Millais encouraged young Browning to set up an easel beside him as he worked on his painting, *Scotch Firs*. Millais was so impressed with Pen's efforts that he suggested the twenty-four-year-old devote himself to art.

Browning was delighted. Pen a painter! Well, he had always envied the life of an artist. He immediately went about trying to set Pen up in his chosen career. With whom should he study? The artist Felix Mos-cheles, yet another Benzon relation, suggested Jean-Arnould Heyermans in Antwerp, and to Antwerp Pen went, taking lodgings above a butcher's shop. The Continent was the obvious place for an artist. Despite the magnificent studio windows in London, those who worked there, like Frederic Leighton, regretted 'the interminable hours, days, and weeks of enforced idleness spent in the continuous contemplation of the ubi-quitous yellow fog, depressing the spirits all the more for recalling the memories of distant lands, where the sun shines in the sky, and sheds its gold over all things, where the fragrance of a thousand blossoms, not the soot of a thousand chimneys, is wafted in through open windows, and where grime does not blot out the heavenly face of nature.' Even at six years of age, Pen had appreciated the difference. After the Brownings'

---

* The following year, 1853, Millais fell in love with – and eventually married in 1856 – Ruskin's wife, Effie, who was from Perthshire.

CLOCKWISE FROM TOP:

The engraving of Robert Browning which hung beside those of Wordsworth and Tennyson in Elizabeth Barrett's Wimpole Street bedroom.

Sarianna Browning, Robert's clever, lively, sensible sister who kept house for him after Elizabeth's death.

The 'good, unworldly, kind-hearted' Robert Browning Senior, the poet's father.

Elizabeth Barrett Browning, a year before her death, with her 'Florentine boy' Pen.

Pen Browning with his father around the time of his matriculation at Christ Church, Oxford, and the publication of *The Ring and the Book*.

Michele Gordigiani's portraits of the Brownings, commissioned by Sophia Eckley in Italy, which later hung in Robert's London dining room.

CLOCKWISE FROM TOP:

W. P. Frith's 'Private View at the Royal Academy' (1881), showing Frederic Leighton in the centre, speaking to the woman seated, Anthony Trollope on the left with catalogue in hand, Robert Browning between them and, on the right, a 'foppishly dressed' Oscar Wilde.

The American sculptor, William Wetmore Story, whose career Henry James was to describe as 'a sort of beautiful sacrifice to a noble mistake.'

Robert Browning and Joseph Milsand studying one of Pen's paintings, 1882.

CLOCKWISE FROM TOP LEFT:

Arabel Barrett, Elizabeth's younger sister and confidante and Robert's 'steadfast friend' in London.

Isa Blagden. No other human being, Browning told Isa after his wife's death, 'can give me one hand – with the feeling on my part that the other holds that of my own Ba.'

Edith Story, William Story's daughter, who thought that Browning was in love with her.

Alexandra Orr, painted by her brother Frederic Leighton. People thought 'there was something tender between Mrs Orr and Browning.'

CLOCKWISE FROM TOP LEFT:

The sensitive and intelligent Julia Wedgwood, whose strong feelings for Browning became the subject of gossip.

The handsome and impetuous Louisa Lady Ashburton 'exploded in all the madness of her wounded vanity' when Browning made clear that his 'heart lay buried in Florence.'

The adoring American Katharine Bronson whom Browning came to regard as 'more than Friend.'

CLOCKWISE FROM TOP LEFT:

Alfred Domett, Browning's Camberwell neighbour whom he immortalised in the poem 'Waring' after Domett's emigration to New Zealand.

'*Waring* came back the other day, after thirty years' absence,' Browning told Isa Blagden, 'the same as ever – nearly.'

Max Beerbohm's caricature of the Browning Society. Browning, depicted sitting down, was gratified but also mortified by the attentions of the Society and its 'Apostles'.

ABOVE: The small party which
gathered in Kent to witness Pen
Browning's marriage to Fannie
Coddington, 4 October 1887.
Sarianna is sitting to the left of the
bride, Robert is behind her.

RIGHT: Robert and Pen Browning
photographed by Constance
Barclay (Evelyn's sister) outside the
Palazzo Rezzonico a month before
the poet's death.

A portrait of Robert Browning taken by his valet turned photographer, William Grove, in 1889. The watch chain, with Elizabeth's ring next to Katharine's coin, is clearly visible.

visit to London in 1855, Pen exclaimed on reaching Boulogne, 'Do you see these houses? all white! Sint [think] of the dirty walls in London. No I sint you dont want to go *bat* never.'⁶⁰ To William Story, Browning wrote in June 1874: 'My best report is to be of Pen. It is now four months and a half since he has been at steady work, and there must be immense good in that .. From Pen's letters, which are unremitting, I can see that he is happier than he ever was in his life. What a load this lightens me of.'

However, in the summer of 1875 a report seems to have gone abroad concerning Pen, which gave Browning cause for concern. Just at this time he spoke to friends of biliousness (always in Browning's case a byword for emotional distress). The problem seems to have arisen when Pen went for a little change of scene to Dinant in May, Heyerman having fallen ill.⁶¹ He took rooms at an inn, La Tête d'Or, and remained in the picturesque Belgian town on the Meuse River throughout the summer. No harm in that. However, by the middle of June the poet felt compelled to call upon his friend, Mrs Eliza Fitzgerald, for help.

Mrs Fitzgerald, a maternal figure three years Browning's senior, was a philanthropist and fellow animal lover who also shared the poet's love of languages and literature. She took a keen interest in Pen and became his 'original patroness', so Browning gratefully described her. According to her diary for 1875, the sixty-six-year-old widow left the comfort of her home, Shalstone, in Buckinghamshire on 22 June to travel to Belgium, where she met Pen and took him away from Dinant for a few days. She returned to England on 12 July. If the problem had been Pen's health, surely Browning would have spoken of it in his letters. Nor does it make sense that Eliza Fitzgerald dragged herself all the way to Dinant for so short a time simply to inspect Pen's artwork. The most likely explanation is that something – a rumour or offhanded remark in one of Pen's letters – had set off alarm bells in his father's mind. At some point talk of a liaison with the Belgian innkeeper's daughter certainly did reach London. Browning must have confided his worry to kind, good Mrs Fitzgerald who offered to go over, assess the situation, and have a word with Pen; as a mother she would have had experience of such matters, after all. As Browning later confessed, friends 'with vigilant eyes enough' had visited Pen from time to time to set his mind at rest.⁶²

Browning was worried sick for the best part of June and July, just the time that he was dashing off *The Inn Album*. He locked himself in his study and threw himself into the poem – the sordidness of the tale matching his mood – so as not to have to think about Pen or Lady Ashburton or any other slanderous gossip. To Domett, who apparently knew nothing of Browning's troubles, it must have seemed as though Robert had reverted to the driven young man whom he and Arnould had known so well. Indeed, Alfred found himself urging his friend to rest when he complained of being bilious while at work on *The Inn Album* – much the same advice he had meted out three decades earlier.

Finally on 14 July, two days after her return, Eliza Fitzgerald had lunch with Robert and Sarianna when she apparently set both their minds at rest. A few days later she recorded in her diary that she was back at Shalstone 'for good' – the implication being: a job well done. By the time Browning laid down his pen, on 1 August, his son had been absolved of any wrongdoing, just like the young man of the tale: 'All's ended and all's over! Verdict found / "*Not guilty*" – prisoner forthwith set free': so reads the poet's rushed scrawl at the end of *The Inn Album*: ' *This young man – / Hem – has the young man's foibles but no fault.*'[63]

Yet, Robert had been badly shaken. He had once told Elizabeth before their marriage that he would endeavour to write to save his soul, even if forced to 'live among lions', although he preferred to do so quietly with her beside him. Well, he had lived quietly with Elizabeth and the verse had not been forthcoming; now he was living amongst lions – in fact, he was one of those lions – and he could not stem the flow of words to save his soul. Henry James wrote at this time that the poet 'is robust and vigorous; more so now, even, than heretofore, and he is more prolific than in the earlier part of his career.' Yet he was wanton, wilful, crude. 'That bard's a Browning; he neglects the form: / But ah, the sense, ye gods, the weighty sense!' exclaims the villain of *The Inn Album*, looking over the verses scrawled in the hotel guest book, the 'album' of the title. This mocking tone, James explained, only made Browning's readers think him graceless and ungrateful.[64]

Browning was angling for a fight. He knew that it was impossible – and, indeed, unwise – to try to combat gossip. As for Pen, there was nothing he could do but wait and see. So, with his next book of poetry he went for the easy target and confronted (gloves off, so to speak) the reviewers, those who had criticised his work, as he put it, 'forty years long in the wilderness'. In 'Of Pacchiarotto and How He Worked in Distemper' (the title poem), chimneysweeps (read 'critics') arrive at the poet's house to sweep out his chimney; they have been trampling over the grass outside his house for 'forty-and-over long years'. The 'neighbours complain it's no joke, sir', the chimneysweeps say; 'You ought to consume your own smoke, sir!' 'Ah, rogues,' the poet replies, 'but my housemaid suspects you – / Is confident oft she detects you / In bringing more filth into my house / Than ever you found there!' Browning threw his biggest punch, however, at the poet and critic Alfred Austin whom he likens to the mediocre yet arrogant Renaissance artist Pacchiarotto. Pacchiarotto works in distemper (paint diluted in water); Austin does too, but it was 'distemper' of another kind – ill temper, even derangement. Browning even made fun of Austin's height – all of five feet – with references to saucy dwarfs, 'so sauced in your own sauce', and the like.

Austin had been 'flea-biting' Browning for years 'in whatever rag of a newspaper he could hop into' – calling him 'muddy and unmusical', misquoting his poetry in order to criticise the metre, claiming his repu-tation was owing to the quantity of London dinners he attended, not the quality of his poetry. Yet, despite the very real provocation, Browning was roundly chastised by both friends and critics alike when 'Pac-chiarotto' appeared. They had overlooked the odd swipe at Austin in earlier works – the 'brisk little somebody' in *Balaustion's Adventure*, 'Dogface Eruxis, the small satirist' in *Aristophanes' Apology* – but this time Browning had gone too far. Robert protested to George Barrett that he had merely been amusing himself with the critics: 'a fit of good humour – and nothing worse'. Just around the time of *Pacchiarotto and How He Worked in Distemper* appeared, in the summer of 1876, he held a luncheon at Warwick Crescent. The 'quite grieving' Frederick Locker took aside another of the guests, twenty-seven-year-old Edmund Gosse, to mourn over the attack on Austin in hushed tones; yet their host seemed cheerful enough. Gosse was one of the many Oxbridge students who had enthused over Browning's poetry in the 1860s, and after the rest of the company had gone, Browning took him upstairs to his study and pulled a volume from the shelf. 'What have we here? Ah! This is the entirely-unintelligible *Sor-dello* . .'[65] He said it so dryly, young Gosse did not know what to think.*

Although Isa Blagden knew that Browning thought Austin 'a filthy

* Browning gained some satisfaction from the fact that between December 1872 and October 1874 the Chicago & Alton Railway Company printed on the back of its timetables what was, in effect, the first complete American edition of Browning's works – including *Sordello*. Ten thousand free copies were distributed monthly. 'This plan of combining high class literature with railway time-cards is adopted in the belief that the traveling public will prefer works of permanent value, and which appeal to the highest culture and most refined taste, to scraps of current railroad history' (*The Official Guide of the Chicago and Alton Railroad*).

little snob', she would have protested against the poet's attack on her good friend in 'Pacchiarotto'.* Nor would she have liked to learn that on her death in 1874, Sophie Eckley had left the two Gordigiani portraits of his parents to Pen. (The pictures had been on display up until then in the Athenaeum Gallery in Boston.) Isa had been no friend of Mrs Eckley. She may have shared Elizabeth's faith in table-rapping and Napoleon III, but she had been in absolute agreement with Robert that Sophie Eckley was pure poison. The Gordigiani portraits had been a particular bone of contention between the two women. Annoyed that Sophie had commissioned the fashionable Italian to paint the Brownings, Isa, together with the rather vulgar but wealthy Ellen Heaton, had asked Elizabeth if she would sit for a second – rival – portrait by the artist Field Talfourd.[66] In 1869 Miss Heaton had presented Browning with a copy of Talfourd's modest chalk drawing (the original then going to the National Portrait Gallery).†

Although the executors of the will would have notified Pen Browning and his father of the legacy soon after Mrs Eckley's death, there was a delay of nearly two years in the delivery of Gordigiani's canvases to Warwick Crescent. Nevertheless, the image of Elizabeth's portrait seems to inhabit – one might say, haunt – a number of poems in *Of Pacchiarotto and How He Worked in Distemper*. It is, indeed, a striking oil painting. Elizabeth's face looks so ghostly pale beneath the dark curls and jet-black gown, and the corners of her mouth are lifted ever so slightly, forming an elusive and mysterious *Mona Lisa*-like smile.

'Still you stand, still you listen, still you smile!' Thus begins 'Numpholeptos', one of the poems in *Of Pacchiarotto and How He Worked in Distemper*. 'Nympholept' was a Greek word which Elizabeth had used in her poetry, defining it as someone embued with 'that mystical passion for an invisible nymph'.‡ In Browning's poem, the narrator is captivated by the spirit before him, a nymph with a smile eerily reminiscent of Elizabeth's expression in Gordigiani's portrait. 'What means the sad slow

---

* So churlish was Robert in this matter that he refused to subscribe to a posthumous volume of Isa's poetry edited by Austin. 'I will be no party to the association of a dearly-loved name with that of Mr Alfred Austin,' Browning told a mutual friend (McAleer (ed.), *Dearest Isa*, xxvi).
† Both portraits of Elizabeth, by Talfourd and Gordigiani, now hang somewhat uneasily next to one another in the National Portrait Gallery, London.
‡ In 1855 Ruskin had complained to Elizabeth about her use of the word 'nympholeptic'. She replied that De Quincey used it, as had Lord Byron. 'We are all nympholepts in running after our ideals' (EBB to Ruskin, 2 June 1855: Kenyon).

silver smile above / My clay but pity, pardon?' But, wait, those lips 'sweet and soft grow harsh and hard − / Forbearance, then repulsion, then disdain. / Avert the rest! I rise, see!' The figure before him demands that the poet go forth into the world, pass through its trials and tribulations, and return once more unscathed, ending his steps 'Where they began − before your feet, beneath / Your eyes, your smile'. For a brief moment the poet rebels, 'No, I say: / No fresh adventure! No more seeking love / At end of toil, and finding, calm above / My passion, the old statuesque regard, / The sad petrific smile!' But he cannot break the spell: 'Ah me! / The true slave's querulous outbreak! All the rest / Be resignation! Forth at your behest / I fare,' returning at end of day, 'To that cold and sweet smile? − which I obey'.

Browning continues his one-way conversation with Elizabeth's portrait in 'St Martin's Summer', which follows 'Numpholeptos'. For those left behind, the world is indeed a treacherous place, full of temptation. Let me dramatise for you what happened at Loch Luichart with Louisa, Robert seems to be pleading before his wife. 'No protesting, dearest!' the speaker of the poem says to his would-be lover, 'Hardly kisses even! Don't we both know how it ends?' She wants too much: 'You would build a mansion, / I would weave a bower.' But, whatever shape it takes, 'Where we plan our dwelling / Glooms a graveyard surely!' 'Love's corpse lies quiet therefore, / Only Love's ghost plays truant.' 'I told her, Ba,' Browning might have gestured to the chimerical portrait on the wall, that 'my heart was buried in Florence.'

But did he really have to justify himself to Elizabeth? After all, she had her share of human frailty and weakness. Just think, that sad sweet smile had once shone on Mrs Eckley, sitting behind Gordigiani's easel as he sketched Elizabeth's face − the poisonous Mrs Eckley whom she had so foolishly befriended despite Robert's protests.* In 'Bifurcation', the poem which immediately precedes 'Numpholeptos' and 'St Martin's Summer' (all written between November 1875 and April 1876), the speaker asks that he be buried next to the love of his life. But, as for their epitaphs, who is to say which tomb 'holds sinner, which holds saint', for has he not had the harder lot on earth, amongst its stones and stumbling blocks?

Browning begins *Of Pacchiarotto and How He Worked in Distemper*

---

* Gordigiani's original version, made in 1858, apparently made Elizabeth look like 'a large buxom radiant matron'; the following year he redid the portrait, and the result was, by all accounts, very like Elizabeth (EBB to Arabel Barrett, [22 January 1859]). Sophie Eckley was present for the first sitting, in 1858, but not for the second in 1859.

with the Prologue, sitting in his study and addressing 'the old wall here', the one at right angles to the study window – perhaps the very one 'embrowned with sin and shame'. By the Epilogue, at the end of a hard day, the poet appears to have returned to the Gordigiani portrait, having lived to tell the tale and toasting his wife's image, glass in hand. ' "The poets pour us wine – "* / Said the dearest poet I ever knew, / Dearest and greatest and best to me. / You clamour athirst for poetry – / We pour.' But, Browning insists, what vintage, sweet or strong, he and he alone shall choose – not the critics, not even Elizabeth. In October 1876, three months after the publication of *Pacchiarotto*, the Gordigiani portraits finally arrived at Warwick Crescent. Browning gave them pride of place in the dining room, to his right as he sat at table with his glass of wine after dinner.† It was said that the poet 'lost himself in contemplation of his wife's picture there'.⁶⁷

Robert was becoming increasingly fretful, but his old friend Alfred Domett could provide no comfort, as he once had thirty years before. In fact, the two men had begun to get on each other's nerves. People had been kind about Alfred's poem *Ranolf and Amohia*.‡ But, although he recouped the cost of publication, Domett could not make up for all those lost years, struggling to make a life in New Zealand when what he had really wanted was fame as a poet. Wherever he went, he found that he was known, not as the author of *Ranolf and Amohia*, but as Browning's 'Waring'. It was bad enough that Browning persisted in calling him by that name, but Domett despaired when he saw himself referred to as such in the American reviews. When the poet Richard Horne, who had spent the years 1852 to 1869 in Australia, confessed that he had once been mistaken for 'Waring', Domett replied testily that 'he was welcome to the honor, if it were such'. His grumblings provoked Robert to write in 1876: 'My dear Domett, you shan't have the last word. You have no right to envy anybody with whom you declined to compete in the race. You stepped aside after other objects while I kept plodding on at the particular one I proposed myself.'⁶⁸

---

* An adaptation of a line from Elizabeth Barrett Browning's 'Wine of Cyprus', a poem which Browning also cited in *Balaustion's Adventure*.

† Domett thought Gordigiani's matching portrait of Robert 'very pleasing' – 'halfway between what I remember him in England before 1842 and his present appearance' (Domett, *Diary*, 28 February 1877).

‡ Arnould said he preferred *Ranolf and Amohia* to Browning's more recent work, with its 'word puzzles', 'sentence-labyrinths', and 'cramped painful style' (Arnould to Domett, 28 January 1873; BL Add. 45560, f. 73). In 1869 Arnould had retired to Naples, then Florence, with his second wife, a Scottish woman, who preferred Italy to England.

The next year Browning accepted the dedication of Domett's collection of verse, *Flotsam and Jetsam*. Some of the poems dated back to their youth, including his spirited defence of *Pippa Passes*. One suspects that Domett's dedication was calculated, at least in part, to draw the critics' attention to his little volume. In thanking him for the book, Robert wrote how he well remembered reading the early pieces as a young man. 'Yes,' he went on, 'I know how you gave me your warmest countenance when most of the faces around me were none of the friendliest.' Browning had, it seems, repaid in full the debt of friendship he owed his old friend. This was the last letter that Domett thought worthy of insertion in the handsome red morocco album devoted to his correspondence with and about Browning, spanning forty years.[69]

Poetry was not the only subject to create a slight frisson between the two men. Domett's son, Alfred Junior, had returned from New Zealand shortly before his father to enrol in the Royal Academy Schools. Once his own son had decided to take up the brush, Browning could not say enough about Pen's brilliant progress whenever the two old friends met. One spring day in 1876, while crossing the street on their way to a dinner engagement, Domett and his son Alfred heard someone loudly calling their names. 'Browning came rushing up. Alf's being a Royal Academy student, made us ask how Pen was getting on.' Browning replied: 'He has had a wonderful success!' and proceeded to tell them how Rudolf Lehmann had offered 150 guineas for one of Pen's early works. When Pen demurred, his father told him, 'Pen, don't be a fool – take it as offered.' 'You will be quite spoilt with all this; you had better get back to Antwerp as fast as you can.' Domett discerned 'a little *practical flattery* to the poet in all this'.[70] Alf was never in danger of being so spoiled.

Pen quite happily continued to divide his time between Antwerp and Dinant, where he set up a studio and left all his things, including a menagerie of pets. Browning had been able to reassure Eliza Fitzgerald several months after her visit to Dinant: 'Well, we continue to hear good news of Pen, – of his work and his pains and continuance in them.' The poet told George Smith that Pen, in his letters, 'speaks of having painted eleven hours a day for the last two days – this time, at a ruined castle. Is not this good news?' It sounds as if Pen was trying very hard not to think of the innkeeper's daughter. 'And at Oxford they could not let "Don't care!" escape coming to a bad end,' so Browning exclaimed to another lady friend. Yet, still he managed to fret about his son. Pen 'will go to his beloved Dinant at the end of the month', he told Annie Smith in October

1876. 'That it is pleasant to go there, I have no doubt: but the stone keeps "rolling"; and I want – perhaps unreasonably – the chances of "moss-growing" to increase.'[71]

That same year, 1876, Robert had decided he wanted a change from his traditional French summer holiday. He and Sarianna, together with Miss Anne Egerton Smith, had tried the Isle of Arran off the Scottish mainland. The Brownings had first met Miss Smith, whom they called Annie, in Florence. A shy but intelligent and independent woman, proprietor of the Liverpool *Mercury*, Annie was Mrs Bracken's sister and therefore linked with Isa Blagden; she had also been a close friend of W. J. Fox and the Flower sisters, with whom, like Robert, she had shared a true love and appreciation of music. Her home in Holland Park Terrace, just north of Holland Park, was not far from Warwick Crescent, and she and Browning regularly attended concerts together in London.

Arran did not particularly suit, and the next year, 1877, Browning, Sarianna and Miss Smith decided to exchange sea breeze for mountain air and travel to the Haute Savoie, a few miles south of Geneva. At first Browning was rather put off by the 'money-grubbing' natives, who were obviously more savvy than the Breton peasants had been. But the peace and quiet of the place, the superb views and mountain streams, soon worked their magic on Browning.[72]

Then, one morning, on 14 September, just a few weeks into the holiday, Robert discovered Miss Smith's body on the floor of her room, 'quite warm – but dead'. She had probably suffered a stroke. It was a dreadful thing. Describing the scene to a friend the next day, he wrote, 'So, have I lost one of the most devoted friends I ever had in my life – a friend of some five-and-twenty years standing.' Browning's grief was intense. So sudden and near was Annie's death, so close her connection, 'I could proceed to nothing else till I had in some way put it all on paper.' Five days after the tragedy, when the dead woman lay buried in the village graveyard and Robert and Sarianna were preparing to return to London, the poet ascended the nearby mountain, La Salève, which he and Annie meant to climb the day she died. It was there that he began to sketch out *La Saisiaz*. (La Saisiaz was the name of their chalet near Collonges.) 'Dared and done: at last I stand upon the summit, Dear and True!' the poem begins, 'Singly dared and done; the climbing both of us were bound to do.' 'I could not tell the incidents of that memorable week more faithfully in prose,' Browning later recalled: how on that fateful morning, 'Up I rose and forth I fared: / Took my plunge within the bath-pool, pacified the watch-dog scared' before thinking to wake Annie, his friend who would wake no more.[73]

Standing there on the summit of La Salève – alone – Robert finds himself asking: 'Does the soul survive the body?'* There, 'within sight of the new-made grave' below, Alexandra Orr surmised in her handbook, 'he re-laid the foundations of his faith, that there is another life for the soul.' At long last Browning was able to grasp what had hitherto eluded him: the gift of faith, that unshakeable belief – free from dogmas and doxies – which had been Elizabeth's. Prove the existence of God and the immortality of the soul? 'That they o'erpass my power of proving, proves them such.' Gone was the life of 'faith diversified by doubt', described in 'Bishop Blougram's Apology'. Robert had so wanted to believe Dante's words when, fifteen years earlier, he copied them into Elizabeth's New Testament. In *La Saisiaz* he repeats them with absolute certainty: 'I believe and I declare – / Certain am I – from this life I pass into a better, there / Where that lady lives of whom enamoured was my soul' – where, Browning adds, thinking of Annie, 'this / Other lady, my companion dear and true, she also is.'

Atop that 'eagle's haunt', as he surveyed Mont Blanc in all its majesty and thought on the enormity of death, Robert had gained a new perspective on life – a sense of proportion. Life's 'fret' dwindled 'into insignificancy before an opening prospect of a new and – so far as the old is concerned – "fretless" existence'. This was how Browning once explained the meaning of the Prologue to *La Saisiaz*, which begins: 'Good, to forgive; / Best, to forget! / Living we fret; / Dying, we live. / Fretless and free, / Soul, clap thy pinion!'[74] Annie Smith, that 'other lady, my companion dear and true', had ascended to take her place next to his beloved wife in heaven – this Robert knew and believed. 'May I never wake / Those of mine whose resurrection could not be without earthquake! / Rest all such, unraised forever!' Why go back over old quarrels between the living and the dead, why torture oneself with guilt and remorse – what good does it do? Rest in peace. This was the poet's 'sad summing-up of all to say'. It was time to return home to Warwick Crescent, to the work which lay before him, and to Elizabeth's portrait on the wall.

'So the poor smile played, that evening: pallid smile long since extinct

---

* Browning and Annie Smith had been discussing a series of articles published that summer in a new journal, *The Nineteenth Century*, on 'The Soul and the Future Life'.

/ Here in London's mid-November!' Thus Browning ends *La Saisiaz.** He dated the manuscript 'Nov. 9, 1877', laid down his pen and sat back in his chair. He had made peace with Elizabeth's ghost – and with his conscience – but was it to be a lasting peace or merely an uneasy truce?

---

* *La Saisiaz* was published together with another poem, *The Two Poets of Croisic*, in 1878.

CHAPTER FIVE

Youthful Echoes,
1877–83

On that mid-November day of 1877 the prospect of a new 'fretless existence' had indeed opened up before the poet, but it was the exclusive province of the afterlife. Elizabeth had attained it, and Robert had resolved to let her rest there in peace. However, he was under no illusion about this life – 'living, we fret', and he had had his share of troubles to fret about in the last few years. The wound inflicted on Browning by the sordid affair of Lady Ashburton and her 'champion', Hatty Hosmer, continued to fester. Sitting for a portrait in Rudolf Lehmann's studio in 1875, Robert had turned 'pale' when his old friend, trying to pass the time with small talk, happened to mention Hatty's name.* (Oddly enough, on seeing the finished portrait, Domett remarked to Sarianna that Robert was 'too pale-looking'.) Three years later (1878), Browning showed utter disdain and contempt when 'Lady A. "tried on" conciliation' (his words) through the Storys.[1] (The parties concerned just happened to meet one day in the Storys' London hotel room.) The noble sentiment expressed in the 'Prologue' to *La Saisiaz* – 'Good, to forgive; / Best, to forget!' – clearly did not apply to Lady Ashburton.

Another matter for Browning to fret over that mid-November day was the disappointing reviews of his latest work. On its appearance a month earlier, the critics called *The Agamemnon of Aeschylus* a too literal, wholly incomprehensible translation. *The London Quarterly Review* told of a

---

* Lehmann was more circumspect in his memoirs, describing the subject of their conversation only as 'a young American sculptress, a pupil of Gibson, who had enjoyed an ephemeral reputation in Rome'. The artist also brought up the name of Home, the spiritualist, which made Browning's face go white as well.

Browning sat again for Lehmann in 1884. In 1905 Pen wrote to his father's biographer, W. H. Griffin, that Lehmann's portrait 'is the one connected with the trousers! – (But that story is between you and me, remember!)', but does not specify which painting (BL Add 45564, ff. 161–5).

young Oxford BA who said on reading it that 'at almost every page I had to turn to the Greek to see what the English meant.' Even the book's dedicatee, Carlyle, told Browning to his face that he could not understand it. The poet had been inspired to translate Aeschylus' tragedy on seeing photographs of Heinrich Schliemann's extraordinary excavations at Mycenae, including Agamemnon's grave. If he had succeeded in his original idea – to render the 'archaic workmanship'* of *The Agamemnon* into English to accompany and complement those stark yet powerful images of ancient artefacts – it might have been a wholly unique and striking production. However, when the translation appeared without illustrations, Browning could only reply to Carlyle 'that all said it was of no use'.[2]

Yet, without doubt, Browning's greatest worry continued to be Pen. Even as Robert sat writing *La Saisiaz* – hostile reviews of *The Agamemnon* leaping off the pages of periodicals piled on his desk – Sarianna was at her own writing table lamenting Pen's latest vagaries in a series of letters to Joseph Milsand in Paris.† In August 1877 his father paid for Pen to pursue his art in Paris; the aspiring artist had the opportunity to draw from a live model in the studio of Jean Paul Laurens. If, back in 1875, Browning had indeed suspected his son of an unsuitable romantic attachment in Dinant, then his worst fears were soon to be realised. Within a month or so of arriving in the French capital, Pen wrote to his father, declaring, apparently, that he intended to make his Belgian landlord's daughter his wife. The move to Paris and the separation from his lady-love had worked to strengthen the twenty-eight-year-old's resolve in the matter. Why shouldn't he? The lady in question was respectable. So what if her father was an innkeeper? He happened to be a very prosperous man of business.

But Browning, like many a father before and after him, declared that he had been cruelly disappointed in his hopes, in his desires, in the very aim of his life. He had 'the right to demand that the sacrifices that he made to help him in his career' – subsidising his son's studies in Dinant, Antwerp and, now, Paris – 'should not serve any other purpose'. In the course of a two-hour walk through the Paris streets that October,

---

* As Browning described Aeschylus' language in his preface to the translation (the manuscript is at Balliol College Library).

† The whereabouts of Sarianna's letters are not known; the story is extracted from Milsand's replies, dated between 20 October and 19 December 1877, which are at the Armstrong Browning Library (with an English translation).

Milsand, who was keeping a vigilant eye on his friend's son, urged Pen to work, to make the most of the opportunity given him to improve his technique under so good a master. The unhappy young man had clearly been neglecting his art. But the Frenchman could not, in good conscience, counsel Pen any further. He reminded Sarianna that he too had come up against parental opposition to his own marriage, and he had chosen to wait (twelve long years) rather than give up: 'It is not for me to urge any man to break or keep pledges of which he is the sole judge.'

'But that was entirely different,' Robert might have exclaimed when Sarianna read this passage aloud to him. What a dreadful mess it all was. No wonder Browning burst forth in the middle of *La Saisiaz*, 'I must say – or choke in silence – "Howsoever came my fate, / Sorrow did and joy did nowise, – life well weighed, – preponderate."'

In early December the matter was still weighing heavily on both brother and sister. Sarianna confided in Alexandra Orr, who remarked (unable to resist the obvious wordplay): 'Pen had the simple manners of a perfect *gentleman*, but that his nature was not *gentle*.'³ Although she found Mrs Orr's words offensive, Sarianna and Robert did indeed feel that Pen had intentionally inflicted pain on the family. Milsand, on the other hand, believed 'that his faults do not come from a deliberate purpose'. 'I attribute them instead,' he wrote to Miss Browning, 'to a weakness, to an incapacity to resist temptation.' Pen had also inherited his father's fiery temper, always 'wanting to talk back'. By mid-December Pen's 'hopes and good intentions' had 'been smashed by M. Laurens', Milsand reported. Laurens had apparently thrown Pen out of his studio owing to a decided lack of application and/or talent. The young man's confidence had been shattered. 'He is like a man who has been thrown two or three times from the top of a building onto the pavement,' Milsand told Sarianna. The Frenchman appealed to both Sarianna and Robert 'not to blame on a voluntary lack of good faith all of the remissness of which [Pen] may be guilty. The distress which a word causes spreads like a spot of grease.'

For all his harsh words, Browning loved Pen and wanted the very best for him. Despite Pen's academic failure, Robert still wanted to believe that his son (Elizabeth's child, after all) had so much potential – if only he would apply himself. The pressure on Pen was unbearable. Since his mother's death, he had yearned for love which was uncomplicated and unconditional, something that he had only ever found in the arms of simple peasant girls abroad. Yet, this was just what Browning dreaded, for he knew that Pen's social position in British society was not secure. Yes, Pen was a pleasant fellow to have at a country-house party: the son of two famous poets and a dab hand with both a gun and a billiard cue. But, he was not in possession of a good fortune; what is more, he was the grandson of a humble and publicly disgraced bank clerk. These were social disadvantages, which he could overcome only by succeeding in a profession or by making a good marriage – and a Belgian girl 'of unexceptionable character and connections', as Browning would later describe her, was not good enough. Once, while discussing the idea of marriage amongst people of different social backgrounds, Browning declared to a rather puzzled Rudolf Lehmann, who had thought the poet a liberal-minded man: 'If ever a son of mine should so disgrace himself, I should certainly cut him off with [*sic*] a shilling.' He may very well have voiced this threat in response to Pen's latest rebellion, for his son seemed determined, in one fell swoop, to destroy his chances of a respectable marriage as well as a career as a painter. He appealed to – and convinced – the girl's father to condemn the match, citing Pen's tenuous pecuniary situation and uncertain prospects.[4] Paternal anguish, disappointment, and wounded pride had led Browning to think the worst of Pen and made him, for a time, insensible to his son's deep-seated insecurities.

Browning tried to put on a brave face before all but his most confidential friends. In early-mid December, when the trouble with Pen was most 'preponderate', he called on Alfred Domett, to whom he had recently sent a copy of his *Agamemnon*. When Domett (who had been out) returned the visit, he was shown up to the drawing room to hear the frustrated poet hurl abuse at his critics, especially the unfairness and ignorance of *The Spectator*. No doubt Robert welcomed the chance to vent his anger over something other than Pen. But then Domett, perhaps to change the subject, asked after young Browning. There would have ensued an awkward moment. It was Sarianna – despite her being 'morally and physically ill' (as Milsand had described her only a few days before)* – who filled the breach. Always ready to defend the family honour, she began to explain that Pen 'was studying painting at Paris under Laurens giving all his attention to *drawing*, as she found he had begun at the wrong end with oil-painting. He had thought of going to Bonnat .. but found he had so many pupils he could give but little instruction or attention to each.' One can almost hear Sarianna saying all this rather

---

* 'Vous êtes moralement et physiquement malade.'

too quickly and nervously – particularly if she happened to recall in the middle of her speech that Domett's son was then one of Bonnat's pupils in Paris. Had rumours concerning Pen been flying around the studios of Paris? Browning did not say a word – perhaps he had left the room by this point. One hopes, for the sake of Sarianna's health, that Domett did not repeat what he had heard from his artist friend, P. H. Calderon, concerning the fast and loose behaviour of both students and 'models' in Paris (unlike their counterparts at the Royal Academy in London where there was always 'a sort of moral Police about in the shape of curators, visitors, or Royal Academicians').[5]

He was not going to confide in Domett, but Robert may have told Henriette Corkran his worries over Pen – either that or the story had got around, for on 31 December 1877 Henriette, who had known the Brownings since she was a little girl in Paris and was now herself an aspiring artist, wrote: 'I must wish you dear Mr Browning a very happy New Year .. I trust you will be spared any kind of sorrow and anxiety and that Pen will show his gratitude to you by following your wishes in everything.'[6] It seems that poor Pen did just that. Before Christmas he wrote an abject letter of apology to his father, left Paris, and returned – not to Dinant but to Antwerp to throw himself into his painting, just as he had done two years before, following the intervention of his father's former emissary, Miss Fitzgerald.

'The day is fine – propitious, I will hope. May it inaugurate a new kind of year,' so began Browning's birthday note, dated 25 April 1878, to Eliza Fitzgerald. He had been much 'harassed' over the last twelve months, he confessed, but 'will hope to "make a new departure" (as the sailors say) this morning, when Pen has just arrived, in good health and spirits'.[7] Both father and son had every reason to be in high spirits that morning, for Pen had come to London to attend, together with his father, the opening of the Royal Academy Exhibition, where his latest painting, *The Worker in Brass, Antwerp*, was to be on show.

Browning had first displayed the picture in Warwick Crescent, where he invited friends to see it. Typical is the note he sent to Thomas Carlyle which begins with the offhanded invitation: 'I hardly dare make the simple mention I am about to do of the fact that a picture by my son will be on view at my house till next Sunday: how much less can I dream of begging you to come and see merely *that*!' But, it is clear that a visit from Carlyle would have meant a great deal to Robert, for the sake of old times as well as Pen's future. 'Should any happy chance,' he continued, 'bring you to this neighbourhood any afternoon, my son's work would be rewarded indeed by your notice. You knew him when a child and were kind as he even yet well remembers' – Carlyle had good-naturedly indulged the two-year-old's antics on a train journey to Paris with the Brownings – 'he is now some years older than was his father when you were more than kind to – Your ever grateful and affectionate Robert Browning.'[8]

Carlyle did grace the drawing-room-cum-picture-gallery of Warwick Crescent. 'How good and dear of you to come! dear Mr Carlyle! How dear!' boomed Browning when, at the end of March 1878, he saw the frail figure alight from the carriage and enter the house on Allingham's arm. The proud father sat Carlyle down in an armchair before *The Worker in Brass*, pointing out certain small details from time to time. After a long silence before the large canvas, the cantankerous old Scotsman merely wondered aloud about the origin of the name 'Antwerp'. He asked a few questions concerning Pen but said not a word about the picture itself. When Carlyle then enquired about the name of Browning's new poem (*La Saisiaz*, due to be published in May), Browning evaded the question, muttering only, 'I'll let it speak for itself.'[9] Neither could have thought it a very satisfactory visit as Browning helped Carlyle back into his carriage.

But there were others who came by invitation to praise the painting, and, by the time of the Royal Academy Exhibition some weeks later, Browning was in the very best spirits, for his son's debut at Burlington House was deemed by one and all a success. On ascending the grand staircase and entering the picture-lined rooms, the poet along with the rest of the crowd saw Mr Pen Browning's substantial canvas hung to great advantage 'on the line' (that is, at eye level). That very first day a perfect stranger had asked the price, but no price had been fixed on. Browning – on his son's behalf – had rushed across the room for the advice of Leighton and Millais, who said £300 should be asked. The stranger was a Mr Joshua Fielden, manufacturer, merchant, and MP for West Riding in Yorkshire, who immediately agreed to pay it. Apparently Mr Fielden knew nothing about art but was 'sure of his own mind', and that was good enough for Browning. When someone remarked that he might not have room enough to hang such a large painting, the MP had declared, to the poet's delight, 'that if his house was not big enough he would build one for it'. Alfred Domett heard the whole story from his old friend as they stood on the street one June day. 'The price was somewhat extravagant, all things considered,' Domett added; 'the friend-ship of the artist-assessors for the father had no doubt some influence on their estimate.'[10]

These two artist-assessors knew well enough how to size up a potential buyer; they had to, for Leighton was financing the enlargement of his 'Arab Hall' in Holland Park, and Millais had recently spent a vast sum (£50,000 Domett had heard) on his new house in Palace Gate, Kensington. They were also both able to assess – in their different ways – what sort of encouragement to give the young painter *and* his father. Millais, the artist who had first recognised Pen's talent – and perhaps his idleness – wrote to Browning a few days after the Exhibition: 'I con-gratulate you both. Pen must now work like a man, refuse dinner, & go to bed early to follow up so good a beginning.' Millais was simply recommending the routine which he himself had followed.*

Leighton wrote to Browning rather more graciously: 'the first sale is an unforgettable event in a young artist's life not for the money's sake but because it lifts his work at once into a new category and makes him feel a yard taller.' He was speaking as an artist who had known disappointment and rejection. One of the low points of his career had been in 1856 when his painting *The Triumph of Music* had, as *The Athenaeum* put it bluntly, been 'anything but a triumph of Art'. 'Poor Leighton – it has been a dreadful overthrow,' Elizabeth Barrett Browning confided to Arabel. Robert, who thought '*all* the mud-pelting of *all* the newspapers' undeserved, had taken young Pen to see it. The painting inspired the six-year-old to write a poem, and Leighton, then only in his mid-twenties, asked the Brownings for a copy to send to his mother. Judging from his kind words on Pen's first sale, Leighton had remembered that precocious little boy, now grown into a rather insecure young man 'too much given to self-mistrust', as the poet confided to George Smith. In November 1878, only a few months after penning his note to young Browning, Leighton achieved the most respected position in the British art world, President of the Royal Academy. 'I wish you joy with all my heart,' Browning *père* wrote to the artist who had designed his wife's tomb nearly twenty years before and to whom he had paid tribute in *Balaustion's Adventure*, 'and congratulate us all on your election'.[11]

---

* Calderon told Domett that Millais 'kept himself in regular training; would rise very early; take a mutton chop and a glass of Claret only for dinner; go to bed at 9 p.m. and studiously avoid all excess or excitement' (Domett, *Diary*, 17 March 1877).

The art critics were kind, if a little snide, about Pen's achievement, but that was to be expected, taking into account his parentage. In *The Academy* William Rossetti mentioned 'a first *debut* to which extraordinary interest attaches; it is that of Mr Robert Barrett Browning, the son of the most illustrious poetess, and one of the most illustrious poets, of our time'. The primary interest of the work was to be derived from its authorship, but it had 'merit'. Most of the reviews were written in this same vein.* Some, such as *The World*, remarked on the £300 price – a 'good round sum to get from a stranger for a first exhibited work' – and *The Times* noted that the painting was 'only sinning in size'.[12]

Pen's picture first appeared before the public on 6 May; Browning's latest work soon followed on 15 May. The literary critics were not so forgiving of the father's performance as the art critics were of the son's. *La Saisiaz* was not a success. Typical was *The Athenaeum*, which, while admiring the pathos of the story, thought that Browning's attempt to convey philosophical truths in metre – *trochaicum tetrametrum catalecticum*,† at that – was simply perverse. No second edition was called for, but Browning did not care. All that mattered was that Pen seemed to be, at long last, on the right track. Just as Elizabeth had taken more pride in her son than in twenty *Auroras*, so Robert took more pleasure in Pen's achievement than in any accolades *La Saisiaz* might have. 'I would renounce all personal ambition and would destroy every line I ever wrote,' the poet later said, 'if by so doing I could see fame and honor heaped on my Robert's head.'[13] 'You must come and see how pleasantly my sister has brightened up the house,' the poet wrote to Eliza Fitzgerald in June 1878: 'We have hung as many of Pen's early works on the walls of my room as will go there, – and very well they really look, – I shall like to raise my eyes from the paper I stoop over, and, like the patriarch, "taste the venison of my son that my soul may bless him".' The poet was here alluding to the Old Testament story of Isaac, who asks his son Esau to kill and prepare a meal of venison for him so that he might bless him

---

* *The Light* had reported that 'Mr Browning's only son – the pretty child who is so charmingly introduced in the chapter in Hawthorne's notebook descriptive of his visit to the Brownings in Florence – will, we hear, exhibit in the next Academy. For a long time it seemed uncertain whether Nature had intended young Mr Browning for any thing out of the common. He did not distinguish himself at college, save the merry manner characteristic of youthful spirits .. But for the timely discovery of his ability by Mr Millais, young Mr Browning would have been a round peg pushed into some square hole, and would never, perhaps, have discovered his vocation.'

† 'the most sprightly of all trochaics' (*The Athenaeum*).

before he dies. Browning was no doubt relieved that he was feasting his eyes upon a selection of his son's paintings and not a set of his hunting trophies.

During that spring/summer, revitalised by Pen's triumph, Browning threw himself back into his London life with gusto. He was an early riser. When his valet Grove carried the hot water upstairs at 7.30 a.m. (8 a.m. in the dark winter months), Browning would already be up, munching an apple or some other fruit that had been left out for him the night before and reading out loud from a book of Greek. He would then climb into the bath and splash violently, singing at the top of his voice, finally pulling the chain to send water cascading down from a tank above, to the peril of nearby bookshelves. Breakfast was served at 9 a.m.; twenty minutes later he turned his chair to the fire, opened the post and read *The Times* and the *Daily News*. Sometimes he would bang on the piano a little. While they were in residence at Warwick Crescent, Browning never neglected to feed and stroke his two pet geese, Edinburgh and Quarterly, who eagerly awaited him in the garden. They would try to follow him up the iron steps into his study, but their legs were too short and they inevitably fell back on to the grass in comical fashion.

Unpoetical it may have been, but the householder was very regular in all his habits, so said Grove; he could set his watch by them. Browning remained in his study from 10 a.m. until 1 p.m. He often began by dashing off brief notes, accepting or declining dinner invitations. 'He would rather do almost anything else,' Pen recalled, than get down to the real business of the morning, poetry.[14] Once he had finally cleared his desk of letters and other such pleasant distractions, he would sit, head on hand, for half an hour at a time before jotting down a line or phrase of verse. During these three hours the servants crept about the house on tiptoe, for the master was not to be disturbed by any noise or interruption. One household member had retained the right to intrude upon the poet's thoughts: his brown owl, Bob. The bird perched on a bust overlooking the desk, his sharp talons making a mess of the carefully sculpted hair, or on Browning's shoulder, occasionally travelling down his arm to give a nip on the hand, perhaps a gentle reminder that it was time to take up the pen once more.*

* In 1875 Browning retired the geese to Mrs Fitzgerald's country house; the owl had died not long before the anonymous author of 'Celebrities at Home' visited Warwick Crescent in 1880. 'Mr and Miss Browning have not ceased to mourn the death' of their owl, which 'was so beloved that he has never been replaced'.

At 1 p.m., having tidied away his notes and papers, Browning took a very light and simple meal, usually comprising a pudding with biscuits and cheese followed by a glass of sherry or claret. Straightaway after lunch he dressed to receive visitors but more often to venture out on afternoon calls or to an artist's studio. He usually went to his club to peruse the weekly papers on a Saturday, and on Mondays he dined with A. P. Stanley, Dean of Westminster, before helping to show tradesmen around the Abbey. The poet walked everywhere. His usual route took him past the grimy bustle of Paddington Station and through Kensington Gardens; from there, the fashionable London world lay open before him – Kensington, of course; to the south Chelsea, Carlyle's home turf; to the east clubland, that is Mayfair and St James's; and, to the west, wealthy artists' houses and studios – foremost amongst them Leighton's – which were springing up in the newly developed area around Holland House. Returning to Warwick Crescent around 6 p.m., Browning dressed for dinner at seven o'clock, which was a four-course meal, accompanied by no more than two glasses of claret, with coffee afterwards. In wintertime the rest of the evening (until around 11 p.m.) was spent with 'book in hand, lamp at elbow, and fire at not too far from footstool', as he pictured for Mrs Fitzgerald.[15]

However, during the London Season (which, for Browning, began with the Royal Academy dinner in early May and continued until the end of July)* his afternoons and evenings turned into a whirlwind – and sometimes, a maelstrom – of social engagements. 'I am indeed a man to be compassionated for his many engagements,' the poet wrote regretfully to the publisher John Murray, ' – since one of them is always standing in the way of some other – and probably – even more attractive invitation – such as your very kind one which is the third I have been forced to deny myself the pleasure of accepting for June the second' (1881). Describing a typical Saturday during the London Season – visitors after lunch (some expected, some not), a musical party in the late afternoon, just time enough to return home and change for Lady Ridley's dinner, then on to the Duchess of Cleveland's party – the poet exclaimed to Eliza Fitzgerald, 'thus runs the world away', and Browning off his feet, one might add. The Sabbath Browning held sacred, but not for the sake of religion; his churchgoing was always irregular. Rather, every Sunday for

---

* At this period, the 'official' London Season began after the Easter recess of Parliament and lasted until Parliament rose, in August.

years he made a pilgrimage to Harley Street, did penance by climbing five flights of stairs, and found his reward in the company of the Procters, old friends from his bachelor days. In the spring the poet dedicated part of the Lord's Day to Art, becoming a habitué of the 'Show Sundays' put on by the Holland Park Circle. Come summer, Sunday afternoons were spent in the gardens of Little Holland House, home of the artists G. F. Watts and Valentine Prinseps (whom the Brownings had known in Italy), with croquet and bowls, tea and strawberries, music and other merriments.[16]

Often was the time that the poet had to pen an apologetic note to a disappointed hostess for not making an appearance in her drawing room; he had, inadvertently, double-booked himself on that particular afternoon or had been too optimistic in thinking he could manage two parties in one evening. The 'bourgeois' Browning, although not very poetical, was good value at a dinner party, with a vast reserve of stories, anecdotes, and opinions. Some fellow diners, like Disraeli, thought him too noisy; when he was in full flow Browning would not let anyone get a word in edgeways. 'I know I am too noisy,' the poet told a friend, 'but I cannot help it.'[17] Nevertheless, he kept the conversation lively and was, therefore, much sought after by London hostesses. His valet Grove marvelled that Browning could stay out every evening, sometimes not returning home until half past midnight, yet still be down for breakfast by 9 a.m.

The truth was, Browning needed the bustle of London society to counterbalance the seclusion of Warwick Crescent. Warwick Crescent was a mausoleum, associated absolutely with Elizabeth and their life together in Italy: the tapestries and heavy Italianate furniture of Casa Guidi; his wife's delicate chair and table beside his desk with her books lining the study shelves; in the drawing room her bust, always with a vase of fresh flowers placed before it; and a picture of her in every room of the house, including Gordigiani's portrait gazing down from the dining-room wall. His reverence for his dead wife was profound, Grove observed, almost a religion to Browning. But the rituals and trappings of religion can be oppressive as well as comforting. It had seemed to Browning, as he sat in his study composing the 'Prologue' to *Pacchiarotto*, that Elizabeth's spirit caused the creeping vine, even the very wall, to 'pulsate', 'tremble', and 'throb'.* The poet treasured

---

* The vine, a Virginia creeper, was from a cutting which Eliza Fitzgerald had sent from Shalstone. 'The most charming adornment of my room,' Browning told her, 'is undoubtedly

these memories, yet they threatened to stifle him: 'though cloistered fast, soar free'. Alexandra Orr remarked that 'the sweet and the bitter lay, indeed, very close to each other at the sources of Mr Browning's inspiration' – and peace of mind. 'Both proceeded, in great measure,' she continued, 'from his spiritual allegiance to the past – the past by which it was impossible that he should linger, but which he could not yet leave behind. The present' – London society and all its charms – 'came to him with friendly greeting.'[18]

Browning's marriage had been sweet, but he had had to endure the bitter also; he had been aware of this for some time now. When William Allingham admitted that he seldom came up to town since moving to the country, Browning remarked that in his early life he had 'much secluded himself, and had often since regretted it'. In the first few years of their marriage, he had, as Elizabeth told Henrietta, 'an extravagant fancy (oh! even *I* call it unreasonable) that, except this walk for his health, he will go nowhere without me – "cannot enjoy it" – and thus he quite lives by my chair. What I cannot do he will not!'[19]

During their winter sojourn in Paris in 1851–2, however, Elizabeth had begun to push Robert out of the door 'with a broomstick' in the evenings; otherwise, she explained to Arabel, they might as well be in Florence. 'Really it's good for him, right for him, & right for me to insist on his going.' Soon the broomstick was not needed, as Elizabeth had reported to Isa Blagden from Rome in early 1859. 'Plunged into gaieties of all sorts, caught from one hand to another like a ball,' she elaborated, he 'has gone out every night for a fortnight together, and sometimes two or three times deep in a one night's engagements'. Meanwhile, Elizabeth, shut up in the house because of the cold, went to bed with a book. The active side of Browning's existence in Italy, as Alexandra Orr put it, had to be 'alternately suppressed and carried on' without his wife. There had been, she added, much 'effort of self-sacrifice on his part' and 'of resignation on hers'.[20] In declining John Murray's invitation that June of 1881, Browning bemoaned the flood of invitations that seemed to come his way, adding in his note to the publisher: 'It all comes, no doubt, of the magnanimity of friends who, taking into consideration my fourteen years spent in Italy, think to pay up all debts of kindness *in full*.'

the creeper which literally embowers the window, just as if it had a purpose' (RB to Eliza Fitzgerald, 9 June 1878).

Some thought Browning had become addicted, as 'Dogface' Alfred Austin put it, to 'the gilded salons' of the fashionable world. 'I am not ashamed to confess that I do enjoy being with cultured folk,' he declared to Henriette Corkran as he rushed out of his house en route to some reception or other; 'besides I find that mixing with others and the friction of ideas are necessary to a writer.' Mixing with others was also necessary to a man who might go mad if left alone with his thoughts. And so, Browning happily threw himself into the rushing torrent of the London Season: gilded salons filled with the great, the good, and the very rich; dinners for twenty people or more; private views hosted by the most fashionable artists; concerts performed by the great musicians of the day: the violinist Joseph Joachim, the great Wagner conductor, Hans Richter, the baritone George Henschel, and Charles Hallé, founder of the Hallé Orchestra. Long gone was the reticence of those first years in London, following his wife's death. Through all the parties and performances, Rossetti observed, Browning 'was vivid and alert – the turn of his head, his footfall on the floor. If he yawned (which he did occasionally), it looked less like a symptom than a dismissal of ennui.'

'He never posed as a Poet nor as a great thinker or distinguished man,' recalled Mrs Dykes Campbell; rather, he came across as a 'man-of-the-world, & one might have known him for years without ever discovering that he had written a line of poetry'.[21] The gulf between the 'two Brownings' – the genius and the bourgeois – became ever wider and people's incomprehension ever deeper.

To Browning's mind there were two hazards, quite apart from fatigue, which he found nearly impossible to avoid during the London Season: stupidity and public speaking. The one made him churlish, the other brought on panic. Although he loved to talk, the poet had an almost morbid fear of public speaking and would avoid any occasion – especially banquets and literary dinners – where he might be called on to return thanks for 'literature' or some such rubbish, so he confided once to Isa. This reaction would not have surprised Isa, knowing how much Robert loathed all cant and affectation, and he certainly wasn't any good at it, as he admitted to Domett in 1885.

As for stupidity, Browning once told Allingham about a 'Mrs P.' whom he had sat beside at a concert the previous evening Could he believe it, she 'knew and cared absolutely nothing about' the music. Allingham suggested that people with sensitive souls – even with little or no ear – might still enjoy the music to some degree. Browning would have none of it, insisting that 'no untrained person could know or feel anything' of Beethoven. The Irishman feared that the poet's look the night before told the poor lady much the same thing when she had attempted to make conversation with her neighbour during a pause in the music. Even more fierce was Browning's reaction when a female dinner partner, thinking him devoted to Shelley, boldly defended Shelley's treatment of his wife Harriet. Another guest at the table, his friend Mrs Campbell, overheard him whispering hoarsely, 'How could you think that because a man was a Poet he is to be excused for behaving like a cad?' He railed at the poor woman before ending: 'And that *you, a woman*, should say such things! It is unbelievable.'[22]

A blessed relief from such poverty of intellect was Browning's visits to Oxford. He was Jowett's guest at Balliol every year for Commemoration, and in the summer term of 1880 the poet attended opening night of a student production of his *Agamemnon* in the college hall. There was, of course, stimulating company to be had back in London. Browning always relished his evenings *en famille* with the Tennysons. When the men were left alone with their port and walnuts, Tennyson's son Hallam witnessed the best talk he had ever heard, full of repartee, quip, epigram, anecdote, depth, and wisdom. After one such occasion, in 1881, Browning reported to Allingham that Tennyson was 'in great force. He said, "this pair of dress boots is forty years old." We all looked at them, and I said it was good evidence of the immortality of the sole.' Browning's special after-dinner trick was to find a rhyme for the most unlikely words: 'toss Eros' for 'rhinoceros' was one.[23]

The two last great poets of the nineteenth century could not have been more different. Tennyson was distant, with his head in the clouds; Browning was affable, his feet firmly on the ground. Typical was the occasion of Hallam Tennyson's wedding at Westminster Abbey in 1884. Squeezed in amongst the distinguished guests, Browning caught Allingham's eye and gave him 'a friendly wink'; the father of the groom entered, 'cool and self-possessed' – as ever. What the critic R. H. Hutton said of their poetry might also be said of their characters: 'Browning trots or gallops; Tennyson walks or canters.' Nevertheless, these 'brotherly poets', as they called themselves, were genuinely fond of each other. Certainly, as a friend remarked, nothing annoyed Browning more than comparisons so often made between himself and Tennyson by people 'thinking to flatter him'.[24] Mary Gladstone described a dinner where the two grown men hurled ridiculous epitaphs at each other; 'the biggest-brained Poet in England' was how Tennyson described Browning to his wife.*

But, as with all brothers, some rivalry did exist between them. Tennyson would rally Browning playfully on his harsh rhythms as well as the length and obscurity of his poetry. One suspects that Browning made one or two pointed but good-humoured remarks relating to moonlit castles and pasty-faced maidens. And he never could understand how Tennyson came to 'wear the livery and take the wages' (the Poet Laureateship), as he once remarked to a friend, a criticism he had also made of Wordsworth years earlier in 'The Lost Leader'.† (Indeed, he often remarked to Sarianna that he would like to be offered the Laureateship, for the pleasure of refusing it.) Tennyson marvelled at Browning's ability to churn out so much verse; Browning wondered at the fact that Tennyson continued to earn so much more by his pen. He calculated (as only Browning would) that Tennyson was paid £6,000 for about 950 lines – a rate of six guineas a line – so he told Domett.‡ Whereas Tennyson could count on making £5,000 annually, in 1881 Browning was earning around £100 in a year from his poetry.[25]

Often friends would call just as Browning was on his way out of the house. No matter; 'Sarianna will be delighted to see you,' he told Henriette Corkran on one such occasion; 'poor thing, she is often alone in the London Season.' Sarianna Browning led a somewhat reclusive life in London. Miss Browning was, according to Grove, a 'stay-at-home', sometimes saying to her brother rather impatiently: 'When are you going to give *me* an evening?'[26] Nor did the Brownings entertain at home. Although Alfred Domett, when he met her again in 1872, had thought Sarianna as lively and friendly as ever, the thirty intervening years had taken their toll. She had been the young Robert's amanuensis, copy editor, and confidante; she had shared his friendships and taken great pride in his early successes. Even after his marriage, Sarianna continued to correct her brother's proofs and took on those of her sister-in-law as

---

* When the historian Oscar Browning met Tennyson for the first time, he shook his hand and said: 'I'm Browning.' The Poet Laureate stared at him, replied, 'No, you're not,' and walked away.
† 'Just for a handful of silver he left us, / Just for a riband to stick in his coat' (see RB to Katharine Bronson, 20 June 1887). Browning's death in 1889 spared him the sight of Alfred Austin as Poet Laureate from 1896.
‡ In terms of sales, Browning's most successful book, *Ferishtah's Fancies* (1884), sold no more than 7,500 copies in the first year; Tennyson's *In Memoriam* (1850) sold 25,000 copies within eighteen months.

well. But, without Robert at home, Miss Browning's life was decidedly more lonely and cheerless. Then came her mother's illness and death, the dreadful widow Von Müller scandal, followed by fifteen years of penal exile in Paris – at least, that is how she saw it at first. Sarianna was careful to protect her father, whose childlike innocence, mercifully, made her task all the easier; but the proud, middle-aged spinster must have felt the shame of it all very keenly.

On her father's death, Sarianna, the most devoted of daughters, now became 'the most devoted sister and aunt': so Mrs Campbell described her; 'she appeared to be entirely wrapped up in her brother & his belongings.' Still high-spirited but long unused to large gatherings, she felt uncomfortable and bored by them, preferring to receive just a few close friends. Elizabeth had once said of her sister-in-law that she was not 'mobile, flexible – she has no enthusiasm in her, & likes chiefly I think what she has been used to, & chiefly because she has been used to it', but she endured her situation in life stoically, for 'her sense of duty, & her excellent sense are so strong.' Within the sanctity of Warwick Crescent, she was Robert's sole and constant companion. She helped him decide which invitations to accept, vetted visitors to the house, and screened any sensitive correspondence (replies to his critics, for example). And she fiercely defended his name and reputation, as well as that of his wife* – she knew how important these were. She clearly resented, for her brother's sake, Tennyson's huge following, and thought him 'rather affected', overdoing his short-sightedness to enhance his other-worldliness and overplaying his helplessness to attract 'a little cosseting'. She told Domett how she once heard the Poet Laureate drawl, as he squinted with a sort of curious admiration at his friend Locker arranging his portmanteau for him, 'Why Locker you seem to have quite a *ge-e-nius* for packing!'[27]

The reclusive Miss Browning would venture out with her brother to dine, just the two of them, at the home of Mrs Orr in Kensington Park Gardens. When Browning had completed a new volume of poetry, he would ask the widow to Warwick Crescent. After dinner, Mrs Orr and Sarianna settled down in the drawing room to hear him read aloud from the proofs. He took their comments to heart and would retreat to his study next morning to make the suggested alterations before returning the sheets to the publisher. According to Grove, Browning always said

---

* It was Sarianna, according to Mrs Campbell, who placed fresh flowers before Elizabeth's bust in the drawing room every day.

that they were his best critics – always excepting Elizabeth – as they did not spare him in any way. These evenings, and the two afternoons a week (Tuesdays and Fridays) when he read aloud to Mrs Orr, laid the foundations for her *Handbook* to Browning's works.

Julian Hawthorne was to describe Alexandra Orr as an intelligent but highly strung woman, 'a little creature in black: her fingers and shoulders jerked nervously, her face twitched'; moreover, 'when one looked her in the face, her eyes seemed to rush away to right and left.'[28] Browning did not seem to notice these irritating little tics, or perhaps he saw beyond them, for he had been acquainted with Mrs Orr and her sad history for many years. Her grandfather, Sir James Leighton, had been physician to the royal family in St Petersburg. Mrs Orr was born in 1828, three years after her family had left Russia and just a few years before Browning's visit to the imperial city; she was the goddaughter and namesake of the Empress Alexandra. Browning had first met Miss Alexandra Leighton in Paris in 1855; he had already made the acquaintance of her younger brother, Frederic, in Rome. Two years later, at the age of twenty-nine, she married Colonel Sutherland Orr and followed his regiment to India, straight into what became known as the Indian Mutiny. Alexandra was caught up in the fighting, trapped on her own in Aurangabad, and only just escaped with her life. Her husband contracted dysentery and died the following year, 1858. The young widow lived in Bath before settling, ten years later, in London, where she kept house for her father.*

By the 1880s Mrs Orr was one of Browning's closest friends. He confided in her, as is clear from the *Life and Letters*, perhaps because she had links to Robert's past – not only through her family's experience of Russia and Frederic's Roman studio, but also through mutual friends, including Isa Blagden. Browning also felt safe in her company, for she had no apparent desire, or designs, to remarry. Nevertheless, there was the usual tittle-tattle. Grove thought Mrs Orr his master's favourite, and, according to Thomas Hardy, people thought 'there was something tender between Mrs Orr and Browning'.[29] Hardy overheard Mrs Procter declare, possibly one Sunday afternoon as she watched Browning descend the five flights of steps back down to Harley Street: 'Why don't they settle it?'†

* Dr Frederic Leighton (1800–92).
† Anne Procter (1799–1888) was known as a sharp-tongued gossip, a quality which Browning did not admire. 'My intimacy has all along been with *Barry Cornwall* [her husband, B. W. Procter],' he told Mrs Fitzgerald (RB to Mrs Fitzgerald, 15 July 1882). Nevertheless, he continued to visit Mrs Procter after her husband's death.

The love and respect that Robert has always displayed towards women, from boyhood through to maturity, made them feel especially comfortable and at home around the poet. A very young Robert (aged seven or eight) wrote in his diary, 'Married two wives this morning.' Fellow expatriate Frances Cobbe noted that during Isa Blagden's evening parties in her Bellosguardo villa, there was always a 'ripple of laughter' round the sofa where Browning, then in his forties, used to seat himself, 'generally beside some lady of the company, towards whom, in his eagerness, he would push nearer and nearer till she frequently rose to avoid falling off at the end!'[30] He 'might have been always in the same company, so far as he recognized any influence from age or condition or sex': so Henry James describes the older Browning's alter ego, Claude Vawdrey in 'The Private Life'; 'he addressed himself to women exactly as he addressed himself to men, and gossiped with all men alike, talking no better to clever folk than to dull.'

For his part, Robert valued the warmth and honesty shown him by women of all ages, often widows, cultivated and intelligent, who sought meaning in their lives. The grey-haired Browning visited these ladies on his afternoon excursions and called them each his very best friend. (Henriette Corkran thought his exuberance of manner amounted to 'gush'.) He also exchanged birthday presents and innocent kisses, Grove silently observed, when they came and when they went away. One imagines the discreet valet raising his eyebrows once or twice as he stood in the hallway of Warwick Crescent, holding the lady's coat. By 1880, Browning had indeed attained the venerable status of 'old man', although the author of 'Celebrities at Home' for the March issue of *The World* that year could not believe it. The anonymous hack – a woman, surely – expressed disbelief that the poet, erect of bearing, square of shoulder, and active afoot, with a well-proportioned, well-preserved figure and strong resonant voice, could be nearly sixty-eight. 'I have been much favoured in friendships – especially from women,' Browning wrote at this time. A few months before her death, Elizabeth had put it another way for Sarianna: women 'adore him everywhere far too much for decency'.[31]

In Florence, Browning's gold wedding ring had shielded him from the well-meaning but misguided attentions of women. In London he thought that his white beard would offer equal protection, but it only encouraged the ladies to impose upon his affectionate good nature. It seems that at times the widowed Mrs Benzon leaned upon Browning a little too heavily as an escort to concerts and galleries in the early years of her widowhood.

'She could hardly do without me,' he writes of a ball she had persuaded him to attend, despite his dislike for them. The gifts with which women friends showered him – often extravagant presents, which the poet knew the giver could ill afford – were something of an embarrassment to Browning. 'Do not again, – if this birthday of mine should repeat itself, – do not attempt to emphasize your kind feeling by a similar gift to this costly and beautiful one,' so he wrote to Miss Emily Harris, a friend of both Lady de Rothschild and Mrs Fitzgerald, who wrote for the *Jewish Chronicle*. He was to pen much the same letter to Miss Harris – and to many other ladies – every year until his death.[32]

Perhaps the most shameless of these gift givers was Mrs Charles Skirrow, wife of the Master in Chancery and huntress of literary lions, who collected some remarkably good specimens. She considered Mr Browning her greatest trophy, and whenever he came to dine, she made certain that he was served port – not sherry, not champagne, nor any other wine – but his habitual port. If this kind hostess could not have the poet beside her at table, owing to matters of rank, 'she would send him affectionate glances from time to time .. little swift noddings, or gentle grimaces,' as if to say, 'I would so rather have your conversation,' or 'I am sorry it is not your *Thirty-four Port*', alluding to a line in the Epilogue of *Pacchiarotto*.[33]

More serious – or, rather, more ridiculous – was an incident described by Henriette Corkran. One afternoon, while Henriette was on a visit to friends, a wealthy American widow rushed in, exclaiming, 'I thought till to-day that Mr Browning only cared for me platonically, but such is not the case, I assure you.' Henriette and her friends all laughed at this and tried to explain to the newcomer that the poet's manner was generally affectionate. The poor deceived widow was not pleased to hear this; 'she had secret hopes,' Henriette reckoned, 'of being the successor of the great Elizabeth Barrett Browning.' The disappointed widow might well have been Mrs Clara Bloomfield-Moore of Philadelphia. (One suspects, however, that this was by no means an isolated incident.)* Browning

* Browning once had a letter from a distinguished doctor, telling him he had a lady patient who believed the poet's voice to be that of God and begging him to see her as she was convinced that his advice was 'necessary to the future conduct of her life'. Browning thought it a great bore and would do no more than write to the poor woman, telling her to follow the doctor's orders. He was, however, amused by the story of one girl who made her 'young man' pass a 'Browning examination' before agreeing to marry him. The candidate was successful, and the poet received an invitation to the wedding (RB to Fannie Browning, 29 May [1888]: Balliol College Library).

first met Mrs Bloomfield-Moore in London in 1879; it was not long afterwards that she conferred on him (and Sarianna too) five shares of stock in the Keely Motor Company: 'Even should the sanguine stock-holders (who expect each share to be worth £10,000) be disappointed,' she wrote, 'I think we are justified in hoping to receive, at least, £1,000 in each share .. may we all live to realize the advantages which Mr Keely's marvellous work' – an engine which worked by compressed air – 'is going to confer upon the world.'* Nor was she Browning's only substantial benefactor. Elizabeth Benzon gave the poet £1,860 worth of stock in the London & Northwestern Railway Company, providing him with a useful annual income of around £72. He was, of course, grateful to these women. However, when Sarianna suggested to her brother that he might marry again, Grove saw the poet look up at Gordigiani's portrait of Elizabeth and reply, 'Never.'[34] Yet, still those same lips 'sweet and soft' would 'grow harsh and hard', compelling him to go out into the world of the living: 'Forth at your behest / I fare.'

That world, however, was shrinking, both at home and abroad. 'My walks are sadly circumscribed. I never go this way for one reason, nor that way, for another,' Browning told Eliza Fitzgerald in June 1878. He still went out of his way to avoid Delamare Terrace, Arabel's former home. Since Annie Smith's death he could not bear to walk past her road, Holland Park Terrace; and nearby Palace Gardens, bordering Kensington Gardens, would also have been closed to him after the death of his friend and benefactor Mrs Benzon in February of that year. London was becoming, for the sixty-six-year-old, a ghost town. As for his holiday that summer, 'where shall we go, I wonder,' mused Browning in his letter to Mrs Fitzgerald, for old haunts abroad were likewise circumscribed. He had no desire to return to Brittany, the scene of Pen's alleged youthful peccadilloes, or to the Haute Savoie, Miss Smith's final resting place. Since the day he had left Florence with the twelve-year-old Pen, Robert had not been able to face Italy. He sometimes talked of going back to Rome one day, but not before Pen had made his own way in the world and no longer needed careful watching. It was as though he feared the possibility – the inevitability – of Italy captivating his heart once more.

But in August 1878, after Pen had returned to Antwerp and directed

---

* J. E. W. Keely of Philadelphia started the Keely Motor Company in 1873, but soon got into financial trouble. Mrs Bloomfield-Moore subsidised him for many years, until 1895, when she withdrew her aid after an official investigation.

his father to collect *The Worker in Brass* from the Royal Academy, have it photographed, packed in its case, and trundled off to Mr Fielden's establishment, Browning felt truly carefree for the first time in a very long while. He had gone to the Exhibition on closing day to stand in front of and savour Pen's painting one last time; the experience, he told Eliza Fitzgerald, had been nothing but 'unalloyed pleasure' to him. To add to his joy, Pen had written to say he would do his best to have something for the Academy and the Grosvenor too. 'Oh, the blessed thing that Work is!' Browning exclaimed. The poet's mind had also been set at rest by those vigilant friends who continued to visit Pen abroad and to report back to London. It was then, for the first time in seventeen years, that he deliberately put himself (and Sarianna) in the way of temptation by arranging to spend several weeks in the Swiss Alps, near to the border with Italy. Then, he coyly told his friend, 'we may follow our inclinations as far as they point toward the Italian side, – the only part of the world I seem at present to fancy might stimulate me a little.'[35]

But Browning had not expected to be so enchanted by the mountains, and in the blissful solitude and clean air of Splügen he found more than enough inspiration. The sacred hours between 10 a.m. and 1 p.m. at Warwick Crescent, at which time the poet locked himself in his study, must have been frequently interrupted by the crash of crockery in the kitchen, delivery boys clambering up to the service entrance to ring the bell, and the like. At Splügen, where both he and Sarianna were 'renewed like the eagles',* isolated as they were on their mountain perch, Robert took up his pen to write at least two – and possibly all six – of the poems which were to comprise his next collection of poems, *Dramatic Idyls*. By the term 'dramatic idyl' the poet meant a succinct little story complete in itself, told by one of its participants. 'I wish he hadn't taken my word Idyll,' Tennyson whined to William Allingham.[36] The subject matter of Browning's idyls was sombre enough – no doubt in deliberate contrast to Tennyson's castles and moonlit towers – and was, for the most part, drawn from Browning's youthful memories: the story, read some fifty years before, of a female spy's fate ('Martin Relph'); the heroic tales associated with the Greek runner Pheidippides ('Pheidippides'); *A Pilgrim's Progress* and other of John Bunyan's works ('Ned Bratts'). Perhaps the glacier which he passed on his favourite walk from Splügen reminded the poet of his ice-bound sojourn in St Petersburg, inspiring him to write

---

* Isaiah 40: 31.

'Ivàn Ivànovitch'. The poem, which tells the dreadful story of a mother who throws her children to the wolves to save herself, beautifully evokes the harsh Russian winter: the 'great solitudes' of white-clad pine forests and the unnatural daylight, 'bred between / Moon-light and snow-light'.

On their daily walk through the mountains or over dinner at the Hôtel Bodenhaus, Robert and Sarianna had great satisfaction in reading and rereading Pen's pleasant letters. 'He seems happy,' Browning told Mrs Fitzgerald, 'full of his art, and regarding it just as I could desire, – aiming at greater work' and about to return to Paris,[37] this time with his head held high, to view that year's Exposition Universelle.* If only, Browning must have thought, dear Nonno – who had spent so many happy hours sketching with young Pen – had lived to see his grandson's picture hanging in the Royal Academy. It is something that the old man himself would have once aspired to – and might well have achieved – if his father had allowed him to pursue his art. How cruel fathers could be, yet children could be heartless in their turn; so might have run Browning's thoughts. Was it only a year ago that he and Pen had fallen out over that business about his marrying? Such harsh words had been exchanged between them. By appearing to sabotage, wilfully, his own prospects in life, Pen had nearly broken his father's heart. Perhaps he had been too hard on the boy. After all, hadn't he himself when a young man refused all well-meant career advice and lived at home, earning nothing, until the age of thirty-four, well past Pen's age. Robert must have seen the disappointment on his father's kindly face when he gave up so easily on a diplomatic career, quit university after only a year, and, most hurtful of all, announced that not even his mother was to meet his future wife before their elopement. Looking back, Browning saw that he had been heartless, although he had never meant to be. Even as a grown man, he had let his temper get the better of him and had let slip an angry word before this good, gentle old man for having allowed himself to be taken in by such a one as Mrs Von Müller. What right had he to judge his father? And had he judged his own son fairly? Conflict between father and child was all too human. Aristotle knew this and told the story of the man who, when he was being dragged along by his son, bade him

---

* When he heard of the death of Millais's son, Browning wrote to the artist from Splügen: 'I know how little good any friends' sympathy can do in such a case, but you have rendered me such an inestimable service in helping to put my own boy in the right way that I feel it impossible to be quite silent now' (RB to Millais, August 1878).

stop at the doorway since he himself had dragged his father only as far as that.*

Pondering it all, Browning decided to use Aristotle's tale as the starting point for the fifth dramatic idyl, 'Halbert and Hob'. Old Halbert and young Hob, father and son, lived couched 'in a growling, grudged agreement' until, one Christmas night 'Came father and son to words – such words! more cruel because the blow / To crown each word was wanting, while taunt matched gibe, and curse / Competed with oath in wager, like pastime in hell, – nay, worse.' So must have seemed to Robert some of the arguments with Pen over money, his career, his future. Finally, Hob seizes his father by the throat and turns to throw him out into the snow when the older man pleads, 'Hob, on just such a night of a Christmas long ago, / For such a cause, with such a gesture, did I drag – so – / My father down thus far: but, softening here, I heard / A voice in my heart, and stopped: you wait for an outer word. / For your own sake, not mine, soften you too!' Hob relents and they return to the room together. The next morning, however, Hob finds his father dead, and he goes mad. At the end of the poem Browning repeats King Lear's cry, after he has tried and judged his daughters, Goneril and Regan, in the farmhouse: 'Is there a reason in nature for these hard hearts?' 'Oh Lear,' the narrator answers, 'that a reason out of nature must turn them soft, seems clear!' By thus obeying his conscience had Robert and his father been reconciled before the old man's death, and such he hoped would be the case with his own son.

Browning took the subject for the last remaining poem in *Dramatic Idyls* from an incident described to him not long before: a bystander, on witnessing a dog save its young master from drowning, proposes to dissect the animal to see 'how brain secretes dog's soul'. It was a plea against vivisection; Browning was Vice-President of the Victoria Street Society for the Protection of Animals. The poem's title 'Tray' reveals, however, that the author was still caught up in thoughts of his own childhood that autumn/winter of 1878. Tray was the name of the family dog in Camberwell. It was probably while reading – or being read – *King Lear* that a very young Robert had come up with the name, for in Act III, Scene 6 – the very same scene quoted in 'Halbert and Hob' – the heartbroken king observes: 'The little dogs and all, / Tray, Blanch, and Sweet-heart, see, they bark at me.' *King Lear* was for Browning an extremely

* *Nicomachean Ethics.*

important and rich work, a play about the true nature of love between a father and his child: he would keep coming back to it throughout his life. Edgar's song had inspired him to write 'Childe Roland to the Dark Tower Came' at a time when Robert, like Edgar, feared for an old man's sanity (his father's following the Von Müller debacle). Lear's heart-wrenching question at the end of 'Halbert and Hob' was the poet trying to make sense of the troubled relationship with his own child.*

So peaceful and productive was his time in Splügen that Browning decided to extend his stay from two to five weeks. Once, he and Sarianna trudged three hours to the top of the mountain pass to catch a glimpse of his former homeland, but not until the third week in September did they descend into Italy – not Elizabeth's Italy, but *his* Italy, the places he had known as a carefree youth when he twice travelled there in 1838 and 1844. His love for the 'woman-country' (as he calls it in 'By the Fire-Side') thus pre-dated his life with Elizabeth. 'Browning has come back from Italy,' Arnould wrote to Domett after his second visit, 'full of Venice, Rome, Naples, & enthusiasm, with restored health, increased spirits & I hope a successful poem or two.'[38]

'My liking for Italy was always a selfish one,' Browning confessed to Isa in 1866, in an effort to explain his complicated feelings for the country; 'I felt alone with my own soul there.'[39] In 'De Gustibus', composed, like 'By the Fire-Side', after his marriage and published in *Men and Women*, Browning speaks of Italy as of an old flame: 'Open my heart and you will see / Graved inside of it, "Italy." / Such lovers old are I and she: / So it always was, so shall ever be!'

In 1838 Robert had gone to Venice to finish *Sordello* amongst the scenes it described. He was enchanted. 'Venice seems a type / Of Life – 'twixt blue and blue extends, a stripe, / As Life, the somewhat, hangs 'twixt nought and nought: / 'Tis Venice, and 'tis Life.' On his return to London, full of enthusiasm for the Queen of Cities, he visited Fox's nonconformist (in every sense of the word) Bayswater cottage and, to the delight of little Tottie, etched on a sheet of blackened paper that had been waved over a candle for the purpose, the forms of light on cloud, palace, bridge, and gondola.[40] Those two weeks in Venice were important not only to Robert's poetic imagination but also to his political outlook.

---

* Sidney Colvin recalled seeing a production of *King Lear* with Browning in 1884. 'Before the end tears were coursing down [his face] quite unchecked. He seemed unconscious of them' (S. Colvin, *Memories and Notes of Persons and Places 1852–1912* (1921), 84).

In *Sordello* the narrator describes, as he sits on a ruined palace-step in Venice, being moved by a peasant girl, a 'sad dishevelled ghost', to notice the plight of the 'warped souls and bodies' all around him. From that moment, he vowed to dedicate his poetry, not to romance, but to the cause of humanity. It was, perhaps, not such a big step for a young man who grew up in a Dissenting (to some, a byword for radical) household, but the experience transformed *Sordello* into a political as well as a poetical manifesto.

His radicalism was further strengthened when, on his second visit, he was made keenly aware of the birth struggles of the Risorgimento, including the Bandiera brothers' doomed uprising against the Austrian navy on the Neapolitan coast in the summer of 1844, just a few months before Browning arrived on the scene. He celebrated the brothers' bravery and the justness of their cause in 'The Italian in England', published in *Dramatic Romances and Lyrics* the following year. Its companion piece, 'The Englishman in Italy', which extols the natural beauty of the Sorrento plain near Naples as the black clouds of the Sirocco pass over it, ends with, as Alexandra Orr puts it, 'a brief allusion to the political Sirocco which is blackening the English sky, but will not vanish so quickly': the storm over the inequitable Corn Laws.* 'Italy was *my* university,' Browning was to say ever afterwards.[41]

Venice and Naples may have educated and enlightened the young Browning, but it was 'sparkling Asolo', as he describes it in *Sordello*, wrapped 'in mist and chill' amongst the foothills of the Dolomites, that first seduced him, in 1838. Robert had then wandered through the elegant arched colonnades of the small town, where the women and children sat spinning silk. He had climbed to the ruined castle above, and had a clear view out over the Veneto to the Adriatic, the campanile of St Mark's, even the domes of Padua. He had imagined the walls around him, now overgrown with wild flowers, as they would have been: covered with bright frescoes at the height of the Renaissance, when the exiled queen from Cyprus, Caterina, together with her secretary Pietro Bembo, made Asolo and its castle a haven for writers and artists. Napoleon, Shelley, and Byron, too, were all names associated with Asolo and its neighbouring towns, Romano, Bassano, Zan Zenone. That day in 1838 atop

---

* The Corn Laws placed a duty on imported corn as a measure to help domestic farmers; but in the face of widespread famine (especially in Ireland) and the high price of bread, many, including Browning, called for their abolition, which came in 1846.

La Rocca, as the exhilarated young poet surveyed the Veneto and thought of all this, he called out for sheer joy, 'Yes, Yes!' waiting breathlessly in silence until he heard the echo repeat his cry. Asolo inspired the story of the little silk weaver, *Pippa Passes* (1841), the first of Browning's poems to appeal to a wide audience, and it became the theme of his one recurring dream. He is travelling with a friend; suddenly he sees the town he loves sparkling in the sun on the hillside. He cries to his companion, 'Look! Look! there is Asolo! Oh, do let us go there!' The friend invariably answers, 'Impossible; we cannot stop.' Each time he awoke, the poet realised that he had been dreaming it all, both the pleasure and disappointment.[42]

One wonders if this dream first came to Robert before or after he and Elizabeth visited Venice in May 1851, when they took an apartment on the Grand Canal for a month. Elizabeth was in relatively good health and in even better spirits, for she loved Venice; its mystery and beauty had far exceeded her expectations. Asolo was only thirty miles north of Venice, yet the Brownings did not venture there. Why? Elizabeth reported to Arabel that, during their stay in Venice, Robert could neither eat nor sleep and suffered continually from 'nervous irritability'.[43] Apparently, so he said, the moist air did not suit him.

More likely, however, he began to hate what he saw reflected in the canals of Venice. Rather than the aspiring twenty-six-year-old poet staring back at him, Browning saw a middle-aged man, just shy of forty, who had not yet succeeded in his aspirations. *Christmas-Eve and Easter-Day*, published just a year earlier, had made no great impression on the public. No longer did he recognise the young radical author of *Sordello*, 'The Italian in England' or 'The Englishman in Italy'. Elizabeth, who before their marriage had encouraged him to voice his political views in these last two poems, had overtaken him in the poetic defence of Italian independence with *Casa Guidi Windows*, published on 31 May 1851 while they were in Venice. Were these some of the thoughts that went through Browning's mind as he sat in the Piazza San Marco, drinking coffee, listening to the Austrian band, and arguing with his wife as to whether two-year-old Penini was too old for frilly caps? Perhaps, Browning mused, he was no better than Wordsworth, whom he had condemned in 'The Lost Leader' (also published in *Dramatic Romances and Lyrics*) for abandoning the liberal cause; his excuse, however, was not 'a riband to stick in his coat' (the Poet Laureateship), but baby hats and a more famous wife. An expedition to Asolo was never mentioned, or if it was, the idea was quietly dropped.

'So can dreams come *false*,' Browning declared to Eliza Fitzgerald from Asolo on 28 September 1878; 'for we got here without hindrance of any kind', neither real nor imaginary. Sarianna had written to her of the journey there, 'but she cannot tell you the feelings with which I revisit this – to me – memorable place after about forty years absence, – such things have begun & ended with me in the interval! It was *too* strange when we reached the ruined tower on the hill-top yesterday, and I said "Let me try if the echo still exists which I discovered here" .. and thereupon it answered me plainly as ever, after all the silence.' Browning had gone to Asolo, according to Mrs Orr, to regain 'the remembrance of his own actual and poetic youth';[44] he listened out for it in the echo calling back to him across the decades. 'And we slope to Italy at last / And youth, by green degrees.'*

Yet, in making his dream a reality, Browning had dispelled the dream itself. 'Sparkling Asolo' was never again to come to him in the hours of sleep; he no longer felt that intense yearning to go there. Moreover, reality is almost always more prosaic than poetic. The sixty-six-year-old found the rowing and screaming over a bargain on market day in the town square below his hotel room a little confusing; a decade later he would recall that his return visit to Asolo after forty years seemed more 'ordinary-life-like'. His next stopover, Venice, elicited nothing like his enthusiasm for Asolo, although he had not seen the 'Queen of Cities' for twenty-seven years, since his visit with Elizabeth in 1851. Rather, he damned the city and his stay there with faint praise. 'Hitherto,' he wrote to Mrs Fitzgerald, 'our journey has been most successful and brimful of interest: so that the events, – not vastly important in themselves, – swell out the time actually consumed.' More likely than not, Browning found the newfangled vaporetti, steam-powered boats that ferried people up and down the Grand Canal, noisy and incongruous. Certainly Henry James thought they robbed the Grand Canal of its tranquillity. Robert and Sarianna had the Albergo dell'Universo – a gloomy hotel on the Grand Canal run by a lady of good birth and fallen fortunes with a ne'er-do-well husband – to themselves, which is to say that Venice was bereft of any stimulating society. The Brackens (Pen's old friend Willy and his wife, whose marriage Browning had disapproved of so strongly seven years before) called on him one day at the hotel. 'I gave W. the kind love I was desired to take in charge [to Pen],' was all he had to say on the subject.[45]

* 'By the Fire-Side'.

The Brownings returned to London in late October, whereupon Robert settled into his quiet winter routine at Warwick Crescent. But when spring came there was excitement enough, both good and bad. Pen, who had continued to please his father by working diligently at his art, had two pictures hung in the Royal Academy Exhibition of 1879: *A Stall in the Fish-Market, Antwerp* and *Dinant, on the Meuse, Belgium*. Browning did everything possible to help his son and to promote his career. Pen did not accompany his paintings on their journey by boat to London. Rather he left it to his father, through the agency of his kind-hearted publisher, George Smith, to arrange for the unwieldy canvases to be picked up from St Katherine's Dock. (*A Stall in the Fish-Market* measured 7'2" × 9'.) In March 1879 Browning told Smith, repeating Pen's instructions, to have his man meet the ship at an early hour. Once the captain had been 'spoken to', – that is, paid – and the mate tipped, he would find them most helpful. 'Pen is as grateful to you as he should be: and I can only trust – as I venture to do from what I continue to hear – that you will find pleasure in the progress shown by the works you help so importantly.'

Smith's hospitality extended to providing, gratis, an empty ground-floor room in South Kensington to display Pen's pictures before they were delivered to the Royal Academy. On 26 March, Browning sent out invitations, the first of many over the coming years, to announce to his friends as follows:

Some new Pictures by
Mr. R. BARRETT BROWNING,
will be on view at
17, Queen's Gate Gardens, South Kensington,
from 2 till 6 p.m.,
On Friday, Saturday, Sunday, and Monday
next.

To Carlyle he added that the venue was 'at a house much nearer your own than that which you honored with a visit on the former occasion'; moreover, the pictures were on the ground floor, so he would not need to climb any stairs. Domett, who went along to the show, saw Browning handing in a rather finely dressed lady with 'some ceremony and much profession of delight at seeing her'. By his exaggerated – and, Alfred thought, somewhat ludicrous – manner, it was obvious he had no idea who she was. When it finally dawned on him, Browning whispered to his old friend, 'That was my *cook*, but I didn't recollect her.' The poet was clearly a little overwhelmed by the occasion, not to mention all the work involved beforehand.[46]

Browning was exhausted but happy. However, there were trials ahead for the poet, quite literally. On 14 June – only a month or so after the opening day of the Royal Academy Exhibition – he appeared as a witness in the trial of Shepherd *v.* Francis.[47] In 1878, Richard Herne Shepherd had produced an edition of *The Earlier Poems of Elizabeth Barrett Browning*, the poems then being out of copyright. In its review of this and previous works, *The Athenaeum* had called Shepherd 'hack', 'insect', and 'literary vampire', and he duly sued the periodical for damages.

'I need not ask who you are,' Mr Serjeant Parry, for the defence, began after Browning had taken the stand. 'I would as soon ask William Shakespeare.'

'I have been before the public some years,' Browning humbly replied. Mr Parry then gave him the opportunity to assure the jury that, had she been alive, Elizabeth Barrett Browning would have objected to the re-publication of these early poems, some written when she was only fourteen. When cross-examined by Mr Waite, Browning declared that 'from what he had now seen of the plaintiff, he thought that the estimate of his abilities formed by the writer in *The Athenaeum* was a very fair one'; he did not think it too strong to speak of the plaintiff as a man who felt 'quite at liberty to defy the wishes of the dead and outrage the feelings of the living'.

Ah, but had not Mr Browning outraged the feelings of Shelley's living son, enquired Mr Waite, when he contributed a preface to the 1852 edition of Shelley's letters – letters which were, in fact, forgeries? Browning had been warned beforehand that the subject might arise, but he was still rattled by it. In his muddled responses to Mr Waite, the poet seemed to imply that he had known the letters to be spurious all along (which, of course, was not the case).

'I have the preface here,' Browning offered lamely, 'and I shall be very happy to read the whole of it.'

'I think not,' the judge remarked, eliciting laughter from the benches.

Browning's embarrassment and humiliation were made complete when, two days later, the jury awarded Shepherd £150 in damages.

'So did Girl-moon, by just her attribute / Of unmatched modesty betrayed, lie trapped, / Bruised to the breast of Pan, half-god half-brute.' With the poem 'Pan and Luna', written within a year of the Shepherd *v.*

Francis fiasco, Browning raged against the man who, in his eyes, had betrayed Elizabeth Barrett Browning's memory while claiming to revere it. More than once had Browning associated his wife Elizabeth with the moon. Pan, the half-brute god of *shepherds*, is R. H. Shepherd, the half-vampire and king of hacks. 'Pan and Luna' retells the myth devised by the Greeks, and repeated by Virgil, to explain the first eclipse of the moon. The unscrupulous Pan entices Luna, goddess of the moon, into the depths of the woods. 'Raked by his bristly boar-sward while he lapped / – Never say, kissed her! that was to pollute / Love's language – which moreover proves unapt / To tell how she recoiled – as who finds thorns / Where she sought flowers – when, feeling, she touched – horns!' With equal disregard were Elizabeth's juvenile poems published, details of her life raked over, her reputation defiled and eclipsed by the literary hacks who professed to love her. Although in Virgil's version Luna followed Pan 'by no means spurning him', Browning knew – or thought he knew – how Elizabeth would have hated it all.

Robert had in mind not only unauthorised editions of her poetry, such as Shepherd's, but also the publication of her letters. On 19 September 1880, not long after the appearance of 'Pan and Luna' in *Dramatic Idyls: Second Series* (June 1880) – and thirty-four years to the day since he and Elizabeth had fled to the Continent as man and wife – Browning wrote to Eliza Fitzgerald regarding his wife's papers. He had just been reading the memoirs of the historian and statesman, François Guizot, compiled by his daughter. The volume included Guizot's private correspondence, something that Robert thought repugnant. He remarked to his old friend: 'Those are fine manly words of Carlyle in his *Life of Sterling* when, speaking of certain intimate letters of the actually dying friend's last moments, he says 'These are of my own, and of the things belonging to no other' – such is at least the sense of what I read so long ago. For my own part – I have intact the long series of letters addressed to me by my wife before our marriage – and *what* letters! I have never opened the box of my own letters [of] which she wore the key round her neck: but one bitter-sweet experience awaits me when – at no very distant day – I shall – for the first and last time – reread them – and then destroy – hers and mine together. However other people feel differently, and the destruction of such crowns and palm-branches will be hard to bear, no question – hence the postponement of it.'

Browning had hoped to capitalise on the success of the first series with a second series of *Dramatic Idyls*, composed in the early months of 1880.

But the collection was not as popular. Most the poems in the first series, which *The Spectator* found strange but full of 'power', 'dramatic force', and 'a touch of grandeur', read like a good story told by an old man round the family hearth, an impression reinforced by the opening lines of the volume: 'My grandfather says he remembers he saw, when a youngster long ago ..' ('Martin Relph'). The 'narrator' of the second series, however, gives the impression of a jaded traveller in the tobacco-stained, whisky-soaked back room of an inn, telling unseemly stories. These reveal the one-time hero of India to be a broken man ('Clive'), debunk Virgil's version of the Pan and Luna myth, advocate 'cleverness uncurbed by conscience' ('Pietro of Abano'), and illustrate the proverb 'Stronger than death is a bad wife' ('Doctor').* The churlish tone is established in the prologue, which begins: ' "You are sick, that's sure" – they say; / "Sick of what?" – they disagree.' The brain, the heart, the liver, the lungs, each doctor suggests in turn, yet they are all ignorant of 'man's whole' and the real cause of sickness, which is 'man's soul' – perhaps the poet's own soul.

The seemingly empty fulfilment of his return to Italy after so long (Browning's subsequent visit to Venice in 1879 passed without comment), the humiliation suffered in Shepherd *v.* Francis: these must have contributed to Browning's ill humour in the first half of 1880. At this time he also began to complain once more of Pen's reticence in his letters and of 'his habitual depreciation' of his art. Pen's pictures continued to be exhibited in London, as well as in Liverpool, Manchester, Leeds, and even Melbourne, Australia. In 1879 *The Unanswered Question*, portraying a saint in the desert, hung in the Grosvenor Gallery (a rival London venue to the Royal Academy since its opening in 1877), followed in 1880 by *Delivery to the Secular Arm*, a huge canvas showing a young girl condemned by the Inquisition. Nevertheless, Browning had begun to realise just how much hard work lay ahead for Pen. 'Before attempting to imagine an angel,' he remarked to Mrs Fitzgerald in September 1880, 'one ought to be able to express a stone or a flower,' and Pen was only now progressing beyond still-life subjects. Moreover, Pen always seemed to make it painfully clear that he felt his father applied too much pressure:

---

* The proverb is derived from Ecclesiastes: 'And I find more bitter than death the woman, whose heart is snares and nets, and her hands as bands: whoso pleaseth God shall escape her; but the sinner shall be taken by her.' One wonders if Browning had in the back of his mind Pen's short-lived engagement to the innkeeper's daughter or, perhaps, his own encounter with Lady Ashburton.

'if he painted an ambitious picture "to please me" – that only meant that, "to please me," he was venturing already a little beyond what he felt justified in doing.'[48]

The epilogue to the second series of *Dramatic Idyls* reveals yet another matter on the poet's mind as he sat at his desk in Warwick Crescent 'drowsed in fog-smoke',* far from the clear air and tranquillity of the Alps: the nature of poetry. 'Touch him ne'er so lightly, into song he broke,' the epilogue begins: 'Soil so quick-receptive' that 'song would song succeed / Sudden as spontaneous – prove a poet-soul!' No, the second stanza argues, 'Rock's the song-soil rather .. Quiet in its cleft broods – what the after age / Knows and names a pine, a nation's heritage.' Contemporaries leaped to the conclusion that in this second part Browning was referring to his own poetry, and certainly it seemed as good a description as any: verse spawned in rock, 'surface hard and bare' where 'few flowers awaken'. Browning balked at this. Several months later he scribbled a parody of the poem in a young lady's album, which pointed to Dante, not himself, as the national treasure.†

And yet .. his sketch of the two types of poetry – the one sudden and spontaneous as a delicate flower, the other as slow-growing and substantial as a tree – tallies so closely with how he viewed Elizabeth's poetry in contrast to his own. Touching upon Browning's bitterness at his long neglect, Alexandra Orr observed that, although he regarded his wife's genius as greater because it was more spontaneous and owed less to life and its opportunities, he judged his own work as the 'more important, because of the larger knowledge of life which had entered into its production'. Browning had merely come round to Elizabeth's way of thinking, for they had debated just this point during their courtship, when she asserted that 'where a poet has been shut from most of the outward aspects of life, he is at a lamentable disadvantage.'[49]

Robert had been musing on Elizabeth's genius around this time. In April 1879, a few months before he was called upon to denounce Shepherd's unauthorised edition of her poems, he advised a Miss Budden on her (not very inspired) attempts at verse. 'It is a strange, perhaps incommunicable art – that of thinking a new thought from these cold heaps of old familiar facts: a page of laborious description fails to do it, –

---

* 'Clive'.
† 'Thus I wrote in London, musing on my betters, / Poets dead and gone ..' Browning wrote this impromptu verse in the album of Edith Bronson (*Poems*, II, 960 and note).

and sometimes the apposition of one word by another sends up a spark that grows to a star.' Robert had hit upon the analogy of a star long before. 'I believed in your glorious genius and knew it for a true star from the moment I saw it,' he had written to Miss Barrett, 'long before I had the blessing of knowing it was MY star, with my fortune and futurity in it.' He returned to the image again in *Men and Women* with a poem simply entitled 'My Star': 'All that I know / Of a certain star / Is, it can throw / (Like the angled spar) / Now a dart of red, Now a dart of blue; .. Then it stops like a bird; like a flower, hangs furled ..' This was the one poem, Browning said, that he could remember, and it often found its way into ladies' albums (three times between October 1880 and April 1881).[50]

Browning was reminded again and again of the public's continued preference for Elizabeth's rich star-blooms over his own prickly pine needles. Even twenty years after her death, the sale of Elizabeth's poems (those still in copyright) continued to bring in more income than his own. The poet wrote to a correspondent in May 1880, just a few weeks after the second series of *Dramatic Idyls* went to press: 'You will be glad to know instead of the poetry of E. B. B. being "almost forgotten," it is more remembered – or, at least, called for in order to be remembered – than it ever was. A note from the Publisher, four days ago, apprises me that the almost yearly new edition of the five volumes is out .. The demand for my own works is nothing like so large.' The only comfort George Smith could give Browning in the face of the hostile reviews of his latest work was: 'You have a certain appreciable number of steady readers who will have what you write, – quite independently of what others [that is, critics] write about it.' He found 'solid satisfaction' in this assurance, so the poet told Mrs Fitzgerald.[51]

But this was not satisfaction enough for Mr Browning's small band of loyal readers, and one night in October 1881 three hundred people crowded into one of the lecture halls of University College, London. Included amongst them were Eliza Fitzgerald and her footman, without whom she never walked abroad in the city. Browning himself was conspicuously absent. The Reverend J. Kirkman stood up and proclaimed: 'Although we cannot and would not shoulder Browning up into a factitious popularity that would be sure to become extinct like fireworks, we may be instrumental in organizing, developing, and cultivating the recognition, which is the first element in our *raison d'être*, that Browning is undoubtedly the profoundest intellect, with widest range of sympathies, and with universal knowledge of many things, that has arisen as a poet since Shakespeare' – indeed, more so, 'as being the all-receptive child of the century of science and travel'. Thus the Browning Society was born. By the end of the first year there were 152 paid up members.[52]

The Browning Society was the brainchild of Frederick James Furnivall, a tireless and rather tiresome individual by all accounts – a vegetarian, teetotal socialist who lectured on grammar to labourers, denounced the House of Lords, initiated plans for the *Oxford English Dictionary*, and founded a whole string of literary societies – seven in all. Browning had the dubious distinction of being the only living author so honoured. Members (or 'apostles', as they liked to call themselves) met once a month to appreciate – and attempt to fathom – Browning's verse.[*] Furnivall asked Domett to become Vice-President of the Browning Society. He declined: 'I did not care to accept the honor of any appointment whatever, the duties of which I should not perform, as I certainly did not intend to "take the chair" at any meeting.' Furnivall responded, in typical fashion, that he must have Domett's 'name' – he was 'Waring', after all – and that he 'never need preside'. Domett threw up his hands in the face of such an onslaught; Furnivall 'was welcome to do what he liked with it'.[53] Frederic Leighton and Milsand were likewise dragooned by Furnivall.

The poet had mixed feelings about both the Society and Furnivall, whom he called his 'trumpet-blower'. As President of Furnivall's New Shakspere Society, Browning had already been caught in the middle of a vitriolic and very public feud between its founder and Swinburne (or 'Fartiwell' and 'Pigsbrook', as they called each other). Browning admitted to Edmund Gosse that he rather disliked Furnivall and thought him 'cracked'. Sarianna certainly did not like Furnivall coming to Warwick Crescent to 'shout and gesticulate and chatter till Browning would admit anything and assent to anything for the sake of getting the terrible fellow out of the house'.[54]

Browning did refuse, however, to attend the Society's meetings, to authorise its monthly printed abstracts, or even to elucidate his poetic meanings. To friends he insisted that he himself was no 'Browningite'

---

* Kirkman somewhat undermined his claims for Browning by dividing his work into two classes: those poems that may be understood and enjoyed and those *'which never will be'*. Furnivall took this to mean those poems that Kirkman liked and those he did not. He himself was certain that the Browning Society would 'soon be able to make all clear' (Peterson, *Interrogating the Oracle*, 117, 171).

and considered the whole idea to be slightly 'grotesque', as he told Edmund Yates. 'Il me semble que cela frise le ridicule,'* he was overheard to remark when the Society's prospectus arrived in the post. It made him feel, he told Eliza Fitzgerald, as if he were 'dead and *begun* with, after half a century'.[55] Half a century . . Did his musings take him back to that evening after the première of Talfourd's *Ion* in 1836 when Talfourd and his distinguished company, including Wordsworth and Walter Savage Landor, had raised their glasses to the twenty-four-year-old Browning, 'the youngest poet in England'? Had the interval of nearly five decades of neglect been simply a bad dream?

No, by now Browning was convinced that his poetry had always been and always would be – certainly in his lifetime – an acquired taste. However, he was not unappreciative of the fact that sales of his works significantly increased as the Browning Society grew, and he greatly relished the evident annoyance it gave his critics of old – 'survivors of the *un*fittest', as he called them. However, Browning rejected his trumpet-blower's call for a 'Shilling Selection' of his works (with a foreword by Furnivall, of course). In 1881 the poet reassured his publisher, George Smith, who had had quite enough of Furnivall's badgering by this time: 'Once for all, – you know whether I have at any time had the least belief in my poems ever getting popular. I hope they will one day justify me in having spent my life in composing them, – a gradual increase of readers is a different thing from a sudden leap into the heads, hands and hearts of the "Public". I am quite contented with the recognition I get already. Of course I should prefer 5000 copies of a cheap edition to 500 of a dear one, if that rate of progress could be kept up unslackened: but the nature of my works makes that altogether impossible. This I know myself.'[56]

Even the existence of a Browning Society did not persuade the poet that he was, or ever could be, as widely popular as Tennyson or, for that matter, Elizabeth Barrett Browning. However, the Society did flatter him into believing that his early dramas for the stage were worthy of attention. Miss Emily Hickey, co-founder of the Browning Society, had been instrumental in introducing Browning's very first play, *Strafford*, to the curriculum of the North London Collegiate School for Girls in 1882. She then, through the Browning Society and with the author's ready permission, set about preparing a new annotated edition of the play, which appeared two years later. 'I feel all your goodness to me – or

---

* 'It seems to me that this sort of thing borders on the ridiculous.'

whatever in my books may be taken for me,' Browning wrote to Miss Hickey on receiving the proofs of *Strafford*.[57]

Yet, Elizabeth considered *Strafford* Robert's 'poorest work of art', as she had confided to Sarianna. By the 1880s Browning seems to have become almost obsessed with those early, ill-fated days as a playwright, prompted in part, perhaps, by Tennyson's recent success on the stage, which, after *Queen Mary* (1875), continued with *Harold* (1876), *The Falcon* (1879) and *The Cup*, to name but a few. The latter, with Ellen Terry and Henry Irving in the lead roles, opened on 3 January 1881 and ran for 130 nights. Judging from the 'Celebrities at Home' article about Browning in *The World*, the poet spent at least half the journalist's visit talking about his own stage dramas, bemoaning the fact that, with all the excisions and alterations made by Macready and the like, his pieces 'did not keep the stage. There is just a faint hint in the tone of these remarks,' *The World* noted, 'which might be taken to imply that the plays would have gone better if they had been less mauled.' When a revival of *A Blot in the 'Scutcheon* toured America at around this time, Browning wrote to Lawrence Barrett, one of the lead actors: 'When I look back to the circumstances under which the piece was brought out in London – forty-two years ago – I may well wonder whether, – if my inclination for dramatic writing had met with half so much encouragement and assistance as you have really gratuitously bestowed on it, – I might not have gone on, for better or worse, play-writing to the end of my days.'[58] Did he recall that Elizabeth had been amongst those who, for better or worse, had actively discouraged him from pursuing a career as a dramatist?

The Browning Society and its activities – not to mention Furnivall's probing questions into his past life and work – stirred up old regrets* and new embarrassments. There were the inevitable caricatures in *Punch* as well as Max Beerbohm's cartoon, 'Mr Robert Browning, Taking Tea with the Browning Society', which shows a well-dressed, dapper Browning seated amongst an assortment of grey, dowdy, ill-humoured figures.

---

* For example, Browning's treatment by his early critics. He told Furnivall in 1881: 'I assure you I shirked no labour but took down and piled up scores of old dead and gone reviews as stale as the dust on them [carefully collected by his father] – "read" them I could not pretend to attempt, so did the sight of their very outsides sadden me – the word is not too strong. So much misconception at best – ignorance at middling, and malice at worst, in those old slaps on my face in order apparently to keep some fellow's critical hands warm! Yourself and those like you are the best suffumigators after this old smell' (RB to Furnivall, 8 December 1881).

It was all rather unsettling. Moreover, the population of ghosts in Browning's London was on the increase. On 29 December 1880, Browning followed George Eliot's coffin to Highgate Cemetery amidst the wind and rain. Within a few months, on 5 February 1881, Thomas Carlyle passed away – the radical thinker who initially took against young Browning's cockney riding coat, yet spent hours talking 'Scotch' with his mother in Camberwell; the narrow-minded critic who advised Robert (and also Elizabeth) to write more prose, yet gave the poet encouragement when it was needed; the old man whom, exasperating as he could be, Browning would hug if he were standing before him, so he told Carlyle's 'Boswell', William Allingham. The bond between these two very different men had been a close one. Not long before his death Carlyle had called at Warwick Crescent, only to find Browning out. 'I should like to see him once more,' Carlyle croaked from his carriage window to Sarianna. Browning returned the visit, stooped over the figure of the dying man wrapped in a shawl on the sofa, and said a word or two. 'He put his arm round my neck,' Robert recounted for Allingham. 'That was all.' The old sage had been anxious to die, the poet remarked when, on the day after the funeral, he ran into Domett on the street in a howling wind.[59]

Perhaps most disquieting of all, because it was so unexpected, news reached Browning by the end of the year (1881) that 19 Warwick Crescent was to be demolished to make way for a railway. Browning had just gone to the expense and trouble that autumn of redesigning his garden, gravelling the path and stocking his garden with shrubs from Shalstone. 'I began by too entirely despising this little house, which has behaved well enough by me for nearly twenty years,' he had told Eliza Fitzgerald in August: 'I never condescended to consider it as other than makeshift: but now I ask myself "what better I deserve" – as Coleridge did, when his tea got cold: and I daresay I shall die here.'*

Although he had been somewhat underwhelmed by Venice in 1878, nevertheless Browning returned there year after year for his annual holiday. The Queen of Cities seemed to provide the ease and contentment, together with a certain continuity, which the poet craved, especially as his London life became more unsettled and disorientated. On his third trip there (in the autumn of 1880) in as many years, he wrote to Mrs Fitzgerald that 'the weather was and continues to be

---

* An anecdote from Thomas Carlyle's *Life of John Sterling* (1851).

delightful – beyond any we remember on former visits to Venice. We shall – I hope – see nothing to prevent our staying two or three weeks longer – the place proving more attractive than ever.' He then asked, did she know Shelley's *Julian and Maddalo*? 'If I had been an unconnected man, / I, from that moment should have formed some plan / Never to leave Sweet Venice: for to me / It was delight to rove by the lone sea.' Venice was in fact one large house party, so Henry James observed, 'in which Piazzo San Marco is the most ornamented corner, and places and churches, for the rest, play the part of great divans of repose, tables of entertainment, expanses of decoration' (*The Aspern Papers*). 'The Storys are capital company, and friendly Americans abound,' Browning enthused to his friend landlocked at Shalstone. 'Somehow, Venetian visiting is a quite different thing from the London laborious "dining-out" – the lulling influence of the sea makes itself felt through the palace walls – and it is helped by one's being waited on at table by gondoliers in their white livery with blue badge and sash.' Moreover, he and Sarianna had 'a jewel of a gondolier who understands our tastes and takes us in and out the most recondite nooks and corners of the city'. And, what do you know: Robert had dined with an American family whose cook was – 'who but my old Ferdinando of Florence', married to his wife's maid Wilson and with them 'up to the very last'. 'The dear old fellow gave us a genuinely Tuscan dinner.'[60]

If Browning had been in more sombre mood, his meeting with Ferdinando might have been a source of discomfort, for any too-close association with his life with Elizabeth in Italy was painful to him. At first, the pain had come with the recollection of all that he had lost; then, increasingly, with the discovery of what he had never had. Ferdinando, who had left Wilson a few years earlier, could only have reminded the poet of Elizabeth's once devoted maid who had grown tiresome and eventually unbalanced. But Robert was in fine spirits. That autumn of 1880 he had rediscovered the charms of Italy and the easy comforts of expatriate living.

But, the real transformation of Venice in Browning's eyes – from a pleasant enough place to pass the time to an 'abode of peace and innocence', as he was calling it by the autumn of 1881 – owed less to the gondoliers and more to the friendly Americans, and one American in particular. In October 1875 the Bronsons, a wealthy, cosmopolitan, New York couple, had decided to leave their mansion in Newport, Rhode Island, and settle in Europe. They crossed the Atlantic on the Cunarder

Bothnia. Henry James, a fellow passenger, recalled that 'the season was unpropitious, the vessel overcrowded, the voyage detestable.' Most people, including James, kept to their cabins during the ten days of autumn storms over the Atlantic. Anthony Trollope, whose name was also on the passenger list, proved more seaworthy. To James's astonishment, he managed to write 'novels in his stateroom all the morning* .. and played cards with Mrs Bronson all the evening', for she was equally unaffected by the boat's pitching and tossing. Trollope was charmed by his female companion. 'I well remember our journey,' he told her years later, 'and our innocent little card playing, and more innocent little suppers.'[61]

After travelling in Europe and the Middle East for some months, the Bronsons alighted in Venice and finally settled down in the delightful if modest Palazzo Alvisi, just at the entrance to the Grand Canal near St Mark's Square. Within a few years, however, their happiness was marred by tragedy; Arthur Bronson suddenly developed a serious mental illness. By the summer of 1880 he had gone to Paris – it is not known whether he lived there on his own or in the care of someone. Although she visited her husband from time to time, Katharine Bronson expunged him from her life and never alluded to his existence amongst her Venetian friends. It was only a few months after this upheaval that Browning came into her life, probably through an introduction by the Storys. Mrs Bronson clearly had the same effect on Robert Browning as she had had on Trollope (and Henry James, once he recovered his land legs).

In 1880 Mrs Bronson was intelligent, generous, pretty rather than beautiful, and sympathetic, for she had clearly known suffering in her life. By this time she had become a semi-invalid and possessed that sort of 'broken-up beauty', like Elizabeth Barrett and Julia Wedgwood, which 'ever took my taste', as Browning had confessed forty years earlier in *Sordello.* Katharine belonged to James's Venice and the world that he evokes in *The Wings of the Dove.* She is Mrs Prest in *The Aspern Papers,* the wealthy expatriate who was 'always interested in the joys and sorrows of her friends'. At the Palazzo Alvisi (renamed the Ca' Alvisi) Mrs Bronson 'sat for twenty years at the mouth, as it were, of the Grand Canal', so the novelist remarked, 'holding out her hand, with endless good-nature, patience, charity to all decently accredited petitioners'.[62] The smaller, more compact rooms of the Ca' Alvisi, in contrast to the larger, grander

---

* Trollope was actually writing his autobiography at the time.

halls of neighbouring *palazzi*, enabled her to create a particular feeling of comfort, familiarity, even intimacy amongst her friends. She also reached out to assist the Venetian poor, especially the gondoliers and their families, those 'warped souls and bodies'* that had so affected Browning as a young man.

Katharine shared with Browning, besides a love of poetry and art, a passion for drama and a sense of humour. She converted one of the drawing rooms at the Ca' Alvisi into a private theatre and even wrote comedies in the Venetian dialect for her daughter and friends to perform. Browning found these comedies immensely enjoyable and encouraged her to publish them.† According to James, Mrs Bronson loved stories and anecdotes, and Browning had a vast repertoire with which to regale her. Moreover, there was a deep and abiding sympathy between them as Katharine was, for all intents and purposes, a single parent of an only child, like Browning. (The beautiful Edith Bronson was as old as Browning's widower-hood; she was born in 1861, within days of Elizabeth's death.) Suffice it to say, the poet always seemed to be 'at his best' in Mrs Bronson's company, as one young Anglo-Italian observed.[63] On returning to Warwick Crescent in November 1881, after only the second 'season' he had spent in her company, Browning wrote to Mrs Bronson: 'You have given Venice an association which will live in my mind with every delight of that dearest place in the world.'

For his part, Browning offered Mrs Bronson the support, companionship, and attentions of a kind, distinguished man, something that she must have sorely missed as a woman separated so recently from both her country and husband. She thought him physically attractive, later recalling 'the perfect outline of his head, the color and brightness of his eyes, or the fairness of his skin, which, with his snow-white hair, made him look as if carved in old Greek marble'.[64] Browning, of course, had always had many close female friends – Isa Blagden, Annie Smith, Alexandra Orr, Eliza Fitzgerald – but he was to them as a loving brother, no more. For Louisa Ashburton, Robert had felt physical attraction without tenderness; for Julia Wedgwood, tenderness without physical attraction. The poet's letters to Katharine Bronson exude both warm affection and sensuality. All the charms of Venice, he assured her in January 1882, converged on the Ca' Alvisi, where he imagined himself

---

* *Sordello.*
† Five privately printed plays by Mrs Bronson survive, dated 1883 to 1894.

'on the low soft chair in the room over the canal with the delicate cigarette-smoke with which I began to be seduced'. The month before, on 4 December, Browning had urged: 'If you just write "I went to the Lido" I shall see the beloved back of the gondolier considerably in the way of my look-out – so that I shall look in – where the cushion is softest and somebody is sitting. Do you know,' he added, 'that our London November has been warm and May-like beyond example,' but, 'golden as is it, may yours be refined and gilded true Venetian for your sake!'

In such a mood one can imagine Browning strolling up and down the newly gravelled path in his garden that November 1881, enjoying the clement, May-like weather, and thinking and dreaming of Katharine Bronson. 'Never the time and the place / And the loved one all together! / This path – how soft to pace! / This May – what magic weather! / Where is the loved one's face? / In a dream that loved one's face meets mine.' But there were so many obstacles. 'The house is narrow, the place is bleak, / Where, outside, rain and wind combine / With a furtive ear, if I strive to speak, / With a hostile eye at my flushing cheek, / With a malice that marks each word, each sign!' Where, Browning pondered, had he room in his life for such a love? And then there were the gossipmongers outside who would latch on to every word, every involuntary show of passion, however innocent. But what was he thinking? Katharine Bronson was a married woman, after all. Since the Ashburton debacle, he had been so certain that he would never be tempted to love again, but now .. 'Do I hold the Past / Thus firm and fast / Yet doubt if the Future hold I can?' As the gravel crunched beneath his feet, the poet thought that he might defy the world or at least continue to dream of her. 'This path so soft to pace shall lead / Through the magic of May to herself indeed! / Or narrow if needs the house must be, / Outside are the storms and strangers: we – / Oh, close, safe, warm sleep I and she, / – I and she!'*

Just at this time, November 1881, Browning told *The Athenaeum* that he had 'written a poem or two', the first in a year and a half.[65] If 'Never the Time and the Place' was one of these poems, then Katharine Bronson was its inspiration. Or, was Robert moved to compose this love lyric in the actual month of May, when his wife was always foremost in his mind, for it was one bright May day, all those years ago, when he had first

---

* 'Never the Time and the Place'.

entered Elizabeth's room on Wimpole Street. Was she the loved one whose face met Robert's in a dream, with whom, defying the storms outside, he slept 'close, safe, warm'? Elizabeth or Katharine: it hardly matters, for Browning had begun in his mind to associate the images of these two women and compound the love he felt for them, past and future.

Mrs Bronson and her daughter made plans to visit London – the following May, as chance would have it. Browning warned her: 'that hurried uncomfortable sort of bird-on-the-branch tarrying in this great distracting London will rather tantalize than satisfy my eyes and ears.'[66] When the time came, the poet was more distracted – and distraught – than usual. On 7 May he turned seventy, an age that inevitably causes people to ponder their own mortality. He was delighted to receive from the Browning Society a uniformly bound set of his own works in an oak bookcase, carved with bells and pomegranates, which he proudly displayed in the drawing room. Yet, even as he admired his gift, he must have been thinking that he would soon have to find a new home for it, owing to the proposed demolition of Warwick Crescent.

Worse, the privacy of Elizabeth's life was being invaded once more. Mr John Ingram had first proposed writing a Life of Elizabeth in 1880, at which time Browning openly discouraged him, claiming that it could not be done properly, nor should anyone try. But Ingram persisted with the project. Two years later the biographer sent a set of proofs to Browning and asked him, three times in the course of May 1882, to correct any errors he might come across. Three times the poet wrote back, insisting that he was compelled, while Elizabeth's brothers were alive, to refuse his co-operation on such a work.[67] Robert's concerns came to the surface when, on 2 May, he wrote to George Barrett regarding Elizabeth's letters – hundreds of which he had collected but never read – which had been safely stored up until now at Warwick Crescent. 'While I live, I can play the part of guardian effectually enough,' he told George, 'but I must soon resolve on the step necessary to be taken when I live no longer – and I complete my seventieth year next Sunday.' He would soon have to inspect the letters, 'ascertain what should be destroyed, what preserved as containing nothing to hurt the living or the dead'. But when he was 'off the scene', who was to be the keeper of her secrets?

With so much weighing on his mind and the inevitable 'bird-on-the-branch-tarrying', Mrs Bronson's visit to London that May was probably not very satisfying for either her or Browning. And, as she was not intending to be in Venice the following autumn, when would they meet again? To accommodate her dear friend, Katharine changed her plans; she would be at the Ca' Alvisi to greet the poet and his sister. In September, after six weeks in the French Alps, near Grenoble, the Brownings duly set out for Venice, where they were to stay for some time before visiting friends, the Cholmondeleys, on the island of Ischia, near Naples. However, in France they had learned of the accidental death of one of Mr Cholmondeley's house guests, a young woman. Browning was shocked and saddened by the event but relieved, he intimated to Eliza Fitzgerald, that he no longer had to make that infernal journey south to Ischia, infernal because it meant passing by Florence and Rome – Elizabeth's Italy. But, as it turned out, he still had to pass through hell and high water to see Katharine's Italy. After leaving France, Robert and Sarianna encountered torrential rain, first at Turin, then at Bologna, causing dreadful delays. After waiting nearly two weeks for the deluge to pass, Browning fell ill. Tired and despondent, he decided to go no further and return to London.

Some time that autumn/winter, safe and well again at Warwick Crescent, Browning picked up his pen, began to write and did not stop writing until 9 January 1883, when he sent George Smith the manuscript of his new volume, *Jocoseria*. It was, he told Furnivall on that same day, 'a collection of things gravish and gayish – hence the title', which was taken from a sixteenth-century book of jests and anecdotes that his father had given him.* *Jocoseria* is, indeed, a mixed bag. The opening poem, 'Donald', revisits a hunting story that he had heard or read more than forty years earlier, although for the detail Browning clearly drew from his son's shoots in the Scottish Highlands: 'The boys were a band from Oxford, / The oldest of whom was twenty,' it starts. 'In our eyes and noses – turf-smoke: / In our ears a tune from the trivet, / Whence "Boiling, boiling," the kettle sang, / "And ready for fresh Glenlivet."' (Did Browning catch a glimpse of the heading 'Shooting Information' at the back of Pen's notebook, which was meant to be a catalogue of his paintings?†) As for the other poems in *Jocoseria*, they delve into rabbinical lore, ancient Greek legend, and eighteenth-century France and England.[68]

---

* Otto Melander's *Jocoseria* (1597), which he had called 'rubbish' in a note to *Paracelsus*.
† While on the Continent, Pen kept up his hunting in the Black Forest, going with a group of friends for the summer months.

Yet, a coherent thread does run through this ragbag of verse, and it is the exploration of love in all its manifestations, the way that men and women dance around one another, and the inevitable misunderstandings between them. In 'Solomon and Balkis', the Queen of Sheba 'through her blushes' admits that she has come to wise King Solomon seeking not truth but a kiss – 'one fool's small kiss'; as for Solomon, 'I confess an itch for the praise of fools – that's Vanity.' 'Mary Wollstonecraft and Fuseli' concerns the pathos and pain of unrequited passion; 'Cristina and Monaldeschi', the betrayal of love and love's revenge. In 'Adam, Lilith, and Eve', two women take fright at a thunderstorm and confess their true feelings towards the man sitting between them, only to claim, once the storm has passed, that it had all been in jest: ' "I saw through the joke!" the man replied / They re-seated themselves beside.'

Katharine Bronson had reawakened in the poet feelings – confused feelings – of love: the light-hearted, light-headed happiness, the physical yearning, the painful doubts and uncertainties, and the guilt. Perversely, his feelings for Katharine made Robert recall what he once had with Elizabeth but had almost forgotten: genuine human warmth between two flesh-and-blood people. Suddenly, he seemed to miss her more than ever, the one woman who had known him – not completely, he understood that now – but better than anyone else. As in all moments of emotional crisis, Browning cried out to Elizabeth: 'Wanting is – what? / Summer redundant, / Blueness abundant, / – Where is the blot? / Beamy the world, yet a blank all the same.' So begins the Prologue to *Jocoseria*. 'Come then, complete incompletion, O comer, / Pant through the blueness, perfect the summer! / Breathe but one breath / Rose-beauty above, / And all that was death / Grows life, grows love, / Grows love!' The poet had always been sure of Elizabeth's love. Did Katharine Bronson reciprocate his passion, or was she simply humouring an old man? To Browning's surprise, the volume was so well received that a reprint was called for immediately. 'This little *Jocoseria*,' the poet wryly commented, 'has had the usual luck of the little-deserving.'[69]

Hidden amongst *Jocoseria*'s pages was 'Never the Time and the Place'. On 10 November 1882, when Browning was hard at work on his little-deserving volume, he took the time to write to Mrs Bronson: 'If I live and do well, be sure, Dear Friend, that I will go as early to Venice next year, and stay as late, as circumstances will allow ... Do believe the simple truth that a word from you, if possible, a word to the effect that you are well again and happy, — will light up November as if it were May.'

This path so soft to pace shall lead
Through the magic of May to herself indeed!

CHAPTER SIX

'In the Silence of the Sleep-time,'
1883–9

In Italy, Browning felt rejuvenated. He had rediscovered his poetic youth, not where he had expected – in the resounding echo atop Asolo's fortress – but in the soft voice of Katharine Bronson, punctuated by the long, slow draw on her cigarette. Both Robert and Katharine each had an especially strong capacity – even longing – for human love, which had been cruelly thwarted; in Katharine's case, by her husband's madness and, in Browning's, by his bereavement and subsequent devotion to the dead. When they were together, able to exchange a certain word or look, they felt they shared a perfect understanding. Yet, when they were apart, they seemed almost at cross-purposes.

When Mrs Bronson wrote to Browning of her efforts to secure the Palazzo Giustinian-Recanati, immediately next door to the Ca' Alvisi, as his new permanent residence, the poet became alarmed and replied on 6 March 1883: 'I must write *at once* about what frightens me somewhat in your kindest of letters – the allusion, – if I rightly understand it, – to my possible acceptance of your proferred generosity in the matter of the *Studio-house*: no, no! Your presence in Venice will always be reason enough for my going there for as many weeks as I can manage.' Even if he were forced to move from Warwick Crescent, he could not give up London as his home. (In any case, the railway scheme had been postponed, indefinitely, perhaps.) The only way Katharine knew how to show her love for the poet was to have him close by her, to pamper and to care for him. Browning channelled his feelings for Katharine into his poetry, unbeknownst to her, rendering their relationship more intimate yet, at the same time, more abstract. Thus he was surprised – almost irritated – when Katharine asked that he send her a copy of his forthcoming volume, *Jocoseria*, due to be published on 9 March. 'Will you please, Madam, to spare me one request for the future,' he replied in his letter of 6 March, 'and take it for granted that you will always find my "last book" go to you humbly for acceptance, without being bidden in advance – as if it did not know its duty!' Did she not know his heart?

Back in London, amidst the cold, the damp and the fogs, the good that he had gained while in Mrs Bronson's care seemed slowly, imperceptibly, to ebb away. The poet had begun to lean even more heavily on his publisher for almost everything, from hunting out his Uncle Reuben's death certificate to filling in his tax returns. And then there was the gruelling London Season. 'I get every day more and more tired,' he told Eliza Fitzgerald in July 1883, 'with this round of dining and what follows it,' the soirées and concerts. As the Season drew to a close, Browning longed for Katharine's Italy, for Venice. Elizabeth's Italy, principally Tuscany, continued to hold painful associations for Robert. 'In no case should I,' he told Edith Story (married since 1876 to the Marchese Peruzzi), 'trust myself in Florence again.'¹ Some memories of their life together in Italy were still too powerful.

Robert and Sarianna left London in August for Venice, stopping first, as was their wont, in the Alps for some weeks to recover their health in the clear mountain air. This time they chose Gressoney St Jean, nestled in the Val d'Aosta, beneath Monta Rosa and its glaciers, on the Italian side of the Alps. They lived in splendid isolation, the only way to reach their hotel being a seven-hour journey by mule in a breakneck ascent. Since Elizabeth's death, Browning had sought out the most secluded retreats for his summer holidays; he found the peace and quiet conducive to thinking and writing. Gressoney St Jean was no exception.

Earlier in the year, holed up in his study at Warwick Crescent, Browning had written a short poem entitled 'The Eagle', loosely based, like so many of his later works, on a book which he had read as a child – in this instance, *Fables of Pilpay* (1818), a sort of Persian Aesop's fables. 'The Eagle' records young Ferishtah's transition from pupil to teacher, or 'dervish'. Meditating on an eagle feeding some orphaned ravens, he comes to understand that God intends that he, like the eagle, should go forth, 'work, eat, then feed who lack'. By the time he reached the Val d'Aosta, Browning had the idea of relaying Ferishtah's teachings – Browning's own philosophical and religious beliefs thinly veiled – in a series of poems entitled *Ferishtah's Fancies*. The inspiration came from several very disparate sources.

The seventy-one-year-old Browning was keenly aware of his own mortality.* Thomas Carlyle, one of his oldest friends, had passed away in 1881, at the ripe old age of eighty-six. But Anthony Trollope had been only sixty-seven, three years younger than Browning, when the latter followed his coffin to Kensal Green Cemetery in December 1882. Robert had counted the novelist as a good friend. Anthony's mother (whom Robert did not like†) and brother Tom (whom he did) had been at the centre of the expatriate community in Florence when the Brownings were there; Anthony's niece Beatrice and Pen were once playmates. When people (Henry James included) met Trollope and Browning in the flesh, they thought them disconcertingly ordinary, so unlike their books. Yet both had been restless, ambitious young writers (and would-be playwrights) who spent much of the 1840s and 1850s in self-imposed exile – Anthony in Ireland, Robert in Italy – before achieving recognition. They belonged to the same clubs, the Athenaeum and the Cosmopolitan, shared a number of close friends, including Millais, George Smith, Kate Field, and, of course, Katharine Bronson.‡ Browning had dined with the novelist at the Garrick Club only two days before he was taken ill. 'We had a gay party, and I thought him in his usual florid health,' Robert wrote to Mrs Bronson, who grieved for her old shipboard companion.

Carlyle and Trollope could not have been more different. The Scotsman, who always saw the glass half empty, could not understand how Browning could be so confidently cheerful and so very content with life.§ This is just how a contemporary might have described Trollope,

* This concern, as well as his interest in Persian lore, is also evident in 'Joachanan Hakkadosh' (*Jocoseria*), based on a Jewish story with a Persian setting. It tells of a rabbi, close to death, whose disciples sacrifice a proportion of their own lives to extend his.
† Browning objected to Frances Trollope's political conservatism and warned Elizabeth, soon after they arrived in Florence, not to receive that 'vulgar pushing woman'. Elizabeth did receive her, although she 'had a longer battle to fight' on this matter 'than any' since her marriage. But people, she told Mrs Martin, 'are better than their books, than their principles, and even than their everyday actions, sometimes' (EBB to Mrs Martin, 30 January 1851: Kenyon).
‡ Millais illustrated and Smith published a number of Trollope's works, and he fell a little in love with the attractive young American Kate Field, whom he met in Florence when the Brownings were there. Although he was not a novel reader, Browning admired Trollope; Trollope, however, did not get on with *The Ring and the Book*, calling the poet a 'stodger' and putting a double exclamation mark next to the title amongst the list of books which he read aloud to his family (Trollope to his son Henry, 23 January 1882 and Appendix C in Hall (ed.), *Letters of Anthony Trollope*). Nevertheless, they each paid tribute to the other in their works: Trollope through Wallachia Petrie, the 'American Browning', in *He Knew He Was Right* and Browning in *The Inn Album*, where a character asks if she is to 'exercise / At Trollope's novels for one month?'
§ Carlyle was not the only one. 'An eminent author,' wrote Sharp, 'of a weak digestion wrote to me recently animadverting on what he calls Browning's insanity of optimism: it required no

who literally died laughing, suffering a fatal stroke while listening to his niece read aloud from a popular comic novel of the day. Browning saw the futility of Carlyle's pessimism and preferred the outlook of that 'good roaring positive fellow', as James Russell Lowell once described Trollope.[2] At some point it occurred to Browning that he had lived long, suffered much, and overcome a great deal. Surely, he had something to say; moreover, the disciples of the Browning Society expected it of him.

The poet's first concern was to make his musings not merely palatable but appetising. 'Pray, Reader, have you eaten ortolans* / Ever in Italy?' So Browning begins the prologue to *Ferishtah's Fancies*, dated 'Maison Delapierre, Gressoney Saint Jean, Val d'Aosta, 12 September 1883'. 'They pluck the birds .. then roast them, heads by heads and rumps by rumps, / Stuck on a skewer. / But first .. comes plain bread, crisp, brown, a toasted square: / Then, a strong sage-leaf: / .. First, food – then, piquancy – and last of all / Follows the thirdling' – the succulent bird. To savour the dish one must 'through all three bite boldly – lo, the gust! / Flavour .. flies, permeating flesh and leaf and crust'. 'So with your meal,' Browning proclaims, 'my poem: masticate / Sense, sight and song there!' My verse is hard at first bite, pungent next, but rich and meaty at the centre.

Ferishtah's encounters with melon-sellers, camel-drivers, and Shahs, told in twelve 'fancies' or fables, reveal Browning's own very personal philosophy of life, which had been formed over the years and was often expressed through his poetry. His conviction, put forth in 'Shah Abbas', that faith is intuitive, the will of the heart, not of the mind, was earlier developed in *La Saisiaz*. The idea that men could or should believe, without proof, that God once took human form – the subject of 'The Sun' – had preoccupied the poet since *Men and Women* ('An Epistle' and 'Cleon'). Robert, who had repudiated the doctrine of eternal punishment in *Jocoseria* ('Ixion')† and promoted the active life over asceticism in 'Rabbi Ben Ezra' (*Dramatis Personae*), did so again in 'A Camel-Driver' and 'Two Camels' respectively. The moral of 'Cherries', that the value of a gift, in God's eyes, lies in the spirit in which it is given, was expressed

---

personal acquaintanceship to discern the dyspeptic wellspring of this utterance' (Sharp, *Life*, 24).

* An ortolan is a kind of quail.

† In 'An Epistle .. of Karshish' and 'Cleon', the central characters, an Arab physician and a Greek poet respectively, witness the birth of Christianity. In Greek mythology, Ixion was bound to a rotating wheel of fire in Hades.

as early as *Pippa Passes* in 1841. In 'Plot-Culture', Browning declares that a man's conscience is a question between himself and God, an idea that had been present in *Fifine at the Fair.*

While Browning was turning over these new poems in his mind, he received news of the death of Miss Teena Rochfort-Smith, Furnivall's secretary – and mistress – as the result of severe burns sustained when her dress caught fire. 'What am I to say,' Robert wrote to Furnivall two weeks into his holiday in the Val d'Aosta, 'to your appalling letter?' He attempted some words of comfort – 'You will know I feel for you in every nerve' – before adding in the postscript: 'I am writing some poetry which will be much influenced by this experience, I do not doubt.' Robert too had known the most heart-wrenching grief, had despaired of any good in the world. In the poem 'A Bean-Stripe', a scholar enquires of Ferishtah, just as Furnivall might have begged to know after Teena's death – 'A good thing or a bad thing – Life is which? / Shine and shade, happiness and misery / Battle it out there: which force beats, I ask?'

Take a bushel of black and white beans, the scholar challenges Ferishtah. 'For beans / Substitute days, – show, ranged in order, Life – Then tell me its true colour!' The 'dervish' Browning responds: 'Of absolute and irretrievable / And all-subduing black, – black's soul of black / Beyond white's power to disintensify, – Of that I saw no sample.' There are those, Ferishtah adds, like the 'the sourly-Sage', who 'found no white at all / Chequer the world's predominating black, / No good oust evil from supremacy, / So that Life's best was that it led to death.' Such a 'sourly-Sage' had been Thomas Carlyle, who at the end had only wanted to die.* Browning had once called the chessboard black as often as white – so Elizabeth had testified – but not any more, not at the present moment. 'Who laughest "Take what is, trust what may be!" / That's Life's true lesson, – eh?' So ends the prologue, dated just three days after Browning received Furnivall's dreadful news. Anthony Trollope's death almost seemed to illustrate this lesson of life.

How had Browning come to don a Persian cloak? The thought may have first struck him while rereading *King Lear*, Act III, Scene 6, that very scene which had inspired 'Halbert and Hob' and 'Tray' (*Dramatic Idyls*): 'You, Sir, I entertain you for one of my Hundred; only I do not like the fashion of your garments: you will say, they are Persian: but let

---

* It was around this time that Browning spoke harshly of Carlyle to Daniel Sargent Curtis (Curtis, 'Robert Browning'.)

them be changed.' Thus appears the address by Lear to the disguised Edgar at the front of *Ferishtah's Fancies*. To be steeped in Eastern art and philosophy, Robert had only to go to Frederic Leighton's house in Holland Park, as he often did to attend concerts, Show Sundays, and evening soirées. In the late 1870s Leighton had extended his house to incorporate the 'Hall of Narcissus', a wide corridor leading to the even more magnificent 'Arab Hall'. Both rooms are lined from floor to ceiling with decorative tiles collected by the artist and his friends (including the explorer Richard Burton) on their travels east to Syria, Egypt, and Persia. To complete the space, Walter Crane designed a series of tiles, which were specially crafted in Venice. Some of the mosaics have animal and flower motifs; others display Arabic inscriptions. The *Art Journal* noted at the time: 'There is about the whole hall the peculiar sense of repose and stateliness, of colour and solemnity, characteristic of the true East.'[3]

Browning could not but have been seduced by its beauty and exoticism, and *Ferishtah's Fancies* seems to reflect these same qualities of repose, stateliness, colour, and solemnity. Moreover, as with Leighton's mosaics, Browning's exotic phrases were for decorative effect rather than deep inner meaning. 'If you will only concern yourself with what is set down,' he told Eliza Fitzgerald when she had confessed herself bewildered by the unfamiliar words in *Jocoseria*, 'regarding a name as a name that explains itself, and a passing allusion as just an allusion and no more.'[4]

Browning had not finished his 'fancies' by the time cooler weather threatened snow in the mountain passes. He and Sarianna made the precipitous, seven-hour descent from Gressoney St Jean by donkey and took three further days to reach Venice by train. They arrived on 4 October in the rain. Katharine Bronson's gondolier Luigi was at the station to meet the weary travellers, 'lighting the way', Robert recalled nearly a year later, 'a few footsteps farther to the more than Friend who had come in the rain to take us and keep us'.[5] 'There is no other such dignity of arrival than by water,' wrote Henry James in *Italian Hours*: 'to float and slacken and gently bump, to creep out of the low, dark *felze**** and make the few guided movements and find the strong crooked and offered arm, and then, beneath lighted palace-windows, pass up the few damp steps', leading into a haven of comfort and elegance.

Mrs Bronson installed the brother and sister next door to the Ca' Alvisi, in the Palazzo Giustinian-Recanati, the very place whose purchase

---

* The cabin at the rear of a gondola.

she had been negotiating for Browning. She decided it would make a convenient guest annexe; Henry James stayed there on a number of occasions. Katharine thought the building 'worthy of a poet's sojourn', owing to its long history and fine façade, with Gothic windows looking out upon a court and garden, and a southern exposure. Browning intended to be home in London at the end of October, so he told Mrs Fitzgerald, 'notwithstanding the witchery of the place and the kindness of our Hostess'. 'Kind compulsion' was the phrase he used when describing Mrs Bronson's charms to the Skirrows. She offered Robert and Sarianna everything they could wish for – all the creature comforts, including their own maid and gondolier, as well as good society. She 'received' most evenings and surrounded Browning with stimulating dinner companions. On leaving the table, the poet would 'talk loud and long, full length in a low chair or sofa-corner, with legs thrust straight out and his hands either clasped behind his head, or plunged into his trousers' pockets'. Sarianna would sit 'erect in her chair, disdaining the support of its back', adding to the conversation every once in a while with an apt observation. One such party was made up entirely of kings, princes, and princesses, Browning told Eliza Fitzgerald – 'all deposed and all as gay as grigs!' At the end of October, when the poet was thinking of returning to London, Mrs Bronson and her daughter Edith persuaded the Brownings to accompany them to Athens, sailing from Brindisi to Corfu and through the islands. This was, Robert told his friend at Shalstone, 'the realization of a dream I have had all my life, and began to despair of finding other than a dream'.[6] In the end, however, they abandoned the idea, for it would have been too taxing on Mrs Bronson's frail health.

Katharine was astute enough to give Browning time to himself while Venice worked its magic on the poet. The weather that autumn was superb. He rose early and walked with Sarianna to the Public Gardens to offer treats and sympathy to the caged animals in the zoo. Sunday mornings were devoted to a local Waldensian chapel.* Each midday brother and sister returned to the Palazzo Giustinian-Recanati to a private repast of classic Italian dishes, such as risotto, macaroni, and even ortolans, followed by seasonal fruits. In the afternoon Mrs Bronson and Edith often set out with them by gondola to tour 'the splendour of the

---

* The Waldensians were a pre-Reformation movement, deemed heretical by the Roman Catholic Church.

great water-way', as James described it on a clear summer's day; 'the sense of floating between marble palaces and reflected lights disposed the mind to freedom and ease' (*The Aspern Papers*).

After a couple of hours exploring the city by water, they would return to a party assembled for tea at the Ca' Alvisi. Browning would sometimes, without stopping for any refreshment, excuse himself for the day and retire to his own apartments. 'He never gave nor was asked his reason for doing so,' the discreet hostess noted; 'it was enough that he wished it.' But Browning, always scrupulously dressed, would appear with Sarianna for dinner at half past seven at the Ca' Alvisi, whether it be a meal *en famille* or a large party. And then there were the sunsets: 'the evenings are inaugurated by such sunsets,' Browning told Furnivall, 'as I believe are only to be seen here – when you float between two conflagrations – that of the sky, reflected in the lagune.' The poet found it hard indeed, as he told Eliza Fitzgerald, 'to extricate oneself from the all-embracing kindness of our Hostess here'. He stayed on well into November. The weather had remained unseasonably warm – as if it were May – and the butterflies still flitted about in the Public Gardens. 'This is said to excuse, or rather explain,' he added, 'our lingering on and unwillingness to return to the fog and cold of which we hear sufficiently.' At long last Browning and Sarianna determined to leave. 'Next Saturday is our doomsday,' he wrote to the Skirrows on 4 December; 'This sounds wickedly – for I have abundant reason for wanting to be at home, (after four months' absence) .. but only a poor creature has just one side to his soul.'[7]

They travelled back to London through Paris, where they stopped over to see Pen, who had gone there to study with Rodin, no less. In Paris, Browning learned that he would not be able to return to Warwick Crescent for some weeks; one of his servants had been taken ill with diphtheria and the house was quarantined. Mrs Fitzgerald offered him the use of her London home in Portland Place for the duration, certainly while she remained at Shalstone. Katharine wrote to Sarianna, just a few days after their departure from Venice: 'I suppose I will one day get used to your absence, but the time has not come yet, & I look with the same sadness across the lonely court every morn'g & evening.' The weather, which had turned cold and grey, added to the sense of melancholy. Mrs Bronson reported on the people whom the Brownings knew in Venice, from the deposed despots of Europe to little Giuseppina, the maid who had special charge of the poet and his sister. 'It is wonderful,' she wrote, 'to hear her stream of talk about you. I wish I c'd transcribe it to make you smile. Her whole monologue may be summed up in the idea that no one has ever been seen to compare with either you or Mr Browning. She says she has a right to judge because she has seen so many forestieri [foreigners] in her life.'[8]

At the breakfast table back in London, Robert and Sarianna would have discussed all their former companions' comings and goings with the keenest interest, in an effort to cling to their memories of Venice. But for Browning the happiness of those two months was inextricably linked to the presence of Katharine, as explained to her on 27 December: 'If I do not dwell more on the loss of those good days and afternoons and evenings,' he explained, 'it is because I hold fast what I gained then, and feel sure that so long as you and I are on earth there will only be so much more or less earth and sea between us: and, for my part, be you as sure that whenever I can overpass these, in the body and not merely the soul, I will once – and if God please – many times again be with you.' He scolds Mrs Bronson about her health, urging her to avoid those small excursions – petty 'taps' – which are nonetheless harmful, 'as the lapping wavelets of the Vaporetti are said to undermine your palaces'. Elsewhere he insisted that she might do better 'could one take the cigarette out of the mouth (well, – I don't think I should like *that*, after all) and induce daily walkings (but – suppose there were no glad and proud companionship immediately available from Palazzo Giustiniani at signal of a whiteness at a window across the Court?) and .. and .. no end of "ands" – all to no purpose, because some things and persons are so entirely well as they are, and one hates to risk interference with them!'[9]

'Those two happy months! – and their good stays with me,' Browning assured Mrs Bronson in January 1884, 'the physical as well as the spiritual good, for, besides the memories, I seem to be living on the strength I stored up there [*sic* for 'then'] and there: I swallow no end of fog and prove unchokable.' He had strength enough to finish the twelve poems comprising Ferishtah's 'fancies'; moreover, he entirely reconfigured the volume, devising a series of love lyrics, one to follow each Persian piece in sense as well as in order. Just as in 'The Eagle', where the young Ferishtah realises that he must mingle with men and women, so the poet exhorts his lover: no woodland paradise for us, no rich-pavilioned splendour, 'Let throngs press thee to me! / Up and down amid men, heart by heart fare we! .. with souls should souls have place.' 'You groped your way across my room i' the dear dark dead of night,' begins the lyric following 'Shah Abbas'; 'At each fresh step a stumble was.' But love, like faith, is intuitive: 'Be love your light and trust your guide, with these explore my heart!'

Both Alexandra Orr and Furnivall had reason to believe that Browning dashed off these twelve lyric poems within a very short space of time. Perhaps his ever-deepening feelings for Katharine Bronson brought home to the poet that he had left out the single guiding principle which held together these 'fancies', so called. To rectify this omission, Browning eschewed all disguise and revealed that love – God's love as manifested in the love between man and woman – is the key to all questions of belief, a doctrine he had long held. The recollection of his Venetian hostess caused his imagination to soar. 'Would I could fly to a home of mine and a housemate beyond the sea,' Browning wrote to Katharine at the end of February, quoting an old Alsatian song;* but 'I must remain here, wingless except in fancy-flights to my own friend of whom I am the own friend while this machine is to him' – an allusion to Hamlet's farewell in his love-letter to Ophelia: 'thine evermore, most dear lady, whilst this machine is to him'.

The affinity between godly and human love is perfectly expressed in the lyric which follows 'Two Camels'. 'Had I no experience how a lip's mere tremble', begins the second stanza, 'Look's half hesitation, cheek's just change of colour, / These effect a heartquake, – how should I conceive / What a heaven there may be? Let it but resemble / Earth myself have known! No bliss that's finer, fuller, / Only – bliss that lasts, they say, and fain would I believe.' Browning seemed to be conjuring up just such a 'heartquake' between them when he wrote to Katharine at the end of December (1883): 'I get into and out of the gondola with you, not unhelped by the fat [gondolier] Luigi, – "Piano, Piano!", – and go through the same quiet delights back again' – the quiet delights of that inadvertent touch as the passing vaporetto caused the gondola to rock like a cradle.

But, whereas God's love is perfect, human love is very imperfect. In several of the lyrics appended to Ferishtah's 'fancies', the poet cries out to be loved, not worshipped. 'Man I am and man would be, Love – ,' so begins one such poem, 'merest man and nothing more. / Bid me seem no other!' Yet he was an 'other' to Katharine Bronson; he was the famous English bard who condescended to accept her hospitality and to read his

---

* The song begins: 'If I were a little bird / And had two little wings / I'd fly to thee.'

poetry aloud to evening gatherings at the Ca' Alvisi. There had been nothing spoken between them. 'Ask not one least word of praise!' the poet begs following 'A Pillar at Sebzebar'. 'Words declare your eyes are bright? / What then meant that summer day's / Silence spent in one long gaze? / Was my silence wrong or right? / Words of praise were all to seek! / Face of you and form of you, / Did they find the praise so weak / When my lips just touched your cheek – / Touch which let my soul come through?' But Mrs Bronson was not the sort of woman to take a man's love for granted.

She could glean nothing from his poetry for, as she observed, he rarely spoke about it, even to his most intimate friends. His prose declarations were, at best, ambiguous. 'You once asked,' Robert wrote in September 1884, 'if I often thought of you: I could answer – by a mechanical contrivance, every five minutes at least. You gave me a dear coin, that issued by the Venetian Republic in '48: I had a ring affixed to it, and that again appended to my watch-chain, – the only other token of love there being my wife's ring. But I think of you between whiles all the same.' Each assurance to Katharine of his love for her only served to betray his devotion to his dead wife. 'The thought of her,' Mrs Bronson later recalled, 'as an angel in heaven, was never out of his mind.' What other form of love was left to Katharine but worship when, on first receiving her gift, all Browning could say was: 'I love this coin as she would have loved it. You know what she felt and wrote about United Italy.'[10]

Robert wanted to believe that his passion for Katharine could be suspended alongside his loyalty to Elizabeth as easily as the coin next to the ring on his watch chain. Yet, there were moments when he felt torn in two. As he had intimated to the Skirrows towards the end of his stay in Venice, 'only a poor creature has just one side to his soul.' Just a few days before he wrote this, as he sat at the open window of the *palazzo* taking in the warm breeze, the optimistic 'dervish' side of his soul had wrestled with the dark, human side. 'Oh, Love – no, Love! All the noise below, Love, / Groanings all and moanings – none of Life I lose!' Thus Browning addressed his dead wife in what was to be the Epilogue to *Ferishtah's Fancies*, dated 'Palazzo Giustinian-Recanati, Venice, 1 December 1883'. It 'seemed to belong to the beloved place where it was penned, – as I wanted to remember – or be remembered rather', so he told Mrs Bronson.[11]

There, alone with his memories of Elizabeth, he felt safe: 'All of Life's a cry just of weariness and woe, Love' – 'How can I, Love, but choose?'

But then, as the poet looks around him, the cloud clears and the moon reveals the faces of 'the famous ones of old' – divined perhaps amongst the ancient stone façades lining the Grand Canal. The 'cloud-rift broadens' and the earth 'displays its worth, man's strife and strife's success: / All the good and beauty, wonder crowning wonder'. This is the uplifting voice of Ferishtah. 'Only, at heart's utmost joy and triumph, terror / Sudden turns the blood to ice: a chill wind disencharms / All the late enchantment! What if all be error – / If the halo irised round my head were, Love, thine arms?' What if the world's good and beauty – the happiness Browning found in Katharine Bronson's company – what if it were all a delusion, merely the afterglow of his love for Elizabeth, and hers for him? In just a few lines Browning had put in doubt all that had gone before, not just in the Epilogue, but in the whole of the *Fancies*. Or was this the point? Even Ferishtah, in his wisdom, had understood that 'all-subduing black, – black's soul of black .. may wreck / My life and ruin my philosophy / Tomorrow.'*

Who knows what tomorrow may bring? Browning and Mrs Bronson had kept up a faithful and lively correspondence throughout the spring and summer of 1884. In April he bemoaned the fact that he had another week of unremitting festivity at Edinburgh, 'whither I betake my tired self to-morrow, when, instead of starting on a nine hours' journey northward, I should like to go to sleep even on the hardest of armchairs .. If heaven please,' he added, 'be the next three months a game at Tennis – of which I am the ball – at the end comes Venice!' The reception given him by the students of Edinburgh made the journey worthwhile. When he rose to receive his honorary degree from the university, the young men stomped their feet and chanted, 'Browning! Browning! Browning!' Nevertheless, it was all so exhausting. The poet did indeed feel bandied about like a tennis ball, and by the end of June he confessed, 'I am wearied out with this London season's hard work called amusement.' Sarianna had been bedridden with a severe attack of peritonitis. They both looked forward to a holiday in the mountains, perhaps the Val d'Aosta again, followed by the delights of Venice and the Ca' Alvisi. However, a cholera outbreak barred the Brownings from entering Italy. They had to content themselves with the kind invitation of Mrs Bloomfield-Moore – she of the Keeley Motor Company – to share the Villa Berry, in St Moritz, Switzerland, from mid-August. Perhaps the

* 'A Bean-Stripe'.

quarantine restrictions would soon be lifted, enabling the brother and sister to proceed to Venice from Switzerland.

But the fates were conspiring against them. Soon after their arrival in St Moritz, the Brownings learned that Mrs Bronson was not in Venice, but in Paris, on 'an errand of mercy', as Sarianna called it, to visit her husband who had become increasingly ill. If that were not enough, Mrs Bloomfield-Moore was then summoned by telegram back to America on business, leaving the Brownings together with her mentally unstable daughter, who seldom showed herself, and a few attendants.* The Brownings made up their minds to forgo Italy and return to London. Towards the end of September a second, more propitious telegram arrived at the Villa Berry. It was from Mrs Bronson. The quarantine had lifted, and she was proposing to change her plans, return to Venice and receive the poet and his sister – if they were not afraid of the cholera. Browning had no fear of cholera, but, he told Furnivall, 'the notion of our friend's making such a sacrifice on our account, was unendurable.' Perhaps, he suggested, she might come to London from Paris. He thought of her often, whenever he checked the time and saw her coin on his watch. 'Here or there,' he wrote, 'at Venice or London, words cannot say how much I am yours.' She would have also been especially on his mind just then, for he had taken the proof sheets of *Ferishtah's Fancies* to St Moritz to correct, and he was happy enough to get back to London to see it through the press. 'I can't at all guess how people will like it,' he remarked to Furnivall, 'but I have managed to say a thing or two that I "fancied" I should like to say.'[12]

We do not know what Katharine Bronson thought – or dared to think – of *Ferishtah's Fancies*. When she received her copy, soon after its publication on 21 November 1884, she had much on her mind. Owing not only to her husband's worsening state but also to her own ill health, she did not visit London. She also ceased directing letters to Warwick Crescent for some time. In February, Browning became concerned and

---

* Mrs Bloomfield-Moore's son-in-law, a Swedish baron, had committed her daughter to an insane asylum in Austria. The mother sought custody but was herself deemed insane. She eventually reversed the decision, but it seems she could be somewhat delusional. As Mrs Bloomfield-Moore left St Moritz, she told Browning, 'Remember, I have loved you with the best and most enduring love – soul love.' She later claimed that the lyric in *Ferishtah's Fancies*, beginning 'Not with my Soul, Love!' was a declaration of the poet's love for her. Browning did indeed send these lines to the publisher after her departure – not as a declaration of love but as a protest against platonic, and rather boring, infatuations like Mrs Bloomfield-Moore's (DeVane & Knickerbocker, 307–8; McAleer (ed.), *Learned Lady*, 184; *Poems*, II, 1101).

wrote to ask why should this be: 'Dearest Friend, I hold fast to your affection, – you must know it, must know,' he insisted, thinking perhaps of all that emotion he had poured into *Ferishtah's Fancies*. Within a month he learned that Arthur Bronson had died, on 2 March 1885. The major obstacle to any union between Browning and Mrs Bronson was gone. 'I had heard,' he wrote a week later, 'with what mingled feelings you need not be told, – that you were in Paris and for what reason. I do not venture to say a word: ... all I know is, I joy in your joy, grieve in your grief, accepting your estimate of both.' A month later he dashed off another brief note to Katharine: 'How I trust all is going well with you, certainly you need no assurance of. Enough that I love you with all my heart.'

How divided – and painful – must Katharine's feelings have been at this time. Browning's words of love and support must have been a great comfort to her. Perhaps she took up the small green-cloth volume, for the hundredth time, letting it fall open to the lyric ending: 'When my lips just touched your cheek – / Touch which let my soul come through'. Had these words really been meant for her? But then she thought of her husband Arthur, whom she had been with in Paris when he died. She had inscribed on his gravestone in the cemetery of St Germain-en-Laye the following lines: 'His last conscious acts were those of loving kindness: / His last conscious words were those of trust in God.'[13] This is very much the sentiment of a wife recalling how happy she had once been with her husband. But, as Browning intimated and she could not deny, his death must have been a relief to her and, probably, a release for him. Then there was so much to do: papers to be drawn up, the additional agony of waiting to hear from lawyers in America, and, most importantly, Edith's financial interests to be secured. Mrs Bronson was exhausted and could think of little else.

She was in Austria, taking the waters to recover her strength in both body and spirit, when she received a letter from Browning, dated 4 September 1885, from 'Hôtel Delapierre, Gressoney St Jean, Val d'Aosta, Italia'. 'You remember,' he appealed, 'this is the wild beautiful place whence we followed you to Venice two years ago, – as our hope was we should do once again. It will be heart-breaking if you are not in Venice.' Indeed, he and Sarianna 'should turn away our heads from the vacant shrine and departed glory' of Venice and the Ca' Alvisi but for Pen. Ever since his father and aunt had returned from their last blissful holiday there, he too wanted to see Venice. 'We cannot disappoint the poor fellow' – they must go to Venice, Browning told Katharine, 'but what will Venice be without you! – All the same, don't fancy me so selfish,' he added, as 'to keep you from your duties – we thoroughly know how glad you would be to make us as happy as before'. Mrs Bronson cut short her rest cure, put off business that had threatened to take her to America, and was back in Venice by the end of September – only seven months after the death of her husband – to receive Browning and his sister. Pen, who planned to arrive a few weeks ahead of them and take a studio there, would make his own arrangements.

'I love you with all my heart,' Browning had written only a few months before.[14] What was the widow's state of mind as she received the poet and his sister at the Ca' Alvisi? She must have wondered why Browning was so eager to see Venice again: to be with her, to comfort her, to ascertain if she might truly be 'more than Friend' – a phrase, although she could not know it, which was full of meaning. Perhaps Katharine had begun to think that she might love, not merely worship, Mr Browning. Alternatively, she might have returned to Italy simply to oblige dear friends. As for Browning, perhaps his desire to return to Venice was simply on account of Pen. Neither knew what was in the other's heart; they were probably not even sure of their own.

One thing was certain, however: Pen was everything to Browning. The father's concern, worry, and occasional anguish had given way to sheer pride and delight in his son. He was not content merely to help further his son's career; for all intents and purposes, he managed it too. Browning continued to organise, with the help of George Smith, exhibitions of Pen's work in Queen's Gate. He sent out invitations and played the showman on these occasions before friends and strangers alike. The poet even took it upon himself to instruct the workmen in the varnishing, crating, uncrating, shipping, and hanging of the canvases.[15]

For six years running, Pen had exhibited his work, statues as well as paintings, at the Royal Academy – a real achievement for a young artist. At one such show in 1881 Alfred Domett spied from across the room a young Oscar Wilde, 'foppishly dressed; long hair to his shoulders, light brown overcoat with curly-furred collar &c'.* Domett's son, despite

* W. P. Frith captured the moment in his painting, *Private View at the Royal Academy*; Browning and Trollope are amongst the crowd along with Wilde. In this same year, 1881, the twenty-seven-year-old Wilde published his first volume of poems. After Browning's death, he said of the poet, 'the man was great' ('The True Function and Value of Criticism', *Nineteenth Century*, 28 (1890); reprinted in *Critical Heritage*).

entering the Royal Academy Schools and studying at Bonnat's Paris studio, only ever had one painting, *The White Rose of York*, chosen for the Exhibition, in 1879. In the *Dictionary of Victorian Painters* this 'flower picture' is listed as his only achievement. Relations had remained awkward between the two old friends. Domett recorded bumping into the poet at Bishop's Road Station, as he often did, in early 1883. Browning asked about Alfred Junior and his painting, after which Domett asked, probably through clenched teeth, about Pen's art. 'Pen had made £1200 last year by his pictures,' beamed the proud father, proceeding then to describe each sale in detail. 'Browning looked well, animated and stepping along sturdily as usual – grown I thought a little stouter,' was Domett's slightly sour comment as he watched the other walk away.[16]

But by 1884 Pen's career had begun to run into trouble. That year the exhibition committee at Burlington House rejected the artist's 6' 4" bronze statue of *Dryope Fascinated by Apollo in the Form of a Serpent*. Pen had paid £16 for a ten-foot python from Senegal to pose with (that is, twine around) his Italian model for hours on end. Certain members of the Academy, however, thought the statue crude. For his old friend's sake, Leighton did his best to reverse the decision but to no avail. The distraught father strode down Piccadilly to Bond Street and banged on the door of the Grosvenor Gallery, beseeching the officials, with tears rolling down his cheeks, to accept the statue. The boy had put so much time and effort into the work; it had been a year in the making. The owner and manager, Sir Coutts Lindsay, also happened to be a friend of his, so *Dryope* was duly exhibited at the Bond Street gallery. Browning forgot all the trouble and heartache when the 'Beaux-Arts' Exhibition in Brussels not only took the statue that same year, despite it being a late entry, but even gave it 'absolutely the best place in the Salle de Sculpture', so he crowed to George Smith.[17] Pen did not exhibit at the Royal Academy again, although his pieces could still be viewed at the Hanover and Grosvenor Galleries.

Most art critics had continued to be generous – for a time, at least – although the size of Pen's canvases elicited comment. In 1879, *The Times* said of *Watching the Skittle Players*: 'As for Mr Browning's pig, we do not know what literal painting could do more with and for a pig than he has done,' adding: 'We do not remember a painter who has ventured on so literal and so nearly life-sized a presentation of a porker as we have here.'*

---

* Even Browning had to admit that 'Pen must learn to moderate this desire for plenty of

William Rossetti, however, had decided early on that Pen Browning was not – and never would be – 'a painter of *genius*', and the rest of the British art establishment eventually came to agree.[18] Tellingly, Pen's chief patrons over the years were his father's lady friends: Mrs Fitzgerald, Miss Egerton-Smith and, most prominently, Mrs Bloomfield-Moore.

Nevertheless, as far as Browning was concerned, where once it had seemed that Pen could do no right, now he could do no wrong. Rudolf Lehmann said of the poet's devotion to his son: 'He never pardoned one of his oldest friends for having formerly expressed a mild doubt about Pen's capacity for steady, hard work.' At times it seemed that Browning had only one purpose in life: to secure Pen's future. Once he had been a 'monomaniac' on the subject of the young man's education; now it was his career. He once told Mrs Bronson how he would gladly destroy every line he ever wrote if by so doing he could see 'fame and honor heaped' on Pen's head. 'In his boy,' Katharine later noted, Browning 'saw the image of the wife whom he adored, literally adored.' He continued to think of Pen as his mother's child. In describing the sale of some of Pen's paintings in 1882, Browning confided to Elizabeth's brother George: 'You well know whose heart would have been rejoiced at this besides mine.'[19]

For Pen's sake Browning even went so far as to make a Faustian pact with the devil – the devil in the guise of one of *The Athenaeum*'s editors and critics, Norman MacColl. He agreed to give *The Athenaeum* advance notice of his forthcoming poems – something that he had previously always refused to do – in return for helpful press coverage of his son's paintings. Thus when in 1881 Browning wrote to MacColl to explain that the rumour in *The Academy* of a forthcoming edition of 'new Idyls' had not originated with him, since he had not broken his part of the bargain, he added nonchalantly: 'I don't know whether there is any interest in knowing that two of my Son's pictures which *The Athenaeum* spoke kindly about .. have just been purchased – the former for the Philadelphia Academy of Fine Arts, – the latter for the American purchaser's [Mrs Bloomfield-Moore] own satisfaction. Gossip about this – which happened last week – *might* get into print elsewhere, so I set it down, – begging you to believe me, &c. &c.'[20]

---

elbow-sweep as he works.' He directed Smith, who had generously offered to display Pen's pictures at his offices in Waterloo Place, not to sell the smaller ones for less than the asking price. But, the larger pictures, 'in case any of them should take folks' fancy – may go at *any* reduction of price – simply because of their *size*' (RB to George Smith, 23 April 1880, 27 January 1883: Murray).

As for Pen's character, people were divided. Although he had more reason than most to resent the young artist's success, Domett still thought him good-natured and unassuming. Others were less kind. 'There was but one novelty in Dinant,' wrote Thomas Westwood, the poet and one-time friend of Mrs Browning, '*Robert Browning, jun.*, and he was a figure of fun' – quite droll in knickerbockers, with short, fat legs and a ruddy countenance – 'the last man in all creation I should have chosen for Elizabeth Browning's son.' At Dinant the artist kept his former 'model', now pet python. Most saw this as a mark of eccentricity, but not his father. To a clergyman friend thinking of visiting Dinant, Browning promised that his son would introduce him, if he liked the acquaintanceship, to his pet python Jean-Baptiste, his owls, dogs, and other members of 'Dinant society'.

After Browning's death, Mrs Bronson would remark that Pen was the poet's 'vulnerable point, the heel of Achilles'.[21] Browning had written much – and probably talked even more – to Katharine about Pen. He was sure that she, the parent of an only child whom she dearly loved, would understand such an obsession. 'Well, you can bear with the talking about them [Pen's paintings and sculptures] you shall undergo,' he had told Katharine in March 1884, when he was still looking forward to Venice that ill-fated summer, 'for we two understand each other, – don't we – Dear, – dearest of friends?' In April he explained to her that he had not written before owing to three weeks of 'busy idleness': 'My son has been and gone, his paintings and sculpture shewn, talked about and finally disposed of. I have toiled like a pack-horse.' On reading this, the thought may have crossed Mrs Bronson's mind that Pen should not look upon his seventy-two-year-old father as a beast of burden.

It was a few months after this that Katharine first met Pen, when she was in Paris. He had taken a studio in Montparnasse. Urged by his father, the artist called upon Mrs Bronson and her daughter Edith in their hotel on the Champs Elysées. When the squat thirty-six-year-old, red faced and balding, was announced as Mr Robert Barrett Browning, mother and daughter were surprised, to say the least. Two other lady friends of Browning (Katharine Bradley and her niece Edith Cooper, who wrote jointly under the pseudonym 'Michael Field'*) first saw Pen around this

---

* They asked Browning to keep the true identity of 'Michael Field' a secret, for 'the report of lady authorship will dwarf and enfeeble our work at every turn' (Sturge Moore (eds), *Works and Days*, 6).

time and called him a 'a fright to behold, his ruddy stumpy face full of cheeriness & mockery'. His figure, his manner, even his speech (he assented to most propositions with a sprightly 'rather!'*) were all very far indeed from the fragile, spirit-like boy described by Hawthorne. Pen looked and spoke the part of an artist no more than did his father that of a poet. How one would have loved to eavesdrop on the conversation between Edith and her mother after Pen bid them farewell that day in Paris. Mrs Bronson went so far as to say to Browning how quite unlike his father the son was. The poet misunderstood (or chose to mis-understand) the force of the remark, commenting only that 'Oh no – Pen is none of mine to outward view, but wholly his Mother's – in some respects, at least.'[22]

Thus, Katharine had already formed an opinion of Pen when at the end of September 1885, in sombre mood and dressed in black, she watched Robert and Sarianna disembark from the gondola in front of the Ca' Alvisi. Browning, in his inimitable fashion, probably began talking even before Luigi had offered him his strong crooked arm to help him on to the damp steps. After his earnest enquiries into Mrs Bronson's health and state of mind, squeezing her hand all the while, Robert might well have launched into the subject of Pen, asking whether he had been to see her yet. Pen had dropped him a line at Gressoney, saying that he was in high spirits. He had, it seems, found plenty of old friends in Venice and felt as though he had lived there for years. He told his father that he wanted to try his hand at Venetian subjects just as they appeared to him, not as convention dictated. No doubt Browning told Katharine that his son's visit to Venice had been noted in the English papers. Certainly he wrote of all this and more to both Furnivall and the Skirrows.[23] Once on the subject of his son, he found it difficult to stop.

That first evening Browning's happiness must have seemed complete. After the previous year's disappointment, he was once more amongst the charms of Venice, anticipating a two-month stay comfortably accom-modated in the Palazzo Giustinian-Recanati, with Giuseppina to see to his and Sarianna's every need; and just across the courtyard presided his 'more than Friend', Mrs Bronson. Best of all, he was to have the pleasure of showing Pen the sights, Pen who had not set foot in Italy since he was twelve years old and had last been in Venice aged two. As father and son floated together in a gondola between the marble palaces and reflected

---

* 'Jolly!' was another term Pen was fond of using.

lights, Browning would have had such memories to share with Pen, memories of that visit in 1851 as well as his own time there when a young man, even younger than Pen.

Yet, just a month later, on 1 November, Browning was writing to Furnivall that he was anxious to return to London 'on many accounts'. A few days later he was wistfully quoting Stendhal's sentiments – 'l'éton-nement du retour' – in a letter to Mrs Fitzgerald. He was, he said, counting the days till he could experience that delight in being back home which always seems to take one by surprise. 'Not that I do not thoroughly love Venice and the friends I am surrounded with,' he quickly added; but 'we do not see many strangers, as during our visit two years ago: Mrs Bronson having lost her husband this year, is in mourning and does not "receive" on the old scale, nor go out as before.' The ragbag of European nobility did not come to dine at the Ca' Alvisi, nor did his hostess join him for those intimate afternoon excursions on the water, although surely Browning sympathised with the widow's need for quiet and seclusion. In any case, Luigi and the gondola were not called out every day, for the weather that autumn in Venice was miserable. He wondered, so Robert told Eliza Fitzgerald, 'how two months can be so unlike the November of two years ago, which was delightfully sunny without interruption, and the present ill-conditioned season'.

There had been some fine days too, the poet admitted. Then Edith had been ill, followed by Sarianna, and eventually Mrs Bronson, all with bad colds. Even so, there had been some unalloyed pleasures that autumn in Venice. In the evenings Browning attended a season of Gallina's Venetian comedies at the Goldoni Theatre, taking great delight in going backstage and greeting Gallina as a brother dramatist. Best of all, Pen had fallen in love with the city beyond all expectation.[24] He was thrilled to see his beloved Ferdinando of Casa Guidi days, and the feeling was mutual, for the old servant assured Signore Browning that he had always loved Pen 'come un figliuolo'.*

So why was Browning so anxious to cut short his stay in Venice? Perhaps Mrs Bronson's reclusiveness, the bad weather, the illnesses – although none alone was a good enough reason – came together in the

---

* Ferdinando had separated from his wife, Lily Wilson – formerly Elizabeth's maid and Pen's nurse – some years before. Browning, who continued to give Wilson £10 annually, once described her as '*insane*, – subject to delusions which are dangerous'. She had even accused Isa Blagden, whom 'she would not call a lady', of helping women seduce Ferdinando (RB to George Barrett, 20 January 1875).

most unfortunate manner, making the seventy-three-year-old long for home. However, one suspects that there were other, more compelling reasons for this sudden change of heart. Perhaps on a dreary afternoon Mrs Bronson, exhausted after attending to Edith, found the poet alone and poured out her heart to him, making him suddenly afraid of his own emotions as well as hers. Or was it he who went too far, frightening them both? More likely, the 'good minute' simply came and went, without any words being spoken at all: 'Just when I seemed about to learn! / Where is the thread now? Off again! / The old trick! Only I discern – / Infinite passion, and the pain / Of finite hearts that yearn.'* Whatever happened – or did not happen – between them, history seemed to be repeating itself. Browning had reached out for a woman's love, going further than he intended or, perhaps, without any clear intention at all, only to draw back again when the intimacy grew too intense. So had ended his relationships with the serious-minded Julia Wedgwood and the impetuous Lady Ashburton.

Pen was part of the problem. More than likely, Browning had got the idea into his head that Pen and Edith would make a handsome couple. He always thought of Pen's happiness before his own; perhaps he found match-making a pleasant diversion from the dark clouds gathering both within and without the Ca' Alvisi. The twenty-four-year-old Edith was an extremely attractive, independently wealthy, and eligible young lady, and nothing would have delighted Browning more than Pen finally settling down with such a girl. One does not know what Pen thought of Edith, but she certainly was in no way attracted to the podgy, balding artist and probably did her best to avoid his company. Browning – not always the soul of tact – might well have made matters worse by a few ill-judged remarks directed at the two young people. Perhaps Edith's prolonged illness was to some degree diplomatic. The clouds grew blacker.

Browning only prolonged his stay in Venice as long as he did – until the third week in November – in order to secure the purchase of the Palazzo Manzoni on the Grand Canal, next to his old hotel, the Albergo dell'Universo. He told Furnivall that he had bought it solely for Pen who had set his heart on acquiring the palace even before his father had joined him in Venice. 'Pen will have sunshine and beauty about him, and every help to profit by these: while I and my sister have secured a shelter when

* 'Two in the Campagna'.

the fogs of life' – and of London – 'grow too troublesome.'[25] How Browning must have enjoyed discussing the details with his son, especially since he himself had, so he told Furnivall, fantasised about owning the Palazzo Manzoni years before. Father and son would have pored over *The Stones of Venice* together, searching for Ruskin's verdict on the building and shutting the volume with glee when they read: 'A perfect and very rich example of Byzantine Renaissance: its warm yellow marbles are magnificent.'

If Browning's plot to bring Edith and Pen together did not further dishearten Mrs Bronson, his talk of the Palazzo Manzoni certainly did. To her he spoke of 'how many windows he could open to the morning sun on the garden, how many balconies could be added toward the south; in fact he may be said to have passed a month, not in building, but in restoring a "castle in the air" hanging over the waters of the Grand Canal'. Even years later, when she wrote this, Katharine sounded dispirited. Most of Browning's friends in Venice, like the American Daniel Sargent Curtis and – no doubt – Mrs Bronson, thought the palace 'too old, too cold, and on the wrong side of the Grand Canal'.[26] Nevertheless, Browning and his son had never got on so well together as in Venice, neutral territory for them both. Browning and his hostess had never seemed so far apart. She knew that if Pen were to set up an independent household in Venice, Browning would, as a matter of course, stay at the Palazzo Manzoni, not at the Palazzo Giustinian-Recanati. She would not be able to pamper him, see to his needs – in a word, love him in the only way she knew how.

Thus somehow, within the space of one month, there had arisen an imperceptible but seemingly insurmountable barrier to the special friendship between the English poet and the American widow.

Browning was also ready to leave Venice as he had work to finish at home. The previous summer he had begun a new poem, which came to wholly occupy his mind. Entitled *Parleyings with Certain People of Importance in Their Day*, it was to be, as he confided to Alexandra Orr, in some degree a biography, a summing up of his intellectual life.

Yet Browning disapproved of the memoirs that seemed invariably to appear after a noted figure's death. 'We are all reading the *Life of Dickens*,'* Browning sneered to a friend in 1871, 'and admiring his sensitiveness at

---

* John Forster's *Life of Dickens* (1872–4) contained long extracts from the novelist's 'auto-biographical fragment'.

having brushed shoes and trimmed gallipots in his early days, when, – did he see with the eyes of certain of his sagest friends, – it was the best education imaginable for the likes of him. Shall I versify? In Dickens, sure, philosophy was lacking, / Since of calamities he counts the crowning, / That, young, he had too much to do with Blacking, / Old, he had not enough to do with —.'²⁷ Trollope had been even more critical of Dickens' outpourings; yet, just a few years later, during that rough Atlantic crossing aboard the *Bothnia*, he had kept to his cabin in the mornings to write his own autobiography, before surfacing to play cards with Mrs Bronson.

The *Autobiography* (published posthumously in 1883), in which Trollope infamously compared the writing of novels to the making of shoes, had its own critics. Browning probably discussed the book with Katharine Bronson; he would have sympathised with his old friend's attitude towards his work. Within two years, Browning was thinking that he too might make a record of his life. For some time now, Browning Society members had been pestering their author with questions concerning his early poetry and its influences. Moreover, the past had been very much on his mind just at this time, even more than usual. In December 1885, just a few weeks after Browning had returned from his unhappy stay in Venice, Furnivall, together with a young and very keen Browning Society member, Thomas J. Wise, paid a visit to Warwick Crescent. They were shown into the front room where the poet was kneeling beside an old trunk that had been dragged from the top of the house. They watched in silent horror as Browning took out old letters and papers, so carefully and lovingly preserved by his father, and threw them on the fire. He then drew forth two copies of his first published poem, *Pauline* (1833). The twenty-six-year-old Wise was too shy to ask the poet then and there for a copy of this already rare item. By the time he got up enough courage, a few days later, both copies were already spoken for.²⁸

Robert had no intention of giving a straightforward prose account of his life and work. He had never been in the habit of talking about his own poetry. But he thought he might compose a new book-length poem, which would in fact serve as 'the autobiography of a mind'.* As Browning watched the yellowed sheets – juvenile poems, letters to his family – curl up and disappear in the flames, he must have looked back over his long life, trying to reconcile past influences and present beliefs, to give his life

* The expression is borrowed from W. C. DeVane, *Browning's Parleyings: The Autobiography of a Mind*, 1927.

some sort of coherence. And this is very much the aim of *Parleyings with Certain People of Importance in Their Day.* Browning chose seven historical figures who 'important in their day, virtually unknown in ours, are with one exception old familiar friends' (from his father's library), Mrs Orr explains in her *Handbook*. He does this, she observed, 'not for the sake of drawing their portraits, but that they might help him to draw his own'.

The first 'parleying', with the Dutch satirist Bernard de Mandeville, supports Browning's protest (first made in *Ferishtah's Fancies*) against Carlyle's pessimism, 'magisterial in antithesis / To half the truths we hold'. The Scotsman was still very much on the poet's mind; on that December day in 1885, Thomas Wise had seen letters of Carlyle go on the fire. Then Browning explores the origins of his artist's credo in three separate parleyings, with a poet, a painter, and a musician. 'The Song of David', by the divinely inspired poet and Bedlam inmate, Christopher Smart, had sparked Robert's belief in poetry's power of revelation. Poetry should act as a moral force – but without moralising. Browning consequently disapproved of the idea of 'art for art's sake' espoused by Rossetti and the Aesthetic Movement. His youthful rebellion against the Dutch painter and writer Gerard de Lairesse's love of beauty and perfection had compelled the poet to delve into the 'morbid psychology of the soul', no matter how sordid and vulgar. The Newcastle organist Charles Avison reminded Robert of his lifetime love of music, so spiritual yet so fleeting.

Browning twisted several of the parleyings to vent his spleen at certain people of importance in his own day. Through the unscrupulous eighteenth-century politician, George Bubb Dodington, Browning revealed his contempt for Disraeli – 'What a humbug he is!' he once told Allingham – and proclaimed his own liberal doctrine of freedom of the individual.* In his parleying with the Italian painter turned priest, Francis Furini, Robert chided the scientists of his day for leaving God out of their equations. He once said of Darwin, 'Whatever his merits as investigator [the poet, in truth, had a poor understanding of Darwin's ideas], his philosophy was of little or no importance.'[29] But Browning reserved his greatest wrath for J. C. Horsley, treasurer of the Royal Academy and the man responsible for rejecting his son's

---

* At around this time Browning wrote a poem 'Why I Am a Liberal' for Andrew Reid's *Why I Am a Liberal, Being Definitions by the Best Minds of the Liberal Party*, 1885.

sculpture, *Dryope*. Horsley had later attacked Pen's picture *Joan of Arc and the Kingfisher* (1886), depicting the girl warrior about to bathe. In *Parleyings* Browning describes this very same painting as by Furini, a painter of nudes, who had also come up against priggish critics, namely his biographer Filippo Baldinucci. Baldinucci – and by clear inference Horsley – is a 'blockhead', a 'scruple-splitting sickly-sensitive / Mild-moral-monger'.*

It was not only his father's papers which Browning had been looking through. At some point he also brought out a dark green, gold-tooled, morocco case in which Elizabeth had placed his correspondence directed to her at Wimpole Street. She had worn the key round her neck while alive, and he had never opened the case. He also unearthed the inlaid box wherein lay her letters addressed to New Cross. Although he had always fully intended to destroy the letters once he had reread them, in the end he could not bring himself to consign them to the flames.[30]

A hundred different thoughts and feelings, many conflicting, must have crossed his mind as Browning again deciphered Elizabeth's small, neatly rounded hand and his own undisciplined scrawl. But it seems that one thing struck him particularly about the letters: they were erudite, playful, loving, certainly, but completely lacking in sensuality. During their courtship and engagement, Robert had never addressed to Elizabeth such sexually charged letters as he had to Katharine Bronson. How could he have? At thirty-two Robert was a passionate but emotionally immature young man. More significantly, Miss Barrett was a confirmed invalid who had convinced both herself and Robert that they would not be able to consummate the marriage. Even so, he had replied, 'I would marry you now and thus . . I would be no more than one of your brothers – *no more*.'[31]

Rereading these letters – for the first time in forty years – the seventy-three-year-old poet began to look on his wish to marry Elizabeth in a very different light. On her death, Robert could only recall his deep and abiding love for his wife; he had forgotten the time before their marriage, when his chief feelings for the invalid poetess were love, yes, but a love born of admiration, respect and, most of all, pity. He had felt it the right – the only – thing to do: to rescue Elizabeth from her tyrannical

---

* Browning really could not understand such priggishness. Once at a Grosvenor Gallery exhibition, when a schoolgirl was looking with some embarrassment at a nude Venus, the poet suggested they make 'a funny rhyme about it', and began: 'He gazed and gazed and gazed, / Amazed, amazed, amazed' (Lady Laura Troubridge, *Memories and Reflections* (1925), 44–5).

father and take her to more temperate climes. Her very life had 'depended upon my acting as I acted', so he swore to Arabel and Henrietta from Pisa. Elizabeth had thought Robert self-deceived as to his feelings for her. 'I have sometimes felt jealous of myself,' she confessed before their marriage, 'of my own infirmities, ... & thought that you cared for me only because your chivalry touched them with a silver sound – & that, without them, you would pass by on the other side.'* Of course, at the time Robert had protested furiously. However, forty years on he seemed to think that she had been right after all. The letters they had exchanged before their marriage had been those of idealistic young lovers (despite their relatively advanced ages), passionate in their intensity and fervour but without the language, experience, or even hope of physical passion.[32]

'A strong sense of sympathy and pity could alone entirely justify or explain his act,' Mrs Orr wrote of Browning's marriage to Elizabeth, ' – a strong desire to bring sunshine into that darkened life. We might be sure that these motives had been present with him if we had no direct authority for believing it; and we have this authority in his own comparatively recent words: "She had so much need of care and protection. There was so much pity in what I felt for her!" '[33] It was almost certainly after rereading the courtship letters that Browning confided thus in Alexandra Orr.

Amongst these letters Browning would have reread Elizabeth's comments on his *Dramatic Romances and Lyrics,* which he had been preparing for publication in 1845. Miss Barrett had especially liked one poem entitled 'The Glove', retelling the story of a woman who throws her glove into the lion's enclosure to test the bravery of her admirer, the duke. The duke retrieves the glove, only to throw it back in the lady's face in protest against her vanity. Schiller and Leigh Hunt had treated the story before. Typically, Browning added a twist to the tale, taking the woman's part. She had sought to test not the duke's bravery but the truth of his amorous boast that he would die for her.

Some elements in 'The Glove' mirrored the young Browning's own situation at the time. A youth, 'eagerly keeping / As close as he dared to the doorway', the only one to realise the lady's worth, steps forward with

---

* 'When griping grief the heart doth wound, / And doleful dumps the mind oppress, / Then music with her silver sound – / With speedy help doth lend redress' (*Romeo and Juliet,* Act IV, Scene 5).

'a certain calm fervour' to serve her; they marry and retreat from court together. So in 1845 Robert, who had been lurking in the shadows at Wimpole Street, finally determined to take the older, world-weary invalid, Elizabeth Barrett, away to the warmer climes of Italy. 'To that marriage some happiness,' says the narrator of the poem, 'I dared augur.'

'As for your "Glove," all women should be grateful,' Elizabeth wrote in October 1845; 'the chivalry of the interpretation, as well as much beside, is so plainly yours, .. could only be yours perhaps.' As always, her observations were astute. The tone of the poem is chivalrous rather than passionate, reflecting Robert's sentiments at the time. He fancied himself Miss Barrett's 'New Cross Knight' (and her father the fire-breathing dragon, no doubt).

Forty years later, Browning felt compelled to return to the story of the woman who withdraws from the world and to retell it in another of the *Parleyings*, this time with the seventeenth-century moralist Daniel Bartoli. The choice of Bartoli is almost incidental. The poet dismisses him straightaway as a hagiographer – flesh-and-blood saints are more saintly than those of mere legend. In this version (based on the eighteenth-century *Mémoires* of the Marquis de Lassay) there is no glove. The woman's dilemma results from her refusing to marry the man she loves and gain the title of duchess thereby if it means dishonour for her husband. She is banished from court but, as in 'The Glove', a young admirer (De Lassay himself) stands by her.

In his parleying with Daniel Bartoli, the septuagenarian Browning discloses much more about this young admirer and his fate, for he knew the end of the story by then – and understood the beginning a little better. He emphasises the hero's immaturity, describing him as a 'fervid youth' and 'big-hearted boy' of ten who 'loved, as boyhood can, / The unduchessed lady'. The 'boy and lad grew man', gained a reputation as a soldier, but still chose to 'outbroke the love that stood at arms so long, / Brooked no withstanding longer', and he wed the lady. He renounced his king and 'dropped off into night, / Evermore lost, a ruined satellite: / And, oh, the exquisite deliciousness / That lapped him in obscurity!' But his beloved wife soon died. He was distraught, 'did his best to die', but eventually 'took again, for better or worse, / The old way in the world, and, much the same / Man o' the outside, fairly played life's game'. The boyish worship had, over time, turned into manly passion; the husband had loved, lost, grieved, and overcome his grief.

And what of the duke? In 'The Glove', as Elizabeth noted with delight,

Browning returned the duke's blow back to him, for he is made to fetch for his new wife – the great beauty of the court – 'those straying / Sad gloves she was always mislaying' just when she is closeted with the amorous king. In his parleying with Bartoli, the duke's fate is not so cleverly construed, but it is more true to life – more true to Browning's life, in any case. The duke 'display[s] erect on his heart's eminence / An altar to the never-dying Past': the memory of Marianne, the woman who had sacrificed so much for him. But, then, 'there came a bold she-shape brisk-marching, bent / No inch of her imperious stature, tall / As some war-engine from whose top was sent / One shattering volley out of eye's black ball.'

Enter Lady Ashburton, with those dark eyebrows and dark flashing eyes that put some 'in mind of lightning amongst thunderclouds'.[34] Suddenly Browning identifies, not with the young man, but with the well-meaning but weak duke. The duke becomes entangled, wrapping himself round with 'love' of her 'black hair, / Black eyes, black every wicked inch of those / Limbs' war-tower tallness'. But have no fear, the narrator declares, 'we'll patch / Some sort of saintship for him – not to match / Hers' – Marianne's (that is, Elizabeth's) – 'but man's best and woman's worst amount / So nearly to the same thing.' This is not the real man you see before you, merely his ghost, the duke cries out to the 'bold she-shape': 'he died since left and lorn, / . . Some day, and soon, be sure himself will rise, / Called into life by her who long ago / Left his soul whiling time in flesh-disguise.' Although his flesh is weak, the duke's spirit has remained loyal to his one true love.

Browning's rage against Lady Ashburton and her 'queenly impudence', as he calls it in 'With Daniel Bartoli', had clearly not gone away, even after fifteen years. In early 1886, while struggling with the *Parleyings*, Robert asked for the return of Louisa's letters to him – full of those 'calumnies . . exploded in all the madness of her wounded vanity' – which he had copied and sent to William Story as an insurance policy. In his letter informing Story of the packet's safe return to him, Browning told how he had on two occasions, one quite recently, chosen 'to volunteer an explanation of the causes of my feeling with regard to her', Lady Ashburton. 'I found that her nearest relatives had undergone precisely similar' – that is, erratic and irrational – 'treatment.' Indeed, one had been called a 'thief' to her face by Louisa.[35]

But why this veiled but nevertheless very public outburst of anger against Lady Ashburton now? Perhaps his love, complicated as it was, for Katharine Bronson had reawakened Browning's sense of guilt for having momentarily given in to his sexual desires that autumn at Loch Luichart. Certainly Katharine was no 'bold she-shape'; nevertheless, were his feelings for her – those of a man towards a woman – really any different than those he had felt for Lady Ashburton? His love for Elizabeth had, in comparison, been so pure and innocent. 'Fancy's flight / Makes me a listener,' Browning says in 'With Daniel Bartoli', 'when some sleepless night, / The duke reviewed his memories, and aghast / Found that the Present intercepts the Past, / With such effect as when a cloud enwraps / The moon' – Elizabeth's symbol – 'and, moon-suffused, plays moon perhaps / To who walks under, till comes, late or soon, / A stumble: up he looks, and lo, the moon / Calm, clear, convincingly herself once more!' What if his premonition two years earlier, which had come to him in the Palazzo Giustinian-Recanati, was right: 'What if all be error – / If the halo irised round my head were, Love, thine arms?'

The year 1886, when Browning was working on *Parleyings*, proved especially difficult. In June, Sarianna had another attack of peritonitis. Robert confided to Katharine Bradley and her niece Edith that she was 'suspended over death by a hair only – I could properly attend to little else'. His work suffered. Sarianna was too weak to travel abroad that summer; also, cholera had returned to Italy; so they spent two months at the Hand Hotel, Llangollen, North Wales.* In addition to Sarianna's health, there was another matter, the purchase of the Palazzo Manzoni, which was giving Browning cause for concern. In May 1886 he told the 'Michael Fields' that the adage, 'qui terre a – guerre a,'† was verified in his case, seeing that he was forced to go to court to prevent the 'rascally marchese' from holding out for more money. Five months later, on 3 September, Browning was writing to the Skirrows from Llangollen that 'our Venice affair is still in strange uncertainty.'[36] As Henry James once noted, 'there could be no Venetian business without patience' (*The Aspern Papers*).

However, the marchese's 'roguery' (as Browning described it to Eliza Fitzgerald) paled into insignificance just three days later, on 6 September, when a telegram arrived at the Hand Hotel informing the Brownings of the death of Joseph Milsand. Without doubt, Milsand had been Brown-

---

* The hotel was recommended by Lady Helena Martin and her husband, Sir Theodore. Lady Martin (Helena Faucit, of old) had been the leading lady in three of Browning's plays and, some said, the object of his affections at the time.
† 'He who has land, has war.'

ing's closest friend – certainly his closest male companion – for nearly thirty years. He was a guest at Warwick Crescent every spring and had often joined the Brownings on their summer holidays in France. The poet invariably sent Milsand the proof-sheets of his latest work for his comments. All the Brownings – Robert, his father, Sarianna, and Elizabeth – had considered the quiet, gentle-mannered Frenchman as one of the family. Despite having mediated between Browning and his son on numerous occasions, the discreet and tactful Milsand had even managed to remain on good terms with Pen. Browning knew that his friend had been ill, but the news of his death came as a great shock.

Nothing seemed to be going right that year. Pen had gone to Venice to inspect the *palazzo* more closely and to meet the lawyers. He saw that the building was in a truly dreadful state of repair and decided that it was a bad bargain; they were best out of it. Browning accepted Pen's advice and stopped legal proceedings, but he was deeply disappointed. In November, while struggling to finish the *Parleyings*, the poet suffered from a bout of coughing and wheezing. (The doctor called it 'spasmodic asthma'.) He felt far from well. He managed to send the manuscript to George Smith, but 'in a roughish state'. He worried that, owing to his ill health and without Milsand's help, he would not be able to correct the proofs properly, 'in which case, I should have destroyed the thing'.[37]

Thus Browning had written to Mrs Bronson. But he persevered, worked at the poem when he could, and returned the copy to the printer on Christmas Day, 1886. He and Katharine had continued to correspond, but their letters were much less frequent. Robert's tone was friendly, but completely lacking in that emotional intensity and sensuality which had once leaped off the page. In the spring of 1886 when Mrs Bronson, with her entire Venetian household (including gondoliers), was preparing to decamp to Hans Place, London, to escape another cholera outbreak, Browning sent a brief, offhanded note, warning her that she might have problems with servants in England. That June both Mrs Bronson and Browning were in Oxford for Commemoration. Browning stayed in rooms at Balliol; Mrs Bronson was across the road at the Randolph Hotel. But her close proximity did nothing to dispel the poet's ennui. He went to Oxford merely for the sake of Benjamin Jowett, whose term as Vice-Chancellor was coming to an end. Generally speaking, he confided to Eliza Fitzgerald, he was 'weary of refusing invitations, almost as much as of accepting them' – Hans Place included, perhaps.[38]

Parleyings with Certain People of Importance in their Day was finally published on 28 January 1887. Browning thought that the volume would represent his best work, but to the critics it was as enigmatic as anything he had written. However, by this time even they had to concede that, despite his (as they saw it) defects of style and the obscurity of his meaning, 'whatever may be his exact place in the poetry of the world, it is a high place somewhere among the immortals' (*The Athenaeum*). William Allingham had come to the same conclusion some years before: 'If you suspect, and sometimes find out, that riddles presented to you with Sphinxian solemnity have no answers that really fit them, your curiosity is apt to fall towards freezing point, if not below it. Yet I always end by striking my breast in penitential mood and crying out "O rich mind! wonderful Poet! strange great man!" '[39]

Certain lines in the *Parleyings* were, however, understood all too clearly. In March 1887, on the pretext of introducing one Mr John G. Shortall of Chicago, Hatty Hosmer – describing herself as 'a very affectionate ghost from the Past' – wrote to Browning. One cannot help wondering if, on reading 'With Daniel Bartoli', she had thought it best to distance herself in the poet's eyes from 'the bold she-shape'. The tactic backfired. Robert copied Hatty's note and enclosed it with a letter to the Storys 'to show how far impudence can go. Pray,' he added, 'do not even reply to this recurrence of mine to a hateful subject – but as you have so lately looked over the letters etc. of Lady Ashburton, you may as well know how the chief agent in that business professes to feel for me whom she slandered.' It seems the 'bold she-shape' recognised herself in the *Parleyings*. One memorable evening, a year after the poem's publication, she gave a confused and extraordinarily hostile account of her affair with Browning to Lord Acton. 'It was a storm unappeased,' Lord Acton told his daughter.[40]

On the day that Browning received Hatty's note, 2 April, he sat down to write to Eliza Fitzgerald. Warwick Crescent had become a hive of activity, for just two days earlier he had completed the purchase of 29 De Vere Gardens. 'A man is engaged at this moment,' he told her, 'on removing the tapestries, which will be sent to Paris for repair' – those same tapestries which had hung in Casa Guidi. 'I have bought a house – Oh, sad descent in dignity – not on *Canal Grande* – the beloved and ever to be regretted,' he had told Mrs Bronson in February, 'but Kensington.' Browning had very mixed feelings on leaving Warwick Crescent; it had been the place where he had been content to be miserable. 'But for the menaced invasion of the railroad' – the Regent's Canal, City & Docks

Company had recently announced it was to go ahead with the compulsory purchase of land* – 'I might be constant to the old place till I went elsewhere "for good",' he wrote a few months later.[41]

But at least a decision had been taken. The threat of the railway had been hanging over Browning's head like the sword of Damocles for five years, since the end of 1881. He had only limited financial resources at his disposal. At one point he had thought he might build a house large enough to tempt Pen back to live with them in London. When Pen fell in love with Venice, the poet had set his heart on bequeathing to him the Palazzo Manzoni. But when that fell through, he had invested the money in De Vere Gardens instead. It was Sarianna who found the new house in Kensington and George Smith who effected the bargain, while Browning claimed compensation from the Company for money spent on the recent renovation and repairs to the house and garden at Warwick Crescent. The poet had only ever leased his former home (at a rate of £92 10s per annum). With the purchase of the freehold for 29 De Vere Gardens for £5,000 he ensured that Pen would inherit a valuable London property.[42]

Although he had chosen the larger and more centrally located house for Pen after his death, De Vere Gardens had its attractions for the poet during his own lifetime. Bordering on Kensington Gardens, it was much more convenient for taking a turn in the park, stopping in at his club and visiting friends on foot. Henry James was renting a flat across the way, at 34 De Vere Gardens, and Millais's mansion was in the next road, Gloucester Terrace. Moreover, for the first time Browning had enough wall space to accommodate all his books and pictures, as well as the tapestries. The street was even being wired with electric cables, although Browning did not think that his household would avail themselves of electric light.

The move took place over the next few months. As he stood outside 19 Warwick Crescent, Robert saw the crates and packing cases emerge from the house, just as he had seen them enter that summer's day in 1862. By June the Brownings were installed in De Vere Gardens. With the new house came a new valet, Richard, whose first job had been to sort out and re-shelve the thousands of books. The faithful Grove had,

---

* The Brownings were not alone. When the Midland Railway's London extension bulldozed its way through North London, including Camden Town, in the 1860s, 4,000 houses were demolished and 32,000 people displaced.

with Browning's blessing and the aid of Smiles' *Self Help* (together with artistic hints from Pen), handed in his notice to pursue a career as a photographer.* Annie Ritchie went to see the Brownings in their new home. 'The servant,' presumably the inexperienced Richard, 'hesitated about letting us in,' she later recalled. Sarianna heard Annie's voice and came out to greet the guests, insisting that they should stay to see her brother. No, 'not into the dining-room', said she, thinking out loud; 'there are some ladies waiting there; and there are some members of the Browning Society in the drawing-room. Robert is in the study with some Americans who have come by appointment. Here is my sitting-room,' she declared, ushering Annie and her companion into the private chamber. Perhaps De Vere Gardens was a little too accessible, and the size of the house too able to accommodate visitors.

Presumably only after Browning had prised himself away from the Americans in his study, uttered a few Delphic phrases to his 'apostles' in the drawing room, and made his excuses to the ladies in the dining room, did he have time for Annie. He seemed to her 'tired, hurried, though not less outcoming and cordial'. She was particularly struck by the amount of correspondence cluttering his study, 'a milky way of letters', as she put it. 'What! all this to answer?' she exclaimed.

'You can have no conception of what it is,' the poet responded wearily, for he received hundreds of letters every week, all begging to be answered. When Katherine Bradley and her niece Edith called at De Vere Gardens, their eyes were drawn to the mantelpiece, '*furnished* with cards of invitation!! Bad old gentleman.' Apart from the usual round of dinner parties and soirées, the poet's presence was also much sought after at weddings. Once, he told them, he found himself about to go off to a wedding: ' – the lady's name I only learned last Monday – the bridegroom's I am still to learn.' On another visit to Kensington, Browning showed his 'dear Binary Star, the complete Michael Field', as he liked to call these two gushing women, his wife's chair, table, and books – all carefully arranged in his study just as before.[43]

The seventy-five-year-old poet had found the whole business – the move and the subsequent rush of visitors – emotionally and physically draining, despite George Smith's help not only with the purchase of the house but also with interior decorating. 'While I write,' he told Mrs

---

* Grove worked first with Hollyer's, then in his own studio at 174 Brompton Road. In 1899 he received a royal warrant and became photographer to the Queen.

Bronson from De Vere Gardens in June, 'two men are hammering – and otherwise confusing what of intelligence is left in me by household cares.' One such matter concerned the final payment for Warwick Crescent. The owner of the property, one William Buddle, sent a bill of £200 to Browning after he had vacated the house, claiming that he had not given the proper six-months notice. Browning's friend Charles Skirrow, Master in Chancery, interested himself in the matter, and, after several months of negotiation Buddle accepted £100 compensation.

Both Robert and his sister desperately needed a holiday. 'Venice, Venice – and again Venice!' he had sighed in his letter to Mrs Bronson. Yet, it was more a sigh of regret for his 'castle in the air', the Palazzo Manzoni, than one of longing for the comforts of the Ca' Alvisi. He did not mean to go to Italy that year. Mrs Bloomfield-Moore had again invited the poet to the Villa Berry, and he and Sarianna duly set out to 'get renovated by St Moritz'. After a couple of months' rest they would go straight back to London to 'try to get snug in our new house'.[44]

It was at the Villa Berry that Browning received a 'surprise indeed, – but a very joyful surprise': his response in August to the letter announcing Pen's engagement to be married. Even more surprising, his father knew the bride-to-be, and she was just then staying near Mrs Bloomfield-Moore's house at St Moritz. Pen, having heard that Fannie Coddington was back in London that spring (1887) after twelve years in New York, had gone to call on her and her younger sister Marie at their hotel. Their father had died the previous year, and they were on their way to St Moritz for the sake of Marie's health. On seeing Fannie, Pen held out both hands and exclaimed, 'Well, *it is* nice to see you again after fourteen years!' Browning waxed lyrical to the Skirrows: 'The smouldering fire was set flaring.' (He only now learned that Pen had proposed to Fannie when she was nineteen.) The truth was, Miss Coddington was now thirty-three and in need of an old friend. Since Pen had last seen her, she had lost not only her father, but also her mother and an older sister, and this warm greeting from a former lover was comforting indeed.* He invited Fannie and Marie to tea at De Vere Gardens and, on hearing that she was to visit her cousins, the Schlesingers, at their summer place in Kent, Pen exclaimed, 'You should tell your aunt to invite me down while you are there.' When Pen duly arrived at Hawkwell Place in Pembury, he

---

* In the 1840s and 1850s the Coddingtons had lost eight children, none older than six. Besides Fannie and Marie, only one other sibling remained, a sister Emily.

showed such sympathy for Fannie's loss; after all, he had known both her parents. His warm memories of her father especially 'touched' the heiress, and within a very short time they were engaged.[45]

Browning was delighted and relieved. 'The kind of life you have been forced to lead for these last years always seemed comfortless and even dangerous to me,' he wrote to Pen from St Moritz, ' – whatever might be said for it as helpful to your art (and *that* it no doubt was).' He never could pass up the opportunity to lecture his son. Yes, at thirty-eight it was high time he settled down and stopped wandering the Continent from studio to studio, taking up with the landlord's daughter (and God knows who else). 'If the lady had been unknown to me,' Browning felt compelled to add, ' – or one of the innumerable pleasant parties to a flirtation and utterly useless for anything else, I should have given you up for lost.' Edith Bronson would have done nicely, but Fannie Coddington, whom the poet had known since she was twelve, was a perfect choice.

Before sitting down to write to Pen, Browning had a visit from the bride-to-be, who ventured forth from her hotel to the Villa Berry. He had always wanted a daughter, he admitted to Fannie. The poet talked of so many things on that occasion, she later recalled. He told her the story of the *Sonnets from the Portuguese*; with tears rolling down his cheeks, he described his wife's death and how she had 'not even giv[en] him any charge about their child, who, as every one knew, was her idol – so absolutely did she trust him'. Browning reported to Pen that Miss Coddington had spoken to him 'with the greatest frankness and generosity of the means she will have of contributing to your support – for my part, I can engage to give you £300 a year: this, with the results of your work – will amply suffice'. Of course, they would take a house and studio in London. Browning and Fannie were already planning Pen's future for him. Sarianna addressed a terse note to her nephew at the end of Robert's letter, agreeing that Pen had had 'quite enough' of hotel life, which was both comfortless and expensive. 'You will not, I trust, work less well for having a happy home.' She too had had a long talk with Miss Coddington in St Moritz. 'She is very different from the fast American girls who abound here,' Sarianna commented, before turning to the weather.

Fannie's first thought was that the marriage should take place in America, but that would be difficult to organise. Above all, both she and Pen wanted to avoid any 'fuss'. Browning quite agreed. The Schlesingers suggested that Fannie might be married from Hawkwell Place. The offer was gratefully accepted. Robert and Sarianna returned home from Switzerland in mid-September. As Pen had gone to his studio in Venice, Browning arranged for the banns of marriage to be published at St Mary Abbotts in Kensington. 'No sort of objection was made to Pen's momentary absence (which I somewhat incautiously mentioned, – not supposing it was of any moment),' he told Henry Schlesinger. The Clerk merely remarked that the groom 'would probably be back in time', adding, as he glared at the non-churchgoer before him, 'You will hear the publication next Sunday if you go to Church.'[46]

Pen returned in plenty of time for the wedding on 4 October 1887. The tiny Pembury church was decked out with pretty autumn flowers for the occasion. Mr Schlesinger gave the bride away. It was certainly an intimate affair with only fifteen or so guests, comprising Browning, Sarianna, the bride's relations and a few American friends. Two American reporters and a number from the British press showed up at the church, but were told nothing. All went well until it came to the signing of the register back at Hawkwell Place. Fannie became hysterical when she was handed a quill pen made from a peacock's feather – supposedly a symbol of bad luck. But she soon calmed down, and the proceedings continued without further mishap. After the wedding breakfast, the couple drove to Tonbridge to catch 'the continental mail' en route to Venice for a brief honeymoon. They then travelled to New York so that Fannie could settle her affairs before returning to live in Europe. His daughter-in-law was, Browning had told the Skirrows, perfectly 'fitted, – if I can judge at all, – to make Pen, with his many peculiarities, the best of wives'.[47]

Just around the time of the wedding, an old thorn in Browning's side reappeared. John Ingram, who had been pestering him for years concerning the details of Mrs Browning's life, announced that he intended to publish an edition of her early poems (still out of copyright) together with a memoir, to be followed by a separate monograph. Browning's reply remained the same: although he had no power to stop such a publication, he would not offer any assistance. Ingram persisted. Had not the poet allowed R. H. Horne to publish his correspondence with Mrs Browning, his collaborator on 'A New Spirit of the Age'? And what about the help he gave to Mrs Ritchie for the article on his wife in the *Dictionary of National Biography*? Browning tried to explain that Horne's correspondence with his wife dated from a period before he could 'pretend to any sort of guardianship'; as for Mrs Ritchie's article, he had only agreed to verify dates for an old friend who had known Mrs

Browning. Ingram then threatened to use as a source Thomas Powell, known to Robert of old as a literary scoundrel and forger, who had never even met Elizabeth.*

Retaliatory tactics were called for. At the end of 1887, to coincide with the publication of *The Poetical Works of Elizabeth Barrett Browning, from 1826 to 1844*, George Smith reprinted Elizabeth Barrett Browning's *Poems* of 1844 to which Robert added a prefatory note, correcting the errors in Ingram's memoir. When his monograph on Mrs Browning appeared in 1888, Ingram published a letter in *The Athenaeum*, challenging Browning's accuracy on several counts. But the poet would not be drawn, replying only that his source was 'indisputable'. That indisputable source was George Barrett.[48] When he first wrote to George, on 5 November 1887, requesting certain particulars of his sister's early life, Robert had made an extraordinary admission: 'Of the genuine biography I know next to nothing: Ba had the greatest disinclination to refer to it' – the death of her mother and brother, her own ill health – 'and I was careful to avoid giving her pain.'

A few years earlier, in 1885, when Browning gave Furnivall his blessing to 'biographize' about both him and his wife for *Celebrities of the Century*, yet another biographical dictionary, he confessed that he did not know the year of her birth: 'The personality of my wife was so strong and peculiar that I had no curiosity to go beyond it and concern myself with matters which she was evidently disinclined to communicate.'[49] He had not even known the day of her birth until a few weeks before writing to Furnivall.† This may have been, in part, female vanity. But Elizabeth, especially since her elopement and the painful separation from her father, had preferred to live only in the present. Robert had been – and continued to be – perhaps overly protective of his wife's feelings.

As for the renegade editions of Elizabeth's early poetry, Browning told George in that same letter (5 November) that he could think of nothing else but to bring out a complete, authorised edition of Elizabeth's work

---

* Powell had entertained Browning and the rest of literary London in the 1840s, but by 1846 the young poet was denouncing Powell's 'unimaginable, impudent, vulgar stupidity' for defrauding the publisher Chapman of £10,000 and committing innumerable forgeries. Powell was prosecuted, committed to an insane asylum, escaped to America, and wrote books on British authors, full of errors. Dickens was so incensed that he exposed Powell's shady past to the New York *Tribune* (RB to Furnivall, 15 October 1883 and note).

† In Elizabeth's New Testament, the same copy in which he inscribed the lines from Dante in 1862, Browning wrote: 'Her birthday, I just discover, was on the 6th of March – in what year, I am ignorant still. Aug. 10. '85. RB' (*Reconstruction*, A232).

to maintain the copyright. A few days later he wrote to George Smith about the matter: 'Is it not time to take some decisive step in the way of bringing out a new edition so as to prevent these disinterested people from declaring; – as I hear they do, – that they merely are forced to supply a general want which we do not choose to attend to?' He would bear any financial loss that Smith might incur in such a venture. Smith preferred that his firm first concentrate on the complete edition of Browning's poems, edited by the author, which was to be published in sixteen volumes in 1888–9. Browning had been working on some supplementary notes, but on 12 November he groaned to Smith: 'I am so out of sympathy with all this "biographical matter" connected with works which ought to stand or fall by their own merits, quite independently of the writer's life and habits, that I prefer leaving my poems to speak for themselves as they best can – and to end as I began long ago.'[50]

The same day that he wrote this to Smith, 12 November 1887, Alfred Domett, the person who (except for Sarianna) knew most about the poet's early years, died. 'There are notices of him in the Papers,' Browning wrote to Pen and Fannie, 'and he proves to have been not other than successful in his life, though not so thoroughly and conspicuously as he might have been.'[51] Domett had been Prime Minister of New Zealand, yet he was a disappointed man, and Browning knew it. They had started off together in Camberwell as two brother poets, but it was Robert, not he, who had acquired fame as a poet.* Alfred might have hoped that his son would succeed where he had failed, but it was Robert Junior, not Alfred Junior, whose work was exhibited at the Royal Academy and elsewhere to some acclaim. Yet Domett, despite the occasional wry look or comment, had valued their old friendship more than Browning, who felt uncomfortable around him. Domett had carefully preserved his correspondence with and about Browning, spanning forty years. As Honorary Vice-President (after some arm-twisting by Furnivall), he loyally attended Browning Society meetings. At one such meeting, in April 1884, the guest speaker, James Russell Lowell, asked to be introduced to Domett. 'So I've found Waring at last,' he remarked as the two men shook hands. The very last entry in Domett's diary, made on 3 June 1885, records an all too typical encounter with Browning. The two men had

---

* At least Domett had the satisfaction of seeing his poem, *Ranolf and Amohia*, go into a second edition in 1883.

run into each other in Kensington Gardens. They talked of Tennyson's recent peerage, and Domett suggested that Browning might be offered one next. The poet said he did not want it, but he had 'vanity enough to be glad' when the Paris Salon made honourable mention of Pen's statue, *Dryope*.*

The Browning Society continued to be a mixed blessing for the poet. Enthusiasm in some quarters waned. *The Academy* reported that at Cambridge University the Girton College girls had proved faithless to Mr Browning. 'They have formally dissolved their Browning Society, and,' to add insult to injury, 'voted that the balance of funds in hand should be spent on chocolates.' Browning commented that it was a better use of money than his 'sour stuff'. The Americans, on the other hand, showed a little too much enthusiasm. One Browning Club in the American West held meetings where everything was brown: brown tablecloth, brown china, brown bread, brown sugar, brown curtains, and brown dresses.† On a visit to London, a party of 'Yankee schoolmarms' spied Browning, let out a 'wild whoop', and chased him round and round the Albert Memorial, finally rushing at him from all sides. 'They were all looking at him with an eager, hungry gaze, as if they were going to preserve his every word – to can them, in fact – and take them back to Boston,' the *Pall Mall Budget* reported.[52]

The London branch, headed, of course, by Furnivall, continued to be active. Lady Dilke (formerly Mrs Pattison), art critic and friend of Browning, recalled with some amusement one meeting that was held at her home.‡ To begin with, Furnivall berated his hostess for not being a paid-up member of the Society: 'A lady then read a bit from *Balaustion's Adventure*, and made a remark to which no one responded; she then tried a second which she addressed to the Chairman and which he received in dead silence.' Lady Dilke turned to the man next to her and asked if the discussion was always as flat as this, to which he replied: 'I was just thinking that I had *never* been present at so brilliant a discussion since the foundation of the Society.'

---

* When Tennyson accepted his peerage, Browning became known as 'our great Commoner' according to Annie Thackeray Ritchie.
† Even Mark Twain held Browning readings throughout America, vowing, 'I can read Browning so Browning himself can understand it' (C. de L. Ryals, *The Life of Robert Browning: A Critical Biography* (1993), 218).
‡ She and her previous husband, Mark Pattison, were supposedly the models for Dorothea and Casaubon in George Eliot's *Middlemarch*.

'After this,' she remarked, 'I subsided and felt more than ever sure that I was not good enough for my company.'[53]

Perhaps Alexandra Orr – a fully paid-up and loyal member – had suffered through too many such meetings, for in 1883 she had suggested that the Browning Society's activities be terminated after five years. An angry Furnivall retaliated by criticising Mrs Orr's *Handbook* (1885) for being not only too expensive but dull to boot, despite its having been commissioned by the Society and 'authorised' by the poet himself. Browning was distraught to find himself caught in the middle of this feud; both Furnivall and Alexandra Orr were such good friends and staunch supporters of his.

Another project sanctioned by the Society was a facsimile edition of Browning's first published poem, *Pauline* (1833). Thomas Wise, who had missed the chance to obtain a copy of the original for himself that December day in 1885, supervised the facsimile in 1886.* Wise was soon using the skills (and the printers) acquired in this undertaking to produce a series of bibliographic forgeries.[54] One of the earliest was a bogus pamphlet of Elizabeth Barrett Browning's *The Runaway Slave at Pilgrim's Point*, with the supposed imprint 'London, Edward Moxon, Dover Street 1849' and 'Bradbury & Evans, Printers'. In 1888 Wise, still not yet thirty, wrote to Browning, claiming that he had a copy of this pamphlet in his possession. Browning had never heard of a separate publication of *The Runaway Slave* apart from its appearance in Lowell's *The Liberty Bell* (1848) and was 'pretty certain such a circumstance never happened. I fear,' he told Wise, 'that this must be a fabricated affair.' But two days later, after inspecting Wise's copy, Robert thought he must have been wrong, after all: 'The respectability of the Publisher and Printer is a guarantee that nothing surreptitious has been done.'[55] One wonders if Wise thought this forgery a just revenge for the poet's wanton destruction of so many manuscripts and letters three years before.†

Browning did not have an inkling of what Wise was up to (no one did) and, although he still was no 'Browningite', he continued to value

---

* Wise, after much hunting, finally procured a copy of *Pauline*, and asked Browning to inscribe the book, which he did: 'I see with much interest this little book, the original publication of which can hardly have cost more than has been expended on a single copy by its munificent Proprietor and my friend – Mr Wise. Feb. 22. '88' (*Reconstruction*, B24).
† One of Wise's most famous forgeries (perpetrated after Browning's death) was the '1847 Reading' edition of *Sonnets from the Portuguese*, which led the poets' early biographers to claim that Elizabeth had first shown Robert the sonnets while they were in Pisa, in 1847, not Bagni di Lucca in 1849.

the Browning Society's interest in – and promotion of – his works. Mrs Orr's *Handbook* proved especially valuable to the poet, for he was able to refer many a curious admirer to its pages for information and elucidation. And Browning could not help but notice the financial benefits: the income from his poetry had risen from just £100 in 1881 to £436 in 1886, £756 in 1887, and £1,252 in 1888. 'I know the difference in the pace of publishers' cheques coming to me since the Society started,' he told Furnivall once: 'And when people have asked me why I don't stop the Society, I tell them that to do so would be just like my putting a policeman at Smith and Elder's door to say to every one coming in, "if you want to buy one of Mr Browning's books, please don't." Surely I am not such a fool as that.'[56]

But perhaps most gratifying of all, as far as Browning was concerned, were the Society's revivals of his plays, *Colombe's Birthday*, *Strafford*, and *A Blot in the 'Scutcheon*.* Although some were more successful than others (the production of *Strafford* was disastrous, owing to Furnivall's altercation with the lead actor/director), Browning still felt that 'the acting of my four plays by professionals, *unpaid*, for the Browning Society, is surely one of the greatest and most wonderful honours ever paid to a dramatic writer.' So he told William Allingham in 1888: 'People burning to have their plays produced – paying to have them produced; if something even of Tennyson's is to be done you hear of the curtain's costing £2000! and here in my case the actors play for love, and give every word of the longest parts, and the audience listen to the very end!'[57] Ironically, Browning's favourite actress in these productions, Miss Alma Murray, was the wife of Alfred Forman, Wise's partner in crime.

The poet was rarely present, however, at the theatre on these occasions. 'It would trouble me with Mrs Malaprop's "chameleon blushes",' he had told Furnivall in 1884 when excusing himself from a performance of *In a Balcony* (a poet/drama first published in *Men and Women*) to be followed by a concert of his poems set to music.[58] Domett, who was there that evening, informed Robert that the songs were not very good. In March 1888, when the Society staged *A Blot in the 'Scutcheon*, with Alma Murray in the lead, Browning expressed the wish to Furnivall that Pen and his wife could be there, but they were in the middle of their voyage home from New York.

---

* *Colombe's Birthday* in 1885, *Strafford* in 1886, and *A Blot* in 1888. The Browning Society planned to stage *Return of the Druses* for the first time in 1889, but the performance never took place.

He was clearly looking forward to having Pen and Fannie in London, going out into society together, attending art exhibitions, co-hosting Show Sundays at Pen's studio, and dining *en famille*. Fannie had suffered a miscarriage in January. 'Don't be disappointed at this first failure of your natural hopes,' Browning comforted his son; 'it may soon be repaired. Your dearest Mother experienced the same misfortune, at much about the same time after marriage.'[59] There was time enough. Soon after the couple's return to London, Pen was elected to the Athenaeum, his father's club. Browning was terribly pleased – and he had not solicited a single vote for his son. They might walk there together some days, when Pen had finished his work at his studio. Pen and Fannie should live near him in Kensington so that he could supervise his son's work. It was still much exhibited and appreciated on the Continent, in Paris and Brussels, but not in London, which was a great shame. Well, once he and Fannie were settled in Kensington, Pen could begin to rebuild his reputation in England – he had such good contacts, after all. These were the thoughts that ran through the poet's mind in the months following the wedding.

But it was not to be. By May 1888, Pen had decided that he and his wife would settle in Venice. Well knowing that this would upset all his father's plans, he left it to Fannie to break the news to him. 'Though apparently disappointed,' Fannie later wrote, he had assured her 'that whatever arrangement *I* was satisfied with, would please him'. At least he would hear Pen's news more frequently and more fully than before, for Fannie was a conscientious correspondent. And she willingly (too willingly, her husband no doubt felt) conspired with her father-in-law to encourage Pen to get on with his painting. 'Fannie, darling,' Browning wrote less than three months after the wedding, ' "stir him up with a long pole" – as we used to say at school!' His sister took the same tone: 'Go to bed at reasonable hours and don't take to smoking!' was a typical piece of advice from Sarianna to Fannie, squeezed in at the end of her brother's letters.[60]

The couple rented an apartment in the Palazzo Dario, overlooking the Grand Canal, for about a year, until they could find something suitable. Pen had never really ceased looking for a residence in Venice. Soon after the Palazzo Manzoni had fallen through, Pen had come upon another 'magnificent affair', Browning told Mrs Bronson at the time, 'only resisted by me (on his account) when I found the price would be far more than I could prudently pay'. He had never thought that Pen's subsequent house-hunting in Venice was anything other than mere curiosity.[61] In any case, it had become a moot point when Browning invested his money in 29 De Vere Gardens. It seems that Pen had been building his own castle in the air, and, happily, his marriage to Fannie was to help him realise it.

Within three months, in early August 1888, Pen had begun negotiations for the Palazzo Rezzonico on the Grand Canal 'under better advice and superintendence than I obtained', Browning told George Smith. 'Yes, the "Rezzonico" is what you Americans call a "big thing",' he told Mrs Bronson, who, of course, kept abreast of Pen's affairs in Venice. When Browning told John Singer Sargent about it, the artist replied in astonishment, for he had once lodged in a room at the top of that very same *palazzo*: 'What, *all* of it?'* In fact, the white marble palace, home of Cardinal Carlo Rezzonico (later Pope Clement XIII) in the eighteenth century, was one of the grandest in Venice. Henry James thought it magnificent; Ruskin, however, had once pronounced it vulgar. Pen, despite being the child of two poets and an artist himself, was surprisingly practical. He had completed the purchase within a month, and at a very good price, so Browning told Henry James whenever he ran into his neighbour in De Vere Gardens: the internal decorations – pillars, statues, painted ceilings (including two by Tiepolo) – were worth as much as the building itself. Browning still felt compelled, however, to warn Pen that too much prosperity could be 'a hindrance to an artist's career'. 'Don't be the little man in the big house!' he urged his son: 'make me happy before I die by proving yourself the son of your wonderful mother, – and you, dearest Fannie, make him show himself worthy of *you*!'[62]

Mrs Bronson astutely observed that it was only after his son had bought the Palazzo Rezzonico that the father was 'really reconciled' to the loss of the Manzoni – and could think of returning to Venice.[63] While Pen's agent was finalising the purchase of the *palazzo*, he and Sarianna spent a month with the young couple at Primiero, in the Austrian Tyrol. Just before leaving London, on 8 August 1888, the poet had written to Katharine, asking if he might stay with her as before. He had not been to Venice for three years; he had not seen her for two, although they had kept in touch by letter and mutual friends' reports. He could go to a hotel, Browning added, but 'you know exactly how much and how little

---

* Sargent had scratched his name together with a little drawing on the wall of his room, which Pen carefully preserved. The residence is also known as the Ca' Rezzonico.

I want'. He was tired, tired of the social whirl of London and its fog; he was also tired of would-be poets wanting his opinion of their merits. 'This time,' he told Katharine, one poetaster 'got an "opinion" so definite as to silence him altogether'. 'If I am to get any good out of my visit,' he added testily, 'I must lead the quietest of lives, and be lulled by the cigarette-smoke of just my friend – not the *chiacchiere* [chatter] of new acquaintance.'

But all such signs of nervous exhaustion disappeared, as they always did, once he was in the mountains. On receiving Katharine's kind assent to his request, he was in joyous – not to say, flirtatious – mood. Apologising for his tiny scrawl in his reply to her, he joked that 'the desire of getting *close* spoils the intended calligraphy. Hear a conundrum to the point: ' "What is Freezing-point? – 32°. What is Squeezing-point? Two in the shade:" and this is the shade, and here are you and I, – and the squeezed writing follows of necessity – and desists through discretion.' A few days later he sent Katharine a box of love-in-the-mist flowers from Primiero with a new poem, 'White Witchcraft', enclosed. Browning imagines the two of them transformed by white magic into animals. He makes her a fox; she, out of spite, turns him into a loathsome toad. Yet, there might be a pearl (Katharine's favourite jewel) 'beneath his puckered brow'; certainly in the toad's adoring eyes 'love lasts there anyhow'. 'White Witchcraft' sounds like a coded message to Katharine – an apology of sorts – that the poet was not going to let anything spoil his stay in Venice this time.

The magic of the place and the kind compulsion of his hostess did indeed work their white witchcraft once more on Browning, as it had four years before, and their one-month stay turned into three. The weather was perfect. 'Such a succession of summer days,' he wrote to George Smith at the end of October, 'with the addition of a bracing autumn-wind, I never experienced before. I have recovered so much health and strength that it seems suicidal in some measure to return at once to London and the fogs.' Robert and Sarianna stayed in the Ca' Alvisi itself, rather than at the Giustinian-Recanati next door, where Katharine might look after her guests even more assiduously. 'I never enjoyed Venice – the place – so much,' Browning wrote to the Skirrows. His routine was as before, although he spent more time walking along the sands of the Lido. Of course, he added, 'the doings of my couple, Pen and his wife, were always calling on me for notice.' Mrs Bronson's gondolier Luigi took Browning along the Grand Canal to 'Palazzo Pen'

(Katharine's sobriquet for the Rezzonico), where his son was 'occupied all day long in superintending a *posse* of workmen who fit the rooms into comfortable inhabitedness'. When he should return to London, Robert threatened the Skirrows, they 'must come and be talked to death to about painted ceilings, marble statues and the like'.[64] Browning was especially touched by the couple's wish to dedicate the palace chapel to Elizabeth's memory, with a copy of Tommaseo's Casa Guidi inscription on the wall. Pen had his ghosts, too. The only mar to the family's happiness was Fannie's health; she had suffered another miscarriage that autumn.

Katharine Bronson must also have been happy with the visit. With Pen safely married and deeply absorbed in his restoration project, she had Browning more to herself, and certainly Edith could relax. In her diary, where she recorded the Brownings' visit, Katharine wrote a poem: 'We each and all hold fast / An ever-living treasure, / Since memory of past / Is surely present pleasure. / So when you're far away / And cruel seas divide us, / We both may truly say – / This joy is not denied us.'[65] For his part, Browning wished to surround himself in De Vere Gardens with Venetian mementoes. How easily did they sit beside the Casa Guidi furnishings? 'The tables, lanterns &c are decidedly approved of,' he wrote to Katharine on 4 January 1889, a month or so after their return to London, 'and fit into the proper corners very comfortably: so that everywhere will be an object reminding us, – however unnecessarily – of Venice. Your inkstand brightens the table by my chair, and the lamp will probably stand beside it: .. I may never see the lovely City again, – but, where in the house will not some little incident of the three unparalleled months wake up memories of the gondola, and the stoppings here and there, and the fun at Morchio's [bargaining for antiques], the festive return home, behind broad-backed Luigi, – then the tea, and the dinner .. oh, the delightful time!' 'I *must* see Venice again,' Browning scrawled, as if crying aloud, 'it would be heart-breaking to believe otherwise!'

However, if he were to return to Venice, he would of course stay with Pen and Fannie; so he explained to Mrs Bronson in June. They both knew that it would not be the same. Katharine had just taken a brief holiday in Asolo, inspired by *Pippa Passes* and Browning's talk of it, and she may already have had in mind the thought of buying a property there when she read his letter. This charming hillside town, so convenient to Venice, would be a perfect country retreat for Mrs Bronson. Moreover, it was a place that she might share with Browning – exclusively. Pen was well and truly ensconced in Venice; more importantly, perhaps, Asolo held no memories of Elizabeth. Except for Sarianna, Robert had always kept Asolo very much to himself, and his reaction therefore to Katharine's plan to return there for the months of July and August was almost churlish. He tried to dissuade her on the grounds that it would be too hot. 'Why not try Primiero,' he persisted, 'a delightful retreat, quite as near Venice, and much more likely to invigorate you than Asolo.' But he overcame his reticence and answered her questions about Asolo and his first visit in 1838. On learning a month later that she had purchased a small house there, La Mura, he told her: 'I shall delight in fancying your life at Asolo, my very own of all Italian towns.' 'Go there,' he sanctioned, 'and get all the good out of the beautiful place I used to dream about so often in old days – till at last I saw it again, and the dreams stopped – to begin again, I trust, with a figure there never associated with Asolo before. Shall I ever see you there in no dream?'[66]

However, at the age of seventy-seven, Browning felt 'disinclined' to leave England that autumn. Pen was trying his best 'to entice' his father and aunt to return with him and Fannie to Primiero, then Venice, the poet told Mrs Bronson in August 1889, 'but the laziness of age is subduing me'. Sarianna was exasperated by her brother's indecision, she confided to Fannie. But travelling was such an effort, and he was so tired. He had continued to promote Pen's work in England, writing to the galleries on his behalf, taking care of any practicalities (framing, shipping, etc.), and inviting friends to see Pen's latest portrait of him on display at De Vere Gardens.* (He also took it upon himself to enquire about English servants for the Rezzonico.) The poet's social calendar during the London Season was as busy as ever. In a letter to Pen that June, after providing an exhaustive – and exhausting – list of gatherings he had recently attended, Browning added: 'To-day, – I have five engagements of one or another kind.' Oh, and then there is the Balliol Gaudy and, after that, dinner at Lord Rosebery's 'to meet the Shah [of Persia] – men only'. One evening at the Rudolf Lehmanns' house, a phonograph – a recent invention and a great novelty – was wheeled out after dinner. One can still hear the energy in Browning's surprisingly high-pitched voice as he shouted and trilled 'How They Brought the Good News from Ghent to Aix' into the receiver.† After a few lines he broke off, saying: 'I'm so terribly sorry but I can't remember me own verses!' He never could recall his own poetry.[67]

* Now at the Armstrong Browning Library.
† This wax cylinder is the earliest known recording of a poet reading his work.

Even now Browning was still trying to advance and safeguard his wife's interests as well as those of their son. He was very gratified when he learned that George Smith had at last agreed to bring out, as he told Pen in June, 'the edition of dearest Ba's works – in six volumes like mine'. Smith was certain that it would sell well; her poetry was still popular. Yet, she had her detractors. 'I chanced upon a new book yesterday,' so the impetuous Browning began an ode to Edward Fitzgerald on 8 July, referring to the recent publication of *The Life and Letters of Edward Fitzgerald*;* 'I opened it, and, where my finger lay / 'Twixt page and uncut page, these words I read / – Some six or seven at most – and learned thereby / That you, Fitzgerald, whom by ear and eye / She never knew, "thanked God my wife was dead." ' (Fitzgerald had actually written: 'Mrs Browning's death is rather a relief to me, I must say: no more Aurora Leighs, thank God!') 'Ay, dead!' Browning continued, 'and were yourself alive, good Fitz, / How to return you thanks would task my wits: / Kicking you seems the common lot of curs – / While more appropriate greeting lends you grace: / Surely to spit there glorifies your face – / Spitting – from lips once sanctified by Hers.' When he had finished this ode, Browning folded the sheet of paper, hastily stuffed it into an envelope – without consulting Sarianna – and posted the letter to *The Athenaeum*'s offices. He regretted his action almost immediately and telegrammed MacColl to stop publication, but MacColl chose to ignore his request. Many disapproved when they saw the poem a few days later (13 July) in *The Athenaeum*; the Tennysons grieved for both Browning and Fitzgerald's family while Julian Hawthorne called his verses 'a feminine screech'; but the poet remained defiant. 'I *did* nothing,' he told Pen, 'only said what I would certainly have done had they been spoken in my hearing.'[68]

It was all too much. Browning was now an old man. His words and actions began to assume an air of finality that summer of 1889. In June, as he sat with Edmund Gosse in the Fellows' Gardens at Trinity, Cambridge, he talked first of his early poetry before falling, 'more in the manner of old men, to stories of early loves and hatreds, Italian memories of the forties, stories with names in them that meant nothing to the ignorant listener'. From Oxford, the poet wrote apologetically to Eliza Fitzgerald: 'I feel myself unable to write the gossiping letters I once was

---

* Edward Fitzgerald, translator of the *Rubáiyát of Omar Khayyám*, had died in 1883 (no relation to Browning's friend, Eliza Fitzgerald).

capable of,' and talked of being tired and washed out. Oxford had begun to have a melancholy effect on Browning, for a year earlier he had described to his Shalstone friend 'a soft sadness about this place, – such a perpetual remembrance is it of the fleeting state of mortal things'. On the occasion of Tennyson's eightieth birthday (6 August 1889), Browning wrote to the poet: 'At no moment from first to last of my acquaintance with your works, or friendship with yourself, have I had any other feeling, expressed or kept silent, than this which an opportunity allows me to utter – that I am and ever shall be, my dear Tennyson, admiringly and affectionately yours.'[69]

On 8 August 1889, just a few days after penning this note to Tennyson, Browning wrote to Mrs Bronson that, it was '*just* a fancy', but 'if I were inclined to join you at Asolo – say, a fortnight hence, – could good rooms be procurable for S. and myself?' Her house La Mura, built into the wall beside one of the town gates, was too small to accommodate them both comfortably. However, Katharine replied immediately that all could – and would – be arranged. Just before he left for Italy, Grove took a photograph of his former master. 'Now William,' Browning said, putting his hand on his shoulder, 'this is the last photograph I shall ever have taken and I hope it will be of some use to you.'[70]

Robert and Sarianna set off on the gruelling journey to Italy: all day and night on a train to Basle, another eleven or twelve hours to Milan, then across the north of the country, stopping off at Brescia, Verona, Castelfranco, then finally reaching Asolo. 'It seemed like a dream when I drove here,' he wrote to Alexandra Orr in early September, soon after his arrival in the hill town; 'a two hours passage through a delightful country, every mile, through the lanes, cooler and cooler.' The road, overhung with marvellous shrubs and mimosa-like trees, began to narrow as they ascended, but La Rocca, the fortress high above the town, always remained in view.[71]

Mrs Bronson greeted the pair and settled them into their lodgings across the way from La Mura.* She had 'out-Bronsoned herself', Browning told Pen, by whitewashing, painting, and furnishing the rooms in preparation for their arrival. Browning soon established a routine, waking early, a cold bath, breakfast at eight o'clock, long walks with Sarianna

---

* A plaque on the side of the house where the Brownings lodged in 1889 reads: 'In questa Casa abito Roberto Browning sommo poeta inglese vi scrisse Asolando 1889.' ('The great English poet Robert Browning lived in this house, where he wrote *Asolando* in 1889.')

about the town to revisit scenes from *Pippa Passes*, a few hours of reading and writing, a light lunch of local Italian dishes, more reading and writing until three o'clock, when they appeared on the loggia of La Mura, with its superb view, for a cup of tea before setting off with Mrs Bronson in the carriage to explore the countryside – the setting for much of *Sordello*. The poet always insisted they return to La Mura in time to watch the sunset from the loggia. In the evenings he would play the spinet, then read aloud to Sarianna and Katharine, except for two weeks when a troupe of actors arrived in town to perform in what was long ago the banqueting hall in Queen Caterina's palace. He still loved a good play and once whispered to Mrs Bronson that his ambition and his hope was to write a tragedy better than anything he had yet done. He thought of it constantly.[72]

Mrs Bronson was more solicitous than ever of Browning's health. On stormy nights, she insisted they not go out to the theatre. On their afternoon excursions in the carriage, she piled blankets over him ('One would think we were going to Siberia,' he grumbled) and tried her best to persuade him to come down off the rickety wooden staircases leading up this tower or that. She consoled him when, after climbing up the steep hill above the town to La Rocca, he could not find the echo which had first answered him fifty years before. 'I should have thought an echo could never fade,' he said sadly. Katharine saw how much Browning had aged in just a year. The least whisper of the romantic love which she might once have felt for him had, like the echo, gone silent. He understood this. As summer drifted into autumn at Asolo, he began to notice 'a presage of decay in the foliage of certain trees. Well, it must come to man and tree!' he wrote to Alexandra Orr.[73]

And yet he seemed to cry out against his fate. He told Katharine that Asolo was even more beautiful to him now than it had been fifty years ago. He had not felt this way just ten years before, when he passed through the town. As in Venice, it was Katharine's presence that made his surroundings seem so precious to the poet. She made him want to cling to life – to love – now more than ever before. While in Asolo, perhaps after their excursion to La Rocca, he wrote a poem, entitled 'Inapprehensiveness', which opens with a man and woman standing 'simply friend-like side by side, / Viewing a twilight country far and wide, / Till she at length broke silence'. 'Has Ruskin,' she asks, 'noticed here at Asolo / That certain weed-growths on the ravaged wall / Seem ..' As he listens to her mundane question, the man's mind wanders: 'Oh, fancies that might be, oh, facts that are!' If only she would let her eyes meet his, 'The dormant passion needing but a look / To burst into immense life!' But, the woman does not turn to him, and she answers her own question.

> 'No, the book
> Which noticed how the wall-growths wave' said she
> 'Was not by Ruskin.'
> I said 'Vernon Lee?'*

Over the past two years Browning had written a number of miscellaneous pieces (including 'White Witchcraft') for a new volume of poetry which, since his blissful stay at the Ca' Alvisi in the autumn of 1888, he had intended to dedicate to Katharine Bronson. Her gondolier Luigi had recounted to Browning the story behind one poem, 'Ponte dell'Angelo, Venice', as they glided past the bridge and the nearby Palazzo Soranzo, known as 'the house of the Devil and the Advocate'. (Browning had never been overfond of Italian lawyers, especially after the Palazzo Manzoni debacle.) On the eve of his departure for Asolo, Robert had written to his hostess that he would 'bring *your* bookful of verses for a final over-hauling on the spot where, when I first saw it, inspiration seemed to steam up from the very ground'.[74] And it did so again in the elderly poet, just as it had done fifty-one years before, when he was twenty-six. In Asolo he added new pieces, such as the Prologue, Epilogue and 'Inapprehensiveness', while refashioning, revising, and rearranging the existing ones. By choosing *Asolando: Fancies and Facts* as the title of this volume, Browning was paying tribute to the town† (*asolare* means to disport in the open air, amuse oneself at random) while also acknowledging a quandary that still plagued him: how to separate fancy from fact.

In one section of *Asolando*, of which 'Inapprehensiveness' is the end piece, Browning was clearly wrestling with his demons. He took up the question he had posed at the end of *Ferishtah's Fancies* while thinking of his wife when amongst the comforts of the Palazzo Giustinian-Recanati: 'What if all be error − / If the halo irised round my head were, Love, thine arms?'

---

* Vernon Lee was the pseudonym for Violet Page, contemporary essayist and novelist, whom both Browning and Katharine Bronson knew.
† Cardinal Bembo, who belonged to Queen Caterina's court in Asolo, published dialogues on love, which were entitled *Gli Asolani* (1505).

'I will be happy if but for once: / Only help me, Autumn weather, / Me and my cares to screen, ensconce / In luxury's sofa-lap of leather!' Thus begins 'Dubiety', a poem which harps back to 'By the Fire-Side'. In 1853 Robert had reflected on what he meant to do 'when the long dark autumn-evenings come'. Yet now that those autumnal evenings had arrived, the poet seemed none the wiser as he sat 'in luxury's sofa-lap of leather'. Dubiety indeed. He appears to conjure up the ghost of his dead wife: 'Let gauziness shade, not shroud, – adjust, / Dim, and not deaden .. If it reach me through dreaming's vapour-wreath.' This is the language of spiritualism, reminiscent of the Epilogue to *Fifine at the Fair.* 'What is it like that has happened before?' the poet asks. A dream, a vision – no, he does not believe in such things – 'but a memory, after all! / – Of what came once when a woman leant / To feel for my brow where her kiss might fall. / Truth ever, truth only the excellent.'

But was truth – fact – enough? The poem that follows immediately after 'Dubiety', entitled 'Now', suggests that the memory of past love, however true, neither dispels fancy nor satisfies longing. 'All of your life that has gone before, / And to come after it, – so you ignore,' the poet declares. Rather, 'make perfect the present .. You around me for once, you beneath me, above me – / Me – sure that despite of time future, time past, – / This tick of our life-time's one moment you love me!' *Now* is 'the moment eternal – just that and no more – / When ecstasy's utmost we clutch at the core / While cheeks burn, arms open, eyes shut and lips meet!'

The next few verses, 'Humility', 'Poetics', 'Summum Bonum', 'A Pearl, A Girl', all seem to convey the same message as 'Now': make perfect the present through love – physical love. Suddenly, this train of thought comes to a screeching halt with 'Speculative'. The poet cries out: 'Minutes which passed' – his time with Elizabeth – 'return, remain! / Let earth's old life once more enmesh us, / You with old pleasure, me – old pain, / So we but meet nor part again!' Browning could not invoke Elizabeth without recalling the pain of separation which he had endured these nearly thirty years: the grief, the despair, the guilt, the longing. Was he also remembering those painful moments in their marriage, which he had come to recognise and accept during this same period?

With the last in this group of poems, 'Inapprehensiveness', Browning's mind had drifted back to that time and place, so long ago and far away, 'By the Fire-Side': 'Had she willed it, still had stood the screen / So slight, so sure, 'twixt my love and her: / .. Friends – lovers that might have been.' Elizabeth had willed it, Katharine had not, and his dormant passion still lay hidden behind the screen, so slight, so sure. Yet Katharine's impression had been that Browning had purposely avoided deep or serious topics. She knew nothing of the poetry he was writing that autumn in Asolo. Infinite passion, finite hearts.

'We shall have flag-signals!' Browning told Katharine with glee, thinking of the property he meant to purchase in Asolo and christen 'Pippa's Tower'. Once part of Queen Caterina's pleasure garden, the old building was across the ravine, but still visible, from La Mura. The telephone was too modern. 'When I ask you to dine,' he continued, 'the flag shall be blue – it is your favourite color; and remember, if the answer is "Yes," you float a blue flag; if "No," it must be a red one.' The poet was building yet another castle in the air. Sometimes, Katharine recalled, Browning would turn very grave and say, 'It may not be for me to enjoy it long,' but Pen and his family could use the tower as their country retreat. Ah, 'but I am good for ten years yet,' he would invariably add. 'Pen must see this' was, according to Mrs Bronson, the poet's constant cry that autumn in Asolo: 'the thought of what would please his son was never far from his mind.' One can almost hear the exasperation in her voice. Pen did drive up from Venice to see Asolo and was as enchanted by the town as his father. He took a lively interest in the plans for 'Pippa's Tower'. (The negotiations promised to be as tortuous as those for the Palazzo Manzoni.) The Storys also spent three days in Asolo at Browning's invitation. After they had said their goodbyes, the poet ran back to the Storys' carriage, stuck his face in at the window and exclaimed: 'We have been friends for forty years – aye – more than forty years – and with never a break.'[75]

After two months, it was time for the Brownings to leave Asolo. The weather had turned, *Asolando* was finished. With *The Ring and the Book* he had fulfilled one vow made to Elizabeth before their marriage – he had produced 'R. B. a poem'. With *Asolando* he had fulfilled another vow, to write a poem entitled 'Now' – 'what is to be done *now*, believed *now*.' Robert posted the manuscript to George Smith on 15 October. The brother and sister left on the last day of that month and proceeded to Venice where Pen's gondoliers, resplendent in red tunics, collected them and rowed them to the broad flight of steps leading up to the lofty and nobly proportioned rooms of the Palazzo Rezzonico. Browning was astounded at the transformation effected by his son: 'I never thought it was in him,' he was heard to say on more than one occasion. Others agreed. 'What Pen Browning has done here,' Henry James wrote,[76] 'transcends description for the beauty, and, as Ruskin would say, "wisdom and rightness" of it.'*

His stay in Asolo had done Browning so much good. Fannie thought him the picture of health when he arrived in Venice. However, another house guest, Fannie's friend Evelyn Barclay, noticed that the innumerable stairs of the palace made the poet breathless. He would spend the mornings at the Lido and the afternoons, once Mrs Bronson had shut up La Mura and returned to Venice, at the Ca' Alvisi. Back at 'Palazzo Pen', Browning took pleasure in talking about 'Pippa's Tower' (negotiations were still ongoing), feeding Jacko the parrot bits of fruit and cake in his aviary conclave, the 'Pope's Room', and going out to buy his son and daughter-in-law little things which they clearly needed, including a sugar basin and cream jug large enough for the house party. Browning dined at *palazzi* up and down the Grand Canal and recited his poetry for hours to his hosts. Somehow he found the time and energy to correct the proofs of *Asolando*, which had arrived in early November. To save his father climbing the stairs, Pen eventually moved Browning's bedroom down to the mezzanine, the same floor where the parrot resided and the family dined. From here the poet wrote to George Smith of the 'Italianly cold': the Italians never lit a fire in the morning and his room did not get the sun.[77]

One Sunday, the first day of December, Browning took tea with Fannie, who was feeling unwell, in her room. She asked her father-in-law to read aloud to her and Sarianna, who was also present, from his new volume. Although he had a slight cough, he read out several poems, the last of which was the Epilogue to *Asolando*. 'At the midnight in the silence of the sleep-time, / When you set your fancies free, / Will they pass to where – by death, fools think, imprisoned – / Low he lies who once so loved you, whom you loved so, / – Pity me?' Just as he had addressed the dedication at the front of *Asolando* to Katharine Bronson, so he spoke to his 'more than Friend' in the Epilogue, 'Oh to love so, be so loved, yet so mistaken!' He had been wrong to let his love for a flesh-and-blood woman – physical passion – torment him. 'What had I on earth to do / With the slothful, with the mawkish, the unmanly?' No, he was 'One who never turned his back but marched breast forward, /

---

* In this same letter James called Pen's restoration 'altogether royal and imperial – but', he added, Pen 'isn't kingly and the *train de vie* remains to be seen'.

Never doubted clouds would break, / Never dreamed, though right were worsted, wrong would triumph, / Held we fall to rise, are baffled to fight better, / Sleep to wake.'

Browning no doubt felt that Katharine – and those others too who loved him, Sarianna, Pen, Fannie – would derive some comfort from these words after he was gone. Gone, not dead. 'I deny death as an end of everything. Never say of me that I am dead!' he told William Sharp. Death was just another stage in life. 'Without death, which is our crapelike churchyardy word for change, for growth, there could be no prolongation of that which we call life.'[78] 'Strive and thrive!' the Epilogue ends, 'cry "Speed, – fight on, fare ever / There as here!" '

Perhaps the most startling thing about this poem is the absence of Elizabeth. Unlike previous poems, there is no indication, no hint, no presentment of Browning being reunited with his wife in the afterlife. Earlier in *Asolando*, in 'Speculative', he had rebelled against the idea of a wholly 'new life in Heaven'; others may need it, but not he. He only asked for 'earth's old life' to enmesh them once more, so that he and Elizabeth might meet and not part again. But this had been only a momentary weakness. No, this painful longing for Elizabeth had been as slothful, mawkish, unmanly – and self-indulgent – as his physical passion for Katharine. Thinking of his dead wife in the wake of the Ashburton debacle, he had told Isa Blagden, 'I shall wash my hands clean in a minute, before I see her, as I trust to do.' That minute had turned into long years, yet he had remained loyal to Elizabeth's memory, difficult as it had been at times, and his hands were indeed clean. But the fulfilment of this pledge seemed, ironically, to have released him from its obligations. He was free. Browning seems to have at last escaped from under that 'strange, heavy crown' imposed upon him by Elizabeth.

As her brother read aloud the Epilogue to *Asolando* that December day in Fannie's room, a cold feeling crept over Sarianna that those lines 'might be a real farewell to life', she later told the Michael Fields, 'as they were'. That very afternoon Browning was diagnosed with bronchitis and a weak heart. He was moved yet again, this time upstairs to the master bedroom so that he might feel the warmth of the sun. That first evening Pen and Fannie stayed up through the night with him. Over the next week or so the doctor came and went; a nurse was brought in; beef tea was sent by Lady Layard and Mrs Bronson. The patient grew steadily worse. Bulletins, always optimistic, about the poet's condition were posted outside the porter's lodge of the Palazzo Rezzonico. Telegrams arrived from friends and admirers. Pen contacted Mrs Orr, who boarded an express train in France to be at her friend's bedside. On 11 December Browning grew very restless, 'talking incessantly in the strangest fashion – often in Italian', Fannie informed Lady Layard. Sarianna, who could hear her brother's rantings from several rooms away, sat 'crushed and broken-hearted'.[79]

The next morning, 12 December, Browning was calmer. Fannie brought to his bedside a parcel that had arrived a day or two before, when he was still delirious, and carefully unwrapped it. The patient seized the book, an advance copy of *Asolando* bound in red cloth. 'That's a little of the work I've done in my lifetime!' Browning told the Italian doctor. After checking one or two details in the book, he presented it to Fannie. 'Under any other circumstances I should give it to Mrs Bronson,' he told her, 'but now I want to give it to you.' Katharine Bronson had not visited Browning at any time during his illness, although Pen had kept her informed of his condition. Perhaps Fannie liked having the care of her father-in-law all to herself; but there is a more likely explanation. Browning's illness had made him incontinent. Fannie confided to Lady Layard that, much to the patient's distress, the bedcover had been spoiled. In his delirium, he insisted to Fannie 'three or four times *he* didn't do it & was so sorry'. Katharine had last seen Browning vigorous and healthy; he did not want her to see him this way. He had already said what he meant to say to her in *Asolando*.

Early in the evening of the 12th, a telegram arrived from George Smith, declaring that the first edition of *Asolando*, published that same day, had already sold out. When Pen bent over to tell his father, Browning remarked, 'More than satisfied. I am dying. My dear boy. My dear boy.' He had every reason to be content. His earthly duties, as he saw them, had been carried out. Pen was settled in his career, financially secure, and happily married. He had said all that he had wanted to say in his poetry. As for Elizabeth, he would have been assured that her verse – and her memory – would live on by the advertisement at the back of *Asolando*, announcing the new edition of Mrs Browning's works to be published uniformly with his own. Browning lost consciousness at around seven o'clock and, three hours later, fell into that deepest of sleep.

The dignities – and indignities – of death soon followed. There was a scramble to find a suitable final resting place for the body. Pen sent a telegram to Florence to ask if his father could be buried next to his mother in the Protestant cemetery; Sarianna particularly wished it. Browning himself had had no strong opinion on the subject. 'Although I have no kind of concern as to where the old clothes of myself shall be thrown,' so he told Elizabeth's brother George in 1866, 'yet, if my fortune be such, and my survivors be not unduly troubled, I should like them to lie in the place I have retained there. It is no matter, however.'[80]

It seems some other poor soul had taken Browning's place, for the municipality informed Pen that the cemetery had become too crowded and no new burials were allowed. Browning had died on a Thursday. Not until the Saturday evening did Pen receive word from the Dean of Westminster Abbey that Browning might be buried in Poets' Corner. While he waited for the appropriate Venetian officials to arrive and certify the body, Pen could not even place his father in his coffin. Messages mourning Pen's loss crossed with those still wishing the poet a speedy recovery. One such letter, which arrived too late, addressed to Browning from William Story, must have been particularly heartbreaking for Pen to open.* In it Story declared how it had 'seemed like old times' in Asolo and describing their trip to Siena after leaving the Veneto, 'so full of old associations with you .. the old terrace was there where we used all of us to sit & talk such happy hours – though only tenanted now by ghosts'. He hoped the poet was 'in good health & strength & jollity'.[81]

Finally, on Sunday, 15 December, the Venetian officials came and went, Browning's body was placed in its coffin, and a private funeral service was held in the *sala* (dining room), located on the still-unfurnished *piano nobile* of the Palazzo Rezzonico. About forty people were present, including Katharine Bronson, to whom Browning's death had been a crushing and sudden blow, and Alexandra Orr, who had arrived in Venice too late to see Browning before he died. The 'Queen of Cities' too paid its respects to the poet. At the end of the service eight *pompieri* (firemen) in blue uniforms and brass helmets carried the coffin downstairs to a waiting municipal barge, ornately decorated in black and gold, as were the gondoliers. At sunset the barge, towed by a steam launch of the Royal Italian Marine, led a cortège of smaller but equally funereal boats down the Grand Canal to the chapel on San Michele, 'the isle of the dead'.

Two days later, Browning's manservant escorted the coffin to London by train, where it was displayed in the dining room of De Vere Gardens until 31 December. On that day, the last of 1889, at about ten o'clock, a

---

* Sarianna wrote beside the address on the envelope, 'Never seen.'

crowd began to gather in nearby Kensington Gardens. Within an hour the numbers had swelled to some hundreds. When the funeral procession left De Vere Gardens en route to Westminster Abbey, the fog was so thick that the end of the road could not be seen. Several vehicles were needed to convey all the wreaths which had been sent by friends and well-wishers. The 'Great and the Good' of English society – Henry James, Holman Hunt, Edward Burne-Jones, and James Whistler – as well as hundreds of ordinary ticket-holders queued outside in the fog as the bells of the Abbey tolled. The pall-bearers included Hallam Tennyson (on behalf of his father, Lord Alfred), Sir Frederic Leighton, and George Smith. Pen and Fannie were present; Sarianna was too ill and distraught to attend.

Edmund Gosse, who sat in the choir stalls next to George Meredith, had to endure the latter going through the list of those still alive, like Tennyson, who coveted a place in Poets' Corner – and those already dead, like Bulwer-Lytton, who did not in his opinion deserve to be there.* 'The music,' Gosse wrote in his diary later that day, 'was long-drawn, dreary, delicate & it floated for an infinite length of time (it seemed), up in the roof of the Abbey.'[82] Just before the interment, a young treble voice pierced the silence with the question posed by Elizabeth Barrett Browning in her early poem 'The Sleep': 'What would we give our beloved?' The choir answered back: 'Let One, most loving of you all, / Say, "Not a tear must o'er her fall"; / He giveth His beloved, sleep.'†

It was an appropriate finale to Browning's life: surrounded in Poets' Corner by the great names of literature, including one, Wordsworth, who had raised his glass all those years ago to 'the youngest poet in England'; honoured by the British public, which had ignored him for so many years; and lulled to sleep by the words of one whose love for him had – for better or worse – transcended even death.

---

* Lord Lytton is actually buried in St Edmund's Chapel in the Abbey, not Poets' Corner, in order to be near the tomb of Sir Humphrey Bourghier, who appears in one of his novels (my thanks to Christine Reynolds of Westminster Abbey Library for this information).
† 'The Sleep' was first published in *The Seraphim and Other Poems* (1838); it was set to music for the occasion by John Frederick Bridge, deputy organist of the Abbey.

Afterword

Within four years of Robert Browning's death, Pen and his wife Fannie had separated. Fannie suffered increasingly from severe mood swings and ill health, probably gynaecological in origin.* She objected to Pen's screeching birds and slithering snakes in the house, as well as a succession of pretty models. There was one in particular, a young Italian woman called Ginevra, who also acted as housekeeper, of whom Fannie became insanely jealous. Pen, who could be overly proud and obstinate, refused to dismiss the girl, and in 1893 Fannie left him. Certain people, such as Katharine Bronson† and Lady Layard, tried to bring about a reconciliation, but others, namely Fannie's sister Marie and to some extent Sarianna, impeded any such attempts. In 1899 the couple made one last effort to live under the same roof, but it was a disaster. His deep-seated insecurities had led Pen to believe that Fannie only ever loved him for his name. Yet she said of Pen following their separation: 'I cannot forget the nice & *the loveable* side of him – Our old old friendship – his loving me when I was 18 – & wanting to marry me then.' Perhaps an Italian friend put it best: 'they were not made to walk the same road – as we say.'¹

After his father's death, Pen had continued to apply his artistic talents (and Fannie's money) to what was clearly his real *métier*: refurbishing and decorating houses. Pen carried out the poet's last wishes and, as well as rebuilding 'Pippa's Tower',‡ he also bought and restored the derelict

---

* Fannie, who had had at least two miscarriages, described her infirmities as 'internal (bodily) affairs' and underwent a serious, but unspecified, operation.
† Katharine remained on friendly terms with both Brownings. She eventually gave up the Ca' Alvisi and lived in Florence to be near her daughter Edith, by this time the Countess Rucellai. Katharine resided in Isa Blagden's former Bellosguardo villa for a time before moving to an apartment in the city, whereas she died in 1901, aged sixty-six.
‡ The town officials of Asolo had agreed to negotiate the purchase of 'Pippa's Tower' on the very day Robert Browning died, 12 December 1889.

silk factory where little Pippa would have worked. After his separation from Fannie, Pen spent less and less time in Venice (eventually selling the Palazzo Rezzonico), but he fell in love with Florence when, in 1891, he visited the city for the first time since his mother's death. He set his heart on reclaiming Casa Guidi (although it was not to be) while acquiring other Tuscan properties. Between his residences in Asolo and Florence, he provided a home for Sarianna (until her death in 1903) as well as the Brownings' old servants, Wilson and Ferdinando. Pen had become caretaker of his parents' memory, although some thought it a dereliction of duty when he published their courtship letters in 1899. Pen died in 1912 at the age of sixty-three. His last public appearance, when he was already ill and nearly blind, had been at the celebrations of the centenary of Robert Browning's birth, on 7 May 1912, in Asolo.

Chronology

1806	6 March	Elizabeth Barrett (EBB) born
1812	7 May	Robert Browning (RB) born in Camberwell, South London
1814	7 January	Sarianna Browning, RB's sister, born
c. 1820–6		RB boards with the Misses Ready, then with the Revd Thomas Ready in Peckham
1824		RB's mother sends the Flower sisters RB's first volume of poetry, *Incondita*; W. J. Fox advises RB not to publish it
1826	May	For his birthday, RB receives from his cousin, James Silverthorne, Shelley's *Miscellaneous Poems* (1826) and, from his mother, Shelley's other works
1827		The Flowers move from Essex to North London, near Hackney, and RB becomes a frequent visitor
1828	October	RB enrols at University College, London
1829	February	Death of Benjamin Flower; RB sees no more of Eliza and Sarah after they become wards of W. J. Fox
	May	RB abandons his studies at University College after less than a year
1832	22 October	RB and James Silverthorne see Edmund Kean perform *Richard III* at Richmond
1833	March	*Pauline* published anonymously; RB gets back in touch with W. J. Fox and the Flower sisters
1834	spring	RB visits St Petersburg
1835	August	*Paracelsus* published
		Alfred Domett and RB probably first meet
1835–6		RB first meets C. W. Macready, Thomas Carlyle, John Forster, and other literary figures
1836	26 May	RB dines with literary luminaries on the opening night of Talfourd's *Ion*
1837	May	*Strafford* published and runs for five nights at Covent Garden Theatre
1838	April–July	RB first visits Italy (Venice and the surrounding area)

1840	March	*Sordello* published; RB becomes notorious for his obscurity
		The Brownings move from Camberwell to nearby New Cross
1841	April	*Pippa Passes* (*Bells and Pomegranates*, No. 1) published
1842	March	*King Victor and King Charles* (*Bells and Pomegranates*, No. 2) published
	30 April	Domett sets sail for New Zealand
	November	*Dramatic Lyrics* (*Bells and Pomegranates*, No. 3) published
1843	January	*The Return of the Druses* (*Bells and Pomegranates*, No. 4) published
	February	*A Blot in the 'Scutcheon* (*Bells and Pomegranates*, No. 5) published; *A Blot in the 'Scutcheon* runs for three nights at the Drury Lane Theatre
1844	April	*Colombe's Birthday* (*Bells and Pomegranates*, No. 6) published
	autumn	RB's second visit to Italy (Naples, Rome, Florence)
1845	10 January	RB's first letter to EBB
	20 May	RB's first visit to Wimpole Street
	November	*Dramatic Romances and Lyrics* (*Bells and Pomegranates*, No. 7) published
1846	April	*Luria; and a Soul's Tragedy* (*Bells and Pomegranates*, No. 8) published
	12 September	RB's marriage to EBB
	19 September	The Brownings leave England for Pisa, via Paris
		Death of Eliza Flower
1847	April	The Brownings move to Florence, where Casa Guidi shortly becomes their home
1849	January	First collected edition of RB's *Poems* published
	9 March	Birth of Robert Wiedeman Barrett Browning (Pen)
	18 March	Death of RB's mothers
	July– October	The Brownings visit Bagni di Lucca for the first time; EBB presents RB with her *Sonnets from the Portuguese*
1850	April	*Christmas-Eve and Easter-Day* published
	July	EBB's fourth and final miscarriage
		EBB's *Sonnets from the Portuguese* published in her two-volume *Poems*
1851	May	The Brownings in Venice, RB out of sorts; EBB's *Casa Guidi Windows* published
	June–July	The Brownings in Paris, where they become close friends of Joseph Milsand and Alfred Tennyson, newly designated Poet Laureate
	July–Sept	The Brownings visit London for first time since their marriage, during which time EBB's health begins its slow, inexorable decline

	October	RB first learns of her father's entanglement with Mrs Von Müller
1851–2	Oct–July	The Brownings in Paris
1852	May	Death of RB's cousin, James Silverthorne
	July	Mrs Von Müller's case against Mr Browning is heard in the High Court, after which Sarianna and her father, accompanied by RB, move to Paris
	July–Sept	The Brownings in London
	October	RB and EBB return to Italy
		Letters of Percy Bysshe Shelley, with an Introductory Essay by Robert Browning published
1853	April	RB's play *Colombe's Birthday* (1844) is staged for the first time at the Haymarket Theatre in London, running for seven performances
	July–Oct	The Brownings in Bagni di Lucca for the second time; William Story and his family are also at the resort
	winter	The Brownings in Rome, where young Joseph Story dies after a brief illness
1854	spring	RB's 'The Twins' published with EBB's 'A Plea for the Ragged Schools of London' for Arabel Barrett's charity bazaar
1855	July–Oct	The Brownings in London; Tennyson and RB read *Maud* and 'Fra Lippo Lippi', respectively, at the Brownings' lodgings
	November	*Men and Women* published
		RB's poem 'Ben Karshook's Wisdom' published in Marguerite Power's *The Keepsake* (for 1856)
1856	November	EBB's *Aurora Leigh* published
		RB's poem 'May and Death' is published in *The Keepsake* (for 1857)
		John Kenyon leaves the Brownings a combined legacy worth £11,000
1857	April	Death of EBB's father
	July–Oct	The Brownings in Bagna di Lucca for third and last time, where they meet Sophie Eckley
1860	June	EBB's *Poems before Congress* published
		RB finds 'Old Yellow Book' in a Florentine market stall
1861	March	Victor Emmanuel crowned King of Italy
	29 June	Death of EBB
	1 July	EBB's funeral
	27 July	RB and Pen leave Florence
	Aug–Sept	RB visits Brittany for the first of many summers with his father, Sarianna, and Pen
	October	RB and Pen move to lodgings in Chichester Place

1862	March	RB publishes EBB's *Last Poems*
	June	RB and Pen move to 19 Warwick Crescent
	winter	*Selections from the Poetical Works of RB* (dated 1863) published
1863		RB publishes EBB's *Selected Essays*
		The Poetical Works (three volumes) published (the first to include *Sordello*)
	autumn	RB first visits 1 Cumberland Place and meets Julia Wedgwood
1864	May	*Dramatis Personae* published
	autumn	RB begins *The Ring and the Book*
1865	March	Julia Wedgwood breaks off friendship with RB
1866	June	Death of RB's father; Sarianna returns to Warwick Crescent to keep house for her brother and nephew
1867	May	RB begins corresponding again with Julia Wedgwood
	June	RB receives Honorary MA from Oxford
	October	RB receives Honorary Fellowship of Balliol College, Oxford
		Pen's entrance examination to Balliol is delayed several times owing to his being ill prepared
1868	April	Pen sits and fails Balliol examination
	June	Death of EBB's sister, Arabel Barrett
		The Poetical Works (six volumes) published (the first to include *Pauline*)
1868–9	Nov–Feb	*The Ring and the Book* published
1869	January	Pen matriculates at Christ Church, Oxford, having failed to get into Balliol
	June	RB possibly hears rumours of Pen's sexual indiscretions
	September	RB's first visit to Louisa, Lady Ashburton's estate, Loch Luichart, and her subsequent proposal of marriage
1870	June	Pen leaves Oxford in disgrace, having failed his Part One examination; RB and Julia Wedgwood exchange letters for the last time
	summer	The Brownings stay at St Aubin, France, near to Joseph Milsand, for the first of several summers
1871	August	*Balaustion's Adventure* published
	2 October	RB's second and final visit to Loch Luichart, leading to a falling out with Lady Ashburton
	December	*Prince Hohenstiel-Schwangau* published
1872	February	Alfred Domett returns from New Zealand
	June	*Fifine at the Fair* published
	summer	RB's annual holiday in St Aubin, in Normandy, where Annie Thackeray is also staying
1873	January	Death of Isa Blagden in Florence
	May	*Red Cotton Night-Cap Country* published

	spring?	Pen Browning proposes to Miss Fannie Coddington but is turned down
	autumn	Pen in Scotland with Millais who encourages him to take up painting
1874		Pen goes to Antwerp to study with Heyerman
		Death of Sophie Eckley; she bequeaths Gordigiani portraits of EBB and RB to Pen
1875	April	*Aristophanes' Apology* published
	22 June–	Eliza Fitzgerald travels to Dinant, Bruges, to see Pen, who
	12 July	has given his father cause for concern
	November	*The Inn Album* published
1876	July	*Of Pacchiarotto and How He Worked in Distemper* published
	October	Gordigiani's portraits arrive at Warwick Crescent
1877	14 September	Death of Anne Egerton Smith when on holiday with the Brownings in the Haute Savoie
	October	*The Agamemnon of Aeschylus* published; Pen declares his intentions of marrying the Dinant innkeeper's daughter against his father's wishes
	December	Pen gives up the marriage
1878	May	Pen's work exhibited at the Royal Academy Exhibition for the first time; *La Saisiaz: Two Poets of Croisic* published
	Aug–Oct	After six weeks in the Swiss Alps, RB revisits Italy, including Asolo and Venice, for the first time since EBB's death
1879	April	*Dramatic Idyls* published
	14 June	RB a witness in trial of Shepherd *v.* Francis
	autumn	RB's annual holiday in the Alps and Venice
1880	June	*Dramatic Idyls: Second Series* published
	Aug–Nov	RB's annual holiday in the Alps and Venice, where he meets Katharine Bronson
1881	February	Death of Thomas Carlyle
	Aug–Nov	RB's annual holiday in the Alps and Venice
	28 October	First meeting of the Browning Society, at University College, London (RB in Venice at the time)
	December	RB first hears of the planned demolition of Warwick Crescent to make way for a railway (Regent's Canal Bill)
1882	May	RB's seventieth birthday; Katharine Bronson and her daughter Edith visit London
	Aug–Sept	RB's annual holiday is cut short when he is prevented from travelling to Venice by heavy rain and ill health
	December	Death of Anthony Trollope
1883	March	*Jocoseria* published
	Aug–Dec	RB's annual holiday, in which he stays with Mrs Bronson

		in her guest annexe, the Palazzo Giustinian-Recanati, in Venice
1884	spring	The Royal Academy rejects Pen's *Dryope Fascinated by Apollo in the Form of a Serpent*; Grosvenor Gallery exhibits it
	Aug–Sept	RB's annual holiday in St Moritz; he is prevented from going to Venice by a cholera outbreak
	November	*Ferishtah's Fancies* published
1885	March	Death of Katharine Bronson's husband, who has been ill in Paris
	Aug–Nov	RB's annual holiday in Venice (with Pen) is cut short; he initiates negotiations to buy the Palazzo Manzoni
	19 November	Revival of *Colombe's Birthday* at St George's Hall
	December	RB burns letters and papers in the presence of T. J. Wise
		RB's 'Why I Am a Liberal' first published in A. Reid (ed.), *Why I Am a Liberal, Being Definitions by the Best Minds of the Liberal Party*
1886	spring–summer	Mrs Bronson and Edith are in London owing to cholera outbreak in Venice
	autumn	RB's annual holiday is in Wales, due in part to Sarianna's ill health
	September	Death of RB's friend Joseph Milsand
	21 December	Revival of *Strafford* under the auspices of the Browning Society at the Strand Theatre
		RB gives up attempts to purchase the Palazzo Manzoni
		T. J. Wise produces a facsimile of *Pauline* for the Browning Society
1887	January	*Parleyings with Certain People of Importance in Their Day* published
	spring–summer	RB purchases and moves into 29 De Vere Gardens, Kensington
	Aug–Sept	RB's annual holiday in St Moritz, where Pen writes to him of his engagement to Fannie Coddington, who is also staying in St Moritz
	4 October	Marriage of Pen Browning and Fannie Coddington
	November	Death of Alfred Domett
1888	15 March	Revival of *A Blot in the 'Scutcheon*
	May	Pen decides to settle in Venice rather than London
	autumn	Pen purchases Palazzo Rezzonico in Venice and begins restoration
	Aug–Dec	RB's annual holiday in Austria with Pen and Fannie; later he is Mrs Bronson's guest at the Ca' Alvisi in Venice
		T. J. Wise produces a forged 1849 publication of EBB's *Runaway Slave at Pilgrim's Point*
1888–9		*The Poetical Works* (sixteen volumes) published

1889	summer	Mrs Bronson purchases a house, La Mura, in Asolo
	Sept–Oct	RB is at Asolo, in lodgings across from La Mura; he initiates purchase of 'Pippa's Tower'
	November	RB stays at his son's *palazzo* in Venice
	12 December	Death of RB in Venice; on this same day *Asolando* is published and Asolo officials agree to negotiate RB's purchase of 'Pippa's Tower'
	31 December	RB is buried in Poets' Corner, Westminster Abbey
1889–90		EBB's *Poetical Works* (6 volumes) republished in a uniform edition with RB's *Poetical Works*

References

Abbreviations Used in References

EBB   Elizabeth Barrett Browning
RB   Robert Browning
ABL   Armstrong Browning Library, Baylor University, Waco, Texas
BL   British Library, London
Murray   John Murray, Publisher, Albemarle Street, London

Contemporary Letters, Diaries and Memoirs

Unless otherwise indicated, references to Browning's contemporaries appear in the works listed below. If the author and date of a letter or diary entry are clear from the context, I have not felt it necessary to repeat the information in a footnote.

For contemporary reviews of Browning's poetry, see B. Litzinger and D. Smalley (eds), *Browning: The Critical Heritage* (1970).

Letters from and to RB and EBB, as well as reviews and supplementary material, up to and including 1847 are to be found in P. Kelley, R. Hudson and S. Lewis (eds), *The Brownings' Correspondence* (1984–; work in progress, fourteen volumes published so far).

Allingham, *Letters*   *Letters to William Allingham*, edited by H. Allingham and E. Baumer Williams, 1911
Allingham, *Diary*   *William Allingham's Diary*, introduced by G. Grigson, 1967
Blagden, Isa   *Dearest Isa: Robert Browning's Letters to Isabella Blagden*, edited by E. C. McAleer, 1951
Barrett, Arabel   *Letters from Elizabeth Barrett Browning to her Sister Arabella*, edited by S. Lewis, 2 vols., 2002
Barrett, George   *Letters of the Brownings to George Barrett*, edited by P. Landis and R. E. Freeman, 1958
Barrett, Henrietta   *Elizabeth Barrett Browning: Letters to her Sister, 1846–1859*, edited by L. Huxley, 1929

Bronson, Katharine	*More Than Friend: The Letters of Robert Browning to Katharine de Kay Bronson*, edited by M. Meredith, 1985
Cobbe, Frances	F. P. Cobbe, *Life of Frances Power Cobbe as Told by Herself*, 2 vols., 1894
Corkran, Henriette	Henriette Corkran, *Celebrities and I*, 1902
Domett, *Letters*	*Robert Browning and Alfred Domett*, edited by F. G. Kenyon, 1906 (including the letters of Joseph Arnould)
Domett, *Diary*	*The Diary of Alfred Domett, 1872–1885*, edited by E. A. Horsman, 1953
Drew, Mary Gladstone	Mary Gladstone Drew, *Diaries and Letters*, edited by L. Masterman, 1930
Field, Michael	*Works and Days: From the Journal of Michael Field*, edited by T. and D. C. Sturge Moore, 1933
Fitzgerald, Eliza	*Learned Lady: Letters from Robert Browning to Mrs Thomas Fitzgerald, 1876–1889*, edited by E. C. McAleer, 1966
Furnivall, F. J.	*Browning's Trumpeter: The Correspondence of Robert Browning and Frederick J. Furnivall, 1872–1889*, edited by W. S. Peterson, 1979
Hawthorne, Nathaniel	Nathaniel Hawthorne, *The Centenary Edition of Works of Nathaniel Hawthorne*, vol. XIV: *The French and Italian Notebooks*, edited by T. Woodson, 1980
Jowett, Benjamin	*The Life and Letters of Benjamin Jowett*, edited by E. Abbot and L. Campbell, 2 vols., 1897
Macready, W. C.	*The Diaries of William Charles Macready, 1833–1851*, edited by W. Toynbee, 2 vols., 1912
Millais, John Everett	J. G. Millais, *The Life and Letters of Sir John Everett Millais*, 2 vols., 1899
Mitford, Mary Russell	*The Letters of Elizabeth Barrett Browning to Mary Russell Mitford, 1836–1854*, edited by M. B. Raymond and M. R. Sullivan, 3 vols., 1983
Ogilvy, Eliza	*Elizabeth Barrett Browning's Letters to Mrs David Ogilvy 1849–1861*, edited by P. N. Heydon and P. Kelley, 1973 (including 'Recollections of Mrs Browning')
Orr, *Life*	Mrs Sutherland Orr, *Life and Letters of Robert Browning*, 1891
Ritchie, Annie	Annie Thackeray Ritchie, *Records of Tennyson, Ruskin and Browning*, 1892
Story, William	*Browning to his American Friends: Letters between the*
Story, Edith	*Brownings, the Storys, and James Russell Lowell*, edited by G. R. Hudson, 1965
Wedgwood, Julia	*Robert Browning and Julia Wedgwood: A Broken*

Friendship as Revealed in their Letters, edited by R. Curle, 1937

General Collections of Letters and Other Frequently Cited Works

Correspondence	*The Brownings' Correspondence*, edited by P. Kelley, R. Hudson and S. Lewis, 14 vols., 1984–
Critical Heritage	*Browning: The Critical Heritage*, edited by B. Litzinger and D. Smalley, 1970
De Vane and Knickerbocker	*New Letters of Robert Browning*, edited by W. C. DeVane and K. L. Knickerbocker, 1950
Garrett, *Interviews*	*Elizabeth Barrett Browning and Robert Browning: Interviews and Recollections*, edited by M. Garrett, 2000
Griffin and Minchin	W. H. Griffin and H. C. Minchin, *The Life of Robert Browning: With Notices of His Writings, His Family, and His Friends*, 3rd revised edn, 1938
James, *Story*	Henry James, *William Wetmore Story and His Friends*, 2 vols., 1903
Kenyon	*The Letters of Elizabeth Barrett Browning*, edited by F. G. Kenyon, 2 vols., 1897
Lehmann, *Memories*	Rudolf Chambers Lehmann, *Memories of Half a Century: A Record of Friendship*, 1908
Lehmann, *Reminiscences*	Rudolf Lehmann, *An Artist's Reminiscences*, 1894
Orr, *Handbook*	Mrs Sutherland Orr, *A Browning Handbook*, 2nd edn, 1887
Poems	Robert Browning, *The Poems*, edited by J. Pettigrew, 2 vols., 1981
Poetical Works	*The Poetical Works of Robert Browning*, edited by Ian Jack *et al.*, 8 vols., 1983–
Reconstruction	P. Kelley and B. A. Coley, *The Browning Collections: A Reconstruction with Other Memorabilia*, 1984
Rossetti, *Reminiscences*	William Michael Rossetti, *Some Reminiscences*, 2 vols., 1906
Sharp, *Life*	William Sharp, *Life of Robert Browning*, 1890
Tennyson, *Memoir*	Hallam Tennyson, *Alfred Lord Tennyson: A Memoir*, 2 vols., 1897
Whiting, *Brownings*	L. Whiting, *The Brownings: Their Life and Art*, 1911
Wise and Hood	*Letters of Robert Browning*, edited by T. J. Wise and T. L. Hood, 1933

The editions used to quote the Brownings' poetry are *The Poems* of Robert Browning, edited by J. Pettigrew (1981), *The Ring and the Book*, edited by R. D. Altick (1981), and *Selected Poems of Elizabeth Barrett Browning*, edited by M. Forster (1988).

Prologue, pp. 3–4

[1] RB to Sarianna, 5 July 1861: DeVane and Knickerbocker; James, *Story*, II, 87.

1: *'A Strange, Heavy Crown', 1861–5, pp. 5–46*

[1] For the description of Browning, see James, *Story*, I, 172; for his house and furnishings, see Corkran, 30, and Ritchie, 300–1; also E. C. McAleer, *The Brownings of Casa Guidi* (1979), 93, quoting Kate Field, and *Reconstruction, passim*.

[2] William Story to C. E. Norton, 15 August 1861: James, *Story*, II, 64; for EBB's writing case, see *Reconstruction*, H418, and McAleer, *Brownings of Casa Guidi*, 99.

[3] *Reconstruction*, A232; for the Brownings, see Ritchie, 157ff.

[4] EBB to Anna Jameson in a letter lost on the *Titanic*, quoted in Maisie Ward, *Robert Browning and His World*, 2 vols. (1967–9), I, 117; RB to Sarianna, 30 June 1861: Wise and Hood; Story to C. E. Norton, 15 August 1861: James, *Story*, II, 66.

[5] EBB to Henrietta Barrett, 7 July 1850; RB to EBB, 21 August 1846.

[6] Orr, *Life*, 140.

[7] Walter Savage Landor to William Allingham, *Letters*, 6 January 1853; EBB to RB [5–6 May 1845].

[8] RB to EBB [13 September 1845]; EBB to RB [15 May, 4 December 1845].

[9] EBB to RB [5–6 May, 20–3 August 1845].

[10] EBB to RB [12–14 November 1845].

[11] RB to EBB [11 February 1846] and her reply.

[12] EBB to RB [15 January 1846].

[13] G. Macpherson, *Memoirs of the Life of Anna Jameson* (1878), quoted in *Correspondence*, XIV, 320–3; EBB to Arabel Barrett [26 September 1846]; EBB to Arabel Barrett [?5]–9 March 1847.

[14] *Correspondence*, XIV, 362–6.

[15] EBB to Arabel Barrett, 8 February [1847]; EBB to Henrietta Barrett, 31 March 1847; EBB to Arabel Barrett, 16–19 December [1850]; EBB to Arabel Barrett [26 September 1846]; EBB to Arabel and Henrietta Barrett, [21–]24 November [1846]; RB to William Allingham, *Letters*, 10 June 1856.

[16] EBB to Arabel and Henrietta Barrett, 24 February 1847; Sophia Hawthorne to Elizabeth Peabody, 25 August 1858: R. H. Lathrop, *Memories of Hawthorne* (1897), 397–8.

[17] EBB to Arabel Barrett, 22–3 December [1847].

[18] EBB to Arabel and Henrietta Barrett, [21–]24 November [1846], 12 April [1847]; C. Carr (ed.), *Harriet Hosmer: Letters and Memories*, (1912), 102–6.

[19] William Story to C. E. Norton, 15 August 1861: James, *Story*, II, 61–7.

[20] So RB recalls the way to Bellosguardo in a letter to Isa Blagden, 19 September 1862.

[21] RB to the Storys, 30 August 1861; Orr, *Life*, 247; RB to W. C. Macready, 18 July 1861: Wise and Hood.

[22] EBB to Eliza Ogilvy, 13 July 1850; RB to Fanny Haworth, 20 July 1861: Wise and Hood.

[23] RB to the Storys, 20 August 1861.

24 EBB to Mrs Martin [October 1855]: Kenyon.

25 RB to J. T. Fields, 6 September 1855, quoted in *Poetical Works*, V, xxiii; RB to EBB, 13 January 1845; EBB to RB, 5 March 1845.

26 G. B. Hill (ed.), *Letters of Dante Gabriel Rossetti to William Allingham, 1854–1870* (1897), 165; William Michael Rossetti discusses Browning in *Reminiscences*, 232–47; M. B. Cramer, 'Browning's Literary Reputation at Oxford 1855–1859', *PMLA*, 57 (1942), 232–40.

27 RB to EBB [11, 26 February 1845]; RB to John Kenyon, 1 October 1855, quoted in *Poetical Works*, V, xxv; EBB to RB, 17 February 1845.

28 EBB to Arabel Barrett, 10 January [1855], [2 March 1853]; RB to EBB [13 May 1845]; EBB to Isa Blagden, quoted in *Poetical Works*, V, 475.

29 EBB to Arabel Barrett, 31 December [1855]; Carlyle is quoted in *Poetical Works*, V, xi, xxxii; D. J. DeLaura (ed.), 'Ruskin and the Brownings: Twenty-five Unpublished Letters', *John Rylands Library*, 54 (1971–2), 314–56.

30 RB to the Storys, 20 August 1861.

31 *Reconstruction*, L3, quoted in Lewis (ed.), *Letters of Elizabeth Barrett Browning to Her Sister Arabella*, xxxii–xxxiii.

32 Nathaniel Hawthorne, 299–301 and *passim*; McAleer (ed.), *Dearest Isa*, 8.

33 EBB to Arabel Barrett, 5[–6] June [1851]; Corkran, 31–2; EBB to Eliza Ogilvy, 24 January, 8 June 1854; EBB to Leigh Hunt, 6 October 1857: Wise and Hood.

34 EBB to Arabel Barrett, 23 January [1850]; EBB to Henrietta Barrett, 4 March 1856; EBB to Arabel Barrett, 3 April [1854].

35 RB to Fanny Haworth, 20 July 1861: Wise and Hood.

36 Orr, *Life*, 255; RB to W. C. Macready, 18 July 1861: Wise and Hood.

37 EBB to Eliza Ogilvy, 24 January 1854; EBB to Arabel Barrett, 5[–6] June [1851].

38 EBB to Mrs Martin, 9 September 1856: Kenyon.

39 M. Ward, *The Tragi-Comedy of Pen Browning* (1972), Appendix E; RB to Sarianna, 5 July 1861: DeVane and Knickerbocker.

40 RB to John Forster [July 1861]: DeVane and Knickerbocker; RB to the Storys, 20 August 1861.

41 Edward Lytton to RB, 1 September 1861: A. B. Harlan & J. L. Harlan, Jr (eds), *Letters from Owen Meredith [Edward Lytton] to Robert and Elizabeth Barrett Browning* [1936].

42 RB to the Storys, 10 November 1861; RB to Edward Lytton, 20 September 1861: Harlan (eds), *Letters from Owen Meredith*.

43 RB to Major Gillum, 17 June 1863, quoted in W. Irvine and P. Honan, *The Book, the Ring, and the Poet* (1975), 422; Ward, *Tragi-Comedy*, 57; RB to the Storys, 3 May 1864, 17 July, 26 November 1863.

44 Orr, *Life*, 254.

45 See M. Stone, 'Bile and the Brownings: A New Poem by RB, EBB's "My Heart and I", and New Questions About the Brownings' Marriage', in J. Woodford (ed.), *Robert Browning in Contexts* (1998), 213–31.

46 EBB to Sarianna [November 1856]: Kenyon; Orr, *Life*, 243–4.

47 See M. Meredith, 'Browning and the Prince of Publishers', *Browning Institute Studies*, 7 (1979), 1–20.

[48] *The Times*, 2 May 1864.

[49] EBB to Henrietta Barrett, 15 November 1855; RB to EBB, 18 September 1845.

[50] William Story to C. E. Norton, 15 August 1861: James, *Story*, II, 67; RB to the Storys, 10 April 1862, 3 May 1864.

[51] RB to the Storys, 5 March, 17 July 1863.

[52] RB to Isa Blagden, 19 September 1862.

[53] RB to Isa Blagden, 19 September 1863.

[54] EBB to Fanny Haworth, 18 May 1860: Kenyon.

[55] Cobbe, II, 14–15; RB to Isa Blagden, 19 December 1864.

[56] RB to Isa Blagden, 19 November 1863.

[57] RB to Isa Blagden, 19 August 1864.

[58] RB to Isa Blagden, 19 July 1862.

[59] Isa Blagden to Mme Mignaty, 16 March [1862]: McAleer (ed.), *Dearest Isa*, xxv.

[60] RB to Isa Blagden, 19 December 1864.

[61] Julia Sterling to Julia Wedgwood, 5 March 1865.

[62] Julia Wedgwood to RB, 1 November 1864; RB to Julia Wedgwood, [4 November 1864].

2: *Fathers and Sons, 1865–8, pp. 47–93*

[1] RB to the Storys, 20 August 1861; RB to Isa Blagden, 18 August 1862, 31 August 1861.

[2] RB to Isa Blagden, 19 August 1865.

[3] EBB to George Barrett, 2 February [1852].

[4] RB to the Storys, 5 September 1863.

[5] Whiting, *Brownings*, 88.

[6] RB to Isa Blagden, 9 September 1861.

[7] RB to the Storys, 11 April 1865.

[8] RB to Tennyson, 13 October 1864: Tennyson, *Memoir*.

[9] RB to Isa Blagden, 19 May 1865, 19 June 1862.

[10] RB to Julia Wedgwood, 19 September 1864; RB to the Storys, 3 May 1864; for a summary of the gossip about Browning, see G. S. Haight, 'Robert Browning's Widows', *TLS* (2 July 1971), although it contains some inaccuracies.

[11] Shelley to Thomas Medwin, 17 January 1820; the artist Elihu Vedder and the writer Charles Lever, in his novel, *The Fortunes of Glencore* (1857); all are quoted in G. Artom Treves, *The Golden Ring: The Anglo-Florentines 1847–1862* (1956); see also P. Neville-Sington, *Fanny Trollope: The Life and Adventures of a Clever Woman* (1997), chapters 12, 13.

[12] W. Thoron (ed.), *The Letters of Mrs Henry Adams, 1865–1882*, (1936); for Hiram Powers, see Hawthorne, 278–81, and *passim*; for William Story, see Hawthorne, 72–4, James, *Story*, II, 224 and *passim*.

[13] T. A. Trollope, *What I Remember*, 2 vols. (1887), II, 190–1; EBB to Arabel Barrett [13–15 November 1852].

[14] Orr, *Life*, 254–5; RB to Isa Blagden, 19 October 1865.

[15] Orr, *Life*, 193; Whiting, *Brownings*, 212; RB to Isa Blagden, 19 May 1865.

[16] RB to the Storys, 5 March 1863; RB to EBB [5 April 1846], 19 January 1846.

17 The series of letters written by RB in Paris to Pen are in Wise and Hood.

18 R. Garnett to W. H. Griffin, 4 December 1904: BL Add 45564, ff. 112–13; RB to EBB [26 August 1846].

19 Griffin and Minchin, 8.

20 Orr, *Life*, 104–5.

21 Griffin and Minchin, 12, 31.

22 EBB to George Barrett [4–5 December 1851].

23 *The Times*, 2 July 1852; EBB to Arabel Barrett [25 October 1852]; EBB to H. F. Chorley, 10 August [1853]: Kenyon.

24 EBB to Arabel Barrett [15–17 January 1853, 25 October 1852].

25 RB to John Kenyon, 16 January 1853: Wise and Hood.

26 EBB to Arabel Barrett, 21 December 1852; Corkran, 10ff.

27 Whiting, *Brownings*, 261; *Poetical Works*, V, xi–xiv; J. W. Chadwick, quoted in W. C. DeVane, *A Browning Handbook* (1936; revised edn 1955).

28 EBB to Mrs Martin, [20?] October 1846: Kenyon; EBB to Mary Russell Mitford, 1 December [1849].

29 Domett, *Diary*, 30 April 1878; Allingham, *Diary*, 5 November 1875; Orr, *Life*, 18.

30 Orr, *Life*, 27–9.

31 Griffin and Minchin, 50; *Poems*, II, 940 and note.

32 Orr, *Life*, 45–6.

33 Irvine and Honan, *The Book, the Ring and the Poet*, 5; C. G. Duffy, *Conversations with Carlyle* (1892), 58; RB to EBB [12 June 1846].

34 RB to Mary Russell Mitford, 9 March 1849: Wise and Hood; RB to Arabel Barrett, 18 March [1849].

35 EBB to Mary Russell Mitford, 30 April [1849]; EBB to Arabel Barrett, 8–16 April [1849].

36 EBB to Arabel Barrett, 14–15 March [1848].

37 EBB to Arabel Barrett, 8–16 April [1849]; EBB to Mrs Martin, 14 May [1849]: Kenyon.

38 EBB to Mary Russell Mitford [18? July 1849]; RB to Sarianna, 2 July 1849: Wise and Hood.

39 RB to Julia Wedgwood, 2 September 1864; EBB to Sarianna [April 1849]: Kenyon; EBB to Arabel Barrett, 8–16 April [1849].

40 RB (and EBB) to Anna Jameson, 11 August 1849: Kenyon.

41 EBB to RB [31 July 1845] and his reply; EBB to RB [15 August 1846].

42 EBB to Arabel Barrett [c. 10 February 1848]; EBB to Mary Russell Mitford, 30 April [1849].

43 RB to John Kenyon, 16 January 1853: Wise and Hood.

44 EBB to Anna Jameson, 21 October [1851]: Kenyon; EBB to Eliza Ogilvy [25 July– 1 August 1851]; EBB to Arabel Barrett [12–14 October 1851].

45 Sarianna to Mrs Wood, 19 November [1851]: ABL; EBB to Arabel Barrett, 18 November [1851].

46 EBB to Arabel Barrett [?20 April 1861].

47 Sarianna to William Allingham, *Letters*, 14 May [1860 for 1859], 19 April 1860; EBB to Arabel Barrett [2–3 July 1853].

48 EBB to William Allingham, *Letters*, 8 November 1858; RB to Isa Blagden, 19 February 1866; Sarianna to Annie Smith, 11 April 1869: ABL.

49 RB to Isa Blagden, 19 August 1865, 19 September 1867; W. H. Grove, 'Browning as I Knew Him, by his Valet', *Sunday Express* (4 December 1927), 9.

50 RB to Isa Blagden, 24 September 1866; Benjamin Jowett to correspondent, 12 June 1865; Meredith, 'Browning and the Prince of Publishers', 13.

51 Sarianna to William Allingham, *Letters*, 28 September 1861; RB to Isa Blagden, 19 May 1866.

52 EBB to Henrietta Barrett, 1 October 1856; EBB to Arabel Barrett, 29–31 August [1847].

53 EBB to Henrietta Barrett, 4 March 1851, 25 May 1850; EBB to Arabel Barrett, 12 April [1858], also EBB to Henrietta Barrett, 14 May 1853.

54 Allingham, *Diary*, 30 June 1864.

55 EBB to Henrietta Barrett, 4 March 1853; EBB to Arabel Barrett [22 January 1859].

56 RB to George Barrett, 28 January 1867; Allingham, *Diary*, 27 December 1868.

57 *Poetical Works*, VII, xxii; RB to Edith Story, 26 July 1865.

58 RB to Seymour Kirkup, 19 February 1867: Wise and Hood.

59 John Maynard, *Browning's Youth* (1977), 51, 268.

60 M. B. Cramer, 'What Browning's Literary Reputation Owed to the Pre-Raphaelites 1847–1856', *ELH*, 8 (1941), 305–21, see also Cramer, 'Browning's Literary Reputation at Oxford'; William Rossetti to Thomas Dixon, January 1859: R. W. Peattie (ed.), W. M. Rossetti, *Selected Letters* (1990); A. C. Swinburne, 'George Chapman', in E. Gosse and T. J. Wise (eds), *Contemporaries of Shakespeare* (1919); RB to Mrs J. E. Millais, *Letters*, 7 January 1867; EBB to Sarianna [c. March 1860]: Kenyon.

61 Allingham, *Diary*, 26 May 1868; *Poetical Works*, VII, xxviii–xxxi.

62 EBB to Arabel Barrett, 12 April [1853].

63 RB to Isa Blagden, 19 October 1865.

64 *Reconstruction*, A355.

65 RB to Isa Blagden, 19 July 1867; RB to George Barrett, 2 April 1861.

66 EBB to Mrs Martin, 5 October [1853]: Kenyon.

67 RB to EBB [25 December 1845]; EBB to Arabel Barrett [21]–24 November [1846].

68 RB to EBB [21 November 1845].

69 EBB to Henrietta Barrett, 14 May 1853; EBB to H. F. Chorley, 10 August [1853]: Kenyon; EBB to Eliza Ogilvy, 9 September 1853.

70 EBB to Fanny Haworth, 14 September 1857: Kenyon.

71 EBB to Mary Russell Mitford, 7 January [1854]; EBB to Arabel Barrett [28–9 November], [16]–19 December [1853]; EBB to Henrietta Barrett, 12 October 1857.

72 EBB to Fanny Haworth, 1 September 1858: McAleer (ed.), *Dearest Isa*, 276.

73 RB to Mrs Story, 26 November 1863.

74 EBB to Isa Blagden, 10 May [1860]: E. C. McAleer, 'New Letters from Mrs Browning to Isa Blagden', *PMLA*, 66 (1951), 594–612; EBB to Arabel Barrett, [13 November 1858]; EBB's correspondence with Sophie Eckley is in the Berg Collection, New York Public Library.

75 EBB to Arabel Barrett, 15 March [1861]; RB to the Storys, 2 May 1863; my thanks

to William Askins for allowing me to see a draft of his paper, 'Women in the Woods: A Reconsideration of the Relationship between the Brownings and the American Friends, David and Sophie Eckley'.

76 EBB to Arabel Barrett, 15 March [1861]; EBB to Isa Blagden, 10 May [1860]: McAleer, 'New Letters'.

77 EBB to Arabel Barrett, 8 February 1847, 5 November [1852]; EBB to Arabel and Henrietta Barrett, 24 February 1847.

3: *'Some Faint Show of Bigamy', 1868–72, pp. 94–141*

1 RB to Lady Colvile, 26 October 1868: BL Add 60632, ff. 18–37; RB to Mrs Millais, *Letters*, 7 January 1867.

2 For the following discussion see Introduction to *The Ring and the Book* in *Poetical Works*, VII; Allingham, *Diary*, 2 January 1872; Hill (ed.), *Letters of Dante Gabriel Rossetti to William Allingham*, 284.

3 RB to W. G. Kingsland, 27 November 1868: Wise and Hood.

4 RB to EBB [3 August 1845]; EBB to Cornelius Matthews [mid-January 1847].

5 EBB to Mary Russell Mitford, 8 December 1847; EBB to J. R. Lowell, 17 December 1846, quoted in Christie's (London) catalogue, 4 June 2003 (now at ABL).

6 RB to Edward Moxon, 24 February 1847: Wise and Hood; EBB to Arabel Barrett, 14–15 March [1848].

7 EBB to Anna Jameson, 1 October [1849]: Kenyon; EBB to Arabel and Henrietta Barrett, 12 April [1847]; RB to H. F. Chorley, 11 March 1850: *Poetical Works*, IV, 318–19.

8 RB to Chapman, 23 February 1852: ABL.

9 RB to EBB [11 March 1845].

10 RB to Leigh Hunt, 6 October 1857: Wise and Hood; Robert Lytton to EBB, 26 December 1856: Harlan and Harlan (eds), *Letters from Owen Meredith*; Orr, *Life*, 270.

11 EBB to Arabel Barrett [27 February 1856].

12 EBB to Anna Jameson, 2 May 1856: Kenyon.

13 EBB to Mary Russell Mitford, February [1853], 15 March [1853]; EBB to Henrietta Barrett, 4 March 1856; EBB to Arabel Barrett, 12 April [1858]; RB to Isa Blagden, 1 October 1871.

14 RB to H. F. Chorley [1860]: Wise and Hood; RB to Isa Blagden, 4 September 1858; EBB to Isa Blagden, 7 January [1859]: Kenyon.

15 EBB to Sarianna, [March] 1861: Kenyon.

16 EBB to Arabel Barrett, [?5]–9 March 1847.

17 EBB to Sarianna, 12 June 1855: Kenyon.

18 EBB to Arabel Barrett [11–12 February 1861]; EBB to Sarianna, [March] 1861: Kenyon; EBB to RB, 20 March 1845; EBB to Mary Hunter, 2 November [1858]: BL Add 45562, f. 4 (copies); Whiting, *Brownings*, 194.

19 RB to Isa Blagden, 19 March 1866; EBB to Arabel Barrett [24 March 1858].

20 R. A. Bosco, 'The Brownings and Mrs Kinney', *Browning Institute Studies*, 4 (1976), 115–17.

21 EBB to Sophie Eckley, undated: Berg Collection, New York Public Library; EBB to Henrietta Barrett, 4 March 1858; EBB to Isa Blagden, 27 March [1859]: Kenyon.

22 EBB to Arabel Barrett [13–15 August 1850]; EBB to Mary Russell Mitford [14? September 1852]; EBB to Arabel Barrett, 31 October [1859].

23 EBB to Henrietta Barrett, 27 April 1855; EBB to Sarianna, [March] 1861: Kenyon.

24 Bosco, 'The Brownings and Mrs Kinney', 67.

25 EBB to Sarianna, [March] 1861: Kenyon; RB to Eliza Fitzgerald, 15 July 1882; DeLaura (ed.), 'Ruskin and the Brownings'.

26 RB to EBB [24 May 1845], and her reply.

27 Quoted in M. Forster, *Elizabeth Barrett Browning* (1988), 328.

28 B. Chevasco, ' "Naughty Books": Elizabeth Barrett Browning's Response to Eugène Sue', *Browning Society Notes*, 28 (2003), 7–17; EBB to W. M. Thackeray, 21 April [1861]: Kenyon.

29 EBB to Arabel (and George) Barrett, [4 October 1856]; Ruskin to EBB, 4 March 1855: E. T. Cook and A. Wedderburn (eds), *The Works of John Ruskin* (1903–12), vol. XXXVI.

30 M. Calcraft-Rennie, 'Wordcraft and the Goldsmiths: Browning and the Castellani', *Browning Society Notes*, 23 (1996), 54–66; Orr, *Life*, 281.

31 RB to EBB, 31 December 1845 [24 May 1846]; EBB to RB [21 August 1846].

32 W. H. Griffin visited and photographed all the places associated with Browning's poetry; see BL Add 74788.

33 EBB to Arabel Barrett [15–17 January 1853]; RB to Mrs Story, 26 November 1863; EBB to Anna Jameson, 2 April [1850]: Kenyon.

34 Quoted in G. Reese, 'Robert Browning and his Son', *PMLA*, 61 (1946), 784–803.

35 RB to Julia Wedgwood, 5 November 1868; J. E. T. Rogers, *Education in Oxford: Its Method, Its Aids, and Its Rewards* (1861); RB to H. G. Liddell, 17 October 1868: Ward, *Tragi-Comedy*, Appendix F.

36 RB to Julia Wedgwood, 8 March 1869.

37 RB to T. Kelsall, 22 September 1869: quoted in Irvine and Honan, 444.

38 See F. Winwar, *The Immortal Lovers: Elizabeth Barrett and Robert Browning* (1950), 306.

39 RB to S. Kirkup, 19 February 1867: Wise and Hood.

40 RB to Mrs Lehmann, 27 July 1869: Lehmann, *Memories*, 118–19.

41 EBB to Arabel Barrett [11–14 December 1851]; EBB to Arabel Barrett, 29–30 May [1852]; V. Surtees, *The Ludovico Goddess: The Life of Louisa Lady Ashburton* (1984), 43.

42 Surtees, *Ludovico Goddess*, 57, 132, and chapter 13; RB to Mrs Story, 26 November 1863; RB to Lady Ashburton, 27 November 1863: ABL.

43 For Browning's encounters with Lady Ashburton, see Surtees, *Ludovico Goddess*, chapter 13, *passim*; James, *Story*, II, 197–8; Sarianna to Annie Smith, 27 August 1869: ABL.

44 EBB to Arabel Barrett, [12]–13 September [1854] *Poems*, II, 955–6.

45 For Rosalind Howard's diary, see V. Surtees, 'Browning's Last Duchess', *TLS* (9 October 1986), 17–18, including Daniel Karlin's comments.

46 EBB to George Barrett, 2 April [1861].

47 RB to William Story, 19 June 1886; RB to Edith Story, 4 April 1872.
48 For example, RB to Isa Blagden, 19 January, 24 February 1870, 29 December 1871, 25 January, 19 February, 30 March 1872.
49 RB to the Storys, 16 November 1869; Ward, *Tragi-Comedy*, 57.
50 RB to Isa Blagden, 19 August 1870; RB to EBB [11 February 1845].
51 RB to Isa Blagden, 30 March 1872.
52 RB to Isa Blagden, 19 July, 19 August 1871, 3 October 1872.
53 RB to Richard Monckton Milnes, 21 December 1870: DeVane and Knickerbocker; Surtees, *Ludovico Goddess*, 143–4.
54 RB to George Smith, 8 August 1871: Murray.
55 Euripides, *The Alcestis*, trans. Gilbert Murray (1915).
56 RB to an unidentified American publisher, 15 April 1870: DeVane and Knickerbocker.
57 RB to Edith Story, 4 April 1872; RB to William Story, 19 June 1886.
58 RB to Edith Story, 1 January 1872; RB to Isa Blagden, 8 November 1871; W. J. Fox said that Elizabeth 'silver-electroplated' Napoleon III: Orr, *Life*, 191; see J. F. McMillan, 'The Empire the French Forget: New Views of Napoleon III', *TLS* (15 March 2002).

4: *Kid Gloves, 1872–7, pp. 142–90*

1 RB to Edith Story, 4 April 1872; Mary Gladstone Drew, 454.
2 Orr, *Life*, 294; see also Orr, *Handbook*.
3 RB to Isa Blagden, 8 November [1871]; for this episode, see J. Marsh, *Dante Gabriel Rossetti: Painter and Poet* (1999).
4 *Poems*, II, 975; the manuscripts of *Fifine at the Fair* and other of Browning's later poems are at Balliol College Library.
5 Orr, *Life*, 46.
6 Sarah Flower to W. J. Fox, 31 May [1827]: *Correspondence*, II, 348.
7 Maynard, *Browning's Youth*, 183; Irvine and Honan, *The Book, the Ring and the Poet*, 24; RB to R. H. Horne, 3 December 1848: Wise and Hood.
8 For the case for Jemima Browning (Robert's half-aunt, a girl his own age) being the possible model for Pauline, see V. Browning, 'The Real Identity of Pauline', *Browning Society Notes*, 13 (1983); Domett, *Letters*, 141.
9 *Reconstruction*, B20 (Browning's own copy of *Pauline*); see the Introduction to *Pauline*, in *Poetical Works*, I.
10 RB to W. J. Fox [?4 March 1833].
11 *Reconstruction*, B20.
12 RB to EBB [10 August 1845]; RB to Count André Victor Amédée de Ripert Monclar, 9 August 1837; RB to EBB [11, 15 January 1846]; RB to George Smith, 27 February 1888: Murray.
13 E. F. Bridell-Fox, 'Browning', *The Argosy*, 49 (1890), 112; Thomas Carlyle to John Sterling, 28 July 1842: C. de L. Ryals *et al.* (eds), *Collected Letters of Thomas and Jane Welsh Carlyle*, 27 vols. (1980–2001); Richard and Edward Garnett, *The Life of W. J. Fox* (1910), 194.

14 Domett, *Diary*, 6; *Reconstruction*, C428.

15 RB to EBB [10 August 1845]; RB to Sarah Flower Adams, 4 February [1835].

16 RB to Domett, 23 February 1845; Arnould to Domett undated: Domett *Letters*, 84; Domett to RB, 30 January 1846: *Correspondence*.

17 M. B. Cramer, 'Browning's Friendships and Fame before Marriage (1833–1846)', *PMLA*, 55 (1940), 207–30.

18 Orr, *Life*, 82; Griffin and Minchin, 77; B. Miller, 'This Happy Evening', *The Twentieth Century*, 154 (1953), quoted in Irvine and Honan, *The Book, the Ring and the Poet*, 64–5.

19 Frederick Young to W. H. Griffin, 25 October 1904: BL Add 45564, ff. 74–6; Bridell-Fox, 'Browning'; the Introduction to *Strafford*, in *Poetical Works*, II.

20 Domett, *Letters*, 67; RB to Count André Victor Amédée de Ripert Monclar, 9 August 1837.

21 RB to John Robertson, [13 April] 1838; the Introduction to *Sordello*, in *Poetical Works*, II.

22 EBB to RB [9 December 1845].

23 RB to Domett, 8 November 1843; EBB to Thomas Westwood, [early] April 1845.

24 Macready (his *Diaries*), 27 August 1840; RB to Eliza Flower, 9 March [1840]; Irvine and Honan, *The Book, the Ring and the Poet*, 66.

25 E. Gosse, *Robert Browning: Personalia* (1890); EBB to RB [12 April 1846].

26 Maynard, *Browning's Youth*, 110; Domett, *Letters*, 20.

27 Domett, *Letters*, 88.

28 Domett, *Letters*, 90; RB to Domett, 13 July 1846.

29 Arnould to Domett, 26 February 1845: BL Add 45560, f. 44.

30 Arnould to Domett, 28 July 1844: Domett, *Letters*; Arnould to Domett, undated: Domett, *Letters*, 67; RB to Frank Hill, 15 December 1884, quoted in Orr, *Life*, 118–23.

31 Domett, *Letters*, 84.

32 Arnould to Domett, 30 November 1846: Domett, *Letters*.

33 RB to EBB [9 December 1845]; Domett, *Letters*, 86; Cramer, 'Browning's Friendships and Fame before Marriage'; EBB to RB [20–3 August 1845].

34 EBB to RB [9 September 1845], 15 January 1845.

35 RB to Domett, 19 December 1841: *Correspondence*; EBB to RB, 1 January [1846]; EBB to Henrietta Barrett, 22 April 1848.

36 EBB to Arabel Barrett [10 July 1851].

37 RB to EBB [11, 26 February 1845].

38 Arnould to Domett, 24 November 1845: Domett, *Letters*; RB to EBB [23 November 1845].

39 RB to Eliza Flower [7 December 1845].

40 Domett, *Diary*, 29 February 1872; this is the first entry.

41 RB to Domett, *Letters*, 1 March 1872.

42 Domett to RB, 6 May 1864: Alexander Turnbull Library, Wellington, New Zealand, quoted in Ward, *Robert Browning and His World*, II, 181.

43 Domett, *Letters*, 143–4.

44 Domett to RB, 6 May 1864: Turnbull Library, Wellington; A. N. Domett to W. H. Griffin, 11 August 1904: BL Add 45564, ff. 23–4.

45 RB to 'Arcturus', letter in Turnbull Library: quoted in Ward, *Robert Browning and His World*, II, 180–4; RB to Domett, 8 November 1843.

46 RB to Domett, 22 March 1872; Orr, *Life*, 101.

47 Mary Gladstone Drew to Lavinia Lyttleton, 9 March 1877; Mrs. T. B. Aldrich, *Crowding Memories* (1921), 178–9.

48 Lehmann, *Memories*, 109–10; Jowett, II, 400–1; J. Hawthorne: *Shapes that Pass: Memories of Old Days* (1928), 139–41; Anon., 'Celebrities at Home', *The World* (17 March 1880), reprinted in *Browning Society Notes*, 27 (2000), 68–72; RB to Eliza Fitzgerald, 10 December 1881; Whiting, *Brownings*, 224; Thomas Hardy to Edmund Gosse, 6 March 1899: BL Ashley 282.

49 L. Edel, *Henry James: A Life* (1996), 224, 240.

50 Cobbe, II, 15; Bosco, 'The Brownings and Mrs Kinney', 63.

51 EBB to Arabel Barrett [5 March 1852].

52 Allingham, *Diary*, 12 May 1873.

53 Domett, *Diary*, 21 March 1874.

54 James, *Story*, II, 94.

55 J. A. Symonds to E. Gosse, 25 November 1875: BL Ashley B264.

56 RB to Edith Story, 4 April 1872; see Surtees, *The Ludovico Goddess*, for the following episode.

57 RB to Hatty Hosmer, 19 October 1857: Carr (eds), *Harriet Hosmer*, 94; RB to Edith Story, 4 April 1872.

58 For the Benzons, Lehmanns, and their wide circle of artistic and musical friends, see C. Dakers, *The Holland Park Circle: Artists and Victorian Society* (1999); Haight, 'Browning's Widows'.

59 *Correspondence*, XI, 329–31.

60 Dakers, *Holland Park Circle*, 240; EBB to Arabel Barrett [23 October 1855].

61 RB to Mrs Skirrow, 16 July 1875: DeVane and Knickerbocker; RB to Felix Moscheles, 12 May 1875: ABL.

62 (Eliza Fitzgerald), McAleer (ed.), *Learned Lady*, 25.

63 The manuscript of *The Inn Album* is at Balliol College Library.

64 H. James in *The Nation* (20 January 1876): *Critical Heritage*.

65 Griffin and Minchin, 260; RB to George Barrett, 12 August 1876; Irvine and Honan, *The Book, the Ring and the Poet*, 483–4.

66 RB to Isa Blagden, 22 March 1870; EBB to Arabel Barrett [15–17 January 1853], note.

67 M. Calcraft-Rennie, 'Robert Browning's Pacchiarotto, Volume: A Reinterpretation and Reassessment,' (Ph.D. Dissertation, University of Southampton, 1985); for the arrival of Gordigiani's portraits, see RB's letters to Annie Smith and George Smith for October 1876: ABL and Murray, respectively; Wise and Hood, xv.

68 Domett, *Diary*, 26 April 1877; Ward, *Robert Browning and His World*, II, 184–5.

69 BL Add 45560.

70 My thanks to the Royal Academy of Arts Library for this and other information about Domett's son; Domett, *Diary*, 30 March 1876.

71 RB to Eliza Fitzgerald, 10 October 1875: ABL; RB to George Smith, 27 August 1875: Murray; RB to Mrs Pattison, 3 January 1876: W. H. G. Armytage, 'Robert Browning and Mrs Pattison: Some Unpublished Browning Letters', *University of Toronto Quarterly*, 21 (1952), 179–92; RB to Annie Smith, 27 October 1876: ABL.

72 RB to Eliza Fitzgerald, 30 August 1877.

73 RB to Mrs Charles Skirrow, 15 September 1877: DeVane and Knickerbocker; RB to J. D. Williams, 30 January 1880: Collins (ed.), 'Letters from Robert Browning to the Revd J. D. Williams'.

74 RB to J. D. Williams, 30 January 1880: Collins (ed.), 'Letters from Robert Browning to the Revd J. D. Williams'.

5: *Youthful Echoes, 1877–83, pp. 191–235*

1 Lehmann, *Reminiscences*, 230; Domett, *Diary*, 1 June 1875; RB to the Storys, 4 April 1887.

2 RB to George Smith, 22 December 1876: Murray; Allingham, *Diary*, 257–60.

3 Sarianna passed on Alexandra Orr's remark to Joseph Milsand, who repeated it in his reply, 2 December 1877: ABL.

4 RB to F. J. Furnivall, 5 January 1882; Lehmann, *Reminiscences*, 320–1.

5 Domett, *Diary*, 17 March, 10 and 11 December 1877.

6 Henriette Corkran to RB, 31 December 1877: ABL.

7 RB to Eliza Fitzgerald, 25 April 1878: ABL.

8 RB to Carlyle, 26 March 1878: Wise and Hood.

9 Allingham, *Diary*, 29 March 1878.

10 RB to Eliza Fitzgerald, 9 June 1878; Domett, *Diary*, 13 June 1878.

11 Millais to RB, Leighton to RB, 10 May 1878: ABL; EBB to Arabel Barrett [26–7 May 1856]; RB to George Smith, 9 May 1878: Murray; RB to Leighton, 14 November 1878: Wise and Hood.

12 Reviews taken from newspaper cuttings kept by Pen in his notebook: BL Ashley 5719.

13 Katharine Bronson, 'Browning in Venice', in Meredith (ed.), *More Than Friend*, Appendix B.

14 For Browning's routine at this time, see Anon., 'Celebrities at Home', *The World*; W. H. Grove, 'My Memories of Robert Browning', MS at Scripps College, Claremont, CA, reprinted in *Browning Society Notes*, 26 (2000), 69–72; W. H. Grove, 'Robert Browning at Home', *Pall Mall Budget*, 19 December 1889, reprinted in Garrett, *Interviews*, 127–30; Grove, 'Browning as I Knew Him'; Lehmann, *Reminiscences, passim*; W. L. Phelps, 'Robert Browning as Seen by His Son: A Talk with Barrett Browning', *Century Magazine*, 85, NS 63 (1913), 419.

15 RB to Eliza Fitzgerald, 14 January 1882.

16 RB to John Murray, 22 May 1881: Murray; RB to Eliza Fitzgerald, 19 June 1880.

17 F. Leveson Gower, *Bygone Years* (1905), 280.

18 Orr, *Life*, 297.

19 Allingham, *Diary*, 10 June 1888; EBB to Henrietta Barrett, 19 December 1846.

20 EBB to Arabel Barrett [11–14 December 1851]; EBB to Isa Blagden, 7 January

[1859]: Kenyon; see also EBB to Mary Hunter, 9 January [1859]: BL Add 45562, f. 7; Orr, *Life*, 148–9.

21 [Alfred Austin,] 'The Poetry of the Period', *The Temple Bar*, 26 (June 1869), 316–33; Corkran, 162–7; Rossetti, *Reminiscences*, II, 235; for this and all subsequent remarks by Mrs Dykes Campbell see her recollections: BL Add 49525B.

22 Allingham, *Diary*, April 1876; BL Add 49525B.

23 Allingham, *Diary*, 20 March 1881; Tennyson, *Memoir*, II, 229–30.

24 Allingham, *Diary*, 25 June 1884; R. H. Hutton, 'Browning and Tennyson', *Spectator* (21 December 1889), 879–80, reprinted in *Critical Heritage*, 507–8; Bronson, 'Browning in Venice'.

25 Sarianna to Michael Field, 3 January 1896; R. A. King, *Robert Browning's Finances from His Own Account Book* [1947], 16–17.

26 Grove, 'Browning as I Knew Him'.

27 EBB to Arabel Barrett, 4 April [1853]; Domett, *Diary*, 14 April 1877.

28 Hawthorne, *Shapes that Pass*, 143.

29 F. G. R. Duckworth, *Browning: Background and Conflict* (1931), 78.

30 Orr, *Life*, 25; Cobbe, II, 14–15.

31 RB to Mrs Skirrow, 15 September 1877: DeVane and Knickerbocker; EBB to Sarianna, [March] 1861: Kenyon.

32 RB to Mrs Henry Schlesinger, 18 May 1876: ABL; see also RB to Annie Smith, 26 October 1876: ABL; Browning's correspondence with Emily Harris is in the Armstrong Browning Library.

33 W. B. Maxwell, *Time Gathered: Autobiography* [1937], quoted in DeVane and Knickerbocker, 190–1.

34 Corkran, 162–7; Mrs Bloomfield-Moore to RB, undated: ABL; Grove, 'Browning as I Knew Him'.

35 RB to Eliza Fitzgerald, 9 August 1878.

36 RB to Mrs Skirrow, 12 September 1878: DeVane and Knickerbocker; Allingham, *Diary*, 20 August 1880.

37 RB to Eliza Fitzgerald, 7 September 1878.

38 Arnould to Domett, 26 February 1845: *Correspondence*, X, 330.

39 RB to Isa Blagden, 19 May 1866.

40 Bridell-Fox, 'Browning', 112.

41 Hiram Corsan, 'A Few Reminiscences of Robert Browning', *Cornell Era*, 40 (1908), reprinted in *Browning Institute Studies*, 3 (1975), 62–3.

42 For photographs of Browning's Asolo, see W. H. Griffin's notes, BL Add 74790–1; Katharine Bronson, 'Browning in Asolo', in Meredith (ed.), *More Than Friend*, Appendix A; see also Allingham, *Diary*, 6 April 1876.

43 EBB to Arabel Barrett, 5[–6] June [1851].

44 Orr, *Life*, 324.

45 RB to Katharine Bronson, 10 June 1889; RB to Eliza Fitzgerald, 12 October 1878.

46 RB to Carlyle, 27 March 1879: Wise and Hood; Domett, *Diary*, 30 March 1879.

47 Trial reported in *The Times* and the *Daily Telegraph*, 16 June 1879.

48 RB to Eliza Fitzgerald, 19 September 1880.

49 Orr, *Life*, 270; EBB to RB [17 April 1845].

[50] RB to A. L. Budden, 6 April 1879: BL Add 48988, f. 37; RB to EBB [9 November 1845]; *Reconstruction*, E267–77.

[51] RB to H. R. Haweis, 11 May 1880: Wise and Hood; RB to Eliza Fitzgerald, 4 September 1880.

[52] *Browning Society Papers*, 1 (1881), 171–90; W. S. Peterson, *Interrogating the Oracle: A History of the Browning Society* (1969), 117.

[53] Domett, *Diary*, 4 February 1882.

[54] E. Gosse to W. H. Griffin, 8 May 1902: BL Add 45563, ff. 147–50.

[55] Curtis, 'Robert Browning'; RB to Eliza Fitzgerald, 6 September 1881.

[56] RB to Mrs Fitzgerald, 4 November 1884; RB to George Smith, 8 July 1881: Murray.

[57] RB to Emily Hickey, 15 February 1884: DeVane and Knickerbocker.

[58] EBB to Sarianna, [March] 1861: Kenyon; RB to Lawrence Barrett, 3 February 1885: Wise and Hood.

[59] Allingham, *Diary*, 10 June 1888; Domett, *Diary*, 11 February 1881.

[60] RB to Eliza Fitzgerald, 30 September, 13, 23 October 1880.

[61] For Henry James, see N. J. Hall (ed.), *The Letters of Anthony Trollope*, 2 vols. (1983), II, 666–7; A. Trollope to Katharine Bronson, 28 May [1882]: Hall (ed.), *Letters of Anthony Trollope*.

[62] Henry James, 'Casa Alvisi', in *Italian Hours*, quoted in Richard Howard (ed.), *Collected Travel Writings: The Continent* (1993), 359–64; 'Casa Alvisi' was first published as a prefatory note to Katharine Bronson's 'Browning in Venice', *Cornhill Magazine*, 68 (1902), 145–71; it was also published, simultaneously, but without the prefatory note, in *The Century Magazine*, 63 (February 1902), 572–84.

[63] For Katharine Bronson, see the Introduction to Meredith (ed.), *More Than Friend*.

[64] Katharine Bronson, 'Browning in Venice'.

[65] RB to Norman MacColl, 24 November 1881: Wise and Hood.

[66] RB to Katharine Bronson, 30 January 1882.

[67] RB to J. Ingram, 21 March 1880, 5, 18, 22 May 1882: Wise and Hood.

[68] BL Ashley 5719 (Pen's art notebook for 1875–81).

[69] RB to J. D. Williams, 17 April 1883: Wise and Hood.

6: *'In the Silence of the Sleep-time', 1883–9, pp. 236–92*

[1] RB to Edith Story, 7 August 1884.

[2] Quoted in N. J. Hall, *Trollope: A Biography* (1991), 226.

[3] Quoted in Dakers, *Holland Park Circle*, 193.

[4] RB to Eliza Fitzgerald, 17 March 1883.

[5] RB to Katharine Bronson, 16 September 1884.

[6] Katharine Bronson, 'Browning in Venice'; RB to Eliza Fitzgerald, 9, 29 October 1883; RB to the Skirrows, 4 December 1883; DeVane and Knickerbocker; Curtis, 'Robert Browning'.

[7] Katharine Bronson, 'Browning in Venice'; RB to Eliza Fitzgerald, 9, 22 October, 8 November 1883.

[8] Katharine Bronson to Sarianna [12 December 1883].

[9] RB to Katharine Bronson, 9 February 1884.

10 For the coin and watch chain, see *Reconstruction*, H472; Katharine Bronson, 'Browning in Asolo'.

11 RB to Katharine Bronson, 7 October 1884.

12 Sarianna to Katharine Bronson [20 September 1884]; RB to Katharine Bronson, 26 September 1884; RB to F. J. Furnivall, 28 September 1884.

13 Meredith (ed.), *More Than Friend*, 65.

14 RB to Katharine Bronson, 8 April 1885.

15 Domett, *Diary*, 27 March 1881.

16 Information on A. N. Domett kindly provided by the Royal Academy of Arts Library; Domett, *Diary*, 27 March 1881, 6 February 1883.

17 C. E. Hallé, *Notes from a Painter's Life* (1909), 189–90; RB to George Smith, 10 October 1884: Murray.

18 Rossetti's diary entry for 26 March 1881, quoted in R. W. Peattie (ed.), W. M. Rossetti, *Selected Letters* (1990), 93.

19 Lehmann, *Reminiscences*, 230; Katharine Bronson, 'Browning in Venice'; RB to George Barrett, 2 May 1882.

20 RB to N. MacColl, 24 November 1881: Wise and Hood.

21 T. Westwood to Lady Compton, 4 October 1880: T. Westwood, *A Literary Friendship: Letters to Lady Alwyne Compton, 1869–1881* (1914); RB to Revd Williams, 26 July 1883: BL Ashley 5768; Katharine Bronson, 'Browning in Venice'.

22 Edith Cooper, 18 May 1886: BL Add 46866, ff. 230–3; RB to Katharine Bronson, 23 October 1884.

23 RB to F. J. Furnivall, 21 September 1885; RB to the Skirrows, 10 September 1885: DeVane and Knickerbocker.

24 RB to F. J. Furnivall, 17 November 1885.

25 Ibid.

26 Katharine Bronson, 'Browning in Venice'; Curtis, 'Robert Browning'.

27 Armytage, 'Robert Browning and Mrs Pattison', 181; *Poems*, II, 957.

28 *The Critic* (2 January 1886), 11; Wise and Hood, xii–xiii, citing A. Muir, 'A Treasure-House of Books: Mr Thomas J. Wise and the Ashley Library', *The Strand Magazine* (September 1929); *Reconstruction*, B17–18.

29 Allingham, *Diary*, 10 March 1876, 10 June 1888.

30 *Reconstruction*, H589, H597; RB to Eliza Fitzgerald, 19 September 1880.

31 RB to EBB [25 September 1845].

32 RB to Arabel and Henrietta Barrett, 24 November 1846; EBB to RB [24 October, 17 November 1845].

33 Orr, *Life*, 142.

34 Lady Walburga Paget: see RB to William Story, 19 June 1886, note.

35 RB to William Story, 19 June 1886.

36 RB to Michael Field, 13 May, 12 October 1886: BL Add 46866; Robert to the Skirrows, 3 September 1886: DeVane and Knickerbocker.

37 RB to Katharine Bronson, 26 December 1886.

38 RB to Eliza Fitzgerald, 26 June 1886.

39 Allingham, *Diary*, 18 February 1868.

40 RB to the Storys, 4 April 1887; Ward, *Robert Browning and His World*, II, 79.

41 RB to Katharine Bronson, 20 June 1887.

42 For RB's compensation claim, see his memorandum of 1888 to George Smith: Murray.

43 Ritchie, 305–6; see Michael Field's journal, BL Add 46866, esp. 257–8, and the printed (edited) version, Sturge Moore (eds), *Works and Days, passim.*

44 RB to the Skirrows, 22 July 1887: DeVane and Knickerbocker.

45 RB to Pen, 19 August 1887: Wise and Hood; RB to the Skirrows, 30 September 1887: DeVane and Knickerbocker; Fannie Browning, *Some Memories of Robert Browning* (1928), *passim.*

46 RB to Pen, 8 September 1887, and his letter to Fannie on the same day: Balliol College Library; RB to Henry Schlesinger, 17 September 1887: Wise and Hood.

47 *Reconstruction,* xix; *The Kent & Sussex Courier* (7 October 1887): my thanks to C. W. L. Wilson for this; RB to the Skirrows, 5 October 1887: DeVane and Knickerbocker.

48 RB to J. Ingram, 24 November 1886: Wise and Hood; RB to Pen and Fannie, 17 December 1887: Wise and Hood; *The Athenaeum* (4 February, 11 February 1888), reprinted in Landis and Freeman (eds), *Letters of the Brownings to George Barrett,* 313–14.

49 RB to F. J. Furnivall, 7 September 1885.

50 RB to George Smith, 9, 12 November 1887: Murray.

51 RB to Pen and Fannie Browning, 12 November 1887: ABL.

52 Peterson, *Interrogating the Oracle,* 174 ff.; G. W. Curtis, 'The Editor's Easy Chair' (1888), reprinted in *Critical Heritage,* 502–3; 'Browning and His Lady Admirers', *Pall Mall Budget* (19 December 1889), reprinted in Garrett, *Interviews,* 131.

53 Memoir of Lady Dilke by her husband Sir Charles: BL Add 43946, 116–17.

54 N. Barker and J. Collins, *A Sequel to .. The Forgeries of H. Buxton Forman and T. J. Wise Re-examined* (1983); J. Collins, *The Two Forgers: A Biography of Harry Buxton Forman and Thomas James Wise* (1992).

55 RB to T. J. Wise, 1, 3 August 1888: Wise and Hood; it is extraordinary that Wise had the nerve to include this correspondence in his edition of Browning's letters.

56 King, *Browning's Finances;* F. J. Furnivall in the *Pall Mall Gazette* (14 December 1889), reprinted in Garrett, *Interviews,* 134–5.

57 Allingham, *Diary,* 10 June 1888.

58 RB to F. J. Furnivall, 11 November 1884.

59 RB to Pen, 25 January 1888: Wise and Hood.

60 Fannie Browning, *Some Memories of Robert Browning* (Boston 1928), *passim;* RB to Fannie Browning, 17 December 1887, RB and Sarianna to Fannie Browning, 14 May 1888: Wise and Hood.

61 RB to Katharine Bronson, 28 January 1887.

62 RB to George Smith, 12 August 1888: Murray; RB to Katharine Bronson, 8 August 1888; RB to Pen, 6 March 1889: DeVane and Knickerbocker; Henry James quoted in Ward, *Robert Browning and His World,* II, 255; RB to Pen and Fannie Browning, 18 July 1888: Balliol College Library.

63 Katharine Bronson, 'Browning in Venice'.

64 RB to Katharine Bronson, 21 August 1888; RB to George Smith, 28 October 1888:

Murray; RB to the Skirrows, 25 December 1888: DeVane and Knickerbocker.

[65] Meredith (ed.), *More Than Friend*, li.

[66] RB to Katharine Bronson, 10 June 1889.

[67] RB to Pen, 19 June 1889: DeVane and Knickerbocker; Sarianna to Fannie Browning, 1 August [1889]: Balliol College Library; the recording of Browning's voice is available on a British Library CD, 'The Spoken Word' (2003).

[68] RB to Pen Browning, 19 June 1889: DeVane and Knickerbocker; Hawthorne quoted in Ward, *Robert Browning and His World*, II, 289; RB to Pen, 16 August 1889: Wise and Hood.

[69] E. Gosse, *Robert Browning: Personalia* (1890), reprinted in Garrett, *Interviews*, 143–7; RB to Eliza Fitzgerald, 23 June 1888; RB to Tennyson, 5 August 1889: Wise and Hood.

[70] 'Grove, 'My Memories of Browning'.

[71] RB to Alexandra Orr, 5 September 1889: ABL.

[72] RB to Pen, 8 and 15 September 1889: BL Ashley B4719; Katharine Bronson, 'Browning in Asolo'.

[73] RB to Alexandra Orr, 28 September 1889: ABL.

[74] RB to Katharine Bronson, 24 August 1889.

[75] William Story to Pen, 13 December 1889: Hudson (ed.), *Browning to his American Friends*.

[76] A. J. Armstrong (ed.), 'Diary of Miss Evelyn Barclay (Mrs G. D. Giles)', *The Baylor Bulletin, Baylor University Browning Interests*, 5th series, 35: 4 (1932); Henry James to Alice James, 6 June [1890]: L. Edel (ed.), Henry James, *Letters*, 4 vols. (1974–84).

[77] RB to George Smith, 30 November 1889: Murray.

[78] Sharp, *Life*, 195–6.

[79] Field, *Works and Days*, 42; Fannie Browning wrote daily bulletins of Browning's condition, which are now in ABL; see also Armstrong (ed.), 'Diary of Miss Evelyn Barclay' and Fannie Browning, *Some Memories*.

[80] RB to George Barrett, 19 October 1866.

[81] William Story to RB, 8 December 1889: ABL.

[82] E. Gosse's account of RB's funeral: BL Ashley A2562.

Afterword, pp. 293–4

[1] Maria Pezze-Pascolato to Anne Leigh Smith, 20 February 1912: ABL. For Pen and Fannie's life after 1889, see James Amory Sullivan (an Asolo neighbour) to N. A. Woychuk, 5 March 1942; Katharine Wormeley to Dana Estes, [n.d.]; notes of Marie Ada Molineux; and the letters of Fannie, Pen and Edith Peruzzi (*née* Story) to Anne Leigh Smith and Lady Layard – all at ABL. See also the introduction to Kelley and Coley (eds), *A Reconstruction*, and Ward, *Tragi-Comedy*.

Bibliography

Abbot, E. and Campbell, L. (eds), *The Life and Letters of Benjamin Jowett*, 2 vols., London, 1897

Aldrich, Mrs T. B., *Crowding Memories*, Cambridge, Mass., 1921

Allingham, H. and Baumer Williams, E. (eds), *Letters to William Allingham*, n.p., 1911

Allingham, William, *William Allingham's Diary*, introduction by G. Grigson, London, 1967

Altick, R. D. (ed.), Robert Browning, *The Ring and the Book*, New Haven, 1981

Anon., 'Browning and His Lady Admirers', *Pall Mall Budget* (19 December 1889), reprinted in M. Garrett (ed.), *Elizabeth Barrett Browning and Robert Browning: Interviews and Recollections*, Basingstoke, 2000

Anon., 'Celebrities at Home', *The World* (17 March 1880), reprinted in *Browning Society Notes*, 27 (2000)

Armstrong, A. J. (ed.), 'Diary of Miss Evelyn Barclay (Mrs G. D. Giles)', *The Baylor Bulletin, Baylor University Browning Interests*, 5th series, 35: 4 (1932)

Armytage, W. H. G., 'Robert Browning and Mrs Pattison: Some Unpublished Browning Letters', *University of Toronto Quarterly*, 21 (1952)

Artom Treeves, G., *The Golden Ring: The Anglo-Florentines 1847–1862*, London, New York, and Toronto, 1956

[Austin, Alfred], 'The Poetry of the Period', *The Temple Bar*, 26 (June 1869)

Baker, J. H., 'The Poet, the Actress and the Shifty Peer: Another Look at the Origins of Browning's *The Inn Album*', *Browning Society Notes*, 24 (1997)

Barker, N. and Collins, J., *A Sequel to an Enquiry into the Nature of Certain Nineteenth-Century Pamphlets by John Carter and Graham Pollard: The Forgeries of H. Buxton Forman and T. J. Wise Re-examined*, London, 1983

Bosco, R. A., 'The Brownings and Mrs Kinney', *Browning Institute Studies*, 4 (1976)

Bridell-Fox, E. F., 'Browning', *The Argosy*, 49 (1890)

Bronson, Katharine, 'Browning in Asolo', in M. Meredith (ed.), *More Than Friend: The Letters of Robert Browning to Katharine de Kay Bronson*, Appendix A, Waco, Texas, 1985 (first published in *The Century Magazine*, 59 (April 1900), 920–31)

Bronson, Katharine, 'Browning in Venice,' in M. Meredith (ed.), *More Than Friend: The Letters of Robert Browning to Katharine de Kay Bronson*, Appendix B, Waco,

Texas, 1985 (first published simultaneously in *The Century Magazine*, 63 (February 1902); and *Cornhill Magazine*, 68 (February 1902), with a prefatory note by Henry James; reprinted as Henry James, 'Casa Alvisi', in *Italian Hours*, in Richard Howard (ed.), Henry James, *Collected Travel Writings: The Continent*, New York, 1993)

Browning, Fannie, *Some Memories of Robert Browning*, Boston, 1928

Browning, V., 'The Real Identity of Pauline', *Browning Society Notes*, 13 (1983)

Calcraft-Rennie, M., 'Wordcraft and the Goldsmiths: Browning and the Castellani', *Browning Society Notes*, 23 (1996)

Calcraft-Rennie, M., 'Robert Browning's Pacchiarotto Volume: A Reinterpretation and Reassessment,' Ph.D. Dissertation, University of Southampton, 1985.

Carr, C. (ed.), *Harriet Hosmer: Letters and Memories*, New York, 1912

Chevasco, Berry, ' "Naughty Books": Elizabeth Barrett Browning's Response to Eugène Sue', *Browning Society Notes*, 28 (2003)

Cobbe, F. P., *Life of Frances Power Cobbe As Told by Herself*, 2 vols., London, 1894

Collins, J., *The Two Forgers: A Biography of Harry Buxton Forman and Thomas James Wise*, Aldershot, 1992

Collins, T. J. (ed.), 'Letters from Robert Browning to the Revd J. D. Williams 1874–1889', *Browning Institute Studies*, 4 (1976)

Colvin, S., *Memories and Notes of Persons and Places, 1852–1912*, London, 1921

Cook, E. T. and Wedderburn, A. (eds), *Works of John Ruskin*, 39 vols., London and New York, 1903–12

Corkran, Henriette, *Celebrities and I*, London, 1902

Corsan, Hiram, 'A Few Reminiscences of Robert Browning', *Cornell Era*, 40 (1908), reprinted in *Browning Institute Studies*, 3 (1975)

Cramer, M. B., 'Browning's Friendships and Fame before Marriage (1833–1846)', *Publications of the Modern Language Association of America*, 55 (1940)

Cramer, M. B., 'Browning's Literary Reputation at Oxford 1855–1859', *Publications of the Modern Language Association of America*, 57 (1942)

Cramer, M. B., 'What Browning's Literary Reputation Owed to the Pre-Raphaelites 1947–1856', *English Literary History*, 8 (1941)

Curle, R. (ed.), *Robert Browning and Julia Wedgwood: A Broken Friendship as Revealed in their Letters*, London, 1937

Curtis, Daniel Sargent, 'Robert Browning', in M. Meredith (ed.), *More Than Friend: The Letters of Robert Browning to Katharine de Kay Bronson*, Appendix C, Waco, Texas, 1985

Curtis, G. W., 'The Editor's Easy Chair' (1888), reprinted in B. Litzinger and D. Smalley (eds), *Browning: The Critical Heritage*, London, 1970

Dakers, C., *The Holland Park Circle: Artists and Victorian Society*, New Haven and London, 1999

DeLaura, P. J. (ed.), 'Ruskin and the Brownings: Twenty-five Unpublished Letters,' *John Rylands Library*, 54 (1971–2), 314–56

DeVane, W. C., *Browning's Parleyings: The Autobiography of a Mind*, New Haven, 1927

DeVane, W. C., *A Browning Handbook*, New York, 1936; revised edn, New York [1955]

DeVane, W. C. and Knickerbocker, K. L. (eds), *New Letters of Robert Browning*, New Haven, 1950

Duckworth, F. G. R., *Browning: Background and Conflict*, London, 1931

Duffy, C. G., *Conversations with Carlyle*, London, 1892

Edel, L., *Henry James: A Life*, London, 1996

Edel, L. (ed.), Henry James, *Letters*, 4 vols., London, 1974–84

Forster, M., *Elizabeth Barrett Browning*, London, 1988

Forster, M. (ed.), *Selected Poems of Elizabeth Barrett Browning*, London 1988

Garnett, Richard and Edward, *The Life of W. J. Fox*, London, 1910

Garrett, M. (ed.), *Elizabeth Barrett Browning and Robert Browning: Interviews and Recollections*, Basingstoke, 2000

Gosse, E., *Robert Browning: Personalia* (London, 1890), reprinted in M. Garrett (ed.), *Elizabeth Barrett Browning and Robert Browning: Interviews and Recollections*, Basingstoke, 2000

Gosse, E. and Wise, T. J. (eds), A. C. Swinburne, *Contemporaries of Shakespeare*, London, 1919

Gower, F. Leveson, *Bygone Years*, London, 1905

Griffin, W. H. and Minchin, H. C., *The Life of Robert Browning: With Notices of His Writings, His Family, & His Friends*, 3rd revised edn, London, 1938

Grove, W. H., 'Browning as I Knew Him, by His Valet', in *Sunday Express* (4 December 1927)

Grove, W. H., 'My Memories of Robert Browning', MS at Scripps College, Claremont, Cal., reprinted in *Browning Society Notes*, 26 (2000)

Grove, W. H., 'Robert Browning at Home', *Pall Mall Budget* (19 December 1889) reprinted in Garrett, M. (ed.), *Elizabeth Barrett Browning and Robert Browning: Interviews and Recollections*, Basingstoke, 2000

Haight, G. S., 'Robert Browning's Widows', in *Times Literary Supplement* (2 July 1971)

Hall, N. J., *Trollope: A Biography*, Oxford, 1991

Hall, N. J. (ed.), *The Letters of Anthony Trollope*, 2 vols., Stanford, Cal., 1983

Hallé, C. E., *Notes from a Painter's Life*, London, 1909

Harlan, A. B. and J. L. Jr (eds), *Letters from Owen Meredith [Edward Lytton] to Robert and Elizabeth Barrett Browning*, [Waco, Texas, 1936]

Hawthorne, J., *Shapes that Pass: Memories of Old Days*, London, 1928

Heydon, P. N. and Kelley, P. (eds), *Elizabeth Barrett Browning's Letters to Mrs David Ogilvy, 1849–1861* (including 'Recollections of Mrs Browning'), New York, 1973

Hill, G. B. (ed.), *Letters of Dante Gabriel Rossetti to William Allingham, 1854–1870*, n.p., 1897

Horsman, E. A. (ed.), *The Diary of Alfred Domett, 1872–1885*, London, New York, and Toronto, 1953

Hudson, G. R. (ed.), *Browning to his American Friends. Letters between the Brownings, the Storys, and James Russell Lowell*, London, 1965

Hutton, R. H., 'Browning and Tennyson', *Spectator* (21 December 1889), reprinted in B. Litzinger and D. Smalley (eds), *Browning: The Critical Heritage*, London, 1970

Huxley, L. (ed.), *Elizabeth Barrett Browning: Letters to Her Sister, 1846–1859*, London, 1929

Irvine, William and Honan, Park, *The Book, the Ring and the Poet*, London, Sydney, and Toronto, 1975

Jack, Ian *et al.* (eds), *The Poetical Works of Robert Browning*, Oxford, 1983–

James, Henry, *William Wetmore Story and His Friends*, 2 vols., Edinburgh, 1903

James, Henry, 'Casa Alvisi', in *Italian Hours*, quoted in Richard Howard (ed.), Henry James, *Collected Travel Writings: The Continent*, New York, 1993; first published London, 1909

Karlin, Daniel, *The Courtship of Robert Browning and Elizabeth Barrett*, Oxford, 1985

Kelley, P. and Coley, B. A., *The Browning Collections: A Reconstruction with Other Memorabilia*, [Waco, Texas], 1984

Kelley, P., Hudson, R. and Lewis, S. (eds), *The Brownings' Correspondence*, Winfield, Kan., 1984–

Kenyon, F. G., *The Letters of Elizabeth Barrett Browning*, 2 vols., New York, 1897

Kenyon, F. G. (ed.), *Robert Browning and Alfred Domett* (including letters of Joseph Arnould), London, 1906

Kenyon, John, *A Rhymed Plea for Tolerance*, London, 1833

King, R. A., *Robert Browning's Finances from His Own Account Book*, Waco, Texas, [1947]

Landis, P. and Freeman, R. E. (eds), *Letters of the Brownings to George Barrett*, Urbana, Ill., 1958

Lathrop, R. H., *Memories of Hawthorne*, London, 1897

Lehmann, Rudolf, *An Artist's Reminiscences*, London, 1894

Lehmann, Rudolf Chambers, *Memories of Half a Century: A Record of Friendships*, London, 1908

Lewis, S. (ed.), *Letters from Elizabeth Barrett Browning to Her Sister Arabella*, 2 vols., Waco, Texas 2002

Litzinger, B. and Smalley, D. (eds), *Browning: The Critical Heritage*, London, 1970

McAleer, E. C., *The Brownings of Casa Guidi*, New York, 1979

McAleer, E. C. (ed.), *Dearest Isa: Robert Browning's Letters to Isabella Blagden*, Austin, Tex., and Edinburgh, 1951

McAleer, E. C. (ed.), *Learned Lady: Letters from Robert Browning to Mrs Thomas Fitzgerald, 1876–1889*, Cambridge, Mass., 1966

McAleer, E. C., 'New Letters from Mrs Browning to Isa Blagden', *Publications of the Modern Language Association of America*, 66 (1951)

McMillan, J. F., 'The Empire the French Forget: New Views of Napoleon III', *Times Literary Supplement* (15 March 2002)

Marsh, J., *Dante Gabriel Rossetti: Painter and Poet*, London, 1999

Masterman, L. (ed.), Mary Gladstone Drew, *Diaries and Letters*, London, 1930

Maynard, John, *Browning's Youth*, Cambridge, Mass., 1977

Meredith, M. (ed.), *More Than Friend: The Letters of Robert Browning to Katharine de Kay Bronson*, Waco, Texas, 1985

Meredith, M., 'Browning and the Prince of Publishers', *Browning Institute Studies*, 7 (1929)

Millais, J. G., *The Life and Letters of Sir John Everett Millais*, 2 vols., London, 1899

Miller, Betty, *Robert Browning: A Portrait*, London, 1952

Muir, A., 'A Treasure-House of Books: Mr Thomas J. Wise and the Ashley Library', *The Strand Magazine* (September 1929)

Neville-Sington, P., *Fanny Trollope: The Life and Adventures of a Clever Woman*, London, 1997

Orr, Mrs Sutherland, *A Browning Handbook*, 2nd edn, London, 1887; first published 1885

Orr, Mrs Sutherland, *Life and Letters of Robert Browning*, London, 1891

Peattie, R. W. (ed.), W. M. Rossetti, *Selected Letters*, University Park, Penn., 1990

Peterson, W. S., *Interrogating the Oracle: A History of the Browning Society*, Athens, Ohio, 1969

Peterson, W. S. (ed.), *Browning's Trumpeter: The Correspondence of Robert Browning and Frederick J. Furnivall, 1872–1889*, Washington, DC, 1979

Pettigrew, J. (ed.), Robert Browning, *The Poems*, 2 vols., Harmondsworth, 1981

Phelps, W. L., 'Robert Browning as Seen by His Son: A Talk with Barrett Browning', *Century Magazine*, 85, NS 63, (1913)

Raymond, M. B. and Sullivan, M. R. (eds), *The Letters of Elizabeth Barrett Browning to Mary Russell Mitford, 1836–1854*, 3 vols., [Waco, Texas], 1983

Reese, G., 'Robert Browning and His Son', *Publications of the Modern Language Association of America*, 61 (1946)

Reid, A. (ed.), *Why I am a Liberal, Being Definitions by the Best Minds of the Liberal Party*, London [1885]

Ritchie, Annie Thackeray, *Records of Tennyson, Ruskin and Browning*, London, 1892

Rogers, J. E. T., *Education in Oxford: Its Method, its Aids and its Rewards*, London, 1861

Rossetti, William Michael, *Some Reminiscences*, 2 vols., London, 1906

Ryals, Clyde de L., *The Life of Robert Browning: A Critical Biography*, Oxford, and Cambridge, Mass., 1993

Ryals, Clyde de L. *et al.* (eds), *Collected Letters of Thomas and Jane Welsh Carlyle*, 27 vols., Durham, NC, and London, 1980–2001

Sharp, William, *Life of Robert Browning*, n.p., 1890

Stone, M., 'Bile and the Brownings: A New Poem by RB, "My Heart and I", and New Questions about the Brownings' Marriage', in J. Woodford (ed.), *Robert Browning in Contexts*, Winfield, Kan., 1998

Sturge Moore, T. and D. C. (eds), *Works and Days. From the Journal of Michael Field*, London, 1933

Surtees, V., *The Ludovico Goddess: The Life of Louisa Lady Ashburton*, Salisbury, 1994

Surtees, V., 'Browning's Last Duchess', *Times Literary Supplement* (9 October 1986)

Tennyson, Hallam, *Alfred Lord Tennyson: A Memoir*, 2 vols., London, 1897

Thoron, W. (ed.), *The Letters of Mrs Henry Adams, 1865–1882*, Boston, Mass., 1936

Toynbee, W. (ed.), *The Diaries of William Charles Macready, 1833–1851*, 2 vols., London, 1912

Trollope, T. A., *What I Remember*, 2 vols., London, 1887

Troubridge, Lady Laura, *Memories and Reflections*, London, 1925

Ward, M., *The Tragi-Comedy of Pen Browning*, New York, 1972

Ward, M., *Robert Browning and His World*, 2 vols., London, 1967–9

Westwood, T., *A Literary Friendship: Letters to Lady Alwyne Compton, 1869–1881*, London, 1914

Whiting, L., *The Brownings: Their Life and Art*, Boston, Mass., 1911

Wilde, Oscar, 'The True Function and Value of Criticism', *Nineteenth Century*, 28 (1890), reprinted in B. Litzinger and D. Smalley (eds), *Browning: The Critical Heritage*, London, 1970

Winnar, F., *The Immortal Lovers: Elizabeth Barrett and Robert Browning*, London, 1950

Wise, T. J. and Hood, T. L. (eds), *Letters of Robert Browning*, London, 1933

Woodford, J. (ed.), *Robert Browning in Contexts*, Winfield, Kan., 1998

Woodson, T. (ed.), *Nathaniel Hawthorne, The Centenary Edition of Works of Nathaniel Hawthorne*, Vol. XIV: *The French and Italian Notebooks*, Columbus, Ohio, 1980

Index